Able-Bodied Womanhood

Able-Bodied Womanhood

Personal Health and Social Change in Nineteenth-Century Boston

Martha H. Verbrugge

New York   Oxford
OXFORD UNIVERSITY PRESS
1988

OXFORD UNIVERSITY PRESS

Oxford New York Toronto
Delhi Bombay Calcutta Madras Karachi
Petaling Jaya Singapore Hong Kong Tokyo
Nairobi Dar es Salaam Cape Town
Melbourne Auckland

and associated companies in
Beirut Berlin Ibadan Nicosia

Published by Oxford University Press, Inc.,
200 Madison Avenue, New York, New York 10016

Oxford is a registered trademark of Oxford University Press

Library of Congress Cataloging-in-Publication Data

Verbrugge, Martha H.
  Able-bodied womanhood.

    Bibliography: p.
    Includes index.
    1. Women—Health and hygiene—Massachusetts—Boston—
History—19th century.   2. Physical fitness for women—
Massachusetts—Boston—History—19th century.
3. Physical education for women—Massachusetts—Boston—
History—19th century.   I. Title.
RA778.V452 1988   613'.04244'09034   88–11284
ISBN 0–19–505124–6

The author thanks Temple University Press for permission to use her
article "The Social Meaning of Personal Health: The Ladies' Physiological
Institute of Boston and Vicinity in the 1850s," published in
Health Care in America: Essays in Social History, Susan Reverby and
David Rosner, eds. (Philadelphia, 1979), as a basis for Chapter 3
of this book.

Portions of the diary of Eunice Hale Waite Cobb are reprinted by courtesy
of the Trustees of the Boston Public Library. Portions of the records of the
Ladies' Physiological Institute of Boston and Vicinity are reprinted by
courtesy of the Institute and of the Arthur M. and Elizabeth Schlesinger
Library on the History of Women in America.

9 8 7 6 5 4 3 2 1

Printed in the United States of America
on acid-free paper

To my mother
and
In memory of my father

Acknowledgments

This project began many years ago in the nether regions of Widener Library at Harvard. As a graduate student in the History of Science, I became interested in medical views and treatment of women and studied "the cult of female invalidism" that pervaded American culture in the late nineteenth century. Browsing through popular magazines and newspapers of the period, I therefore was surprised to find images of healthy women—young girls playing croquet and badminton, ladies exercising at home in loose-fitting garb, college students riding bikes and rowing boats. Perhaps the delicate female, real or imagined, had an able-bodied sister. That simple question led to this book. I welcome the opportunity to thank the many people who contributed to its completion.

My greatest debt is to Barbara G. Rosenkrantz, my mentor and friend. Her capacity to listen, guide, and stimulate is remarkable. I have gained immeasurably from her incisive intellect, her extensive knowledge, and her abiding support and counsel. To Barbara go my warmest respect and gratitude.

Other scholars too offered help and criticism along the way. Robert H. Wiebe commented on early drafts of the work; Regina Markell Morantz-Sanchez read portions of the manuscript and gave timely advice and encouragement; and Stephan Thernstrom reviewed the entire manuscript, as did Gerald N. Grob more than once in recent years. I have benefited from friendships with other historians of medicine and American society, including Allan Brandt, Susan Reverby, and David Rosner. Finally, my colleagues in the History Department of Bucknell University helped me rethink the central issues of the book.

Historical research is impossible without the aid of dedicated librarians, and I encountered many during my work. Of particular note are the staffs of the Arthur M. and Elizabeth Schlesinger Library on the History of Women in America, the Francis A. Countway Library of the Harvard Medical School, the Boston Public Library, and the Harvard University Archives. With resourcefulness and good cheer, Wilma Slaight of the Wellesley College Archives greatly facilitated my study of the Boston Normal School of Gymnastics and of physical education at Wellesley.

Special contributions were important to several chapters. The officers and members of the Ladies' Physiological Institute allowed me to examine the organization's surviving records, and agreed to donate them to the Schlesinger Library. Mrs. Calvin L. Gardner of Swansea, Massachusetts, was especially eager to talk about the Institute's history and kindly gave me access to privately held materials. George K. Makechnie, former dean of the Sargent College of Allied Health Professions at Boston University, discussed Dudley Allen Sargent and the history of physical education with me. Betty Spears, Professor Emerita of Sport Studies at the University of Massachusetts, Amherst, shared her considerable knowledge of the Boston Normal School of Gymnastics.

I am indebted to numerous sources for financial support and other services. The National Science Foundation and the Danforth Foundation funded my doctoral program. The National Endowment for the Humanities awarded a summer stipend in 1979 and the American Council of Learned Societies provided a grant-in-aid in 1980. During 1981–82 I was a fellow at the Charles Warren Center for Studies in American History at Harvard University. Bucknell University has been especially generous, with a faculty development stipend in 1982 and additional resources and release time through the years. The secretaries who helped me at the Charles Warren Center and at Bucknell were always skillful and efficient. At Oxford University Press, I was privileged to have the excellent advice of Sheldon Meyer and Joellyn Ausanka and the expert copyediting of Stephanie Sakson-Ford. I completed the book in 1986–87 during a sabbatical, which I spent as a Visiting Scholar at Carleton College, my alma mater. I appreciated the college's hospitality and assistance.

Every project brings its full share of joy and doubt. My family and some special friends kept me company through it all. Their encouragement and understanding were invaluable. My parents, in particular, never wavered in their confidence or support. My father died before the book was finished. He took pleasure in helping people do what was important to them, and I owe him more than I ever said.

Northfield, Minnesota   M.H.V.
May 1987

Contents

Able-Bodied Womanhood

Introduction

Personal health has become a national obsession. Around the country, bookstores are crammed with guides about nutrition, exercise, alternative medicine, and self-help psychology. Each year Americans spend billions of dollars on vitamins and natural foods, athletic equipment, and health club memberships. Special clinics teach the habits of health from A to Z, from aerobic dance to Zen meditation; employees run laps and pump iron in corporate gyms; restaurants offer "light" meals for calorie-conscious patrons. What accounts for this phenomenal concern about physical well-being? What do Americans hope to gain from their quest for health?

The answers must lie in the social history of America during the past twenty years. Yet how do such developments as the Vietnam War, economic crises, and a shifting political climate explain this country's preoccupation with health? The puzzle is easier to solve if one generalizes the question and lengthens the time frame. The issue at stake is, Why do people become interested in their physical well-being? What does the ideal of "health" mean to them and why do they pursue it? Those questions may not have a universal answer; attitudes about health vary according to their historical and cultural context.

In America, for example, popular concepts of health have changed significantly since colonial times.[1] During much of the seventeenth and eighteenth centuries, settlers in the New World tolerated the precariousness of their lives. Faced with numerous illnesses and limited medical resources, many regarded disease as inevitable. In New England, Puritan doctrine explained sickness as a natural, even necessary event in a world of human sin and divine judgment. Health drew little attention, as a theoretical standard or practical goal. A good life was long, not necessarily comfortable; a town, despite its risks, was considered salubrious if it grew in size. Modes of eating, dressing, and working were simply daily routines, not deliberate steps toward well-being.

During the early national period, some leaders began to discuss health in new terms. Thomas Jefferson, Benjamin Rush, and others declared that health, much as truth or progress, was a likely, even inevitable condition. They argued that America's physical environment, political institutions, and social ideals were uniquely conducive to health. America's growth in population, they claimed, was testimony of the new republic's political and economic prosperity. The Jeffersonian view cast health in collective, not personal, terms and continued to measure it quantitatively. There are few signs that average citizens shared their leaders' patriotic vision of health.

Between the 1820s and 1860s, however, Americans' fatalism gave way to the belief that physical well-being was possible. In concert with the perfectionist philosophy and social reforms of antebellum times, optimism about health swept the Northeast. Advice literature, voluntary societies, and schools popularized the lessons of human physiology, coached Americans about the habits of self-improvement, and promised a new era of personal fulfillment and social harmony. The resemblance between the zealous crusade of the mid-nineteenth century and present-day America is unmistakable.

Over the last third of the nineteenth century, interest in personal health remained keen. The wealth of books, journals, and institutions that promoted fitness is ample proof. Compared to antebellum times, however, Americans of the late 1800s regarded health as more tenuous and its benefits less sweeping. Once the road to a new millennium, physical well-being was now a buffer against the forces of modern society. To understand and practice the laws of physiology would save people, not perfect them; health enabled one to participate in the world, not to change it. Stripped of romantic language and reformist goals, health became a pragmatic adjustment to the demands of urban, industrial life.

During the first half of the twentieth century, other aspects of health gained importance. Apparent threats to national vigor, within and beyond American shores, heightened the belief that health was a civic duty and the emblem of a responsible life. Organized recreation and sports served as training for productive workers, true citizens, and sturdy men and women. Mixing competition with cooperation, athletics and supervised play taught discipline while releasing physical energy. In addition, discoveries in nutritional science and bacteriology focused more attention on diet and personal hygiene. Physical educators, doctors, and others cautioned Americans about unwholesome foods, improper exercise, and unsanitary habits.

At first glance, few historians would find those changes over the past three hundred years surprising. Most would argue that popular attitudes about health are a function of science, medicine, and physical conditions. Through the centuries, developments in the study of human physiology and pathology modified theories about health and sickness. As expert knowledge was popularized, Americans learned to define and to pursue health in different ways. Moreover, concern about health would seem to depend on the quality of one's physical life and the availability of effective medical care. With progress in life expectancies, mortality rates, and therapeutics, Americans naturally became more optimistic about their health.

On closer examination, however, the historical pattern does not look so simple or predictable. In particular, physical experiences and the status of medicine, though relevant, are not sufficient explanations. For example, the fervent crusade for health of the mid-nineteenth century accompanied epidemics, ineffective therapeutics, and worsening death rates in urban areas such as Boston. Disenchanted with regular medicine, Americans experimented with health reform and nonorthodox therapies, believing that personal vigilance would guard against illness. Yet what encouragement did they actually have that health, rather than disease, was humankind's natural condition, and that preventive measures would bring physical, much less social, improvement? Faith and exuberance were hardly logical responses to the status quo, unless we accept the witticism that "there was no place to go but up" as adequate historical analysis.

For a more complete answer, we must look beyond medicine and beyond the quality of people's lives.[2] Physiological events gain coherence only when we construct intellectual models to differentiate and explain them. Because health and sickness are physical experiences, our concepts of them are necessarily biological. By describing internal conditions scientifically, we aim to separate functional states from those which are impaired. That process of interpretation is an evaluative one; the labels of "health" and "sickness" themselves distinguish between "good" and "bad" states. Thus, we are forced to decide what is desirable, or normal, or functional in a human's life. Such judgments are relative, not absolute; they are bound as much to cultural values as to biological criteria. The dividing line between health and sickness varies by time and place.

Concepts of health and sickness are also directive. They enable both the lay population and professional healers to identify goals and measure success. Invariably, people's agendas for a healthy life include not only physical qualities, but standards of appearance and behavior as well. Society's expectations, more than biological considerations, often determine which traits are viewed as ideal. A simple but dramatic example is the changing norm of physical size and shape, especially for women, over time. Because they judge and prescribe, concepts of health and sickness are necessarily value-laden.

A survey of American history supports that conclusion. From colonial times to the present, definitions of health and disease have carried far more than biological information. They have identified what is "right" or "wrong" about individual citizens and American culture as a whole. Models of health and sickness have helped diagnose personal shortcomings, analyze social problems, and reinforce moral behavior.[3] Throughout the last three centuries, private concerns and social values have shaped popular attitudes about health in America. One purpose of this book is to dissect the relationship between intellectual content and social context, between concepts of health and their cultural environment. What judgments, what expectations have ideas about health conveyed in this country?

Social factors also influence how important physical well-being is to people. Major changes in one's family, workplace, or community can be unsettling; they test one's ability to understand and adjust to new circumstances. In effect, one experiences dis-ease. The term is appropriate for more than physical disorders; it connotes a general sense of vulnerability and apprehension. During certain eras, Americans tried to alleviate their dis-ease through a commitment to health. For some, the language and philosophy of health enabled them to make sense of external events, and the practice of good habits restored order to their lives. One way Americans comprehend and cope with the world around themselves is through the world within. Whereas other problems seem remote and intractable, the matter of health is concrete and accessible. This book examines the forces that heighten concern about personal health. It argues that interest in health is a barometer that responds to private anxieties and social developments.

That was especially true during the nineteenth century. This study focuses on the years between 1830 and 1900 because of major shifts in the content and context of ideas about health through that period. During the Jacksonian era, perfectionism challenged Americans' earlier fatalism; after the Civil War, the country's outlook became more realistic and more secular; when Progressivism arose in the 1890s, pragmatism emerged as a dominant attitude. Those changes were evident in the language of health. During antebellum times, crusaders for health preached Christian physiology in moralistic, sometimes millennial, terms. In 1900, their counterparts spoke of "fitness" and "efficiency," rhetoric that signaled a more scientific and bureaucratic age.

The structure of health reform also changed between 1830 and 1900. During the middle decades of the nineteenth century, a wide assortment of Americans exhorted their fellow citizens along the path of health. The movement included practitioners of nonorthodox medicine (such as botanics, homeopaths, and hydropaths), dietary reform advocates (such as Sylvester Graham and other vegetarians), and popular writers and lecturers on physiology (ranging from self-taught lay people to esteemed regular physicians). By the last third of the nineteenth century, however, many of the reformist journals, organizations, and medical institutions established in the antebellum period were struggling to survive or had folded, and a new generation assumed direction of the movement. Between 1870 and 1900, as before, many prominent figures in health reform were self-proclaimed experts in exercise, diet, and hygiene. Increasingly, though, national leaders carried professional credentials—either from orthodox medicine or from the maturing fields of public health and physical education.

Finally, the social context of health differed significantly in antebellum and late Victorian times. During the nineteenth century, the agrarian economy of America slowly converted to an industrial one; the roles of men and women continued to diverge; urbanization created new opportunities and new hazards; developments in science and technology reshaped the way Americans thought and lived; and two waves of immigration, one before mid-century and the other in the late 1800s, changed the country's portrait. In large measure, concern about physical well-being persisted in America because of, not despite, those profound transformations.

The relationship between social change and ideas about health becomes concrete when one examines it in a particular setting. Nineteenth-century Boston is especially inviting as a case study. The city had a long record of professional and public attention to matters of health and an abundance of people and resources committed to popularizing physiology and hygiene between 1830 and 1900. Moreover, Boston experienced the demographic, social, and economic changes common to cities in the Northeast during the 1800s.

But was "the hub of the universe" (as one Boston Brahmin

dubbed the city) the prototype of health reform? The question is difficult to answer at this time. Current scholarship in the field consists primarily of biographies of notable health crusaders, histories of various medical sects, and wide-ranging surveys of the movement's ideas and activities. Complementing such work, this book contributes a new perspective by tracing health reform in one locale over a long period of time. Without comparable studies about other communities, one cannot say if events in Boston were representative or unique. (I suspect that both conclusions are, in part, true.) This study, therefore, should be read as an example, not a paradigm.

The main characters in the book are middle-class Bostonians, who served as the primary leaders and audience of the city's personal health movement. A crisp definition of middle class is hard to give. For the purposes at hand, the common nineteenth-century phrase "the middling condition" is the most suitable. The term referred to the many ordinary Americans whose families were neither rich nor poor. In the antebellum period, the middling condition ranged from independent tradesmen to entrepreneurs and professionals; in late Victorian times, it covered the families of white-collar clerks to those of fairly prosperous businessmen. Although different in some respects, the lives of middling Americans between 1830 and 1900 were fundamentally similar. Because of shared experiences and fears, a variety of middle-class Bostonians rallied around the cause of health. It became a focal point for them in a way not evident among the city's elites or working class.

Middle-class women, in particular, were central figures in nineteenth-century health reform. One reason was the country's distress about female health. Girls and women seemed prone to both ordinary and peculiar ailments; treatment for female disorders was ineffective, if not grueling; medical and popular literature cultivated a stereotype of feminine delicacy and invalidism. Whether accurate or not, the perception that women were unusually, perhaps innately, sick generated a cult of female frailty. What prompted such a dire diagnosis? For investigating the origins of concern about health, the case of nineteenth-century women is an instructive one.

In part, fears ran so high because of the relationship between health and women's roles in nineteenth-century America. As wives and mothers, as caretakers of sick friends and relatives, as school teachers and nurses, middle-class women supervised other people's physical lives. Women's knowledge of physiology and their own well-being were essential to those responsibilities. As one health reformer declared in 1855, a woman "should not only *know her duty, and have a disposition to perform it,* but she should possess the requisite power and energy."[4] If imaginary women were considered weak, real women were obliged to be fit. Middle-class women sought practical information and personal reassurance, and the literature and programs of health reform addressed those needs. In nineteenth-century America, popular instruction about health was often a movement of, by, and for women.

Meanwhile, the daily lives of middle-class women changed significantly between 1830 and 1900. Opportunities for a young woman to be educated or to work outside the home grew; the birth rate among white females declined; technological innovations transformed household chores. The country became embroiled in "the Woman Question," as traditionalists, advocates of female rights, and other Americans debated the status of women. Developments in women's private lives, in American society, and in general attitudes about health recast the discussion about women's physical condition. For some people, the issue was no longer How sick are women? but How well could they be? What constituted an able-bodied woman? Neither the question nor the answer was merely biological. "Able-bodied womanhood" had cultural as well as physical meaning. As an example of how social values and concepts of health intersect, the evolution of ideas about women's health in nineteenth-century America is a rich case study.

By folding together people's attitudes and experiences, this book combines intellectual and social history. A comment on sources and methodology is warranted. The work incorporates local history, prescriptive literature, institutional studies, and, wherever possible, the reflections of individual women. Background information on nineteenth-century Boston reveals the condition of the city's middle-class residents, and suggests the nature of their dis-ease. Magazines, books, and other published materials articulate contemporary ideas about health. More specifically, such literature explains the origins of health and sickness as perceived by nineteenth-century doctors, popular physiologists, and physical educators. It is tempting, but misguided, to assume a connection between those sets of data; what Bostonians worried about and did in private may not have corresponded to the observations and rules of health reformers. To see if there is any relationship between common life and prescriptive rhetoric, the historian needs other sources. One option is the study of social institutions, where public activities serve to express people's private concerns. The book examines several educational programs, in clubs and schools, through which middle-class women in Boston learned about and taught health. With profiles of groups and individuals, this study explores how some nineteenth-century women viewed personal health and used physiological instruction. Though institutional studies are imperfect tools, they do allow the historian to move a step closer to people's private lives and values.

In sum, the book analyzes the relationship between personal health and social change in nineteenth-century Boston. It asks why middle-class Bostonians worried about health, and what the search for well-being signified to them. Ideas about health are powerful because they help people interpret and organize their lives. Such models, though, are also flexible and ambiguous. Once committed to health, Bostonians discovered that the concept had no uniform meaning, and their quest had no single conclusion. In particular, the nature of able-bodied womanhood remained open to debate well after the cult of female invalidism had faded. Health is not so much a fixed, biological state as it is an exploration. As personal concerns and social values change, so do our expectations of health.

1

The Etiology of Dis-ease: Life and Death in Middle-Class Boston, 1830–1860

Popular and medical writers in the mid-nineteenth century were both discouraged and hopeful about the likelihood of human health. On the one hand, health reformers and doctors lamented the prevalence of disease. Mankind "literally groans in agony!" exclaimed Orson Squire Fowler, a leading phrenologist. "Poverty, wretchedness, loathsome and distressing sickness," he noted, "the heart-rending decease of friends, children, and companions, and even premature death itself, tearing its victims from life and all its pleasures, torment most mankind!"[1] Within that vast domain of suffering, the plight of women seemed especially grave. Catharine Beecher, an advocate of female health and education, declared that women's feebleness was increasing so rapidly that doctors feared "ere long, there will be no healthy women in the country."[2]

Such writers also maintained that health was a possible, even natural state of life. At the very least, it represented the absence of discomfort. As one noted doctor asserted in 1848, Nature intended "that we lead long, full, and happy lives; that, from the beginning to the end, we have neither sickness, nor weakness, nor discontentment."[3] At the very most, personal health was individual and social perfection. It was testimony of physical, moral, and intellectual harmony within a person and the foundation for piety and order in society.

The prospect of able-bodied womanhood was especially welcome. Health literature acknowledged that the responsibilities of a wife and mother were as demanding as they were crucial. In the view of the *American Journal of Education*, ill-health regrettably was making American females "less qualified for the daily active duties of life."[4] The best insurance that a woman could fulfill her domestic chores without fatigue, much less illness, was through "the general healthful activity of mind and body."[5] The *Ladies' Magazine* added that awareness of "the simple principles of healthful life" would also prevent a mother from "becoming the murderer of the comfort or health of her child."[6] Only women's application of physiological knowledge, the magazine urged, would enable America's "pale, puny, and sickly generation [to] be renovated."[7]

Gloom and optimism were complementary sides of a widespread concern for health during the mid-nineteenth century, as many Americans became anxious about their physical well-being. Antebellum advice literature urgently disseminated the laws of life and health. Itinerant lecturers exhorted their audiences to forsake every excess by eating, working, and exercising in moderation. Around the country, private schools and some public ones introduced courses in anatomy and physiology and periods of supervised exercise. Voluntary associations organized lectures, libraries, and conferences devoted to popularizing the message of health. Private gymnasia offered programs to help adults and children recover their health.

That interest ran so wide and so deep indicates that people's concerns transcended physical health. By diagnosing their bodily ills, antebellum Americans also formulated a moral and social pathology of their times. By promoting physical health, they sought to mitigate less tangible disorders in their lives. Using the experiences of middle-class Bostonians, especially women, this chapter explores the relationship between the ideal of health and the realities of daily life in the mid-1800s. It suggests how the concept of personal health became a panacea, a comprehensive philosophy through which some Bostonians understood and adjusted to the shifting contours of urban life. The second chapter describes in detail what their prescription for health entailed.

Dio Lewis, a well-known health reformer who lived in Boston during the 1860s, portrayed Americans as a collection of "drooping forms, feeble chests, dyspepsia, decayed teeth, putrid breath, cold extremities, crazy nerves, brains on fire."[8] He found no standard, human or otherwise, by which his fellow citizens were healthy. "The birds, the squirrels, the cows, are well; we are sick," he despaired.[9] Lewis's conclusion was as dire as it was graphic.

Were the realities of life and death in Boston as depressing as Lewis believed? Local data show that life expectancy at ages 0 to 4 for males and females born between 1826 and 1835 was 37.8, and 38.1 for those born between 1839 and 1841. For those born between 1859 and 1861, the comparable figure for males was 34.8, and 37.8 for females.[10]

Annual crude mortality rates in Boston were also quite stable during the first half of the nineteenth century.[11] From 38 deaths per 1000 live population in 1774, the city's mortality rate dropped to an average of 22 between 1812 and 1821. The figure held relatively steady for several decades: 20.5 between 1821 and 1830, 21.5 between 1831 and 1840, 20.3 between 1841 and 1845; followed by a modest increase: 25.2 between 1850 and 1854, and about 24 between 1855 and 1860. Contemporaries attributed most short- and long-term changes in death rates to epidemic diseases. Lemuel Shattuck, a vital statistician and public health advocate in Boston, determined that between 1811 and 1840, deaths due to cholera, typhus, and other epidemic conditions rose, while those from "sporadic diseases" of the nervous, respiratory, circulatory, and digestive systems declined.[12] Later data also revealed the impact of epidemics. In 1849, for example, the mortality rate reached 38.5 following outbreaks of cholera, dysentery, scarlet fever, and measles.[13] Nevertheless, as Shattuck and others recognized, the most consistent causes of death were nonepidemic conditions. Shattuck estimated "that from *one-fourth* to *one-seventh* of all the deaths in the Northern and Middle states, and perhaps throughout the whole Union, and the civilized world, are caused by consumption."[14] However sweeping a generalization, Shattuck's observation did hold true for Boston, where consumption accounted for 15 to 25 percent of all deaths between 1811 and 1845.[15]

By modern standards, such figures for life expectancy and annual mortality are grim. From the vantage point of the antebellum period, however, the statistics were merely discouraging, not catastrophic. The vital data of Boston had improved since colonial times and did not worsen significantly through the first half of the nineteenth century, unlike the experience of other northern cities. In that sense, the dismal pictures drawn by Lewis and others look exaggerated.

Whatever the facts, Bostonians perceived their situation to be a perilous one. To explain their city's condition, Bostonians applied the model of health and disease that was popular in antebellum times. Three factors determined whether an individual enjoyed health or became sick. The first, biological endowment, included the general vigor of one's constitution as well as any inherited weaknesses.[16] For example, one might be born with a poor heart, a sensitive stomach, or a predisposition to consumption. Though remediable to some extent, such unfortunate tendencies put an upper limit on a person's chances for a long and healthy life. With the impact of heredity being so large, health advocates urged parents to bestow upon their offspring the best possible endowment and advised everyone to invest their biological inheritance wisely.

The second determinant of health was the quality of one's physical environment. Because the size and character of their city changed so rapidly in the 1800s, Bostonians had good reason to be apprehensive of their surroundings.[17] From a population of about 18,000 in 1790, Boston grew to 49,000 inhabitants in 1822, when it was incorporated as a city, and to nearly 178,000 by 1860. Despite various land reclamation projects and the settlement of outlying areas, the city remained crowded and the problems of garbage, sewage, water drainage, and nuisance-producing trades seemed only to worsen. As a journal in Philadelphia observed in 1832, with the "glare of light," "loud noises and discords," inadequate sun, and impure air, "no sense receives in a suitable degree its appropriate stimulus" in a city.[18] Amidst the crowding, Boston's population also became more segregated and more mobile. By mid-century, the city was a tightly packed checkerboard of neighborhoods, divided by class, ethnicity, and race. At the same time, the city was fluid. As many as half of its residents moved each year, particularly within city boundaries. So much congestion and activity created an unpleasant, if not unsanitary, environment, fertile conditions for both endemic and epidemic disease.

For all their importance, heredity and environment were hostage to personal behavior, the final component of health and sickness. Good daily habits could compensate for a weak constitution and an unsanitary environment, whereas careless practices might undermine a strong inheritance and favorable surroundings. With so much room for error and with the consequences being so crucial, health advocates preached caution and responsibility in people's daily conduct.

The model of biology, environment, and behavior made sense to nineteenth-century Bostonians because it explained patterns of health and sickness in their own lives. In particular, it accounted for the vulnerability of certain groups in the city. No one doubted, for example, that children were unusually fragile. Especially among immigrants, Shattuck remarked, "death seems . . . to be abundantly supplied with new materials to work upon; and his agents are able to make easy victims. Children seem literally 'born to die.' "[19]

Vital data confirmed that alarming impression. Shattuck, for example, determined that children under age five accounted for one-third of all deaths in the city between 1811 and 1820 and close to one-half between 1841 and 1845.[20] Dr. Josiah Curtis, a Boston physician, concluded that nearly one-quarter of all deaths in Boston between 1850 and 1854 occurred among infants (under age one).[21] Since those calculations did not factor in the age distribution of Boston's population, a more informative statistic is age-specific mortality rates. Shattuck discovered that between 1830 and 1845 the death rate among children under the age of five grew from 64.8 to 75.9 per 1000.[22] Without question, Boston's children became ill and died at an extraordinary rate.

The reasons seemed equally apparent. "The miseries of infants commence even before birth," observed Mary S. Gove (later Nichols), a lecturer on popular health.[23] Many newborns, she explained, enter the world "with deteriorated constitutions, and predisposition to disease," a penalty inherited from unhealthy parents.[24] In addition, every infant was innately frail and dependent; proper supervision was their only protection against illness, even death. Because a mother was the caretaker of her family, she was a likely, however unwitting, culprit in the failing health of her children. Gove spoke for many health advocates and doctors when she concluded that some mothers "literally 'killed with kindness.' "[25] After poisoning their own systems with medicine and alcohol, she claimed, mothers insisted on nursing their newborns, oblivious to the harmful substances being transmitted. Unaware that vitiated air could suffocate, Gove continued, women bundled their young ones in layers of blankets and tucked them into hooded cradles. Many popular physiologists and doctors agreed that infants were victims of circumstance: born with physical weaknesses and subjected to ill-advised care. Whether that explanation was valid or not, the young were among Boston's most endangered classes.

A second group that drew attention was the city's immigrant population. Native Bostonians regarded foreigners as both victim and villain in the battle against sickness; immigrants succumbed to disease at an extreme rate, especially during epidemics, and their high morbidity appeared to jeopardize the rest of the city. As one Boston official argued in 1845, local conditions among immigrants " 'are extended to the population in the neighborhood; and epidemics are generated, which are, no doubt, injurious to the general health of the city.' "[26] Immigrants seemed to be encroaching upon native Bostonians with disease as well as sheer numbers.

However exaggerated those fears were, the foreign population was growing and its level of health was dismal. Whereas 95 percent of the city's residents in 1830 had been born in America, between 40 and 45 percent were native-born of native parents in 1860.[27] Immigrants in Boston had both a higher birth rate and a higher death rate than native-born residents.[28] As Shattuck pointed out, they fared worse both in typical years and during epidemics. In the late 1830s, for example, over two-thirds of the city's Catholic (and presumably Irish) population did not live to age five, and during the cholera outbreak of 1849–50, immigrants accounted for roughly 54 to 59 percent of all deaths in the city, while constituting around 46 percent of its population.[29]

Native Bostonians speculated that both environmental conditions and personal habits accounted for the immigrants' predicament. Their problems seemed endless: poverty, intemperance, ignorance, squalor, poor hygiene, crowded tenements, impure air. In itself, each condition was a potent source of illness; together, they made disease virtually inevitable. Analyzing Boston's census of 1855, for example, Dr. Josiah Curtis described "the low, dark, damp habitations grouped in badly drained and almost unscavenged neighborhoods where thousands, and we think we might safely say tens of thousands of our population dwell, amidst all the impurities of a polluted atmosphere, and personal uncleanliness. These are the hotbeds of typhus, dysentery and other epidemics, as well as diseases peculiar to children."[30] The causal relationship between environment and behavior, however, remained unclear to native Bostonians. Did poor sanitary conditions breed bad habits, or did personal negligence create an unhealthy environment?[31] Either way, foreigners seemed locked into a cycle of plentiful births and plentiful deaths.

If Bostonians mourned the loss of children and feared immigrants, they deplored the condition of girls and women. Health reformers, doctors, and others alleged that the frailty of American women in the nineteenth century compared unfavorably with the robust health of earlier generations and of contemporary women in other countries.[32] Catharine Beecher, for example, was unable to recall, in her "immense circle of friends and acquaintance all over the Union, so many as *ten* married ladies born in this century and country, who are perfectly sound, healthy, and vigorous."[33] The belief that females were inordinately, even inherently, delicate became so pervasive in antebellum times that a cult of female invalidism developed. The phrase "female sickness" came to seem redundant.

Were women as sick as popular opinion maintained? Vital statistics from the period do not permit a definitive answer. Accurate morbidity data, for example, are virtually unknown. Even if they indicated a prevalence of female illness, the information would not be conclusive. The assumption that women were unhealthy may have been so extensive as to be self-perpetuating; for doctors and women alike, it may have been a source, as well as the result, of female complaints and disorders. Other kinds of information, such as life expectancy and mortality data, are more available. Though incomplete and somewhat unreliable, they do shed light on the relative health or debility of women in the mid-nineteenth century.

For example, life expectancy rates for women in antebellum Boston surpassed men's, a phenomenon common to many other places and time periods. Moreover, differential mortality rates indicate that, disregarding age, the risk of death for a male was greater than for a female. Lemuel Shattuck reported that in 1835, for example, one in thirty-nine males in Boston was apt to die, compared to one in forty-eight females.[34] Finding the identical pattern from 1811 to 1845, Shattuck concluded that "the agents of death are uniformly more active among males than among females."[35]

As Shattuck recognized, differential mortality rates become even more informative when age distribution is considered. "At certain ages," he observed, "a greater proportional mortality prevails among males, and at other ages among females."[36] Although Shattuck did not complete the necessary calculations himself, one can use his data on mortality and population in Boston to compare proportional deaths among males and females in various age ranges with proportional representation of the sexes in each age cohort. In 1830, for example, male deaths were disproportionately high in all age groups except ages ten to thirty.[37] Life expectancy and mortality rates, at least, suggest that women were not necessarily the weaker sex.

How did perception fall so out of line with fact? The answer emerges as one examines how Americans explained the supposed frailty of women. Health reformers, doctors, and other observers believed that illness was symptomatic of fundamental disorders in women's lives; it betrayed not only physical weakness, but personal and social disturbances as well. Fear, more than fact, gave the cult of female invalidism its intensity.

Based on the model of health and sickness popular at mid-century, concern about women's condition focused on biological constitution and personal behavior. As many historians have recounted, popular and medical literature of the nineteenth century portrayed women as unusually fragile creatures.[38] Compared to a man's, the refrain went, a woman's muscles were weaker, her bones and cranium smaller, her skin softer, her tissues more delicate, and her nerves more sensitive. Though distinctly and endearingly "feminine," those characteristics were said to limit a woman's strength, intellect, and resistance to common ailments. Of course, the distinguishing feature of a woman's anatomy and physiology was her reproductive system. It defined her nature and her destiny; to function properly, it required considerable amounts of vital energy and personal attention; through reflex actions, it was often responsible for complaints in remote parts of the body. Marked by frailty from birth, a woman's constitution seemed incapable of withstanding ordinary disruptions and was uniquely liable to problems associated with menstruation, pregnancy, and childbirth. The female body was an unsteady structure ready to collapse at any moment.

The breakdown usually began with improper habits. Health literature of the mid-nineteenth century recorded a long list of practices that supposedly triggered illness and infirmity among women. Many examples dealt with social customs or historical developments that were virtually beyond women's individual control. With little choice about certain conditions affecting their lives, reformers conceded, women found their health in jeopardy. Physical activity was a case in point. Convention prohibited rough-and-tumble play among young girls, limiting them to more refined pastimes. The prevalence of "hot-house" education penalized them even further. Confined to their school desks in awkward positions for long stretches of time, America's pupils were said to be physically stunted, though mentally proficient.[39] Because a boy was " 'permitted the indulgence of his natural powers as far as he is willing,' " he found relief at home and during free periods at school.[40] A girl, on the other hand, never fully recovered because she was " 'prevented by reason of her sex, from those very exercises which gives [sic] her brother health and enjoyment.' "[41]

Adult women seemed to have an equal disadvantage. According to one physician in New England, urban life lessened the healthfulness of domestic chores. The modern disdain for work and the availability of labor-saving machinery, wrote Dr. Abel L. Peirson in 1839, "extinguished some of those active employments which conduced to the health of females."[42] Spinning, "an admirable fortifier of the muscles," he explained, had been replaced by "the sedentary occupations of the needle and the lace frame."[43] Concluding just the opposite, some observers argued that new household technology actually increased the time and energy spent on domestic chores, and promoted ill-health. Whether "labor-saving" devices appeared to curtail or multiply women's activities in the home, the consequence was physical degeneration. There was no question that women's mental condition was deteriorating as well. Catharine Beecher, for one, bade farewell to the days when "all the details of [domestic] life were simple, and easy, and comfortable."[44] "The numberless and perplexing *cares* of nursery, kitchen, and parlor," she observed, now severely taxed a woman's mental and nervous systems, leaving her exhausted and distraught.[45] The weight of social custom and domestic change was not easily ignored; nor, in the view of health reformers, did it contribute to women's well-being.

The analysis of female ill-health also included examples of behavior for which women were more accountable. Whatever social pressures existed, health literature insisted, women could decide if their daily habits of eating, hygiene, and rest would follow or disregard the laws of health. A firm believer in personal responsibility, Mary S. Gove (Nichols) challenged her female audiences to acknowledge their shortcomings:

> Let each consider whether she has clogged the wheels of life, and barred out the influx of Heaven by excessive eating, by improper food, and poisonous drinks; by neglect of healthful employment and exercise, by neglect of bathing and cleanliness, or whether she is wasting life by excessive labor, nervous abuses (which comprehend the abuses of amativeness, whether its action be social or solitary), and all the train of wrong habits which our present state of civilization produces.[46]

In these matters, the force of culture was no excuse for misguided behavior.

Another of Gove's favorite examples was women's habits of dress. "During the day, and often a large portion of the night," she protested, women "are loaded with clothing of a fashion the most absurd and ridiculous."[47] Virtually every health advocate joined Gove in condemning female dress, from tip to toe, from hats to shoes. The practice of tight-lacing, or women's heavy, close-fitting corsets, appalled physiological reformers the most. The dreadful consequences ranged from displaced organs and bones in the torso to the functional impairment of the lungs, heart, and stomach. "A multitude of painful and protracted diseases, by which thoughtless females, in this age, are hurried to an early grave, have their origin in this horrible custom of wearing stays," declared one Boston physician in 1841.[48] Already marked by nature as delicate, the female constitution fell victim to the tyranny of fashion and, even more so, to women's own lack of good sense.

If the effects of poor eating and restrictive dress were self-evident, the damage from other habits was more insidious. Some popular physiologists claimed that women ruined their health more through moral failures than by physical abuses. Urban women of the middle and upper classes were a particular concern. They seemed irresponsible, frivolous, and self-indulgent. "For want of rational and healthful employment," the *Journal of Health* complained, the average young lady "becomes indolent, nervous, and low spirited."[49] She develops "a pernicious taste for shows and public amusements" and her "curiosity is directed to vain and dangerous objects."[50] For health writers and others, this alleged selfishness and laziness of American women was far more than a source of physical impairment; it exposed what they considered serious disorders in women's lives.

The diagnosis was a complicated one. Were women merely ignorant of the laws of health? In that case, physiological instruction might correct their errors. Were women lost amidst the disarray and temptations of urban life? If so, reminders about moral principle might steer them back on course. Or did irresponsible behavior signal a profound weakening of women's character and self-control? This was the most troubling possibility. Whatever answer they settled upon, popular physiologists and other commentators agreed that women's mistaken habits aggravated an already delicate system.

By system, they meant American society as well as the female body. Though sympathetic to women's private pain, health reformers and doctors also feared the social implications of ailing womanhood. In their eyes, it jeopardized the strength of families and the stability of the nation. Following her travels around the country, Catharine Beecher reported that "there was a terrible decay of female health all over the land, and that this evil was bringing with it an incredible extent of individual, domestic, and social suffering, that was increasing in a most alarming ratio."[51] In practical terms, invalidism left women unable to bear and raise vigorous children, in whose hands the future of the country lay. In moral terms, it seemed to reflect an erosion of values and resolve among the principal guardians of the home and family. Female ill-health became a symbol of and, at times, a scapegoat for the upheavals in American society in the middle decades of the nineteenth century.

The larger meaning of female sickness can be seen in the responsiveness of middle-class Bostonians to antebellum health reform. For many, women's ailments, and sickness in general, demonstrated the precariousness of urban life: the city teemed; children passed away; immigrants proliferated, spread epidemics, and died; women became invalid and infertile. That was physical evidence of deeper problems. Along with others in the urban Northeast, middle-class Bostonians sensed that their world was shifting: familiar routines held true less and less; traditional roles and values were strained; the structure of work, home, and neighborhood began to change. Dis-ease was a social as well as physical condition; the vulnerability of the body mirrored the insecurity of one's private world. Literally and figuratively, middle-class Bostonians came to fear for their lives.

Economic and social forces changed the character of life for both men and women in Boston during the mid-nineteenth century. While remaining a financial and commercial leader, Boston also developed a considerable industrial base.[52] Located in both the central city and the outlying areas, new enterprises created opportunities for middle-class men, especially among clerical and salesworkers. The middle-class professions, too, gained in strength, though less consistently. In contrast, the old middle class saw its importance wane. The day of the independent artisan was near an end, and the number of small shopkeepers and managers barely grew after 1830. By midcentury, large-scale businessmen monopolized power and wealth in Boston, and unskilled and skilled laborers prevailed in absolute number. Measured in terms of either property holdings or occupational mobility, "success" for middle-class men was uncertain and often fleeting.

As was true in cities throughout the Northeast, changes in domestic life complemented those of the workplace in Boston. The urban middle-class family was not a self-sufficient unit; increasingly, it depended on productive labor outside the home for economic support and on external sources for daily commodities. As the worlds of work and home divided more sharply, the roles of middle-class men and women grew further apart as well. According to Lemuel Shattuck's rough survey in 1845, a male over the age of twenty was far more likely to work outside the home than was his female counterpart (73 versus 17 percent).[53] The disparity was especially clear in white-collar occupations; only about 10 percent of all female workers held jobs in such areas as education or health.[54] Most of those female workers were probably single.[55] The norm for a middle-class woman in her mid-twenties was to be married and occupied in the home. At mid-century, the average age of first marriage for Massachusetts women was about twenty-four.[56] Around 80 percent of native women who were born in Massachusetts in antebellum times and who lived at least to age twenty eventually married.[57]

The average middle-class female in the mid-1800s took her place in the family. In some ways, women's domestic lives had not changed since the early national period or even colonial times. Despite some new practices of childbirth, pregnancy and delivery still caused considerable fear and pain.[58] Moreover, wives and mothers continued to oversee the daily affairs of the home and the health of their families. In other respects, though, familial life in cities changed significantly during the first half of the nineteenth century. For example, technological developments began to transform the nature of domestic chores, including cooking, cleaning, and sewing.[59] Manufactured goods replaced articles once prepared in the home, and "labor-saving" devices, from egg-beaters and apple-parers to enclosed stoves and hand-driven washing machines, not only changed women's daily routines, but may have increased their expenditure of time and energy in the process. Meanwhile, the urban family became smaller, more private, and more mobile. Crude fertility rates in east-central Massachusetts declined steadily between 1810 and 1850, paralleling changes throughout New England and the nation as a whole.[60] Whereas a colonial wife might have borne seven or eight children, the average among native white women around the country fell to five by 1860 and four or less by 1890.[61] Obviously, couples practiced some form of birth control more frequently; women faced the risk of maternal death less often; and given life expectancy rates and the relative scarcity of divorce, women spent fewer years rearing children and more in the company of their husbands or as widows.[62] In crucial ways, the cycle of family life for a woman in the mid-1800s was quite different from that experienced by her grandmother or even mother.

The mixture of old and new circumstances was not easy to handle. Told that her health was innately delicate, a wife had to deal with birth control and pregnancy as well as routine ailments. Offered little training beyond informal apprenticeship when young, she had to manage numerous responsibilities while household technology changed. Discouraged from working outside the home, she devoted whatever education and skills she had to the supervision of her home and family. Excluded from the worlds of business, law, and politics, she satisfied her intellectual and social aspirations through church affairs and cultural events. From every angle—physical, psychological, and practical—the life of a middle-class woman was problematic.

Although their situations were dramatically different, middle-class men and women shared a profound uneasiness. Urban life promised self-fulfillment and security, but often delivered frustration, instability, and sickness. The men and women of Boston's middle class felt not so much betrayed as uncertain.

They also had a measure of confidence. However powerful and distant, the forces affecting their lives seemed open to some degree of control. Middle-class Bostonians believed that individual actions molded the character of society. When summed over every member of a community, personal rectitude and self-governance yielded a morality of the whole; individual discipline and exertion translated into common wealth; personal vigor brought public health. Similarly, private dissolution complemented social disorder, just as mediocre work disrupted economic stability and personal negligence encouraged endemic and epidemic disease. The answer to Boston's many ills, then, could be found in the regeneration of its citizens.

Individual reform was a common theme during the middle decades of the nineteenth century. As the Second Great Awakening spread romantic evangelicalism through the Northeast and as liberal denominations gained ground in New England, the notion of predestination gave way to a belief in personal salvation.[63] From the new Methodists and Baptists to the Unitarians, many Protestants maintained that individual faith, not a wrathful God, determined the course of one's spiritual life.

That sense of freedom and optimism pervaded many facets of antebellum life. A belief in self-determination and human perfection, for example, lay at the heart of many social crusades, including temperance, abolition, and moral purity.[64] Convinced that individuals were responsible for change, advocates of romantic reform assumed that moderate doses of moral suasion, education, and example would guide Americans toward improvement. Political democracy also gained more favor as a principle, though not uniformly as a practice. By mid-century, virtually every white adult male was eligible to vote; supporters of abolition and women's suffrage argued for the extension of that basic civil right to disfranchised groups.

If people could shape their own destinies, popular rhetoric continued, they had little need for specialists. Increasingly, lawyers, scientists, and doctors found their claims to exclusive knowledge and skills challenged. Elitism violated democratic principles, and, as medicine in particular showed, the promises of self-proclaimed experts were often empty. With doctors unable to cure most common ailments, let alone serious disorders, alternative medicine and health reform flourished in the mid-nineteenth century.[65] Citing the severity and ineffectiveness of orthodox treatment, a variety of reformers called upon the lay populace to become keepers of their own health and healers of their own diseases.

In the decades preceding the Civil War, the most popular nonorthodox therapies included Thomsonianism, homeopathy, and hydropathy. Each of those sects, to some degree, endorsed self-medication at home. In the early 1800s, Samuel Thomson, a New Hampshire farmer, founded a medical system that replaced the bloodletting, blistering, and mineral drugs of regular physicians with botanic remedies. Thomson believed that nature provided the most trustworthy cures and that ordinary citizens had the right (even necessity) to be their own doctors. During the 1820s and 1830s, Thomsonianism became a commercial success as agents sold "Family Rights" and manuals for the practice, especially in rural areas. When botanic medicine began to fade, two other sects, homeopathy and hydropathy, gained favor. Imported from Germany during the 1820s, homeopathy was based on two beliefs: the law of similars and the law of infinitesimals. The first principle stated that an illness could be overcome by administering a drug that reproduced the symptoms of the disease in a healthy person. The second law maintained that the more dilute a medicine was, the stronger it became. Dosages as small as one-millionth of a gram were not unheard of. Though homeopaths naturally urged patients to consult one of the sect's trained practitioners, they did support domestic kits, which included prepared medicines and an instruction booklet, so that Americans could diagnose and treat their own ills. With numerous followers in the Northeast and Midwest, homeopathy posed a significant challenge to orthodox medicine prior to the Civil War. Unlike botanics and homeopaths, the advocates of hydropathy shunned drugs altogether, and prescribed only natural remedies, such as fresh air, sunshine, proper diet, exercise, and water. During the 1840s and 1850s, ailing Americans, especially in the Northeast, visited water-cure sanitaria in order to bathe, shower, sweat, douche, and plunge their way back to health. At the risk of losing clients, some hydropaths did approve self-treatment at home for conditions that were not serious or urgent. More crucial than domestic medicine, though, they added, was an understanding of physiology and hygiene, which would allow people to preserve their health and avoid disease.

The importance of knowledge was a common conviction among the many health reformers who lectured and wrote for the public during antebellum times. While medical sectarians tried to heal the sick, popular physiologists hoped to forestall disease by re-educating Americans about diet, exercise, alcohol, tobacco, and sex. Two leaders of that crusade in New England were Sylvester Graham (1794–1851) and William Andrus Alcott (1798–1859). An evangelist minister, Graham gained notoriety in the 1830s by promoting temperance, vegetarianism, and wholesome bread, baked at home from unbolted wheat flour. (Contemporaries called him "Bran-Bread Graham." We now, unwittingly, memorialize Graham by eating crackers that bear his name.) Meanwhile, Alcott, a physician who trained at Yale, set out in 1830 to cure his chronic pulmonary ailments through a natural diet, rather than artificial drugs. Pleased with the results, Alcott decided to prepare advice books for the general public. By 1859, when he died, Alcott had written some eighty-five guides on wide-ranging topics and edited several health journals. Just as he had emerged from "the wilderness of pills and powders,"[66] Alcott hoped that his fellow citizens would take responsibility for their own well-being by obeying the laws of life and health. Graham, Alcott, and other health reformers agreed that knowledge and vigilance were essential to personal health. During the middle decades of the nineteenth century, they instructed and coaxed the American public from lecture platforms, at physiological clubs, and in countless books and magazines.

In the Northeast, New York and Boston were major centers of the health movement. For example, Graham's lectures in New York during the cholera epidemic of 1832 drew national attention to his ideas. Leading hydropaths, such as Joel Shew, Russell T. Trall, and Mary S. Gove (Nichols), opened sanitaria and schools in New York during the 1840s and 1850s. From the beginning, Boston too was a hotbed of hygienic reform. Alcott lived and worked there from the 1830s on; Graham arrived in 1835; the American Physiological Society, an early health reform association, was founded in Boston in 1837; a Graham boarding house, where residents practiced a strict regimen of vegetarianism and clean living, was established there in

1837; Gove attracted hundreds of Boston women to her lecture series on anatomy and physiology during the late 1830s. In Boston, as elsewhere, the call to self-improvement had numerous messengers and disciples during the mid-nineteenth century.

In many respects, antebellum health reform simply extended the prevailing cultural theme of self-reliance from religion and politics into the physical domain. Americans were also free to manage their own health and disease. For some Bostonians, however, health reform had even broader significance. It was not merely insurance against physical ills or a substitute for useless medicine, but an antidote for the problems of urban life as a whole. By removing the causes of disease, middle-class Bostonians hoped to alleviate conditions beyond the physical body that jeopardized their well-being—urban filth, economic instability, moral fluidity, domestic change. In their eyes, no other solution held such promise.

A central purpose of this book is to understand the power of the concept of personal health. What features made it so effective an explanation and answer for the concerns of middle-class Bostonians? A number of factors seem important. First, the management of health offered immediate practical dividends for both men and women. Improving one's personal habits was an investment toward physical vigor, which increased the odds of a productive life, uninterrupted by fatigue or illness. Moreover, since the physical, moral, and social worlds were connected, the anticipated benefits from health were extensive. As a program that specified values and behavior, a healthy regimen was also an organizing principle for one's conduct in both the private and public sphere. The pay-off was psychological as well as practical. The rules of health were scientific guideposts toward security and virtue in an era of uncertainty.

Personal health had symbolic meaning as well. Economic and domestic change placed new demands on middle-class Bostonians; old patterns of life and norms of conduct eroded in the process. As external events came to seem confusing and unmanageable, middle-class Bostonians turned inward; they focused on the one parameter of life that was still amenable to control. The pursuit of health, they believed, would help them understand and solve their own dilemmas. Health became a physical metaphor for self-preservation.

The middle class declared, in fact, that they alone could achieve genuine health. Luxury, they argued, simply bred uselessness and atrophy, while either a rugged outdoor life or urban poverty offered none of the comforts essential to health. In contrast, the lives of farmers, shopkeepers, and other "decent citizens" were "freest from those physical and moral evils which curtail and embitter life."[67] Health was both means and end as middle-class Bostonians attempted to stabilize their lives. As the next chapter describes, the popular definition of health in the mid-1800s was a portrait of middle-class concerns in physiological garb.

2

Moral Physiology and the Habits of a Healthy Life

As with other crusades in antebellum America, self-regeneration was the central tenet of health reform. Believing that personal change accumulated to bring social progress, health advocates focused on the shortcomings and betterment of individuals. The main obstacles to self-improvement, physical or otherwise, appeared to be ignorance and negligence. In Catharine Beecher's words, "the two grand causes" of ill-health were "first, a want of *knowledge* of the construction of the body and the laws of health; and, next, a want of *thought* and *conscience* on the subject."[1]

The conclusion was a familiar one during the mid-nineteenth century. Commenting in the *North American Review* in 1855, for example, A. A. Livermore recorded his amazement that having "inhabited the earth for at least sixty centuries," people did "not yet know how to eat, drink, dress, dwell, travel, sail, work, exercise, breathe, after the true dictates of nature."[2] Even more distressing was the indifference of people who understood the laws of life and health, but chose to violate them. "Multitudes abuse their bodies because they do not know the mischiefs they are perpetrating," Beecher asserted. "Perhaps as many more go on in courses that they know to be injurious," but do not relinquish because healthy habits "are never urged on their attention and conscience as matters of *duty*."[3]

Both knowledge and conscience were essential to the campaign for health. Without the guidance of truth, good intentions might go awry; uninformed by morality, knowledge invited abuse. As a writer in the *Moral Reformer and Teacher on the Human Constitution* observed in 1835, "There is something else necessary, besides mere light. Knowledge furnishes motives, it is true; but how powerless they are without principle—without moral courage!"[4] The agents of health reform were heat and light, inspiration and information.

This chapter explores the knowledge and incentives embedded in the concept of health during the middle decades of the nineteenth century.[5] What principles and rules did Bostonians learn as they read health tracts, attended physiological lectures, or visited local gymnasia? How did health advocates motivate their audiences for the arduous journey of self-improvement? Their message was a simple one: be well by being good. The antebellum model of health was a blueprint for middle-class values and behavior. It helped codify those standards of conduct that sociologists and historians label "bourgeois" or "modern," including persistence, self-reliance, and self-control.[6]

Although one can easily locate those themes in nineteenth-century health tracts, it is much harder to gauge their impact on readers' lives. By charting the course to health, advice literature addressed the uncertainties of the middle class. An attentive audience, however, is not necessarily a compliant one. As social historians have come to appreciate, description cannot be inferred from prescription. The following discussion does not attempt to determine the extent to which middle-class Bostonians heeded the advice in health literature. Rather, it identifies those elements in the model of personal health that resonated with their concerns. What guidance did physiological reform offer to middle-class Bostonians who sought a cure for the disorders in their lives?

The effect of health literature is also difficult to assess because its contents were not uniform. Although most writers agreed on certain general principles of health, they differed on how personal well-being might be achieved and identified. While such variety may have confused readers, it also created choices for them. Though normative, in its effort to direct middle-class Bostonians toward propriety, advice about health was also ambiguous enough to invite experimentation. As this chapter will illustrate, differences of opinion were especially evident in discussions about women's health.

The concept of personal health during the mid-nineteenth century was grounded in three components of American thought: commonsense realism, Christian moralism, and natural science.[7] Derived from Scottish realism of the eighteenth century, commonsense philosophy was a familiar feature of academic thought in the Northeast before the Civil War and had a popular counterpart in the moral framework of middle- and upper-class Bostonians. It posited that people intuitively knew right from wrong, could easily test those principles in daily experience, and would exercise choices accordingly.

Middle-class Bostonians believed that a moral context existed for every thought and deed. Though evident in the course of natural events and everyday life, the moral code was established and monitored by a wise divinity. It was the responsibility of mortal beings to live according to God's precepts; in part, an individual's fate, both temporal and final, rested on the character of his or her conduct.

Natural law existed in concert with the moral principles of life. God had so designed the universe that the laws regulating physical events were consistent, even intertwined, with those of human virtue. The natural world, from the processes of the physical earth to the workings of one's body, was an orderly creation that required as much attention, if not reverence, as did the spiritual realm. The tool for unveiling the mechanisms of nature was science. Although middle-class Bostonians may have distrusted its practitioners, they began to accept science itself as an explanatory system. It was a method of inquiry, an analytical model, a language, and an authority. Far from being sacrilegious, the search for a physical interpretation of any phenomenon was an indirect means of appreciating God's handiwork and the organic character of human life, that is, the regular interplay of its physical, moral, and social dimensions.

Commonsense realism, Christian moralism, and natural science were interwoven, rather than competing, views of life. The theoretical and practical lessons of science meshed with the conclusions of moral philosophy and the imperatives of rectitude. In constructing a model of health, no stronger components than those three could be found. Natural science described the structure and function of the human body; Christian moralism squared the rules of health with goodness and decency; commonsense philosophy explained why an individual ought to pursue physical well-being.

The particular science that guided antebellum health reform was physiology, or, in the parlance of the times, "the science of human life" or "the laws of life and health." Physiology was both theoretical and practical, both descriptive of the human body and prescriptive about its care. Its scope, wrote Scottish physician Andrew Combe, was nothing less than "the basis of every thing having for its object the physical and mental health and improvement of man."[8]

Popular physiology of the mid-nineteenth century was an amalgam of contemporary medical knowledge and the idiosyncratic views of American health reformers. Physiology was by no means a unified body of thought in the 1800s. Questions still existed about respiration and digestion, the origins of body heat, the action of the nervous system, and the material or vital character of life forces.[9] The more responsible health reformers in America based their work on reputable sources and reflected the central debates of their time. For example, Sylvester Graham's system of physiology resembled the ideas of several European medical theorists of the eighteenth and nineteenth centuries; he claimed to have read the works of the anatomist Bichat and the pathologist Broussais.[10] At the same time, many American health advocates held unusual views about human physiology and endorsed marginal practices, such as hydropathy and botanic medicine. Those commitments colored their assessment of contemporary physiology. For example, Graham's vegetarianism led him to dispute the research of American physiologist William Beaumont, whose experiments on gastric processes purportedly showed, among other things, that food from animal sources was easier to digest than vegetable food.[11] Thus, the popular physiology that middle-class Bostonians encountered in books, magazines, public lectures, schools, and gymnasia was a mixture of both orthodox and nonorthodox knowledge about the human body.[12]

Two major themes characterized popular physiology in the midnineteenth century: the principle of appropriate action and the principle of interdependence and harmony. The first stated that the perfect functioning of any system in the body required careful regulation of its use. As Dr. John Collins Warren, a prominent Boston physician, observed, "Action is the object for which organization was created" and, conversely, good organization is developed through appropriate action.[13] Dio Lewis, a noted health reformer, agreed when he declared that "motion is the great law of the universe. . . . The degree of life may be measured by the amount of normal motion."[14] Exercising an organ allowed it to function properly, whereas the absence of activity brought degeneration.

According to physiologists, there were two requisites of healthy action: first, an organ had to be constitutionally receptive to stimulation, or, in a word, excitable; second, it had to receive stimuli that were suitable in type and amount. The concept of stimulation or excitement was central to both academic and popular physiology in the eighteenth and nineteenth centuries.[15] There was no consensus about the material or vital origins of excitability, but theorists agreed that it was essential for bodily processes.

Too much or too little stimulation, whether from internal or external sources, was harmful to an organ. In *Thoughts on Physical Education,* Dr. Charles Caldwell applied that rule to the stomach:

> Let that organ receive suitable aliment, in proper quantities, and at
> well-regulated periods, and it will be . . . improved. . . . Suitable
> exercise, indulged in to the proper extent, strengthens it, while ex-
> cessive and deficient action weakens it, and unfits it for its func-
> tions.[16]

There was equal danger from an improper stimulus in moderation
and a healthy stimulus in excess. For example, a faint, but abrasive
noise and lovely music that was too loud were as damaging to the
ears as the complete absence of sound.

If the body required activity, it also needed time to rest. Some
theorists described the cycle of use and recovery as a physical process
whereby the body's materials were depleted and then restored. The
circulation of blood, they explained, served to remove waste products
and to replenish the body with fresh particles.[17] Other physiologists
viewed the alternation of exercise and rest in vitalistic terms. Sylvester Graham, for example, suggested that activity expended an organ's
supply of excitability and, thereby, the body's overall reserve of vital
force, the intangible principle of life.[18] Whether subscribing to mate-
rialism or vitalism, health reformers agreed that the balance of action
and recovery was the first law of life and health.

The second main principle of popular physiology was the law of
interdependence and harmony. According to health reformers, the
body was not a collection of unrelated structures and processes, but
a dynamic unit in which constituents relied on each other. As Sylvester Graham explained in 1839, "Each organ has its particular function to perform,—yet no organ can perform its function independently
of the others; and no organ can sustain itself by its own function."[19]

Few American health advocates or other physiologists of the
period understood the mechanisms of interdependence. Oftentimes,
they invoked the law of stimulation and depletion. On the one hand,
organs depended on each other for excitation; only a healthy organ
could send the right stimuli to its partners. For example, a good digestive system was the body's sole source of life-sustaining nourishment. On the other hand, the impairment of any one function caused
widespread harm. Overuse of an organ diminished its ability to produce the stimuli that other vital systems needed and also appropriated
the energizing force of the nerves and blood, thereby withdrawing it
from other organs. The result was general debilitation of the body.
Physiologists used the vague concept of "sympathy" to suggest those
direct and indirect means whereby the condition of one organ was

communicated throughout the body. Certain organs, such as those for digestion and reproduction, appeared to have exceptional powers of sympathy because of their rich concentration of nerves and blood vessels.

The theory of sympathy reinforced the conviction that harmony was essential to health. Interdependence assumed cooperation between the various parts of the body. Health was not possible if constituents competed for or monopolized vital resources. As Sylvester Graham concluded, the body "is more of a republic or a confederation than an absolute monarchy."[20]

The principle of interdependence extended beyond the physical processes of life. Health reformers viewed the material body as the vehicle for a person's mental, moral, and emotional powers. Rather than separate qualities, Dio Lewis declared, the human body, mind, and soul "are interlinked and interwoven so completely that they are *one* and not *three*."[21] In that case, popular physiologists reasoned, the law of mutual assistance must connect all human faculties. As Dr. Thomas S. Lambert elaborated in *Hygienic Physiology* in 1852,

> It is clearly proved that the cultivation of the intellect and disposition, in a proper manner and to a proper degree, improves health, adds beauty to strength, and increases the happiness of man, while it lengthens his days; and on the other hand, paying proper attention to the welfare of the body, not only gives it health, but tends to produce as well, a healthy and happiness-causing state of the intellect and disposition. . . .[22]

This was merely a lengthy restatement of the old aphorism *"mens sana in corpore sano."*

The opposite also held true: the body, mind, and soul were bound together in debility as they were in health. The literature of popular physiology in the mid-nineteenth century abounded with examples of mutual impairment, intended to scold the delinquent audience. In his physiology text for schools and families in 1853, for example, Dr. B. N. Comings illustrated the relationship between emotional states and physical processes. "Melancholy, or depression of spirits from any cause whatever," he wrote, "will often produce disease and derangement of the liver; and, on the other hand, a derangement of the liver will almost always insure melancholy, though no other cause exists."[23] In 1838, Dr. Elisha Bartlett explained the connection between immorality and physical abuses in his lecture on "Obedience to the Laws of Health, a Moral Duty":

It is almost invariably true, that those violations of the physiological laws, consisting in intemperate and sensual excesses, ultimately becloud the intellect, and enfeeble the moral sentiments, while they stimulate into a blind and fearful activity, the selfish and animal powers. The sot has a besotted mind. The miserable victim of strong drink, the luxurious lover of high living, the decrepid [sic] debauchee, tainting the very air with corruption, each and all, totter on to the grave, the light of intellect feeble and dim, the pure and radiant glory of the moral and religious feelings extinguished and gone forever; but with their several ruling appetites, strong from indulgence, still burning in their bosoms,—lurid and murky fires of an unquenchable hell,—the unappeasable gnawings of the worm that never dies.[24]

Even without their dramatic imagery, such examples would be unsettling. The sensitive interaction of body, mind, and soul made life seem both sturdy and delicate: the cooperation between human faculties provided strength, while the escalation of small disturbances into serious disorders left people alarmingly vulnerable.

If proper stimulation and internal harmony were so crucial to health, then people had to manage their lives very carefully. In order to spell out the practical implications of physiological theory, health writers of the mid-nineteenth century devoted volumes to advice about diet, exercise, hygiene, work, sleep, and other daily habits. Although the specifics varied, the regimens outlined in health tracts agreed on a number of general rules that applied to everyone in every setting.

First, popular physiologists advised that daily routines be thorough and balanced. Since the neglect or abuse of any bodily process was harmful to the entire system, every function had to be exercised judiciously. Dr. Edward Jarvis opened his 1848 primer on physiology by listing the requirements of human life: "Every one must supply himself with food of the proper quantity and quality," "supply his lungs with pure air to breathe," "cleanse his skin from all impurities," "exercise his muscles sufficiently to keep his body in good health," "exercise his mind sufficiently for the life and health of the brain and nervous system," and "govern all his passions and appetites, so that they may always subserve the purposes of life."[25] Jarvis's rules affirmed the value of a full, but prudent life. Even the veiled reference to sexual functions was an endorsement, rather than outright prohibition.[26]

A natural corollary to balanced use was the principle of moderation. Temperate behavior, health reformers insisted, was the only protection against oversight or indulgence. For example, as Dr. Charles Caldwell warned in 1834, physical exercise "ought not to be very severe."[27] Strenuous or violent activity, he explained, "diminishes vitality . . . instead of augmenting it. Like excess in every thing else, it is wrong and injurious, *because* of its excess."[28] Discussing "Health and Education," an author in the *Massachusetts Teacher* noted that self-control was equally necessary for emotional well-being:

> There is nothing so conducive to health as equanimity; and, in a life chequered by the ordinary amount of cares and trials, equanimity can be secured only by habitual control (not suppression) of the feelings, and by habitual and intelligent application of the mind to worthy and dignified pursuits.[29]

Catharine Beecher described the importance of temperate eating. To live well, she observed, one does not require frequent, or complicated, or rich food. "The more a person will limit a meal to *a few articles,* and these of the *simplest kind,"* Beecher suggested, the better he or she will feel.[30] "Is not here the place," she asked, "to practice the Christian 'daily' duty of 'self-denial?' "[31] Whatever the activity, health advocates saw moderation as both physiological necessity and moral virtue.

As Beecher's example of diet showed, simple habits were the best means to a temperate life. The third rule of health urged people to avoid artificial practices, that is, any activity contrary to physical nature or moral principle. According to popular physiologists, the external world provided every material necessary to sustain life, including air, sunshine, nourishment, and various stimuli. Manufactured medicine, processed foods, cosmetics, and other artificial products were unhealthy by virtue of being unnatural.

The call to simplicity rang loudest among partisan groups, such as vegetarians, hydropaths, and botanics. The *American Vegetarian and Health Journal,* for example, believed that people are what they eat: "If a pure, healthy, strong, calm body is required, then must a pure, healthy, calm fruit and farinaceous diet, with pure cold water, be presented to the builder."[32] On the other hand, if Americans wish "a nervous, irritable frame," they need only drink tea and coffee.[33] If they seek "the cankerous scrofula and its hideous pain, let [them] resort to the flesh of swine, or some other foully-fattened creature. So may butter nurture a cancer, salt stiffen to a rheumatism, and gluttony realize the gout."[34] If vegetarianism was the journal's standard recipe, simplicity was the key ingredient. "We are convinced by the more healthful condition of the simple treated body," the author asserted, "that such a life is more in accordance with its true nature, than a complicated and luxurious one, which entails on the poor frame a host of in-eradicable diseases."[35] No antebellum health reformer would have disagreed. Sectarians and nonpartisan writers alike believed that living well meant living naturally.

As a final admonition, advice literature noted that personal health was an ambitious, even elusive, goal. "The *beau ideal* of health has seldom, if ever, yet been attained," declared one author in the *Teacher of Health*. "There is no person so healthy but that he might be healthier, and consequently happier."[36] Far from denying the possibility of health, the observation that it was relative allowed for unlimited human development. It also imposed a considerable burden. Since people's quest for health would never truly be over, their commitment must never flag.

Health literature in the mid-1800s was a translation of middle-class ideology into physiological terms. Moderation, self-control, and persistence were standard themes in the prescriptive rhetoric of the period. Codifiers of middle-class norms declared that self-governance would enable people to endure social change; that the habits of temperance and simplicity would replace confusion in daily life with control; and that virtuous behavior, if widespread and sustained, would solidify the values of America's middling population and the roles of its men and women. As did other ideologues, health reformers recommended self-management as a buffer against private apprehensions and social upheaval. They depicted health as the perfect solution; its vehicle was nothing more than a moral life, and its benefits were nothing less than order and security.

However attractive a prospect that was, the endeavor itself was difficult. What motives would sustain someone during such a long, demanding journey? Health advocates found the answer in common-sense realism and Christian moralism, which proposed that prudence and conscience guided people's choices in life.[37]

Grounded in self-regard and directed at happiness, prudence was considered a rational power. Following the laws of life and health was obviously the right course because the advantages were so great and the alternatives so unpleasant. As Cyrus M. Burleigh declared in the *American Vegetarian and Health Journal,* "OBEDIENCE is the path of safety, health, happiness, and life, and disobedience the way of danger, suffering and death."[38] Similarly, J. W. Colburn of

New Hampshire, describing "an obstinate case of dyspepsy" in the *Graham Journal* in 1838, asserted that "obedience to each law is attended with its own reward, and disobedience with its own punishment. Those who obey reap the reward of health and vigor of body and buoyancy of mind; those who disobey are punished with languor, sickness and death."[39] Faced with such distinct choices, Colburn believed, rational people would dedicate themselves to "plain living" and labor, "as a source of pleasure, as well as to avoid the consequences inflicted on those who neglect" such practices.[40] The calculus of obedience and error was persuasively simple.

Popular physiologists cautioned, however, that good behavior did not bear fruit quickly. Dr. Abel L. Peirson dramatized the value of patience with an anecdote about exercise:

> In taking up a prejudice against exercise from the ill effect of single, ill-judged efforts, . . . [people] reason like the honest Hibernian, who, having heard of a feather-bed, thought he would first try a feather betwixt him and the floor, and exclaimed, as he stretched his aching limbs, "if a single feather is so hard, what must a whole bag full be?"[41]

Health reformers urged people to disregard momentary hardships and to anticipate the more lasting rewards of health.

They also warned against the false hope that occasional mistakes were acceptable. Physiological reformers insisted that the pursuit of health demanded absolute diligence and tolerated no lapses. As Dr. Edward Jarvis proclaimed in 1848, "We can relax in no required exertion, omit no necessary supply, and indulge in no wrong appetite or propensity. However small the error, the ever-watchful sentinel of life visits it with proportionate punishment, either of positive pain or lessened enjoyment."[42] Self-interest became a moral, not simply rational course. As a complement to guilt and fear, prudence measured the strength of one's will-power and the limits of one's commitment. To live healthfully was as much a test as an opportunity.

Success, then, depended on conscience as well as prudence. Derived from one's moral sense and confirmed by rationality and intuition, conscience was regarded as one of the higher human faculties and a quality more noble than mere expediency. According to moral philosophers and physiological reformers, conscience propelled individuals to choose the right path for its own sake. "There is, in every soundly constituted mind," asserted Dr. Elisha Bartlett in 1838, "an innate consciousness,—a quick and irrepressible instinct,—a feeling . . . ,—of right and wrong."[43] With respect to health, obeying physiological law was not simply a personal choice, but a moral imperative; what one might do became what one had to do.

First, health was a personal duty because individuals were responsible for their own well-being. As a correspondent to the *Graham Journal* proclaimed in 1838,

> *Every man is the keeper of his own health.* We cannot throw off this responsibility upon the regular doctor, the nurse or the quack; upon chance, or fate, or the Divine decrees. We are ourselves accountable for the health of our bodies as well as our souls; . . . and were not our ears closed to the truth, we should hear in every pain we feel, as unequivocally as conscience sounds remorse in the ear of the morally guilty, a voice saying, "THOU ART THE MAN!"[44]

Old excuses for ill-health were no longer valid. In particular, health reformers declared, people could neither blame heredity, nor defer to God, nor plead ignorance when explaining their illnesses.

Conventional wisdom at mid-century stated that each person was born with certain capacities, disabilities, and predispositions. Given the prevalence of Lamarckianism, Americans believed that acquired traits were heritable; in other words, characteristics that parents developed during their lives could be transferred to their offspring. Popular thought, however, also maintained that judicious intervention, such as education and proper habits, could temper one's liabilities and strengthen one's better qualities. With such influence over their own welfare and the condition of their children, health advocates concluded, no one could fix the blame for ill-health on heredity.[45]

Nor could people hold God responsible. Physiological reformers viewed the attribution of misfortune and sickness to "Divine Providence" as a common, but useless gambit. The subject was a favorite one in the anecdotal repertoire of Dio Lewis:

> A young scape-grace snatched a piece of mutton from a neighbor's table, and tried to swallow it without chewing. He was choked to death. The ignorant cried out that he was killed by a mysterious Providence; but the doctors found upon examination that it was not a mysterious Providence that killed him, but a chunk of mutton. The mutton was bigger than the boy's swallow, and so it choked him.
>
> The lesson of the event was, not that "God moves in a mysterious way," etc., but that people must not swallow big chunks of mutton.[46]

Without Nature or God to impute, no legitimate excuse remained. According to advice literature of the mid-1800s, conscience marked health as an inescapable duty to oneself.

Personal health was an obligation to one's family and community as well. Much as the human body was an alliance of physical organs, so too a stable society relied on the contributions of every member. In his arguments for physical culture, for example, Dio Lewis often pointed out the social as well as personal value of health:

> Every one of those pale, feeble, crooked little ones who now swarm in our streets at the hour of school dismissal, would be changed into an erect, vigorous, elastic, ruddy, and happy child. Every one of those sunken, nervous, fainting young ladies now lying in wait to break the hearts of the men who become their husbands, would be transformed into a healthy, happy woman, and prove a joy and blessing to husband and children. And every one of that miserable, premature, nervous, tobacco-cursed class, known as "Young America," would become decent, manly, and useful.[47]

Lewis's contrasts were sharp: a sick person was burdensome and unproductive, while a healthy one was a pleasant companion, a virtuous individual, and a valuable citizen. Conscience alerted people to their familial and social obligations; health allowed them to fulfill those responsibilities.

Finally, one had a duty to God to be well. Although God did not rule directly over people's physical lives, health advocates noted, He had established the laws governing the human body. The principles of health carried as much authority as did any other holy decree. "The commandments which God has written in the constitution of these mortal bodies," declared Dr. Elisha Bartlett in 1838, "are as obligatory as are those which were graven by his finger on the tables of stone."[48] To practice the lessons of physiology was to obey the divine order, while to violate them was to repudiate a moral duty and, in effect, to sin. Although New Englanders came to question their belief in an autocratic and intrusive God, their assertion of personal control, ironically, made little difference in their conduct. They were free to shape their own destinies, yet obligated to follow sacred rules. As William A. Alcott observed, "God has indeed left us free agents; but in leaving us free, he has not left us at liberty to disobey him—at least with impunity."[49] Quite simply, one was free to behave.

In fact, correct behavior became the preferred measure of health in the mid-nineteenth century. With health now considered a natural and desirable state, Americans needed new ways of recognizing their progress toward that ideal. Some indicators were self-evident. For example, if health was a physical condition in its own right, one should be able to feel it. Health was the experience of positive sensations, such as pleasure and vitality, not simply the absence of discomfort or disease. To be healthy, explained William A. Alcott, is "not merely to be free from pain, . . . but to have vigorous muscles, a good brain and healthy nerves, a strong heart, capacious lungs, a sound stomach, and a good skin."[50] When functioning properly, an organ conveyed a sense of enjoyment to its owner. As one Bostonian rhapsodized in 1861, "Health is perpetual youth."[51] To experience true health "is to feel the body a luxury, as every vigorous child does."[52]

A qualitative description of health diminished the value of most quantitative ones. Although longevity, population growth, and low mortality continued to be important signs of collective well-being, some popular physiologists distrusted strictly numerical measures of individual health. Dio Lewis, for one, tried to blunt the enthusiasm for equating quantity with quality:

> It is not true that you can determine a man's physiological condition by the tape line. He may have a very large, muscular arm, and be in a bad way. Most pugilists die early of disease of the heart and lungs; the strong man of the circus is notoriously in variable health, and, almost invariably, short lived. . . .
>
> In brief, they who regard big *muscle* as the alpha and omega of Physical Culture have but very crude notions on the subject— quite as crude and imperfect as those of the man who claims that mathematics constitute a complete intellectual culture.[53]

For Lewis and others, health was an independent state, not merely freedom from disease, and was to be judged qualitatively, not by physical bulk or strength.

Outward appearance was another mark of well-being. Advice literature observed that healthy people had such features as clear skin, good physical proportions, and a sound carriage. Most discussions about the relationship between looks and health focused on women. Such interest was hardly novel, since female features, both real and ideal, had been an object of attention in literature and art for centuries.[54] American health reformers in the mid-nineteenth century concluded that contemporary standards for women's looks were unhealthy and, therefore, objectionable. The *Journal of Health,* for example, found little appeal in either rural or urban womanhood:

> . . . [W]e are no admirers of barn-door beauties, with great bluff, ruddy cheeks; nor city beauties, puffy, punchy, and unwieldy, as if they were Falstaff's great-granddaughters; nor hot bed beauties, ghost-like, bloodless, and fleshless, with neither roses nor lilies to boast of, in their pale and unsunned faces.[55]

Physiological reformers favored the sort of beauty that derived from health. They asserted that good looks in the absence of well-being were a delusion, and that unattractiveness was no barrier to genuine health. As Dio Lewis explained, "A sick woman's face may be exquisitely moulded; she never appeals to our imagination. But even an ugly face all aglow with health and spirit, and with sparkling eyes, becomes beautiful."[56] Simply put, "beauty in woman is, in considerable part, a matter of health."[57] A woman need not sacrifice her desire to be attractive in order to be healthy; she could now look good by living well.

Neither inner sensations nor outward appearances, however, were adequate testimony of personal health. According to popular physiologists, the true litmus test of health was behavior. On the one hand, they argued, good character and conduct were necessary for well-being. One's every exertion, whether physical, mental, or emotional, influenced one's body. By living in accord with moral precepts and social norms, a person met the first condition of health. The converse held true as well. Since cleanliness and godliness were synonymous, health was the cornerstone of propriety. " 'Many of the fundamental Christian virtues—gentleness, patience, contentment, hope, cheerfulness, courage,' " declared the Reverend Henry Ward Beecher in 1860, " 'are so largely dependent on health, that in all but exceptionable [sic] cases they are not to be looked for in the unhealthy.' "[58] In sum, health was both the source and the product of respectability. As one observer concluded in 1835, health may be regarded "as one of the first requisites to usefulness and happiness; Temperance, Order, and Activity, as indispensable to procure and preserve it."[59]

With this behavioral yardstick, the normative content of health became explicit. To measure health, one need only ask to what extent an individual satisfied the moral code of the day. The answer depended on who a person was as much as on how well he or she behaved. Since people did not share the same physical requirements or social positions, one could neither expect nor condone uniformity of habits. For example, a child, a shopkeeper, a longshoreman, and an invalid needed different amounts of food and rest. The appetite of a farmer was not expected among refined ladies, nor was the spirited play of a youngster proper exercise for a grown woman.

To account for those differences, health reformers devised the notion of appropriate hygiene, that is, of tailoring the general rules of health to the special circumstances of people's lives. "Appropriate" was at once a social and physiological judgment. Suitable hygiene specified acceptable behavior, and identified which activities offended either cultural norms or the laws of nature. A healthy man was ambitious and resolute, not lazy or tentative; a healthy child was polite and obedient, not ill-mannered or defiant. The distinction between natural and normative often vanished in antebellum advice literature. Popular physiologists explained what behavior was suitable according to age, sex, and class by merging scientific principles and social conventions.

The question of what appropriate hygiene meant for girls and women seemed especially important. As other historians have shown, a new standard of true womanhood was articulated in America during the middle decades of the nineteenth century. From Sunday sermons to ladies' magazines, popular rhetoric depicted the ideal female as nurturant, submissive, and pure.[60] Such qualities complemented the independence and authority ascribed to men. The assumption of gender-specific traits posed a dilemma for health advocates: could girls and women gain health without losing femininity?

For some, the answer was straightforward. Healthy behavior for females was equivalent to the ideals of true womanhood. By being sweet and unselfish, a woman achieved both health and femininity. Or, as William A. Alcott elaborated, "The young woman who truly governs herself will be at once *cheerful, discreet, modest, diffident, vigilant, courageous, active, temperate* and *happy.*"[61] Similarly, her daily habits should be consistent with both the rules of health and the canons of womanhood. When asked, for example, how often and in what manner women should exercise, some health reformers advised activities that were gentle, even genteel. Dr. Charles Caldwell believed that "masculine feats" such as foot-races and wrestling suited neither women's "taste, delicacy, nor intended pursuits."[62] Instead, "as a duty to themselves, their contemporaries, and posterity," Caldwell recommended that women should "indulge in graceful and becoming exercise, in the streets, gardens, fields, lawns, roads, and pleasure-grounds" to an invigorating, but not unseemly degree.[63] For Dr. Caldwell and like-minded reformers, the dictates of nature and the expectations of society governed physical habits; women's innate character and social position determined how their health was to be achieved and recognized.

Other writers moved beyond personal attributes and related health to function. Excluded from business, politics, and the professions, what social value did women have? The answer resounded from pulpits, lecture stands, and books: as wives and mothers, women held a central place in human affairs. The home was portrayed as an intimate school where children learned virtue and obedience, and a moral enclave where adult men found refuge from the corrupting world of work. Women were responsible for preserving that environment of goodness and love. As shepherds, not merely custodians, they had control over the well-being of their families and the future of society. In short, a cult of domesticity complemented the antebellum romanticization of womanhood.[64]

The ideal of service was incorporated into antebellum measures of female health. A person's well-being, suggested the *Ladies' Magazine* in 1832, should be judged, among other things, "by the opportunities it affords of being useful in our social relations, and communicating happiness, and doing good."[65] Catharine Beecher, a chief architect of the cult of domesticity, applied an operational test. When Beecher investigated the condition of American women during the 1840s and 1850s, the highest rank in her scale, "a 'perfectly healthy' or 'a vigorous and healthy woman,'" was reserved for that subject "who can through the whole day be actively employed on her feet in all kinds of domestic duties without injury, and constantly and habitually has a feeling of perfect health and perfect freedom from pain."[66] In brief, how long and how well could a woman meet her familial duties? For some health reformers, domesticity and able-bodied womanhood were one and the same.

Others, however, questioned certain features of the cult of true womanhood. Their quarrel was not with femininity per se, but with societal limitations on women's interests and activities. Breaking ranks with conservative health reform, a sizable number of popular physiologists encouraged middle-class women to widen the perimeter of their separate sphere, for the sake of both womanhood and health.

For example, some health advocates opposed any restrictions on female exercise, especially among the young. Dio Lewis declared that "the noblest women I have personally known, were 'regular tom-boys' in their girlhood."[67] Among the women who assisted during the Civil War, he continued, "not one began with being a *'proper' young lady!"* There is nothing wrong if a girl "breaks through the trammels of propriety, rides the saddle astride, climbs fences and trees, joins a baseball club, or acquires distinction in any roystering game." She is more likely than her meek sister to achieve "strong womanhood." Just as a colt or a boy, "if quiet and staid," is not "likely to accomplish anything very grand in this world," Lewis concluded, neither will a girl who "is prim and nice and proper" amount to much in life. Lewis urged parents and educators to ensure healthy womanhood by allowing girls to play freely.

Some health reformers also deplored young women's preoccupation with marriage. What "prejudice" in modern society, Dio Lewis asked, "says to an unmarried woman of the better class, If you do anything except stay at home and wait for a man, you shall be ostracized?"[68] It is unfair, Lewis insisted, for women to be educated and given "large and noble views of life," only to be denied any goal except "to charm the beaux" and "any occupation except that of fascination."[69] The bright, healthy young women of America, he argued, were capable of becoming bank clerks, proofreaders, gardeners, and carpenters, jobs well suited to the feminine qualities of dexterity, neatness, patience, and conscientiousness.[70] Although his list of female attributes was not unusual, Lewis did object to the limits that social custom imposed on young, unmarried women.

Other physiological reformers focused on women's range of activity during marriage. They noted that women spent their time primarily on domestic chores which, however necessary, could be degrading. Confined to the kitchen, amidst the " 'everlasting din of pots and kettles and frying pans,' " for example, women labored to satisfy other people's physical needs.[71] Ignoring the value of simple meals, they were "chiefly employed in perverting—spoiling our food and drink—instead of making it better."[72] Such slavish toil in the home, one female author contended, frustrated women's higher purposes in life:

> Woman should be something more than Fashion's doll, or a cooking-machine. Their ambition should aim at something higher than the gratification of depraved appetite. . . . Woman should live for something higher and nobler than cannibal tastes, good appearance, costly furniture, or fine equipage.[73]

Home exercises for women in the mid-nineteenth century. Source: *Harper's Weekly* 1 (July 11, 1857): 436.

Examples of Dio Lewis's calisthenics with dumbbells. Source: Dio Lewis, "The New Gymnastics," *Atlantic Monthly* 10 (Aug. 1862): 139.

Women are intended, another writer explained, "to be the educators of our race; to educate their minds and hearts, as well as their bodies."[74] Far from denying the ideals of womanhood, such health reformers yearned for the day when wives and mothers would be free to exert their natural moral power, without the shackles of domestic drudgery or material pretense.

Using the issue of dress and public display, Dio Lewis made a scathing analysis of women's secondary status in society. Men establish standards of female body size and fashion, Lewis argued, in order to control women, literally and figuratively. Corsets and small shoes, he pointed out, limit women's ability to breathe and walk. "The compressed vital organs and the encumbered feet mean, that women are dependent and helpless. . . . While the nudity of the arms and bust signifies a slavery to man's passions."[75] A man prefers to treat his wife as "a pet or a toy," which he can decorate, summon, and rely upon for companionship and amusement.[76] Lewis left no doubt about the patriarchal and economic roots of women's suppression:

> The real but unconscious pleasure with which men regard women with little feet, little waists, and little figures, is that these fix her dependence. A woman with contracted feet, contracted waist, and contracted size, may fret a man by her nervousness, but she can never seriously challenge his authority. Many a man would prefer to sit up half the night to support a helpless wife than to hear from a strong, helpful one, a demand for a fair division of the family treasury.[77]

If petiteness marked subordination to men, such physical slavery would disappear, Lewis concluded, as women gained their full rights. "No one supposes," he proclaimed, "that when woman becomes a citizen, and man's equal, she will compress her lungs, fetter her legs, or appeal to his passions by any immodest exposure of her person."[78] For Lewis, physical norms were both symbol and substance of women's bondage to men.[79]

Lewis arrived at his opinions by asking the same question as troubled other physiological reformers: What sort of life was both womanly and healthy? Virtually every health advocate, whether conservative or radical, believed that the essential female qualities were moral and nurturant, and that the best gauge of personal health was behavioral. The matter under contention was the exact meaning of able-bodied womanhood; how could one achieve it and identify it? For some popular physiologists, the rules of healthy behavior followed directly from social expectations; a healthy female was a proper one, and vice versa. Other reformers, however, were convinced that certain cultural norms violated female nature and diminished women's health. If a woman exercised, dressed, and occupied herself as tradition demanded, they claimed, she would actually jeopardize, not improve, her health. Insisting that convention yield when it interfered with health, Dio Lewis and like-minded reformers supported aspirations for women that stretched, even broke, social custom. They argued that independence and other "unseemly" qualities were compatible with being female and were essential to being well. Discussions of appropriate hygiene and female health reveal the ambiguity of antebellum health reform. The movement reinforced the emerging code of true womanhood as well as proposed alternatives; its diagram of propriety was sprinkled with examples of nonconformity and invitations to self-discovery.

Overall, antebellum health reform prescribed self-governance to alleviate the problems of urban life. The world seemed unmanageable to Boston's middle class. Sickness, personal insecurity, social change abounded; transformations in the home, the workplace, and the city strained old codes of behavior and the familiar routines of daily life; institutions and customs that once guided conduct eroded under the force of new social conditions; a sense of order, not human perfection, was the immediate concern. In an unpredictable and seemingly uncontrollable world, Boston's middle class looked inward for stability. Self-control appeared to be the most reliable, perhaps only, mechanism for restoring order. That was the central message of health reform. The theme of self-management underlay every piece of advice, every firm admonition, every appeal to prudence and conscience. This was not exuberant individualism or democratic physiology so much as a search for control and the acceptance of one's obligations. If disorder was the problem, personal responsibility seemed the necessary and sufficient answer.

Around the cornerstone of self-governance, health reformers laid out the rules of good living. Their guidelines were general ones, and each was eminently reasonable: be thorough, temperate, simple, persistent. Those made particular sense to a middle-class audience, who hoped to check the turmoil of the outside world by regulating the internal one.

Health literature also explained how individuals should modify those universal principles according to the specific circumstances of their lives. During a period of social upheaval, the concept of personal health helped clarify norms of behavior, by sex, age, and occupation. It translated social expectations into physical images; the self-made man, the attentive woman, the dutiful child were pictures of health.

On occasion, those portraits became blurred. In particular, health reformers disagreed about what constituted able-bodied womanhood and how it might be attained. Advice literature gave no uniform sketch of the ideal, healthy woman, her behavior, or looks, or aspirations. If health reform helped codify and disseminate behavioral standards in antebellum America, it challenged them as well. Alongside the demands about propriety were opportunities for self-development. The history of the Ladies' Physiological Institute of Boston and Vicinity illustrates how some middle-class women dealt with that ambiguity.

3

"Know Thyself":
The Ladies' Physiological Institute of
Boston and Vicinity,
1848–1880

As both audience and agents, women played a major part in American health reform during the mid-nineteenth century. Advice literature, lecture series, and programs in schools, clubs, and gymnasia were often directed toward girls and women. Given widespread concern about female ill-health and the need for knowledgeable and able-bodied mothers, such attention is not surprising. More intriguing is women's role as promoters of health reform, in both the public and private realms. As speakers, authors, and educators, some women helped popularize the theories and rules of physiology. As wives and mothers, many applied those lessons in the supervision of their families and homes. What prompted women to enlist in the cause of physiological reform?

The history of the Ladies' Physiological Institute of Boston and Vicinity provides some insight into women's experiences in health reform. The Institute was a voluntary association devoted to the self-improvement of its members through physiological instruction. Mid-century America was a nation of organizers and joiners. Alexis de Tocqueville, the young Frenchman who arrived in 1831, exclaimed that "Americans of all ages, all conditions, and all dispositions constantly form associations."[1] That was especially true, he observed, "if it is proposed to inculcate some truth or to foster some feeling by the encouragement of a great example."[2]

While some Americans united to advance temperance, abolition, and women's rights, others banded together to learn, practice, and disseminate the laws of life and health. Throughout the 1830s and 1840s physiological societies sprang up in small communities such as Bangor, Maine, and North Brookfield, Massachusetts, as well as in major cities, including Boston and New York.[3] The American Physiological Society, founded in Boston in 1837, was one of the most visible and well-documented health associations.[4] Besides typical projects, such as running lecture series and a library, the group established a health food store and a short-lived physiological boarding house.

Women comprised nearly a quarter of the American Physiological Society and, as the annual report of 1838 noted, they got "in the habit of holding monthly meetings for conversation and discussion."[5] In addition to its regular gatherings at members' homes, the "Ladies' Physiological Society" sponsored public courses for women taught by Mary S. Gove (Nichols), a supporter of Grahamism and hydropathy. Similar groups for women appeared during the 1840s and 1850s elsewhere in Massachusetts (Charlestown, Gloucester, Millbury, and Worcester), in Providence, Rhode Island, and in Bangor, Maine.[6]

A social institution such as a physiological club has both advantages and limitations as a historical subject. On the one hand, an organization is at least one step closer to people's inner lives than is the prescriptive literature discussed earlier. By its very nature, a voluntary association serves and, thereby, reveals the concerns of its members. Survival depends, in part, on the reciprocity between collective activity and individual needs.

Admittedly, though, the history of an organization offers only a partial view of members' private worlds. One frequent problem is the scarcity of materials. Most antebellum physiological societies were ephemeral groups with obscure memberships that left scant documentation. Basic questions, such as who attended meetings and what topics were addressed, often defy historical study. The Ladies' Physiological Institute of Boston and Vicinity is a rare exception, since its records, albeit spotty, have been preserved.[7]

Another difficulty with institutional studies is that whatever materials do exist may give incomplete, even misleading, information. Contemporaries and historians alike learn only what appears in club minutes, published records, and other documents. As semi-public or public sources, those may not accurately reflect the private thoughts or behavior of individual members. To examine those, the historian can, in the best of circumstances, consult diaries, letters, and other private memoirs. The journals of a founder of the Ladies' Physiological Institute opened such a window in this study.[8] Less personal material can also enrich the historian's understanding of an organization. In this chapter, obituaries, city directories, and related sources helped develop portraits of individual members and a group profile of the Institute. With that range of information, one can explore the concerns that brought middle-class women to the Institute between 1848 and 1880. What forms of dis-ease did they hope to cure? What vision of health and womanhood did they hold, and how did physiological reform affect those perceptions?[9]

The Ladies' Physiological Institute of Boston and Vicinity was organized in the spring of 1848. Still extant, it is one of the oldest continuous women's organizations of any sort in America. While there is some evidence that members had gathered informally for nearly five years prior to that time, the Institute's official birthdate was April 1848. The catalyst was an offer by Charles P. Bronson, an elocutionist and itinerant lecturer, to deliver a course of talks to a female audience " 'who should form themselves into a Society for the promotion of useful knowledge among their own sex, proposing to present them with his apparatus (Model of Woman, etc.,) valued at $700, provided $1,000 were raised.' "[10] Biographical details are sketchy, but when Bronson arrived in Boston during the 1840s, he proclaimed himself to be a "professor of elocution" and the originator of a system of speaking.[11] Although the local medical community questioned Bronson's credentials, the women of the Institute regarded him as a philanthropic teacher and gentleman.[12] With the revenue from two public lecture series and a fair, the women met Bronson's condition and even elected him president, a post he held for two years.

The Institute had nearly 200 charter members and included 454 women at the close of its first year.[13] The first article of the Institute's constitution explained the group's purpose:

> The objects of this Society are, to promote among *Women* a knowledge of the HUMAN SYSTEM, the LAWS OF LIFE AND HEALTH, and the means of relieving sickness and suffering.[14]

To fulfill its mission, the Institute established a pattern of activities during the 1850s that lasted for decades. Interrupted only by a summer break, the women held weekly lecture meetings, presided over by an invited speaker or Institute member. "Conversational" meetings, usually conducted once a month, were more informal discussions when "all shall be free to speak & ask questions."[15] On occasion, the women made trips to places of mutual interest, such as an exhibit or gymnasium.

The Institute also maintained a library for its members. Beginning with 27 volumes in January 1849, the collection grew steadily to 330 volumes by May 1857.[16] In addition, the Institute acquired a substantial number of models, charts, and apparatus. During its third year, for example, the society purchased "a Phrenological Bust, a most beautiful colossal model of the Ear, capable of dissection, & models of the Eye" and "received donations of two embryonic specimens & one lobe of a Brain, properly preserved."[17] The collection also included a "Model of Woman, full size, capable of dissection," a female skeleton, detailed models of various organs, "a prepared Foetus, three months old," and numerous anatomical drawings and charts.[18]

In surveying the record of Institute lectures, books, and apparatus, one is struck first by their scope. As did other antebellum health advocates, the women construed the term "physiological" broadly. Lectures covered a wide range of theoretical, practical, and philosophical subjects.[19] During the 1850s, speakers discussed the rudiments of human anatomy and physiology, including the heart, the brain, the skin, respiration, and digestion. Others explained the principles of phrenology, hydropathy, and mesmerism. Numerous lectures addressed the source and care of specific diseases, such as consumption, cholera, and typhoid fever. Members also heard talks on such general questions as "Health & Religion," "Self Conquest," "Beauty," the "True Dignity of Woman," and "Music & Morals." On November 13, 1850, Charles Bronson spoke on "the laws of harmony governing individuals & societies; showing causes of discord, & the remedy."[20] Among the issues covered at conversational meetings were cancer, women's dress, and the "decision of character." During the 1860s and 1870s, the subject matter of lectures and discussions continued to be wide-ranging. Topics included the lungs, rheumatism, "the marriage bond," "Hereditary Intemperance," the "Health of Woman," and "the Past and the Present."[21]

The Institute library was equally diverse. It included popular health journals such as the *Water-Cure Journal* and the *Graham Journal of Health and Longevity,* as well as the *Boston Medical and Surgical Journal,* the organ of local orthodox physicians. It had scores of books on human anatomy, hygiene, and disease, ranging from general texts by George Combe and Dr. Calvin Cutter to practical guides on "Ladies Exercises" and "Water Treatment in Cholera." Finally, there were numerous treatises on natural history and physical science, moral and social philosophy, and such general issues as the "Improvement of Society" and "Woman: Her Education and Influence." For the Institute, physiology embraced every facet of the laws of life and health, whether physical or social.

A natural corollary was the Institute's belief in the unsurpassed value of physiological study, another basic tenet of health reform. First, Institute members noted the religious significance of their work. Physiological instruction helped them observe God's wisdom and power as revealed in Nature. As the recording secretary elaborated in 1850,

> We have met from week to week, & studied the handiwork of God,— traced His finger in the beautiful workmanship of our bodies,— learned the nice relations of the parts to each other, & to the whole, —been shown the intricacy & simplicity of this system of body, mind & soul,—we have seen that all is here governed by fixed laws, as in other parts of God's creation. . . .[22]

The teachings of physiology gave Institute members indisputable evidence of a " 'First Great Cause.' "[23]

It also laid bare the natural principles that directed the processes of health and disease, life and death. Along with other health reformers, members never doubted the necessity of studying life scientifically. For them, science was a reliable explanatory system, and physiology was the one body of natural law that rested "at the foundation of all others."[24] In particular, physiology was accessible knowledge, which made sense of daily experience and enabled people to improve their lives. As the secretary proclaimed in 1857,

> You stand as a Physiological School, professing to teach scientific truth. It is no less than the science which relates to the laws of life; the study of the human body,—to learn its structure, its functions, its derangements,—to learn the means to correct those derangements and to prevent suffering,—to learn the laws which govern life and health, are the pursuits to which your attention has been turned. What pursuits more ennobling? What objects more entitled to support than ours? As we look about us, on either hand, we see disease marking its prey; taking for its victim the budding infant, the blooming youth, as well as the man of declining years; and, as the funereal note strikes our ear, we catch the words, "Mysterious Providence!" and then all is silence.[25]

Eunice Hale Waite Cobb (1803–80), a founder and long-time leader of the Ladies' Physiological Institute. Source: *Ladies' Physiological Institute. Semi-Centennial Report* (1900?).

Instead of living in confusion or blaming inscrutable forces, the student of physiology "traced effects to their cause"[26] and learned to distinguish between the paths of sickness and health.

Institute members believed that disease was a punitive, and avoidable, condition caused by people's ignorance or neglect of natural law. Eunice H. W. Cobb, for example, concluded that a lingering illness in the late 1870s was "occasioned by undue exercise, and eating, for supper, something I had not aught to have done, New bread [?], and fried over potatoes. *I knew* the *right,* but still the wrong pursued. The good Father took me in hand, and dealt perfectly right with me. . . . A *lesson* has been taught me, that I shall not forget."[27] The Institute reiterated the same lessons of causality and culpability for other members. Institute women anticipated the day when "disease shall be disarmed of its power, [and] humanity, restored, perfected—made whole."[28]

Thus, a great deal was at stake. Physiology, the Institute's secretary observed in 1851, has "an intimate bearing on all the phases of Society," from "the more retired duties of life" to "the general relations we sustain to each other in the organized forms of society."[29] The prevalence of sickness and premature death signaled for members a profound dissonance between the human condition and the divine plan. They viewed physical degeneration as both a cause and a symptom of the general turmoil in America at mid-century. Physiological enlightenment would restore piety, moral rectitude, and social order. Thus, "the sphere of our usefulness," the secretary concluded in 1851, "is neither small nor narrow."[30] In 1852, her successor forecast what kind of legacy the Institute might leave:

> Although no structure of Granite or of marble shall be reared, to commemorate these our efforts, or mark the place of our first beginning, yet, a more noble structure shall be reared, shall appear in the ages, the structure of the human form, shall come forth, in its Loveliness not as now, marked and marred by deformity, disease and suffering; but shall appear in its completeness, harmonious in its proportions, perfect in its developements [sic], fitted and trained for usefulness. . . . The "Golden Age" is before us, and as a signal, we would present . . . our "Ladies' Physiological Institute" as destined to prepare the way, to usher in that golden period so long foretold by bard and sage; and in the fulness of time, bringing man into harmony with nature and with God.[31]

Through physiological study, members would understand the potential of humanity and gain a powerful tool for social betterment. Just as their work was immediately useful in daily life, so too was it a long-term antidote for social ills.

Members considered physiological instruction a natural, even necessary, activity for women. Their reasoning followed that of other antebellum health reformers. First, they noted that women's biology and upbringing were in conflict. Ignorance of their own bodies and mistakes in daily life spelled misery for most women: "Fondled at our birth, . . . nursed without the knowledge on this subject which should have guided the steps of our youth, we were educated according to the prevailing mode in every thing but a knowledge of ourselves, till as a natural sequence, we had hardly a true habit accordant with the design of our being."[32] Implicitly, women's suffering would not end until their physical nature and personal conduct were reconciled through education.

In addition, Institute members shared with other reformers the conviction that human regeneration was the special province of women. After all, they declared, a woman was the "sculptor" who molded the "mind & character" of her family.[33] Her power, in fact, extended well beyond the domestic sphere. As the Institute secretary explained sincerely, though awkwardly, in 1851, physiological knowledge is

> pre-eminently useful to the mother, in the care of her family, & affecting the welfare of a large part of the community.—for who can estimate the influences exerted by Woman, through the minute radiii [sic] of the *home circle*—instruction to her in the necessity of reform is felt world-wide, if her heart responds to the teachings.[34]

Throughout the Institute's early years, the assumed link between physiological reform and women was vital to the group's continuity.

Convinced of the magnitude of their cause, Institute members took their studies seriously. Although attendance records were not kept, the regularity of meetings (weekly for nine to twelve months of the year) is evidence of the women's commitment. In 1850, for example, the Institute met for a lecture on Christmas Day, indicating that neither winter weather nor special occasions could interrupt their program.[35]

Moreover, the Institute rarely strayed from the subject of physiology, and then only reluctantly. Lectures on political or economic issues, such as Otis Clapp's discussion of postal reform in 1856, were infrequent. In 1878, after attending a lecture that "was more *classical,* than *Physiological,*" Eunice Cobb noted in her diary that it had "a little too much of '*Shakespear,*' [sic] for my *taste.*"[36] The Institute avoided identification with causes beyond physiological reform. In 1856, for example, the recording secretary suggested that the organization thank Massachusetts Senator Charles Sumner for "his fidelity to Freedom[,] to his Country & to Humanity" by contributing ten dollars to a Boston anti-slavery fund.[37] After a month-long debate, a special meeting was arranged for those members who wished to make private donations.[38] Was the Institute afraid of controversial issues or merely steadfast in its course? A combination of misgivings and dedication kept members' attention on physiology.

If their subject matter was focused, the women's resources were diverse. Since the laws of life were open to everyone, members regarded physiology as communal property. No person or group held exclusive rights to the study of health. Anyone who could share some scientific knowledge or experience was welcome on the Institute's platform. Speakers during the 1850s, for example, represented the full spectrum of contemporary medical beliefs.[39] Among the most frequent lecturers were Charles Bronson; Dr. William Cornell, a regular physician who supported popular physiology; Dr. Ezra W. Gleason, a homeopath; Dr. George Hoyt and Dr. Edward A. Kittredge, who belonged to the Massachusetts Medical Society, but practiced hydropathy; and Dr. Enoch C. Rolfe, a regular who promoted women's medical education. Other speakers included Dr. Wooster Beach, a prominent eclectic; Dr. Walton Felch, a leading hydropath; Orson Squire Fowler and J. S. Grimes, two of America's chief phrenologists; Dr. Walter Channing and Dr. J. V. C. Smith, two of Boston's most eminent regular physicians; and an assortment of other local doctors, ministers, and health lecturers. During the 1860s and 1870s, the Institute continued to invite homeopaths, phrenologists, and other nonorthodox practitioners, as well as members of the regular medical community.[40]

The Institute's unwavering, but almost unconscious eclecticism is noteworthy in light of the sectarian clashes that divided American medicine during the mid-nineteenth century. The distinction between "regular" and "irregular" was crucial to the medical practitioners vying for scientific credibility, collective identity, and public acceptance.[41] Many regular physicians claimed that nonorthodox systems were devoid of any intellectual basis or practical worth and were the work of vultures, preying on an anxious public. Many sectarians, on the other hand, viewed orthodox medicine, or allopathy, as a corrupt monopoly that valued money and power more than the public's well-being and that relied on arid book-learning instead of experience and common sense.

Curiously, the Institute seemed unconcerned as the battle raged in the medical literature and professional societies of mid-century America. For example, in the spring of 1851, Dr. Ezra W. Gleason felt compelled to defend his credentials before the Institute. A recent convert from allopathy to homeopathy and a frequent lecturer before the group, Dr. Gleason "proceeded to refute the reports circulated that he was not a regular physician, by displaying his Diploma from the Medical College of Philadelphia, & also, the Certificate he had received from the Medical Association of Massachusetts."[42] Obviously, Dr. Gleason sought both the respectability of orthodox training and the independence of sectarianism. Institute members politely thanked him for the information and noted that "the fact which he had established had not been called in question by the Institute."[43] Though somewhat ambiguous, the Institute's response indicates that it was not very interested in disputes about credentials or affiliations. With only occasional exceptions, the Institute maintained good relations with a variety of nonorthodox speakers and seemed indifferent to their marginal status.

Similarly, the Institute rarely thought about its work in relation to the plight of orthodox medicine. It did not regard its program as a challenge to regular medicine or as a vehicle for medical reform.[44] Nevertheless, its initial dealings with some leading orthodox physicians were uneasy. At issue were the Institute's interest in physiological study and doctors' responsibility to that undertaking.

The controversy surfaced in 1849 when Dr. Martha A. Sawin, a recent graduate of the New England Female Medical College, a charter member of the Institute, and its president in 1858 and 1859, wrote a letter to the *Boston Medical and Surgical Journal*. Among other things, Sawin reproached regular doctors for slighting popular health instruction, especially for women. Have physicians, she asked, "done what they could for the advancement of true scientific knowledge among females?"[45] Mistakenly, the editor interpreted Sawin's question to mean that Institute members had tired of "listening to stuff that has already nauseated them" and were seeking more nourishing fare.[46] Having recognized that "knowledge vaunteth not itself, neither is it puffed up," he continued, the women were ready to enlist the services of those "professional gentlemen in the city, who never make presents of manikins, but who really have intelligence, and more substance than sound."[47] The editorial was not so much a genuine offer to work with the Institute as a sarcastic suggestion that the ladies display their "usual good sense and discrimination" by requesting the help of orthodox physicians.[48] In fact, while it did welcome irregular practitioners, the Institute had never snubbed orthodox medicine, at least its individual representatives.

Within a few years, the public tension between the Institute and the local medical press lessened. In 1853, Dr. Jerome V. C. Smith, the editor of the *Boston Medical and Surgical Journal,* paid tribute to the Institute. "With limited pecuniary means," he wrote, "the members have made themselves known and respected for their intelligence, and their praiseworthy determination to study the art of promoting the health of themselves and others."[49] Dr. Smith, who first lectured at the Institute shortly before writing his editorial, observed that the group relied on "the teachings of the best lecturers and writers on the laws of physiology."[50]

The journal's turnabout is informative. The stinging editorial in 1849 indicates the regulars' suspicions about popular instruction when conducted by those whom they considered charlatans. Dr. Smith's conciliatory remarks in 1853 show that approval was contingent upon evidence that popular physiology was a serious scientific activity for audience and lecturer alike. The best proof, needless to say, was the involvement of reputable instructors.

Antebellum medical literature repeated the same line of argument many times over. Thus, a short digression seems worthwhile, in order to examine the general attitude of regular doctors toward popular physiology. A convenient point of departure is the *Boston Medical and Surgical Journal,* whose editorials, letters, and articles between 1828 and 1870 frequently discussed the issue, in hopes of distinguishing between good and bad instruction.[51] Few commentators in the *Journal* opposed popular physiology outright, preferring it to public ignorance. As "Medicus" argued in 1850, "Though a 'little knowledge is a dangerous thing,' I have ever found that ignorance is a great deal more dangerous."[52] Doctors agreed that, in principle, the public should understand the laws of life and health to the degree it could. "Surely no subject is of more importance to the whole community," exclaimed the editor in 1846, "than a general knowledge of the complicated mechanism of the human frame."[53] To dismiss that idea would have been neither defensible nor politic. Instead, doctors took a stand that was both civic-minded and self-serving.

Writers in the *Boston Medical and Surgical Journal* specified what kind of popular instruction was acceptable. Physicians have always encouraged such lessons, the editor claimed, "so far as they are conducted by competent and discreet men, and are limited to such topics as it is every man's and every woman's duty to know."[54] Emphasizing that the laws of life and health were essential to women, some articles commended instruction whose content was both simple and decorous. Despite some reservations, for example, the journal's editor supported the work of Mary S. Gove because there was "nothing objectionable or indelicate for one woman to tell another those important facts which men study with a view to ameliorating their sufferings and promoting their health and longevity."[55]

The benefits of suitable education seemed considerable. First, it had practical value in helping people maintain their health, thereby facilitating "long life, happiness and prosperity."[56] Second, it would enable the public to distinguish between good medicine and quackery, between "the well-informed physician and the ignorant pretender."[57] One author elaborated by analogy:

> Give a valuable watch to a man who knows nothing of its structure, and if it stops running he may try to repair it himself, or apply to a *blacksmith* for advice; but let him see its wheels, and learn something of its movements, and he would neither meddle with it himself, nor allow any one but a *regular* watchmaker to repair it.[58]

Other commentators agreed with Dr. Finch "that medical quackery thrives and fattens upon *ignorance*."[59] "There is nothing," one doctor concluded, " . . . that would so soon and so completely rid the community of charlatanism, as a good knowledge of some of the first principles of medical science."[60]

The consequent advantage to regular doctors was obvious. As "quackery and medical humbugs . . . retire before the light of science and truth," one writer observed, "the well-educated physician will be more and more respected and appreciated."[61] That would be a major victory given the profession's admittedly low status at mid-century. Confronted by intractable diseases among their patients and by a host of medical competitors, many orthodox doctors hoped that popular physiology would improve their public image. Writers in the *Boston Medical and Surgical Journal* urged their fellow regulars to support popular instruction, thereby "adding . . . to the solid reputation of their brethren."[62]

To do otherwise, the argument ran, was to leave popular physiology in the hands of diverse, but uniformly dangerous charlatans. Most commentators assigned the name "quackery" to virtually every kind of irregular medicine, itinerant lecturing, and health reform. Failing to make even simple distinctions, many orthodox physicians adopted a two-level taxonomy, with themselves as the superior species, and homeopaths, hydropaths, Grahamites, mesmerists, medical clairvoyants, popular health writers, and nonorthodox traveling lecturers as the inferior one.

Their objections to popular physiology among irregulars were threefold. First, the pronouncements of "quacks," whether in books, journals, or public lectures, were, at best, misleading intellectual fluff and, at worst, harmful absurdities parading as truth. "The present age," declared the editor of the *Boston Medical and Surgical Journal* in 1851, "is characterized by being fruitful in learned nonsense, which some are so bold as to thrust upon the community with a strange confidence that shadows are quite as good as solid materials."[63] Humbug and hoaxes seemed rampant. Orthodox physicians railed against bran-bread reformers and "no-meat eaters"; against *"eminent female physicians, who have no more knowledge of diseases than they have of the quadrature of the circle"*; against "all these self-styled 'doctors,' going about preaching their balderdash 'physiology,' aided by innumerable newspaper puffs, certificates from (yet unborn) M.D.s and humbug mannikins"; and against those traveling mesmerists and "clairvoyant females, who look into the interior of their customers' bodies with shut eyes, declaring they see disease, and then indicate the remedy."[64] It was curious, the regulars observed, that each quack claimed to know the panacea for human ills, yet never provided scientific explanations or medical proof. "Are their propositions legitimate deductions from any known principles in any science?" one doctor asked rhetorically.[65]

Second, orthodox physicians maintained, popular physiology often violated common decency and exploited people's curiosity. According to Dr. I. F. Galloupe, the popular lecturer was "a sycophant, a feeder of vulgar ignorance, of base prejudice and baser passion."[66] Skillful lecturers "make easy dupes of silly women and weak-minded men," and can become "the pets of thousands of soft-headed dupes."[67] Doctors singled out the exhibition of mannikins as a particular "abomination, inasmuch as they excite a vulgar curiosity to see and to hear things that only belong to professional eyes and ears."[68] Displaying "specimens appertaining to the delicate subjects of conception, gestation, manual and instrumental labor, deformed genitals, &c.," before mixed audiences, one writer asserted, "has been and continues to be demoralizing and mischievous, especially to the young."[69]

Finally, critics assailed the motives of popular instructors. "Could there be any selfishness in taking the humble pittance of *twenty-five cents* a head . . . ?" asked one doctor. "Is it possible that there can be any inordinate degree of hankering for notoriety . . . ?"[70] Others complained that charlatans were able "to line their pockets with such earnings as years of patient labor can hardly command for the honest and reliable practitioner."[71] Little more than greed and the pursuit of fame, regulars alleged, inspired "this shameful system of sponging."[72]

In sum, regulars contended that popular physiology was usually "a superficial show of superficial things, and far too often by very superficial persons in pursuit of pence."[73] Their argument was a calculated effort in public relations and self-protection. The exchanges between the *Boston Medical and Surgical Journal* and the Ladies' Physiological Institute were but one round in the regulars' campaign to equate their professional abilities and the public interest; popular instruction in health was a legitimate need, best served by orthodox practitioners. Criticism of the Institute dissolved when regulars concluded that the group was serious and discriminating, that is, open to reputable lecturers.

Relationships with its speakers, orthodox or not, were the Institute's only formal contact with the Boston community at large. The group, however, had not intended to be so isolated. Members believed that physiological reform must begin in their own lives, then radiate to their families, the city's youth, and society as a whole. Having learned the laws of life, one secretary inquired, how should the Institute meet those broader responsibilities? "The answer intuitively follows; —by a practical Life; by living those principles which we advocate; . . . by using our influence to discard those false customs, in society . . . ; by instilling into the young mind, the principles of physiological truth. . . ."[74] Despite those goals, the Institute rarely initiated public activities. The group had no regular publication, failing even to print all of its annual reports as promised in Article XI of the constitution. It sponsored no exhibitions devoted to health. Some members even criticized its occasional fund-raising fairs for compromising the Institute's commitment to physiological reform.[75] As for making its resources available to nonmembers, the Institute was somewhat more diligent. The group periodically opened its lectures to the female public for an admission fee of ten to fifteen cents per person. (During the 1850s, paid attendance averaged between ten and twenty women, sometimes reaching fifty.) Notices of open meetings and lecture series appeared regularly in local newspapers, such as the Boston *Daily Transcript*. During 1851 a series of six free lectures was held as a gesture to show "a liberal policy" and afford "a means of a more general knowledge of our aims & progress."[76] The group apparently never carried through with its intention "to extend to *Female Teachers* and their *Pupils* the benefits of this institution," as stated in Article V of its constitution.[77]

Finally, formal contact with other organizations was infrequent. (Exceptions will be noted later.)

The Institute took its slogan "Know Thyself" literally. Maintaining a low public profile, it was a self-contained group devoted to self-improvement. Given the Institute's broad vision of physiological reform, the group's insularity is striking, if not paradoxical. It raises the key issues of who joined the Institute and why.

On first consideration, those questions do not seem very soluble. Although Institute records contain the names and, occasionally, addresses of many members, few clues about their personal lives are immediately available. A collective profile is one means of overcoming that limitation and of understanding the group's composition. Starting with names and residences, one can trace many Institute women through local documents such as the city directories, tax assessment lists, and newspaper obituaries of nineteenth-century Boston. However helpful, those sources do present difficulties, especially when used to identify women. For example, city directories in the 1800s were not complete snapshots of an urban population; they tended to be most accurate in covering geographically stable, adult, middle- and upper-class white workers and heads-of-household. Women did not have independent listings unless they held a job or headed a household as a spinster or widow.[78]

A collective profile of the Institute was constructed from two sources: a published list of 385 members from the first year (1848–49) and a sample of the most active and identifiable members (256) between 1850 and 1857, drawn from the Institute minutes. Both suggest that the organization was comprised mainly of white, nonworking, married or widowed women whose husbands were middle- to upper-middle-class.

The charter list shows that 60 percent of the original members lived in Boston, East Boston, or South Boston, and that about 75 percent were married or widowed. A survey of city directories uncovered nineteen women listed as widows and twenty-six as workers (or roughly 5 percent and 7 percent of the total membership, respectively). The workers included teachers, medical practitioners, small proprietors, and skilled workers. Seventeen of the workers were single, while nine were married (none widowed), representing 17 percent of all single members and 3 percent of all married members.

The above figures reveal a bias toward marriage and nonemployment outside the home. Comparative data help put those numbers in perspective. First, only 20 percent of the women born in

Massachusetts in 1830 and surviving beyond twenty years did not marry before the age of 50.[79] If one estimates that half of the single Institute members in 1848 were young and eventually married, then one may conclude that the group was fairly representative of marriage patterns in the state before mid-century. Second, the members' level of employment also seems typical. Carl N. Degler has estimated that the proportion of white women working outside the home was about 5 percent in 1800 and 10 percent in 1850, and that a great majority of those women were single.[80] With about 7 percent of its members working outside the home and a high proportion of them single, the Institute's employment figures were normal for the time.

Women without separate listings in city directories were traced through a husband, father, or brother. For that process, a subset of the charter membership, namely, the 230 from central, East, and South Boston, proved the most feasible. Of those women, 122 were located through a man's listing. Nearly 80 percent of the men (primarily husbands) were either skilled artisans or fairly prosperous businessmen, while about 13 percent were professionals or white-collar workers. Compared to Peter R. Knights' portrait of antebellum Boston, the Institute was significantly more middle- and upper-middle-class than the city's overall population.[81] A noteworthy percentage of the men appeared on the city's published lists of major taxpayers. A survey of those lists for 1842, 1847, and 1855 revealed 10, 17, and 18 percent, respectively, of the Boston cohort's families. Some of them were quite wealthy, judging from Knights' scheme of tax assessment groups (in which $10,000 in property value separates upper-middle from upper class).[82]

A final measure of the social status of the Institute's original membership is residence. The women tended to live in districts that were predominantly middle-class in the 1840s and 1850s, such as the West and South ends of the city proper and the harbor communities of East and South Boston.[83]

A second profile of the Institute, one based on the manuscript records, confirms the above conclusions. Although the archival sample of 256 members spanned seven years and emphasized the Institute's most active women, the resulting group profile resembles that of the charter membership. About 75 percent were married or widowed. Among the women whose residences were known (175 of 256), about 75 percent (or 132 women) lived in the city proper, East Boston, or South Boston. This residential subset came from comfortable, even well-to-do families in which the husbands or fathers were engaged in business or skilled trades (66 percent), white-collar jobs (11 percent), or professions (9 percent). The Boston cohort also included five widows and fifteen workers, or approximately 4 percent and 11 percent, respectively, of the subset. The workers were employed in teaching, medicine, dressmaking, and art.

While the sample from the 1850s is similar to the charter membership, it also has some unique features. In particular, the women who served as officers stand out. Besides Charles Bronson, the early presidents included Eunice Cobb, the wife of a Universalist minister and religious editor (1850, 1853–55, and 1860–62), and two female physicians, Harriot Kezia Hunt (1856–57) and Martha A. Sawin (1858–59).[84] A native New Englander, Cobb (1803–80) participated in church activities and charitable causes around Boston, in addition to caring for her family and friends.[85] Hunt (1805–75) was a self-taught physician and well-known social activist on behalf of women's rights, anti-slavery, and popular physiology.[86] Sawin (1815–59) was one of the first graduates of the New England Female Medical College.[87]

During the 1850s, the other offices were held by an assortment of women, fairly representative of the Institute as a whole. Several women in leadership positions, though, were distinctive. For example, Caroline H. Dall (1822–1912) was a noted author and reformer, particularly in women's rights. She joined the Institute in 1856 and was quickly appointed to several important committees.[88] Carolina Marie Seymour Severance (1820–1914) was a lecturer and social activist, especially well known for her work in women's rights and anti-slavery. Severance served on a number of Institute committees and was corresponding secretary during the late 1850s.[89] This array of officers suggests that, although it shied away from political issues, the Institute willingly associated with some prominent, even controversial, figures.

Overseeing Institute decisions and activities was the board of directors, a group of fifteen women. Among those who served on the board the longest were widows, wives, and daughters of Boston's elite. They clearly outranked the average membership in terms of social class and status, and were valuable additions to the Institute. Commenting on one director, Eunice Cobb said that she "was one of our original, and most devoted members of the Inst[itute] and did much to advance its early success."[90] Precisely what such contributions were is unclear. Still, wealthy board members must have brought an extra measure of respectability and security during the Institute's early history.

Continuity within the leadership was important, since the membership roll was so unstable during the Institute's first decade. Upon reaching 454 after one year, membership plummeted to 130 by May 1854, prompting the secretary's dismal conclusion that the roll was declining "as the square of the distance in time has increased."[91] Membership climbed to 300 by May 1857, fell to 100 in 1866, and, apparently, stood at 500 in 1871.[92]

Year-to-year rates of turnover dramatize the Institute's fluidity. Once admitted, a woman could renew membership by paying annual dues (at first, fifty cents; then one dollar in the late 1850s). Despite such easy provisions, the dropout rate, or the percentage of women who failed to renew membership, ranged from 23 to 57 percent during the Institute's early years. It then stabilized between 10 and 20 percent.[93]

The problem disturbed the leadership. As the secretary noted in 1857, 1,015 different women had been members since the group's inception. "I find," she wrote, "that few are with us to-day who assembled with us on our first anniversary. Of the three hundred members of to-day, not more than fifty have been with us more than three years."[94] Officers believed that several causes were at work, including the normal decline when members left the Boston area, confusion about the rules governing annual assessments, and the transient participation of women who joined "from an interest in the lectures alone, without any view to the organization, which was to be the means of continuing" the Institute's program.[95] Trying to encourage more responsible membership, the secretary likened the group to a majestic river that was "dependent on the little rills & streams which unite to form its volume & furnish its means of irrigation."[96]

The Institute somehow survived the ebb and flow of its membership. Though unstable in the short term, the Institute was remarkably persistent in the long run. The group's resiliency and longevity are its most intriguing puzzle. Recent trends in scholarship about women shed light on the Institute's durability. In particular, studies of female organizations in nineteenth-century America have begun to analyze the connection between women's private experiences and public activities, between their personal needs and social commitments. What expectations did women bring to voluntary associations, and what political impact did groups have on their members?

What relationships developed between domesticity and social activism, between sorority and feminism, between the personal and the political?

Such questions never arose before. Older generations of historians deemed women's voluntary societies unimportant. They certified that by simply omitting women's clubs from the historical literature.[97] With today's burgeoning interest in women's history, scholars have begun to examine the forgotten subject of female associations. Some have overcompensated for past neglect by virtually enshrining women's organizations, portraying them as the cutting edge of nineteenth- and twentieth-century feminism and social change. One scholar, for example, has argued that women's voluntary associations, in general, "created a vibrant feminist ideology" during the 1800s and that the history of benevolent societies, in particular, "is the chronicle of the origins of woman's emancipation."[98] If some historians believed that women's groups did nothing at all, others have asserted that they could do no wrong.

Neither position does justice to the meaning of women's organizations. At least two important insights have emerged from more sophisticated studies. First, the connection between private and public, between personal and political, is more complicated than most literature has implied. Through much of the nineteenth and twentieth centuries, social ideology in America maintained that the home and family were a woman's proper sphere and that her most valued traits were domesticity, selflessness, and service. In a word, her domain was private. For women and historians alike, that prescriptive model created a seemingly irreconcilable tension between private and public. Older historians reasoned that women's public (nondomestic) activities must necessarily be inconsequential. Recent champions have assumed that women's voluntary societies must have been strident political responses to the constraints of personal life.

As Estelle Freedman and others point out, however, there is no simple relationship, much less antagonism, between women's private and public lives. Although the concept of separate spheres for the sexes exiled women to the home, it could also inspire and legitimize their entry into the public realm. Elements of women's separate culture, such as domestic values and female friendships, could support social activism as well.[99]

That observation has been crucial to recent studies in women's history. Nancy F. Cott, for example, has explored how American women in the eighteenth century developed group awareness and justified wider roles through the very expectations that restricted their lives; bonds of sisterhood and activism grew out of the bonds of domesticity.[100] Through her biography of Catharine Beecher, Kathryn Kish Sklar has illustrated the personal and political nuances of "true womanhood" in the life of one middle-class woman in antebellum America.[101] A conservative educator and writer, Beecher intended both to codify the emerging ethos of female domesticity and to project women into roles that carried personal autonomy and social value. Other scholars have found evidence of a similar interplay between the private and public in nineteenth-century female voluntary associations. Karen J. Blair, for example, argues that clubwomen in Victorian America sought sincerely, but shrewdly, "to leave the confines of the home without abandoning domestic values."[102] They "utilized the domestic and moral traits attributed to the ideal lady," Blair writes, "to increase autonomy, assert sorority, win education, and seize influence beyond the home in the forbidden public sphere."[103] Other scholars have joined Blair in documenting the practical skills, self-confidence, companionship, and influence that members gained from women's organizations.[104]

To identify positive consequences, however, is not to locate feminism. As Freedman and Mary P. Ryan remind us, women's political awareness, whether private or public, need not be feminist. One unsolved issue among historians concerns the net political impact of women's associations. Were they, as Berg and Blair argue, quite radical in intent and outcome? Or, for all their value to members, did women's groups further institutionalize female domesticity? In a study of moral reform societies, for example, Ryan wonders about "the convoluted and ironic history" of organizations through which "Victorian women were guided into domestic confinement by members of their own sex."[105] Similarly, in her study of women's evangelical and temperance societies, Barbara L. Epstein observes that the extension of domestic roles into the public realm often fell short of feminism and gave women influence, but not necessarily power. With their commitment to Victorian morality and the sanctity of the family, members rarely challenged the traditions of male domination and female submission.[106] All of these scholars have found connections between women's private interests and their public activities. Where some see clear-cut feminism, though, others find a ledger whose bottom line is harder to read.

That divergence of views suggests a second concern about studies of women's organizations. Many works have presented a fairly monolithic and static picture of women's experiences. They have described associations as if members shared the same expectations and outcomes, and as if the political direction of a club, whether conservative or progressive, was uniform. As Ryan and Carroll Smith-Rosenberg have shown, women's groups were not monolithic; at any given time, a particular group may have served different, even contrary, ends.[107] Moreover, women's societies evolved; original motives and platforms may have changed as members reassessed their own and their community's situation.[108] Gradually, historical literature is appreciating that women's associations were variegated, dynamic institutions. No single conclusion about a group's significance can be drawn for all members or for all times.

One can apply those general lessons of women's history to an analysis of health reform, which, as suggested earlier, could serve either conformity or change. Organizations such as the Institute provided a forum in which to learn, share, and grow with other women. Did sorority evolve into feminism? Did self-improvement as wives and mothers alter women's perceptions of domesticity? In considering those questions, studies about health reform have diverged in a manner similar to scholarship about female institutions. Some historians have proposed that health reform was both a source and product of nineteenth-century feminism. Stimulated by the women's rights movement of the 1840s, they argue, health reform was an arena in which, by word and deed, women challenged the conventional limits of female life.[109] Less convinced that health reform was universally feminist in intent or consequence, other scholars have emphasized the practical and psychological value of physiological instruction, and also its prescriptive content.[110] The following discussion is a step toward resolving that seemingly polarized debate.

As with all voluntary associations, the Institute's survival was tied to the needs and experiences of its members. It attracted and retained women who believed that their interests were being addressed. It lost those who felt either very satisfied or very disappointed. Looking as deeply into members' hopes as the records permit, one finds that both personal and practical concerns drew women to the Institute. Specifically, members sought female companionship and useful information. Both needs reflected the uncertainties of women's private lives at mid-century. Health reform in general and the Institute in particular served to lessen their isolation and confusion.

The development of women's organizations such as the Institute built on long-standing patterns of female interaction. In recent years, historians and sociologists have begun to explore the many layers of sisterhood among American women from the seventeenth through twentieth century. Casual contact through letters, visits, and church was always common. The scattered societies for women in the colonial and early national period and their more numerous counterparts in the nineteenth century were, in part, formal structures that extended a tradition of female companionship.[111]

Despite the fluidity of its membership, the Institute functioned as an intimate and complex network of friends. During the 1850s, for example, the organization included many clusters of relatives and friends, such as mothers and daughters and next-door neighbors. They often joined together, and then proposed other kin or friends for membership as well. When a key member moved or passed away, the remaining women paid tribute in their annual reports. We are "a band of sisters," observed the secretary in 1851.[112] By acknowledging a loss or sending condolences to a bereaved family, the Institute showed that "the association on scientific interests extended to the more endearing & intimate relations of affectionate & sympathizing regard for each other's joys & afflictions."[113] Such personal warmth must have appealed to new members and sustained older ones.

A spirit of sorority also pervaded the Institute during the 1860s and 1870s. As indicated in Eunice Cobb's diary, the Institute still consisted of networks of friends who shared many activities with one another, including visiting, shopping, attending exhibits and fairs, exchanging overnights, and tending one another during illnesses. During her more-than-thirty-year association with the Institute, Cobb missed remarkably few meetings, in part because she cherished the fellowship of the group. On a stormy day in 1871, for example, Cobb ventured out to Charlestown for a board of directors meeting. Reflecting on the pleasantness of the gathering and her overnight stay, Cobb exclaimed in her diary,

> How many such kind attentions, and marks of friendship and respect I [have been] made the happy recipient of! . . . I have a host of friends, who seem to vie with one another, to see who shall add the most to my happiness.[114]

There was also a melancholy side to companionship. As Cobb wrote after an Institute sociable in 1872,

> I would not care to attend these meetings were it not for my friends, who so much urge me to be present. I have been with them so long a time, that I am missed when away. So many, who used to meet

with us, are now, no longer with us. I am lonely, and would prefer
to be quiet at home.[115]

Whether delighted or sad, Cobb found the Institute a place of en-
during friendship.

Her experience may be typical of the Institute's busier members. If a woman combined intellectual and cultural pursuits with
shopping and visiting, her social life could become a whirlwind of
activity. For example, the Institute was but one of Eunice Cobb's
many interests from the 1840s to 1870s. She also subscribed to the
lecture series of the Boston Lyceum, visited reform institutions, supported temperance, served as a director of the North End Dispensary
and Mission, and attended numerous fund-raising fairs and exhibits
for various causes. On October 12, 1865, for example, she sand-
wiched the Institute's lecture on consumption between a morning visit
to an art exhibit and lunch with her husband, and afternoon tea with
a friend, an evening lecture on education by a fellow Universalist,
and the writing of two letters.[116] On most of her outings, Cobb's companions were other women. The names of female friends and relatives
recur throughout Cobb's diary, indicating that she shared her private
and social life with a close circle of women. The Institute extended
friendships she already enjoyed among her relations and neighborhood and through her church and other institutions. For Cobb and
similar women, the Institute added another link to already large
chains of female friends and shared experiences.

For other members, regular contact with familiar women may
have been rare. The size and mobility of Boston's population made
relationships more difficult to sustain than in former times or in
rural communities. It is likely that many urban middle-class women
felt isolated in their small, privatized families, cut off from kin and
social events. For them, the Institute was a welcome source of interaction, if only for a short span of time.

Whatever their motives for seeking companionship, the Institute
prompted members to explore the meaning of sisterhood. As an
organization of and for women, the Institute inevitably faced decisions that required it to define that identity. Two episodes in the
group's early years suggest that members were conscious, even protective, of the Institute's female character. At issue in both cases was
the participation of men in Institute affairs.

In the spring of 1849, a crisis arose over the presidency of
Charles Bronson. While details about the incident are scarce, the

secretary did note in her annual report that this early "dividing point" caused "many to withdraw," but left "a band of strong and determined hearts."[117] With the dissidents subdued or gone, the Institute re-elected Bronson for another year and, at the end of his term, presented him with a suit in gratitude for his service.[118] The controversy appears to indicate that sorority was an active question for the Institute. Bronson was the first and last man to hold an office in the group, and no man ever became a regular or honorary member.

The second problem concerned the admission of men to Institute lectures. The discussion began in 1851 when the directors agreed to invite "husbands, Clergymen & Physicians" to occasional lectures.[119] The idea gained some support on the grounds that permitting mixed sessions would counteract the "erroneous impression [that] has gone abroad in regard to our lectures."[120] (Apparently, some Bostonians were suspicious about what transpired at meetings restricted to women.) Moreover, "fathers as well as mothers" would benefit from physiological instruction, and men's attendance would boost the Institute's revenue.[121] The proposal lay dormant until Carolina Severance revived it in the fall of 1856, and secured its adoption. (The records do not reveal if the plan was ever implemented.) What that five-year delay meant is ambiguous. It may show a reluctance to disrupt the privacy of the Institute by admitting men. On the other hand, the issue may not have seemed urgent enough to warrant prompt resolution. In the end and for whatever reasons, members decided that the idea did not seriously threaten their integrity as a group of and for women.

The Institute's spirit of sisterhood was consistent with emerging concepts of friendship in the first half of the nineteenth century. According to Nancy Cott, "relations between *equals*–'peer relationships'–were superseding *hierarchical* relationships as the desired norms of human interaction."[122] Female friendships were considered the most meaningful exchanges for women. As Cott notes, such group identity lay the groundwork for political awareness. Thus, the Institute's debates over Bronson and mixed lectures were not simply explorations of sorority but political statements as well. The Institute affirmed that community among its members was not merely appropriate but essential. Men were unwelcome intruders in a circle of warmth and understanding among peers. Regarding female friendship as comfortable and precious, members maintained the Institute as, first and foremost, an association of ladies. That position is an indisputable sign of the women's collective awareness and desire for independence, which is one layer of feminism. To what extent, however, did those episodes reflect more radical sentiments? Did some members perceive men not merely as trespassers but as thieves of women's voice and power in the Institute? Why certain members objected to full-scale participation by men is not known. Though signs of militant feminism are absent, the Institute's decisions do reflect a politicization of sorority.

As a setting for friendship, however, the Institute was hardly unique. Whatever their objectives, most women's organizations during antebellum times depended on and contributed to the growth of sorority.[123] Yet the decision to join the Institute rather than another group was a deliberate one. A cross-check of the Institute's membership and that of other voluntary associations in Boston during the 1850s revealed little overlap, even within the leadership.[124] Some reason, more specific than companionship, must have drawn women to the Institute.

President Eunice Cobb identified the Institute's special appeal in her inaugural address of May 9, 1855. Though cognizant of the value of friendship and personal growth, Cobb believed the Institute's real mission was educational:

> [I]f other good had not resulted, our extension of valuable acquaintance and mutual good-fellowship, and our discipline in the rules of good order and self-government, are acquisitions of no inconsiderable value.
>
> But *these* benefits are incidental. . . . We have derived useful knowledge from the varied instructions which our Institute has provided. We know more of the laws of life and health, and are better fitted for the duties of our responsible relations.[125]

Unlike so many contemporary associations, the Institute was not dedicated to the moral uplift or social regeneration of other people; it offered self-improvement by way of physiological instruction.

Middle-class women in Boston turned to the Institute because it offered precisely the right sort of "useful knowledge" at the right time. No longer self-sustaining clusters integrated into stable communities, urban families were small, mobile units in an increasingly complicated environment. Architects of the emerging industrial order and bourgeois values singled out the family as a key institution for moderating the strains of modern life. The cult of domesticity placed responsibility for the family's well-being on the shoulders of women. Nevertheless, many women entered marriage and the domestic sphere with little guidance about managing their duties as wives and mothers. Sickness, pregnancy, and death were recurrent dilemmas, and technology changed the character of everyday chores.

The Institute relieved women's confusion. By receiving physiological instruction and sharing their experiences, members learned how to care for themselves and supervise their families and homes more effectively. Meetings during the 1850s, for example, covered topics in female physiology, including menstruation, parturition, midwifery, menopause, and "Water Cure applied to Female Diseases." Lectures on such subjects as whooping cough and "chronic diseases & their treatment" informed members about tending infants and the sick. Dr. Harriot Hunt's lecture on "The Temperaments" in 1850, for example, "alluded to the wrong management of mothers & others having charge of youth, & pointed out the responsibility resting on those, who have been enlightened on the subject of Physiology, to counteract the tendencies of present customs at variance with the laws which govern our bodies & minds."[126] Other sessions focused on personal hygiene and habits, including "the great evils resulting from improper modes of dress of ladies" and "the effects of Tobacco."[127] Many lectures during the 1860s and 1870s were equally relevant, discussing such topics as the "Health of Woman" and "Hereditary Intemperance."[128]

Subjects conspicuously absent from the Institute's program were sexuality and birth control. Given the women's concerns, it is unlikely that such matters never arose during lectures or conversational meetings. The minutes may simply have omitted, or discreetly veiled, any reference to them. The only explicit mention of those topics appears in the records for 1850, after Dr. Frederick Hollick, an infamous proponent of sex education, donated two copies of his "new work" (probably *The Marriage Guide, or Natural History of Generation*) to the Institute's library. Regarding the information as extremely delicate, the Institute agreed to exclude the title from the library's catalogue and to place "the books in the hands of the Directors, to be lent by them to such persons as their judgement approved."[129] (On a later occasion, the board also decided to oversee the display of the Institute's anatomical models. Members should learn physiology systematically, they argued, not by rapid and perhaps shocking exposure.[130]) If the Institute covered sensitive subjects, it did so with a discretion, even reticence, consistent with the public customs of their social class.

Whether or not intimate discussions occurred, the Institute obviously addressed many of its members' practical concerns. As the secretary inquired in 1850,

> What mother among us does not recur to the period of her first maternal responsibilities, with regret that the knowledge which has been here acquired, was not possessed at that time, thereby preventing much physical suffering & mental anxiety[?] . . .[131]

The Institute, she concluded,

> is eminently adapted to our wants, & is designed to provide the kind of instruction, which will fit us for an intelligent performance of our duties, as wives, mothers, nurses, & guardians of youth.[132]

A concrete illustration is found in the life of Eunice Cobb. Problems of sickness and health interested Cobb from her early role as a minister's wife until her final years. The many hours she spent tending family members and friends were mixtures of kind solicitude and medical experience. What Cobb called her *"errands of love"* were occasions to increase and apply her medical knowledge as well.[133] During her husband's lengthy illness in the 1860s, for example, Cobb kept extensive notes about his symptoms and treatment. After the reverend's death in 1866, she recorded a detailed pathological description of his heart, following an autopsy to which she had readily consented. Not inclined to be ignorant or squeamish, Cobb dealt with her own ailments with equal inquisitiveness, good sense, and self-confidence. Cobb's diary reports the professional diagnosis and treatment of her illnesses, as well as her own analysis of the symptoms and their origins. To break a cold or fever, she used common remedies such as "an old fashioned sweat" induced by a hot mustard footbath or steamed bricks on her back.[134] For bilious attacks, she would give "the stomach a good rinsing out" with hot water washes, and would also apply external mustard baths.[135] On occasion, Cobb agreed to more novel treatments, such as the use of ether when a doctor repaired her dislocated shoulder and homeopathic medicine during a bilious attack; her reactions to both were very favorable.[136] Convinced that illnesses were explicable and treatable, Cobb never stopped learning or experimenting. For Cobb, organizing the Institute was a logical means of reinforcing those beliefs, and of communicating them to other women.

The Institute was more than a source of practical information. It also alleviated some of the uncertainties and stress that attended domestic life. Neither their upbringing nor advice books gave women adequate guidelines for handling their duties. In contrast, Cobb's self-assurance reveals a woman who was emotionally, not just intellectually, equipped to meet her responsibilities. For example, when her daughter had a large uterine tumor removed in 1871, Cobb observed, "[My] knowledge of the whole matter was of incalculable value, and gave me strength for the occasion."[137] Through useful instruction, the Institute fostered personal confidence as well.[138]

In the process, Eunice Cobb and other members may have perceived their female duties to be more gratifying than they originally thought. Relieved of their ignorance and uneasiness, members assumed their roles as wives and mothers more confidently, and even felt empowered by them. If women came to the Institute out of confusion, perhaps they left feeling quite literally like the "sculptors" of their families, now armed with the scientific tools to accomplish the job more successfully. Domesticity came to represent authority and self-respect. That was no small consequence in a culture that denied women most forms of power and self-esteem.

How far did members' new perceptions of womanhood go? Did their attitudes about sorority and domesticity evolve into a feminist critique of women's status? Those questions are difficult to answer, if only because the views of most individual members are unknown. Nevertheless, there are some clues about the Institute's overall political tendencies. For example, the Institute certainly enlarged its circle to include nonmembers. By its very nature, the group had occasion to associate with other women involved in physiological reform. Its record of support for female lecturers was a vigorous one. Besides using its own members as speakers, the Institute frequently invited women from the Boston area or the lecture circuit in the Northeast. The speakers list in the 1850s included a Mrs. Fergus, a local mesmerist and phrenologist; Madame Sarti, who ran an anatomical museum in Boston with her husband; Dr. Nancy E. Clarke, a young graduate of the Cleveland Medical College who practiced in Boston and unsuccessfully tried to gain admission to the Massachusetts Medical Society; Dr. Lydia Folger Fowler, a graduate of the Central Medical College in Syracuse and the wife of a famous phrenologist; Paulina Wright Davis, an activist on behalf of physiological reform and women's rights; and Mrs. M. A. W. Johnson, another familiar itinerant lecturer in antebellum times.[139] Besides conferring honorary membership on such guests, the Institute praised their efforts in terms exceeding the usual thanks for an interesting lecture. In 1851, the Institute agreed to publish a resolution in local newspapers "commending Mrs. Johnson to the public, as an interesting expositor of truth" on physiology.[140] Members also applauded Lydia F. Fowler's "noble work of ameliorating the condition of our sex, and in the developing and perfecting of humanity."[141]

Impressed with such dedication, the Institute secretary hoped in 1851 that "many from our ranks will yet embark in this branch of instruction. The voice of woman is needed to be heard, to call her sisters' attention to the great dangers threatening them from their blind adherence to false customs & habits. . . ."[142] At least one member of the Institute did answer the call. As a minister's wife and then widow, Eunice Cobb addressed ladies' groups and general conventions of the Universalist church throughout the mid-nineteenth century. During the same period, she began speaking at the Institute and soon became a popular lecturer on physiology and related subjects, traveling from Saratoga Springs, New York, to Bridgeport, Connecticut, to Dover, New Hampshire. Entries in Cobb's diary reveal a mix of budding confidence and anxiety about her new role. Prior to the nineteenth century, women really were "unaccustomed to public speaking" because tradition, and sometimes law, prohibited it. Along with other antebellum reform groups, the Institute broke new ground by giving its members and other women a public platform.

Support for female medical practitioners was a logical corollary to the Institute's encouragement of female lecturers. Members believed that their programs enlarged the knowledge and usefulness of the nurses who joined the group.[143] It also prepared a list of the nurses' names and references for the benefit of other members.[144]

The Institute's contribution to medical education for women was modest but noteworthy. The issue of female physicians was controversial during antebellum times and thereafter.[145] Amidst a rhetorical battle in the general and medical press, a number of groups, especially in the Northeast, took steps to offer medical training for women. One of the earliest efforts was the establishment of the Boston Female Medical College in 1849.[146] At first, the Institute kept a cautious distance between itself and the College. As its published report of 1850 stated, "This Institute is not at all connected with the 'Female Medical School,' located in Boston, . . . under the patronage of the 'Female Medical Education Society.' "[147] The primary reason for the disclaimer was confusion: first, public uncertainty about the difference between the Institute and the Society, since they received charters from the state legislature at the same session, and second, members' uneasiness about the exact name and purpose of the group that ran the College.[148] Nevertheless, some of the founders and faculty of the new school were favorite lecturers at the Institute during the 1850s and were allowed to use the Institute's hall for other purposes. Such personal contacts continued through the College's troubled history, but Institute records reveal no other ties between the two organizations.

During the mid-1850s, a campaign developed in New York to establish a hospital that would provide health care for women as well as training and staff positions for female doctors.[149] The leaders were three pioneering women physicians, Drs. Elizabeth and Emily Blackwell and Dr. Marie Zakrzewska (friends of Dr. Harriot Hunt and Carolina Severance, both Institute officers at the time). During a visit to Boston in the fall of 1856, Dr. Zakrzewska attended a meeting of the Institute and appealed for help.[150] Two months later the Institute donated articles valued at $300 to a fund-raising fair in New York, prompting a letter of thanks from Dr. Elizabeth Blackwell.[151] What became of the Institute's relationship with the New York doctors is not known, but the organization's early support is significant. It demonstrates the Institute's interest in the community of women beyond its own walls.

Some members made women's concerns a life-long project. Harriot Hunt and others were widely known activists on behalf of women's rights, and undoubtedly championed the cause at Institute meetings. Most, however, had a more limited view of sorority and reform. Eunice Cobb probably represented the norm in the Institute. Based on what she considered women's best interests, Cobb advocated balancing change and tradition. For example, she endorsed dress reform on the grounds of improved health. After attending a church meeting on a wickedly hot day in 1879, Cobb wrote,

> [I wore a] light Muslin dress, and black lace shawl, and kept myself very comfortable, while others, with their *thick black dresses*, seemed entirely overcome. O, what a slave *fashion* is! I am glad that I am independent of its uncomfortable influence, and study *comfort*, instead of *look*, and remarks of others.[152]

Cobb, however, refused to support major reforms in women's social position. For example, she did not approve of female ministers and found the suffrage movement too extreme. In 1870, Cobb visited a bazaar sponsored by suffragists, and noted: "The 'strong minded women' are pretty strong in their effort for what they consider so all important, but I do not fully sympathise with the movement. . . ."[153] Cobb believed in "the 'rights' of woman to make every thing 'right,' in the 'right' way."[154] Neither strictly conventional nor strikingly radical, she perhaps exemplified the intermediate position of many Institute members, something akin to what historians call domestic feminism. Cobb wanted to dignify women's special qualities and separate sphere, not to gain autonomy from or equality with men. Her goals were more woman-oriented than woman-defined; that is, she sought to improve women's health, authority, and self-esteem within the bounds determined by her (male-defined) society.[155] Nevertheless, Cobb stretched the fabric of true womanhood and domesticity to accommodate ideas and roles that many Americans at mid-century would have considered unfeminine. To regard Cobb as a conservative reformer does not deny that the Institute politicized its members. The label is a relative one, based on the political philosophies extant in Cobb's lifetime. If she was typical, then the Institute as a whole was more progressive than some women's organizations, but significantly less radical than others.

The ideals and realities of domesticity were central to the Institute's existence. Their roles as wives and mothers compelled women to join the Institute. Members created an extra-domestic group of peers that helped them manage the demands of familial life. If the notion of a separate sphere for female influence legitimized their weekly gatherings, it also drew them back into the home. Members believed, without hesitation, in the primary significance of their domestic and maternal duties. They were middle-class married women who set out to understand their roles more fully and to bring some order and control into their lives. At the same time, the cult of domesticity opened doors for them. Institute members gained new knowledge, skills, and self-esteem. They no longer were fragile and dependent females, but able-bodied and competent women. The Institute nourished stronger personal identities while it filled in the outlines of domestic womanhood.

In the process, it served a larger social function. The Institute's work incorporated the basic ingredients of middle-class ideology in the mid-nineteenth century. It reinforced the belief that self-management, domestic order, and adherence to natural law and social arrangements were the building blocks of personal happiness. It endorsed education and self-reform, not the redesign of society, as the first steps in the search for progress. The Institute did not impose such an outlook on its members. Rather, the women fashioned an organization that both reflected and advanced already firm, or at least emerging, convictions.

The early years of the Institute reveal the interwoven functions of physiological reform, within voluntary associations in general and women's groups in particular. In order to survive, such organizations had to represent their members' concerns. If internal or external changes limited its responsiveness, a group was apt to fold. Despite its unstable membership between 1848 and 1880, the Institute persisted by serving women's needs. It did so through single-minded devotion to physiological instruction and self-reform in the company of ladies. There were other ways of finding sorority than by joining a club; there were other means of learning physiology than by attending lectures. The Institute's distinction was in combining those two interests, thereby satisfying personal and practical concerns at once.

In 1880, several months before her death, Eunice Cobb wrote a farewell poem to her friends in the Institute. It read, in part:

> I will speak of times long past,
> Whose memories will always last.
> Times, when we have met together,
> In *pleasant* and in *stormy* weather.
> We've met to do all that we could
> Which we have thought for others good,
> To help our friends to study health,
> Which is to all a priceless wealth.
> We have been favored by the Lord,
> And have received a full reward.
> *Yes, my friends,* we've lived to see,
> That we have gained the victory;
> And much, dear ones we have enjoyed,
> While this our time has been employed.
> And now *my friends* oft may you meet,
> And in love, each other greet.[156]

Cobb's poem captured the dedication and idealism, the quiet intimacy, and the practical benefits that sustained the Institute over its first three decades. As the next chapter will show, the poem also marks the closing of an era for the Institute, and for American health reform in general.

4

In Private and In Public:
The Ladies' Physiological Institute,
1880-1898

In 1886, novelist Henry James wrote *The Bostonians,* a satire about the city's women and their social causes.[1] The reader meets, for example, Miss Birdseye, a long-suffering philanthropist, who "belonged to any and every league that had been founded for almost any purpose whatever."[2] James mocked the incessant activity of that "rather suburban and miscellaneous" set of women "who trotted about, early and late, with books from the Athenaeum nursed behind their muff, or little nosegays of exquisite flowers that they were carrying as presents to each other."[3] On the street, Boston's crusading women were "always apparently straining a little, as if they might be too late for something."[4] One obligatory date was their discussion club. "They form an association for meeting at each other's houses, every week, and having some performance, or some paper read, or some subject explained. The more dreary it is and the more fearful the subject, the more they think it is what it ought to be."[5] One can almost see members of the Ladies' Physiological Institute sitting down to discuss neurasthenia or consumption.

Whether James had the Institute in mind or not, his caricature hardly does justice to that organization, or to other women's clubs in late nineteenth-century America. The history of the Institute during the 1880s and 1890s is both significant and complex. The Institute broadened its role as a women's group devoted to physiology. While continuing to provide education and companionship for average members, it also became a public platform among women for whom health ranked high on a long agenda of social needs. That development within the Institute reflected general trends in American attitudes about health in the late 1800s. By the last quarter of the century, changes were underway in how the middle class defined personal health and where hygienic rules and values fit into their daily lives. A new perspective on health emerged in late Victorian Boston, as shown by the inner history of the Institute.

During the 1880s and 1890s, physiological instruction remained the Institute's primary activity.[6] Adjourned over the summer months, the organization averaged more than thirty meetings a year. Following tradition, weekly lectures and "conversational" meetings covered a wide range of subjects. Some sessions dealt with the basics of anatomy and physiology, including the brain, the nervous system, the kidneys and liver, the eyes, and respiration. Others focused on specific diseases and disorders, including colds, diphtheria, congenital malformations, and insanity. A large number of the meetings were practical, teaching members how to preserve health and care for the sick. They learned about the evils of alcohol and opium, proper habits of eating, exercise, and sleep, the techniques of first aid and resuscitation, and rules for raising infants and children. The Institute also enjoyed topical subjects, such as faith healing, "Florida as a sanitarium," the Swedish movement cure, and the medical aspects of President Garfield's assassination. The Institute still considered any issue related to physical well-being a legitimate part of its program.

Moreover, it continued to invite a variety of speakers to its platform.[7] Distinguished members of Boston's medical community appeared, as did an assortment of less prominent orthodox physicians, such as the superintendent of a home for reformed drinkers. The Institute also welcomed a considerable number of sectarian doctors, especially homeopaths, and other nonorthodox practitioners, including a massage therapist and electric bath operator. The remaining speakers were a collection of educators, ministers, and civic leaders from the Boston area. As in earlier years, Institute members rarely differentiated between lecturers on the basis of background or medical philosophy.

Other signs too suggest that the Institute was as vigorous as during its first decades, if not more so. For example, between one-third and one-half of the members checked out books from the Institute's library each year.[8] (While those numbers seemed disturbingly low to some officers, they do reflect members' interest in pursuing their studies at home.) In addition, the group's total size fluctuated quietly between 150 and 200 members during the late nineteenth century, in contrast with the seesaw figures of earlier years.[9] More important, turnover rates were notably low. During the early 1880s, for example, an average of nearly 80 percent of the women renewed their memberships at the close of each lecture season.[10] The Institute had achieved a degree of continuity unknown in its formative years.

At the same time, there are indications that the group, however stable, was hardly unified. The most troublesome issue was a basic one: the Institute's purpose with respect to its individual members and to the larger community of Boston. Usually concealed, differences of opinion surfaced abruptly during the Institute's annual election of 1884.

In the spring of that year, the Institute faced the unhappy job of replacing its departed president, Dr. Arvilla B. Haynes. A homeopath and leader in several women's groups, Haynes served as the Institute's president for twelve years.[11] Normal procedure was forsaken during the annual election when two slates of candidates for the major offices were filed: one favored by the nominating committee, the other proposed as a minority report. Institute members decided that both should go before the voters, and an unusually high proportion (53 percent) turned out to cast ballots on May 1, 1884.[12] The key difference between the slates was the contest for president, which set Dr. Salome Merritt against Dr. Helen B. O'Leary. The two women held contrasting views about the Institute's agenda; Merritt hoped to lead the group in new directions, whereas O'Leary stood for a more traditional program.

Dr. Salome Merritt was born in Templeton, Massachusetts, in 1843, the youngest of eleven children.[13] After attending local public schools and an academy in Rhode Island, Merritt taught in her hometown from 1864 until 1871. She then apprenticed under a physician in Boston and completed a three-year program in just one year at the New York Free Medical College for Women. After teaching at her alma mater for two years, she established a private practice in Boston. Over the next twenty years, Merritt became known as a competent and generous pediatrician, who even helped sew clothes for her patients' babies.

Merritt's attentiveness illustrated a general concern for human growth and knowledge. Her chief causes were instruction in proper infant care for new mothers and sex education for the young. (She regarded "sex-shame" as one of the last and most unnatural superstitions of modern civilization.[14])

In turn, Merritt's interest in health education was only one of her many social projects. As a local newspaper commented after her death, Merritt was "conspicuous" in Boston for "her many efforts to protect the interests of the young, to obtain larger opportunities for the neglected classes of society and to enlighten the ignorant as to their duties and privileges."[15] She was a member and officer of the Women's Charity Club, the Women's Educational and Industrial Union (WEIU), the Moral Education Society, and the Committee of Council and Co-operation, a coalition of Boston's moral reform societies. She was a charter member of the Woman's Suffrage Association of Massachusetts, and its president for five years. A self-appointed watchdog over municipal affairs, Merritt organized a citizens' group to monitor the Boston School Committee, in hopes of keeping it nonpartisan and nondenominational, and she spearheaded efforts to have a permanent board of citizens help review the administration of correctional institutions. Finally, she promoted local legislation related to health problems, from better sanitary conditions in public schools to the availability of chairs at work counters for tired salesclerks.

Several themes wove through Merritt's diverse activities. She believed that education was the primary agency for personal development, self-respect, and freedom. She campaigned against any form of intolerance and injustice, and worked for any measure that encouraged individual and social purity. For Merritt, physiological instruction offered an important, but not isolated, means to her ends, and social reform was a necessary counterpart to self-improvement.

Merritt represented the new perspective on health that evolved in America during the late nineteenth century. Philosophically, she was both an old-fashioned moralist and a modern pragmatist. As much as Merritt believed in the unity of cleanliness and godliness, she also understood the concrete benefits of health, for individuals and their society. In addition, Merritt relocated health in the matrix of personal and social goals. During antebellum times, some Americans had regarded health as a direct source of happiness and success. For Merritt, health was a vital, but only intermediate aim in life; along with economic security and civil justice, physical well-being contributed to the general social good. Both the substantive and the symbolic meaning of health had changed since mid-century and new strategies for promoting health were required. Although self-improvement remained important to Merritt, she viewed other means of education and reform as equally crucial. If the Institute followed Merritt's lead in 1884, it would become less a private organization devoted to self-knowledge and more a public agent of social change.

Although the nominating committee preferred Merritt, the Institute's membership voted in favor of her challenger, Dr. Helen B. O'Leary, by the resounding margin of 75 to 25 percent. The result was qualitatively decisive as well, since O'Leary represented a different vision of the Institute's work. O'Leary's credentials, both professional and social, appear to be impressive.[16] While details about her training and practice are not known, both of her parents and her husband were doctors. O'Leary was a Mayflower descendant and a member of the Daughters of the American Revolution. A devoted physician, she was also noted for her ease in public speaking and her love of travel. O'Leary participated in relatively few organizations; she was a long-time member and lecturer of the Institute and a member of the WEIU, chairing its Hygiene and Physical Culture Committee in 1885.

O'Leary was older than Merritt by more than ten years and had been a familiar face in the Institute since the 1860s. During her inaugural address in 1884, O'Leary emphasized the difference with a none-too-subtle analogy:

> In that terrible disaster to the "City of Columbus," [a recent shipwreck] . . . it was thought the Captain left the Steamer too much in the young mates [sic] hands. He did not keep it far enough out at sea, and it struck upon the rocks.
>
> We want our Physiological ship manned by experienced hands, who will keep it sufficiently far out into the sea of knowledge so that we may free ourselves from the bitter rocks of contentions, bickerings and personalities, for if we continue to strike these, we shall surely go down.[17]

Just what conflicts O'Leary meant and whether she exaggerated them is unknown, but her election was a clear vote for seasoned leadership. Institute members viewed O'Leary as a source of continuity and experience.

O'Leary's plan for the Institute also set her apart from Merritt. O'Leary maintained that the group's primary functions were educational and sororial. In her inaugural address of 1885, for example, O'Leary reminded members that "physiology is our theme here, it is our business to study it."[18] As president she took steps to improve the quality and use of the library and to revive the practice of conversational meetings. O'Leary also believed that the Institute should be a congenial setting in which to maintain friendships and to sample topics other than physiology. After a course of "substantial science," she once declared, "we can have a dessert of literary matter."[19] It is entirely appropriate, she continued, to have "our entertainments, our gala days."[20] In word and deed, O'Leary pledged herself "to be true" to the Institute's principles and, thereby, to its tradition of instruction and companionship.[21]

Her program, however, was not simply a throwback to the Institute's early days. O'Leary encouraged the group to embark on more public activities. "We must not hide our physiological light under a bushel," she said, "but let it so shine, that others may feel its beneficent influence."[22] She thought that Institute members might visit the sick and poor, and should organize lecture meetings for special audiences, including Boston's children, young ladies, and the husbands and brothers of members.[23] Compared with Merritt's intentions, though, such ideas strayed little from the Institute's original design. O'Leary considered physiological instruction the members' primary need and, thus, the Institute's central focus. Regarding self-improvement through education as the chief means of effecting change, she advocated a mixture of activities in which the private still outweighed the public. As evidenced by the large turnout and conclusive results of the 1884 election, a substantial majority of Institute members agreed.

The decisiveness of the vote seems to diminish when other facts are considered. O'Leary's tenure of four years was notably short compared to the twelve years that both her predecessor and successor held office. Although those women's deaths terminated their service, O'Leary resigned in 1888 and lived until 1916, well beyond her presidential tenure. What prompted O'Leary's decision is not known, but it seems to have been of her own making, not the Institute's. Even after her first year, O'Leary had contemplated leaving the post, believing that she had fulfilled her promises and feeling the weight of professional obligations.[24] Thus, O'Leary's resignation cannot be seen as a repudiation of her views. Nor was the subsequent election of Merritt, O'Leary's rival in 1884, a dramatic turnaround for the Institute. However much the members respected Merritt, they did not fully endorse her agenda even when she presided over the organization between 1888 and 1900.

The election of 1884 was a visible tug-of-war between two tendencies in the Institute: one fairly traditional and centripetal, the other quite new and centrifugal. Those inclinations, in turn, derived from two separate constituencies: the rank and file, and the group's most active lay and medical members. As social conditions in Boston changed and as new concepts of health developed, the Institute survived the late 1800s by leading a double life.

To understand the first of the Institute's two sides, one can begin with the membership list published in the group's semicentennial booklet.[25] Although the 152 members in 1898 came from nearly every community in the immediate Boston area, nearly 60 percent lived within a six-mile radius of the Institute's meeting hall. Being the easiest cohort to trace, that subset of eighty-nine women (who lived in the city of Boston and its recently annexed suburbs) is the basis for the following profile.[26]

Slightly more than half of the women (54 percent) were married, while the rest were widowed (27 percent) or single (19 percent), a third of whom apparently were spinsters.[27] The group included a large number of older and/or unmarried women, an important feature when ascertaining the Institute's role.

A modest number (around 6 percent) were employed outside the home in 1898. Comprising 24 percent of the single women and 4 percent of the widows, they worked in such common fields for women as teaching and dressmaking, and also less conventional jobs, such as physician and doorplate manufacturer. Although none of the married women were employed, many of the widows had worked prior to 1898. The small overall proportion of job holders and the higher representation of nonmarried than married women among the workers conformed to general employment patterns among white women in America during the late nineteenth century.[28]

The married women came from Boston's middle and upper-middle class. Over three-quarters of them had husbands who were white-collar, half in business and the rest divided evenly between the professions and clerical and sales positions.[29] The contrast with Boston's overall population is striking. In 1890, about 33 percent of the city's entire male labor force was white-collar, and about 47 percent of all native white working men were white-collar.[30] In disproportionate numbers, Institute husbands represented the middle and upper rungs of Boston's socioeconomic ladder.

The husbands' career profiles were typical for their class and generation. Information about the men's occupations, taken at five-year intervals from city directories and supplemented by obituaries, showed that few experienced major leaps or falls over two to three decades. Holding the same or a similar job for a long period, the men tended to remain in one occupational stratum during their careers. That pattern followed the occupational stability of many

white-collar male workers in Boston during the late nineteenth century.[31]

The members' residences give the same impression of security.
Although the Boston cohort represented many districts of the city,
they generally came from the comfortable, though not wealthy, neighborhoods in each area. For example, Institute families in the South
End lived between the exclusive districts of the Back Bay and the
lower South End near Chester and Union parks.[32] Moreover, Institute families were not very mobile. A spot-check of their addresses
over a thirty-year period indicated that Institute families moved in-
frequently and then within, rather than into or out of, city limits.
Their peers were equally settled. Between 1880 and 1890, for example, 80 percent of high white-collar workers and 71 percent of low
white-collar workers remained in the city.[33] In contrast, more than
one-third of Boston's population in 1890 were recent in-migrants,
whereas Institute families were ten- or twenty-year residents by
then.[34]

In sum, the ordinary Institute member in the late nineteenth
century was the wife or widow of a white-collar worker, whose socioeconomic position was fairly comfortable and secure. Many may
have resembled Mrs. George W. Spaulding of Dorchester, whose husband was a wholesale hat merchant for more than fifty years. Born
in Scituate in 1843, she taught school in South Boston for eight years
and married in 1870. The Spauldings had two children and lived in
Dorchester, moving only once between 1880 and 1910. Besides holding membership in the Institute, Mrs. Spaulding was active in her
local church. Her daughter, Miss Elsie W. Spaulding, also joined the
Institute and was still single when her mother died in 1930.[35]

Among the many widows in the Institute in 1898, the lives of
Mrs. Rebecca H. Christian and Mrs. Rebecca M. Pope were typical.
Mrs. Christian's husband had been a salesman and then merchant
before he died around 1870. She lived with a son, a newsdealer, at
the same family address for the next thirty years.[36] Similarly,
Mrs. Pope was the widow of a prominent lumber dealer, who had
been active in municipal politics, the Masons, and a literary association, as well as serving on the board of financial and insurance companies. Between 1879, when her husband died, and 1900, Mrs. Pope
moved a couple of times before settling down in West Roxbury with
one of her sons.[37]

Miss Vadilla A. Damon was representative of the older single
women in the Institute. When she died in 1930, Miss Damon had

lived in the South End for sixty-four years and had been a member of the Institute for "fully fifty years."[38] Her obituary noted no other outstanding interests or activities.

Together, the group profile and personal stories suggest what concerns brought the average member to the Institute in the late 1800s. First, the organization remained a source of practical information about personal health and sickness. Sessions related to public health were rare, as the Institute continued to focus on topics closest to members' private lives. In the 1880s, for example, one out of every ten lectures dealt with female physiology, including menstruation and menopause, pregnancy and childbirth, sterility, and cancer. Other meetings considered women's responsibility for "scientific marriage" and heredity, and the problems of female fashion and posture. Even more common were sessions devoted to the management of the family and home, especially the health and education of children and proper care for the sick. As in earlier years, the Institute was a dependable counselor in personal matters, whether members were young or old, single or married.

At the same time, the Institute's program reveals that members' attention span was shortening and their interests were diversifying. Unlike its intensive studies of earlier decades, the Institute sponsored few long lecture series on specific topics at the end of the century, and individual speakers rarely visited the group more than five times during the 1880s. Instead, subjects and lecturers changed from week to week, and the Institute relied on its own medical members to conduct many sessions. In addition, topics unrelated to personal health appeared approximately once in every ten lectures or conversational meetings. Some offered little more than light entertainment, as illustrated by a local minister's anecdotal talk in 1881 on the graphic nature of words.[39] Occasionally, discussions closed with a "dessert," such as a literary recitation.

That does not mean, however, that frivolous matters occupied the Institute's time. A majority of the miscellaneous talks covered substantial topics, including history and political issues. In fact, about half of the nonmedical lectures addressed the social condition of women in America and abroad. For example, members learned about famous female authors, social reformers, and scientists, and about the position of women in Zulu, from "amusing incidents relating to the marriages of the girls" to some "instances of horrible cruelty to Woman and degredation [sic] in which they were placed."[40] Sometimes, then, the message was unmistakably political, as speakers from female organizations and colleges advocated improvement in the education, employment, and status of women. In 1886, for example, Dr. Salome Merritt considered the "Labor Question" from an economic, physiological, and moral perspective. She argued that a woman worker was "entitled to wages enough to supply her with all the necessaries of life with [without?] departing from her virtue."[41] Whether a program dealt with women or not, Institute members certainly grew accustomed to female speakers. During the 1880s, female doctors, educators, social activists, and other women conducted about half of all the lectures and discussions.

It is difficult to generalize about members' responsiveness to lectures on social issues. Some undoubtedly felt comfortable with such a program. A likely example is Mrs. Alden Frink, who supported many causes, "especially those relating to the care and guidance of young girls."[42] She served on the boards of the New England Hospital for Women and Children and the New England Helping Hand Society and was a member of the New England Moral Reform Society and the Roxbury Woman's Suffrage League. Unlike Mrs. Frink, though, most members of the Institute tended not to join reform groups. A survey of women's cultural, charitable, and political societies in late Victorian Boston brought forth the names of only a handful of Institute members.[43] Apparently, ventures that were less practical, less personal, or more political than the Institute were unattractive. The average member enjoyed the Institute because its profile was low, its program educational, and its politics ambiguous. (For instance, discussion of women's suffrage was barred for many years, because of the opposition of older members.[44])

To label the Institute safe and conservative would be fair, yet somewhat misleading. Its very insularity may have enabled members to grow politically. The combination of wide-ranging lectures and a nonthreatening atmosphere gave members an opportunity to discern connections between their private lives and external conditions. If personal issues remained paramount, at least members were not ignorant of the social problems and political debates of their era.

One cause and effect of the Institute's relative seclusion was its sense of community. Members preferred to share their time and concerns with peers, not with strangers. Patterns of membership and retention during the late nineteenth century demonstrate that female companionship remained integral to the Institute. As before, clusters of relatives, friends, and neighbors joined during the 1890s. For example, Mrs. Spaulding of Dorchester and her daughter, Elsie, were members along with a close neighbor, Mrs. C. E. Littlefield. During the early 1890s, Mrs. J. H. Scott of the Institute had also been their neighbor; she then moved to the same house as yet another member. Turnover rates during the 1880s were very low, and the overlap between membership in the mid-1880s and 1898 was substantial. Perhaps as many as one-fifth of the 152 members in 1898 had been in the Institute for at least fifteen years; some memberships extended over fifty years.

For the average member, the Institute was a satisfying activity beyond her private home and family. She gained some useful knowledge, expanded her intellectual and political horizons, and maintained important friendships. Those had been the Institute's functions since mid-century. Their significance in the late 1800s was different, however, because social conditions in Boston had changed. During the late Victorian period, members' lives became more comfortable, as their families' social and economic positions stabilized. Middle-class life, though, was not as calm as it appeared to be on the surface. Economic security did not protect middle-class women from certain disquieting issues. Some of their concerns—about female physiology, reproduction, and health care—were personal. Other questions bridged the private and public spheres. The Institute exposed members to the country's growing debate about women's rights and status. They could not have listened to such discussions without reflecting on their own circumstances. The Institute no longer promised self-enrichment and social perfection as a panacea. Its program merely helped members interpret their private experiences and the social condition of their sex. If the Institute's ambitions were more limited than before, its role was no less meaningful. Interested in practical information, eager for female companionship, and willing to study social problems, the rank and file enjoyed the traditional features of the Institute and endorsed the program of Dr. Helen B. O'Leary.

Simultaneously, the Institute addressed the concerns of a second constituency, its lay leadership and female physicians.[45] Between 1875 and 1900, at least forty-six lay women served as the Institute's chief officers. Their personal backgrounds resemble those of the general membership. During their period of service, at least 22 percent were widows, around 9 percent were single, and about 30 percent were married; the remaining 39 percent were either married or widowed.[46] Only two (or 4 percent) were employed outside the home.[47] Nearly all (93 percent) of the husbands of married officers were white-collar (primarily businessmen), and the husbands of at least 70 percent of the widows had been businessmen as well.[48]

What distinguished the lay leadership was their participation in other women's and reform organizations.[49] Mrs. Dora Bascom Smith, for example, an Institute vice president for over twenty years, was an early member of the Women's Educational and Industrial Union, the New England Helping Hand Society, and the Woman's Charity Club, which operated a hospital for destitute women. She was an officer in the National Woman Suffrage Association of Massachusetts and, along with Dr. Merritt, a member of the Committee of Council and Co-operation.[50] Similarly, Mrs. Mary Ann Hobbs, a charter member of the Institute who served on its board of directors in the 1880s, was a well-known figure in the city's charitable associations, including the Female Samaritan Society, the Helping Hand Society, and the Boston Provident Association.[51] At least six other Institute officers were active in the WEIU, and a number joined the New England Moral Reform Society as well.

During the 1880s the Institute also included at least twelve female physicians. Among them were seven homeopaths, three regulars, one "electrician and eclectic," and one of unknown background.[52] Along with the lay leadership, the medical members supported a variety of other organizations. During the 1880s, for example, eight of the twelve were officers or members of the WEIU, especially its Hygiene and Physical Culture Committee. A couple were members of the Moral Education Society and also promoted women's suffrage.

Through the efforts of lay officers and medical members, the shell that had enveloped the Institute during its first quarter-century broke open. Activist members connected the Institute to a network of local women's groups. The Institute also became affiliated with the Massachusetts State Federation of Women's Clubs and sent representatives to various national expositions and conferences, including the meeting of the National Council of Women in 1895.

The leadership represented the second of the Institute's two faces. They benefited from the organization in significantly different ways than did the general membership. As during antebellum times, the Institute and other voluntary associations continued to bridge the domestic and public realms for women. The values ascribed to womanhood in the home legitimized female participation in social causes, and opened the door to new experiences. Women's clubs groomed organizational skills, bred confidence, encouraged autonomy, and gave access to social power. The Institute taught its lay leadership not only physiology, but political know-how as well. For them, the organization was one of many public commitments that fostered independence and influence.

The Institute had many advantages for its medical members as well. As Regina Markell Morantz-Sanchez and Mary Roth Walsh have shown, the late nineteenth century was a period of dramatic gains and impending losses for women doctors in Boston and around the nation.[53] Many female physicians believed that the only way to ensure equality in medicine was by fully integrating women into the field's educational and professional institutions. Entrance into male-dominated medical schools and societies, however, proved very difficult. The Massachusetts Medical Society, for example, accepted its first female member in 1884, having originally considered the matter in 1850 and again in the 1870s. By 1893, women could attend three of Boston's four medical schools; Harvard did not yield until 1945. Facing such resistance, women established separate training programs between 1850 and 1900.[54] By the turn of the century, many of the women's medical schools offered a curriculum equal to that of men's colleges. In addition, female physicians formed their own professional societies. Among the earliest was the New England Hospital Medical Society (later called the New England Women's Medical Society), founded in 1878 by a dozen women doctors around Boston, most of whom were associated with the female-run New England Hospital.[55] Such groups offered women doctors a chance to discuss medical matters, to present papers, and to build an independent professional community.

Despite their significant accomplishments, though, women physicians had marginal status in medicine during the late 1800s. They accounted for between only 4 and 5 percent of the profession at the turn of the century.[56] Their representation among Boston's physicians (18 percent) was the highest for the country's major cities in 1890.[57] Moreover, progress was short-lived, as the transformation of medicine into a full-fledged science and profession during the early twentieth century further restricted women's opportunities. Women's medical schools closed; the number of female medical students and practitioners dropped; appointments on hospital staffs or medical faculties were limited.[58] In all phases of their careers—from training to practice to professional activities—female doctors faced considerable adversity in the nineteenth and twentieth centuries.

Women's organizations, such as the Ladies' Physiological Institute, eased those hardships to some degree. For example, membership in a club afforded female doctors public visibility and, thereby, new clients. Although Dr. O'Leary once disclaimed looking upon the Institute "as a place to obtain practice,"[59] she and other physicians probably benefited from contacts made in local clubs.

Voluntary associations certainly provided women doctors in Boston with an alternate professional network. The Massachusetts Medical Society and the New England Hospital Medical Society admitted only regular doctors; one of the Institute's three orthodox physicians in the 1880s joined both groups. Three of the Institute's seven homeopaths were members of the Massachusetts Homeopathic Medical Society. The remaining eight regular and irregular practitioners apparently had no affiliation with a professional society. The Institute and other women's clubs helped female doctors, whether involved in a medical society or not, to maintain personal and professional relationships with their colleagues.

Finally, women's organizations were an arena for public education and social activism. From the antebellum period on, supporters claimed that women doctors would extend the "female" values of sensitivity and service from the domestic sphere into the public realm. Women's unique attributes seemed increasingly desirable as medical theory and practice became more impersonal.[60] Historians continue to debate whether or not such rhetoric became reality; did women physicians treat their patients, especially female ones, more compassionately than male doctors did?[61] However that question is resolved, it is clear that many women physicians, from antebellum times through the Progressive era, expected to "feminize" medicine and to reform American society.

Women's clubs offered one path toward that goal. In the mid-nineteenth century, female physicians promoted health reform and various political causes through voluntary associations; at the turn of the century, women's societies continued to serve as a platform for doctors interested in preventive medicine, public health, and popular physiology.[62] Membership in a club gave women doctors a means of expressing their social concerns and exerting public influence. Along with their lay counterparts, the Institute's medical leaders used women's organizations to fulfill personal needs and to advance social aims.

The Institute also had significance beyond the value that individual members derived. It signaled the development of new attitudes about personal health. For some Americans at mid-century, health had been a magnet for every private worry, and a panacea for every social disorder. During the last quarter of the century, both the personal and social meaning of health began to change. Through physiological knowledge, lay members still hoped to resolve practical questions about their health and hygiene. Moreover, they gained new insights into their private experiences and social position as women. An understanding of health might reassure members about difficulties in their lives, but it would no longer cure every problem. The Institute's social mission also changed during the late 1800s. Compared to antebellum times, its vision was less perfectionist and more practical. According to Institute leaders, personal health was neither an immediate nor comprehensive solution to major public dilemmas. Physical well-being protected individuals against the strains of modern life, and enabled them to be reliable citizens and productive workers. Along with economic justice, moral uplift, and sanitary control, then, health was another element in social cohesion.

Perhaps more than ordinary members did, Institute leaders recognized that individual experiences and social conditions were inseparable. Personal health contributed to the public good; conversely, a stable society enhanced private well-being. Institute officers and medical members must have been especially aware of the interaction between women's private lives and social position. Through the subject of health, the Institute and other organizations focused attention on the relationship between women's personal interests and larger social developments. In the process, they addressed "the Woman Question," a national discussion about women's status and, invariably, female health during the late nineteenth century.

Because most of its activities were private, the Institute did little as a group to popularize the new outlook about health. Through their work in the Institute and other organizations, however, individual members were quite visible in that effort. Many voluntary societies in Boston were more systematic than the Institute about health education, the descendant of physiological instruction. What the Institute undertook among its own members, such groups as the Massachusetts Emergency and Hygiene Association achieved for a larger public audience.

However insular, the Institute did reflect general trends in Boston and the country. In particular, the Institute's 1884 election revealed that a transition was underway in the personal and social meaning of health. The presidential slate offered one candidate with traditional views about physiological instruction and another with more forward-looking ideas. In the life of the Institute, the contest symbolized the group's flexibility. The Institute was so durable in the late nineteenth century precisely because it served quite diverse, even antithetical, needs. From a broader perspective, the events of 1884 signaled the emergence of less romantic, more pragmatic ideas about health in a changing urban environment.

5

Fitness of Body and Mind: Personal Health in Late Nineteenth-Century Boston

During the latter decades of the nineteenth century, Americans continued to worry about their health, and a new generation of popular physiologists stepped forward to counsel them. The areas of concern—diet, exercise, hygiene, and medical remedies—were familiar ones. In other respects, though, the character of popular health changed after the Civil War, as new problems and solutions replaced those of antebellum times.

Late Victorian health reform focused on the country's most prevalent disorders, such as dyspepsia, debility, tuberculosis, and nervous exhaustion.[1] According to some popular physiologists, the main culprits in the nation's ill-health were meat, alcohol, and tobacco. Dietary reformers argued that simple nourishment and the avoidance of stimulants were necessary for well-being and longevity. Many Americans, however, chose a shorter road to health. Home cures, from bottled mineral water to electrotherapy devices, were common products after the Civil War, and patent medicines entered their golden age in the 1890s. Those who could afford more expensive treatment visited sanitaria in the countryside, which promised to clear tubercular lungs and to soothe ravaged nerves. In many facilities, vacations masqueraded as medicine, as comfortable baths and elegant meals replaced the arduous regimens of hydropathy and vegetarianism. New medical sects, such as osteopathy and chiropractic, claimed that sound structural alignment was the key to physical health, while Christian Scientists and adherents of New Thought, or positive thinking, regarded correct mental attitude as the source of well-being. Concern about nervous exhaustion and related disorders in America coalesced into a mental hygiene movement, led by psychiatrists and social reformers. Increasingly, health also seemed dependent on personal cleanliness and domestic sanitation. With rapid discoveries in bacteriology during the late 1800s, Americans became even more apprehensive about the dangers that lurked in their environment. For some, the solution was to purchase water filters, bathtubs, special commodes, and other equipment to control various poisons and germs in the home. Exercise also became more popular during the last quarter of the nineteenth century as recreation, sports, and physical education grew. The modern "safety" bicycle arrived in America during the 1880s, and riding "the wheel" soon became a craze; local clubs and men's colleges organized athletic contests; municipal governments and private entrepreneurs opened gymnasia; numerous companies sold equipment for home exercise; and bodybuilders toured the country championing muscle development. There certainly was no shortage of ways to treat illness or improve one's health in late nineteenth-century America.

Events in and around Boston illustrate those trends.[2] The city government, for example, contributed to the personal health of the populace. Classes in physiology and exercise became more regular at all levels of public education, especially during the 1890s. Boston also began to set aside land for recreation and sports. Before the Civil War, the only general play area in the city was the Common. By World War I, in contrast, Boston had an array of public parks, playgrounds, outdoor gymnasia, bathhouses, and beaches. The corridor of parks that graced the city's landscape was the first such public system in the nation, and thousands of youths and adults patronized local playgrounds each year, while millions visited the beaches and public baths.

Private groups were among the strongest lobbyists for those municipal facilities. Voluntary organizations, such as the Massachusetts Emergency and Hygiene Association (MEHA), supported the city's efforts while also sponsoring their own educational programs in health. The MEHA was established in 1884 to continue independently a series of lectures initiated by the Woman's Educational Association.[3] For some thirty years thereafter, the MEHA conducted both free and private instruction in first aid, personal hygiene, and sanitary science. Audiences included police and firemen, machinists and factory operatives, employees of railroads, department stores, and libraries, school teachers, church groups, matrons of charity homes and asylums, and the destitute or working women who visited local missions and working girls' clubs. The MEHA also supervised recreational facilities such as playgrounds and sandgardens, especially in poor neighborhoods, and ran a public bathhouse in the city's Italian district. Although the city government contributed some funds, most of the financial support came from the dues and donations of MEHA members, who included some of Boston's leading civic reformers, orthodox physicians, and wealthiest citizens.

Health education was an important function of many organizations in Boston. Women's groups such as the Young Women's Christian Association (YWCA), the Women's Educational and Industrial Union (WEIU), and Working Girls' Clubs (WGC) dealt with every facet of their beneficiaries' lives—economic, moral, and physical. Founded in 1867, the Boston YWCA ran gymnastic classes for working girls who found "themselves at the close of the day too worn and tired for even the walk home which they so much need."[4] The WEIU sponsored lectures in physiology and personal health, opened a hygiene room where poor women could receive free advice and medical care, and conducted several investigations into the sanitary conditions of businesses where women worked.[5] Local branches of the WGC offered many educational and personal services for young working women, including medical consultations, health instruction, and exercise classes.[6]

Perhaps the greatest promoters of recreation in the city were Boston's sports clubs. Private athletic groups flourished after the Civil War, and virtually every sport was represented, from rowing and walking to baseball and tennis. During the 1880s and 1890s, for example, dozens of bicycling clubs encouraged the wheeling craze in Boston.

Wherever the government or organizations left an opening, individual entrepreneurs soon entered. Beginning in the 1860s, for example, private gymnasia were quite common in the city. Among the earliest proprietors were George B. Windship, M.D., a famous strongman who popularized weightlifting and marketed exercise apparatus, and Dio Lewis, M.D., the prolific writer and lecturer on health reform. City directories between 1875 and 1895 listed nearly a dozen private gymnasia in Boston, as well as thirty different facilities for steam, hot air, and other types of baths. Several publishing houses in the city joined the *Boston Journal of Health* (1887–93) and *Health: A Monthly Magazine* (1890–94) in teaching the general public about hygiene, diet, and exercise. Nearby, Mary Baker Eddy organized Christian Science, which emphasized the connection between religious purity and physical health, and Lydia E. Pinkham began selling her Vegetable Compound for women's ailments, which became one of the country's most successful patent medicines. In late Victorian Boston, the search for health was a spirited one.

A Rhode Island newspaper was both impressed and amused by the fervor of its neighbors:

> If Bostonians are not thoroughly conversant with the theory and practice of physical culture, it certainly must be because they can neither see, hear nor act. Every paper you take up has its daily offering of matters athletic, physical or psycho-physical.[7]

Interest in health certainly had not waned since antebellum times.

Such widespread concern, though, reflected as much anxiety as it did zeal. Compared with their predecessors, Bostonians of the late nineteenth century were less confident about their prospects for health. Physical well-being seemed increasingly tenuous, and its benefits less extensive than was once believed. The vitality of women appeared to be declining. Why did middle-class Bostonians worry about health between 1870 and 1900, and what hazards did they consider to be the most serious? What solutions seemed the most promising to leading health reformers?

Popular and medical literature painted a gloomy picture of urban health in the late nineteenth century. Some observers described the failing condition of America's boys and men. William Blaikie, a fitness enthusiast, stationed himself at Broadway and Fulton Street in New York. "Scarcely one in ten" of the men who walked by, he reported, was "either erect or thoroughly well-built."[8] They had bad posture, were asymmetrical, and moved awkwardly. Worn-out minds and nerves troubled commentators as well. An article in the *Boston Journal of Health* in 1888, for example, lamented the "high-pressure" and "feverish life" of most businessmen, which resulted in nervous exhaustion, "chronic brain weariness," and "nervous derangement of the heart."[9]

Blaikie and other observers found even less to applaud among the country's girls and women. Popular literature of the late 1800s depicted women as vulnerable creatures whose physical complaints and nervous disorders made them virtual invalids. Oftentimes, female characters in Victorian fiction were pallid young ladies, draped in flowing gowns, languishing on settees, literally consumed by tuberculosis and nervous exhaustion. Medical reports gave an equally dismal account. According to Dr. Edward H. Clarke of Boston, sick women abounded in the city:

> On the luxurious couches of Beacon Street; in the palaces of Fifth Avenue; among the classes of our private, common, and normal schools; among the female graduates of our colleges; behind the [store] counters of Washington Street and Broadway; in our factories, workshops, and homes,—may be found numberless pale, weak, neuralgic, dyspeptic, hysterical, menorraghic [sic], dysmenorrhoeic girls and women. . . .[10]

As did many contemporaries, Dr. Clarke believed that women's sorry condition was a recent development. "Our great-grandmothers," he declared, "are pointed at as types of female physical excellence; their great-grand-daughters as illustrations of female physical degeneracy."[11] Only two or three generations earlier, he argued, the nation's women had been robust and fecund. Dr. Clarke also made the familiar claim that American women were inordinately sick compared to their European sisters. During his many trips abroad, Dr. Clarke was "always surprised by the red blood that fills and colors the faces of ladies and peasant girls, reminding one of the canvas of Rubens and Murillo; and [was] always equally surprised on my return, by crowds of pale, bloodless female faces, that suggest consumption, scrofula, anemia, and neuralgia."[12] The frequency and tone of such remarks suggest that concern about female health had become even more urgent than during antebellum times.

The simplest explanation for such dire reports is that people's health actually declined during Victorian times. Perhaps sickness and premature death were more prevalent in Boston than before. Vital statistics reveal the inadequacy of that hypothesis. By some measures, the quality of life in Boston did improve over the last quarter of the nineteenth century. For example, life expectancy for men and women rose.[13] Crude annual death rates were lower than at mid-century, but somewhat higher than during the first quarter of the century.[14] The proportion of all deaths in the city due to contagious disease dropped from roughly one-third in the 1870s to less than one-fifth from the mid-1880s through the 1890s.[15] The virtual disappearance of cholera and the relative infrequency of smallpox, diphtheria, and scarlet fever, however, were offset by a rise in constitutional and local disorders. By the mid-1890s, the former accounted for more than one-fifth of all deaths in Boston (even though tuberculosis was abating) and local diseases (especially pneumonia, heart disease, and bronchitis) were responsible for nearly one-half of all deaths.[16]

Another important indicator is mortality among the young. As Boston's Board of Health noted, the fate of children was "an excellent test of the city's sanitary condition."[17] The board claimed a passing grade, because deaths attributable to children under the age of five dropped from roughly 41 to 35 percent of all deaths in Boston between 1871 and 1896.[18] Those figures, however, did not factor in the changing age distribution of the city.[19] More informative measures include what demographers now mean by infant mortality, namely, deaths under age one per 1000 live births, and other age-specific death rates (such as number of children five years and younger who died per 1000 in that age range). By those standards, Boston's children were actually more vulnerable in the late nineteenth century than during previous generations.[20]

These examples demonstrate the ambiguity of vital statistics. First, because some indicators improved while others worsened, there was no uniform trend in Boston's healthfulness after mid-century. Second, numbers may not lie, but they can deceive; depending on how certain figures are calculated, one gets a favorable or discouraging picture of the city's well-being. Finally, and most importantly, the above data catalog facts; they do not necessarily represent how individual Bostonians perceived their own circumstances. In order to explain why city residents were concerned about health, one needs to look beyond the statistics and examine the relationship between experience and perception, between reality and understanding. What did Bostonians believe their condition to be?

Fears about women's health in the late 1800s graphically illustrate how fact and belief interact. Given widespread reports of female frailty, one might conclude that women actually became sicker during the nineteenth century; in other words, that perception accurately mirrored reality. Testing that hypothesis is difficult. Not only is reliable information scarce, but the available data relate primarily to mortality, not morbidity. If the familiar observation that "women get sick and men die" held true then as it does today, the data would conceal many acute, nonfatal illnesses among women.[21] Despite that limitation, mortality figures in Boston offer a partial gauge of women's condition.

Crude death rates for all Boston females were somewhat higher in the late 1800s than at mid-century. Using Lemuel Shattuck's data on the number of female deaths and total female population in the city, one can determine that the annual female death rate was 21.67 in 1810, 22.79 in 1825, 20.70 in 1835, and 20.15 in 1845.[22] According to an analysis of census data by Dr. John S. Billings, deputy-surgeon general of the United States Army, the death rate among all Boston females in 1890 was 23.57.[23] That represents a 17 percent increase over the preceding forty-five years. Billings also reported female death rates according to race and ethnicity: a composite figure of 23.37 for all white females (native and foreign) in 1890, which reflected rates of 18.03 for white women born to American parents, 26.28 for native-born white women with either one or both parents of foreign birth, and 21.77 for foreign-born white women.[24]

Trends in death rates by age group are ambiguous. Based on Shattuck's data, one can estimate that the annual mortality rate in 1845 for women ages 20 to 30 was 10.15, and 13.54 for women ages 30 to 40.[25] Billings reported the following death rates for Boston females in 1890: 8.99 for ages 20 to 25, 12.06 for ages 25 to 35, and 15.09 for ages 35 to 45.[26] Without further information, one cannot draw a firm conclusion about mortality trends among Boston's adult females between the middle and late 1800s.

Another way of evaluating women's health is through a comparison of their experiences with men's. Calculations based on Shattuck's data reveal that the death rate for all Boston males was 23.96 in 1825, 25.67 in 1835, and 20.78 in 1845.[27] Billings's analysis showed the comparable figure in 1890 to be 26.08.[28] Male death rates exceeded women's in each of those years, and between 1845 and 1890 male mortality rose significantly more than women's (26 versus 17 percent). Billings's statistics about age-specific death rates by sex in 1890 indicate that mortality among white males surpassed that of white females in every age group except ages 15 to 20.[29] Comparable data for whites born to American parents show the same disparity between the sexes, except for ages 25 to 35.[30] Overall, this information suggests that men were at greater risk than women at most stages of life, and that their degree of risk increased more rapidly than women's during the second half of the nineteenth century.

A final indicator of relative health is distribution of deaths by sex. In 1890, men constituted 48.5 percent of Boston's white population, but accounted for 51.1 percent of all deaths among the city's whites. Analyzing patterns of death by age as well as sex, one finds a similar imbalance in virtually every age category: white males comprised 51.1 percent of the population under age 1 and 55.4 percent of deaths in that age group; 50.9 percent of the under-five population and 54.7 percent of its deaths; 48.3 percent of whites aged 15 to 45, but 51.3 percent of the deaths; and 46.4 percent of those over 45 years and 47 percent of the deaths, a negligible difference. The only case in which females died disproportionately to their share of the population was in the age range 5 to 15 years. The imbalance, though, was not significant: white females constituted 50 percent of that cohort and 50.9 percent of its deaths. In most age groups, white males died in numbers slightly disproportionate to their representation in the population.[31]

Inevitably, the daily occurrence of deaths among females, young and old, distressed Bostonians in the late 1800s. Yet the data do not seem to justify excessive fear about women's health. Adult women probably were not at greater risk than their counterparts earlier in the century, nor were white females of most ages more vulnerable than their male peers. Only a somewhat higher death rate for all females indicated a decline in women's condition since mid-century. Mortality data do not support the frequent lament that women were unusually and increasingly unhealthy in late Victorian Boston. If anything, the higher risk of death among males in most age groups and over time warranted concern.

That does not imply that women enjoyed unqualified health in the late nineteenth century. On the contrary, female mortality figures, although favorable for their own time, were markedly higher than today's. Moreover, morbidity data, if available, might show a significant incidence of acute disorders. In lieu of systematic information about morbidity, historians must rely on impressionistic reports from doctors and from women themselves. Women's accounts of their own lives, ranging from private letters to published autobiographies, reveal a steady battle against ordinary and severe ailments.[32] Pregnancy and childbirth were especially difficult, even frightening, experiences.[33] Letters to health magazines from female readers expressed considerable weariness and a despair about finding expert help.[34] Correspondence to the offices of Lydia E. Pinkham's Vegetable Compound, a leading proprietary medicine of the time, related poignant tales of physical illnesses and the inability of regular doctors to cure them.[35] Some historical studies have also concluded that orthodox treatment of gynecological and other disorders was, at best, ineffective and, at worst, brutal.[36]

What conclusions can the historian draw from sources as diverse as clinical reports in medical journals and women's private letters? No interpretation is valid unless the accounts themselves are credible.

Did the physical conditions actually exist, and were reports about them accurate? Those two questions are interrelated, rather than distinct. Illness is both a biological experience and an intellectual construct. We search for patterns or configurations among physical symptoms, and codify them under the name of a disease or condition. Reality and perception are intertwined: the disease label would be meaningless without the symptoms, and the experience would lack coherence without the designation of illness.[37] To understand nineteenth-century accounts of female sickness, the historian must appreciate the multiple origins and meanings of illness. For both women and their doctors, female ailments were "real."

A useful example is the case of Alice James (1848–92), the younger sister of William and Henry.[38] For years, Alice endured neurasthenia, dizzy spells, and mental fitfulness and fatigue. She tried medical treatments ranging from pills and rest to therapeutic exercise. Denied the systematic education and encouragement granted her brothers, Alice James gave her life meaning through a confrontation between her body and her mind. The former was female, representing evil, "violence, upheaval, dissolution"; the latter was male, the seat of "will power, self-control, muscular sanity."[39] Accepting that the forces of evil would eventually win, Alice adopted an air of detachment, which "enabled her to submit and resist at the same time. It was as if she ceded her body to the 'feminine' principle of frailty and submission, while cultivating with her mind a 'masculine' strength and indifference to pain."[40] Though characterized as a fragile neurasthenic throughout her life, Alice died of an organic disease (cancer) in 1892, facing that last challenge to her body and mind with great fortitude.

The experiences of Alice James reveal the complexity of women's physical and nervous disorders in the late nineteenth century, and of any sickness at any time. The most general source of ill-health was (and remains) a universal one: the interaction of a specific human organism with illness-producing conditions in the body or environment. A prolapsed uterus may have resulted from naturally weak abdominal muscles. Influenza developed when fatigue compromised the body's immune system. Cholera and tuberculosis, nineteenth-century rhetoric notwithstanding, were triggered by pathological agents, not moral indiscretion.

Sometimes the cause of illness is less tangible. Modern etiological models link cardiovascular disease and even certain types of cancer to personality traits—for instance, how people handle stress or convey their emotions. Through a complicated sequence of chemical events, habitual behavior is translated into life-threatening physical problems, such as high blood pressure. Psychosocial conflicts can also disrupt a person's equilibrium, culminating in such simple ailments as a cold or complex conditions in the class of anorexia nervosa. As today, the tension between a restrictive culture and women's search for a genuine self became evident during the nineteenth century in physical and emotional disorders.

Consciously or not, the "victim" can be an accomplice in the development of sickness.[41] The designation of illness can help a person manage life's difficulties. Perplexed by the physiological changes and social strains of being female, Victorian girls and women found solace through their complaints and order through their disorders. The diagnosis of illness legitimated their uncertainties, and etiological models and therapeutic regimens explained their predicament. Although sickness often fosters dependency, it can also be an assertive act, through which people express frustration and exert control. Common female illnesses in late Victorian times, such as hysteria, could have been a demonstration of anger, a ploy for gaining attention, or a means of abandoning traditional roles and relationships in the family. Finally, some female conditions may have derived, in part, from learned behavior. Much as they do today, female adolescents at the turn of the century may have coped with insecurity by adopting a prevalent disorder, such as chlorosis, a form of anemia. Whatever its source or function, illness was a real phenomenon for women themselves.

Female sickness had several meanings for doctors as well.[42] Many female complaints baffled male physicians. Disorders related to menstruation, pregnancy, and menopause, and nervous conditions such as hysteria were especially mysterious. Their symptomatology was often irregular; their causes seemed elusive; the prognosis and required treatment were ambiguous. The reigning model of female physiology, which reduced most symptoms to problems in the generative system, provided a simple framework for explaining virtually any condition. The theory relieved doctors' personal uneasiness while satisfying their professional obligation to interpret and treat illness systematically. In addition, doctors may have resented female disorders as deviant behavior, an affront to the male norm of strength and stoicism, and a dangerous opportunity for women to gain authority over their families and physicians. Medical diagnosis and treatment helped restore conventional relationships; if delinquency brought ill-health, then responsibility and virtue were the cure. More than simply a physical event, female sickness carried professional, psychological, and cultural import for doctors as well. Given that constellation of meanings, physicians were more apt to perceive illness in women, and the act of diagnosis made it real for them.

The issue, therefore, is not whether nineteenth-century reports of female ill-health were accurate or exaggerated. Such a question presumes that the historian can separate perception from reality, an unlikely, if not impossible job in this case. Fact and impression were interwoven: the occurrence of illness supported the belief that women were physically weak; conversely, assumptions about female frailty made sickness a more likely event. The result was a widespread belief that women were frequently, and perhaps inevitably, sick.

The interplay of fact and perception is not limited to the case of women's ailments. It is a general explanation for apprehensions about ill-health during the late nineteenth century. Morbidity and mortality rates alone did not make life seem tenuous to the residents of Victorian Boston; historians cannot assume a simple correlation between vital statistics and contemporary fears. Perception blended with experience to undermine people's optimism about leading long and healthy lives. To decipher the concerns of middle-class Bostonians, one must examine more than composite data on illness and death in the city; one must ask why people considered health to be so precarious and what risks they regarded as the most serious.

Much as earlier generations had, middle-class Bostonians of the late nineteenth century concluded that physical well-being depended on many factors. Three elements seemed the most crucial: biological constitution, personal habits, and environmental conditions. Their bodies, their daily lives, and their surroundings appeared to be the major sources of health or harm. Those were familiar concerns, but their meaning had changed somewhat since mid-century.

First, Bostonians continued to believe in the power of inherited characteristics.[43] One's innate biological nature, from sex and race to specific proclivities and weaknesses, helped determine the likelihood of health or sickness. Medical and popular opinion about the peculiarities of female physiology, for example, remained much the same as before. A woman's distinctive features, including her smaller skeleton and musculature, more delicate nerves, and complicated reproductive system, were thought to predispose her to a host of organic and emotional ills.[44]

Increasingly, however, middle-class Bostonians expressed concern about more universal human experiences. Perhaps more than previous generations had, they viewed processes inherent to life as a source of trouble. Some natural appetites, such as hunger, were necessary for survival and had to be satisfied, within reason. Other sensations and emotions were more problematic because their supervision, even suppression, seemed requisite for health. If allowed free play, for example, anger could lead to physical and emotional exhaustion; if unchecked, sexual feelings could destroy both health and morality.[45] Still other signals in the body were completely deceptive. When any physical function is abused, health writers cautioned, the body's messages become garbled. A favorite example was the false testimony of a sick stomach. "The appetite," wrote Dr. Charles H. Stowell in 1896, "is not always a safe guide, because by irregular habits, by overeating, and by eating improper articles of food, it becomes variable, and is then an unreliable test."[46] "The *feelings* of the dyspeptic," concurred Dr. George H. Taylor, "are entirely untrustworthy" and such a person must learn "to *distrust his sensations* scrupulously."[47] Each feeling, then, had to be scrutinized to determine if it was genuine or distorted, and what the appropriate response would be. Apparently, numerous enemies—autonomous needs, overwhelming feelings, tempting sensations—lay ready to ambush each human being. Middle-class Bostonians came to fear the mischief of their own bodies.

Second, they worried about the strains of daily life in a modern, urban world. While applauding the technological advances of their time, middle-class Bostonians and other Americans believed that progress exacted a heavy toll on both physical and mental health. "We are all sorely tempted to do more than our bodies can stand," observed a writer in *Mind and Body* in 1897.[48] A leading physical educator, Luther H. Gulick, agreed: "Our lives are more rapid and intense. We do less physical and more mental work. We worry as no generation ever did."[49]

Such concerns were not unfounded. During the last quarter of the century, technological developments transformed the character of the home and workplace in Boston. In 1880, the use of electricity for light, power, and communication was barely underway in the city.[50] Most homes relied on gas, not steam heat, and few had full plumbing prior to 1880. Municipal services, such as water, sewers, and garbage disposal, were poorly organized and hardly adequate to meet the city's needs. As Boston grew, however, the city government invested heavily in upgrading and equalizing its utilities. Similarly, private companies extended gas service and began developing electricity and telephone systems. The first Boston Edison power station opened in 1886 and telephones also appeared on a wide scale throughout the 1890s. The horsedrawn, and then electrified, railway system also arrived during that time. The point is not that Boston was less comfortable in Victorian times than today, but that the introduction of electric power, telephones, streetcars, and other conveniences changed the tempo of everyday life in the city.

The impact of new technologies was clearly evident in the home. Industrialization brought new consumer products, and transformed domestic activities such as cooking, sewing, and cleaning. As caretaker of the home, the average wife and mother experienced a revolution. Far from relieving women of household work, the introduction of new commodities placed greater demands on their time and health.[51] Simple matters became complicated: for example, new cleaning machines led women to spend more time and effort on their families' laundry.

Industrialization also affected the lives of people who worked outside the home.[52] Boston remained a financial center in the late nineteenth century, but lost some of its prominence as a seaport and shipbuilding area. The wholesale and retail trade expanded, and the industrial and commercial sectors continued to diversify, bringing more factories, warehouses, and offices into the city. But seesaw growth made the city's economic condition unstable. Following the trauma of the Great Fire in 1872 and the depression of 1873, the city recovered somewhat in the 1880s. The mid-1890s, however, brought further economic setbacks.

The fortunes of the working population varied by class and ethnicity. In terms of size, the blue-collar class still dominated the city, while the financial and business elite wielded the most power. The middle class had neither the numbers of the blue-collar workers nor the clout of the wealthy managers and bankers.[53]

One can also ask if the occupational status of various Bostonians improved or declined during the late 1800s. Stephan Thernstrom has studied occupational continuity and mobility as a means of comparing the fate of different groups in the city.[54] His work reveals a more fluid history of jobs for some Bostonians and a more rigid one for others than might be anticipated.[55] Blue-collar workers, ranging from unskilled laborers to skilled tradesmen, could expect the largest occupational shifts during their lifetimes. In contrast, career patterns of white-collar workers, especially professionals and major businessmen, showed the greatest stability. Rarely slipping beyond low white-collar jobs, they tended to remain in the same general stratum throughout their working lives.

Parallel trends occurred among ethnic groups.[56] Native residents were more likely than the foreign-born population to hold middle-class jobs, and they also fared better in the boom-and-bust economy. Concentrated in the blue-collar sector, many immigrants could expect rather dramatic changes during their own lifetimes and across generations. Such gains, however, were temporary, leaving the immigrant population as a whole "disadvantaged in comparison with their Yankee rivals."[57] The small black population in Boston fared the worst of all.[58]

Judged solely by occupational stability, the livelihoods of middle-class Bostonians were safe. That fact, however, did not remove the anxieties of the average white-collar male worker. He did not know if his job was secure, if an immigrant would displace him, if his business would survive an economic panic, or if his income would hold steady. Although the odds were in their favor, native middle-class men remained uncertain about their futures.

It was technological change, in part, that upset the lives of both middle-class women and men in Boston. The revolution was as much psychological as physical. Industrialization not only affected activities in the home and in the workplace, but also produced emotional stress. Increasingly, technological developments forced Americans to " 'live upon [their] nerve.' "[59] Daily life seemed more unsettled and more demanding. However welcome in some respects, the new routines of urban life were also a potential source of physical and personal dis-ease.

The industrial revolution took place in a city whose own physical character was dramatically different as well. Increasingly, middle-class residents worried that Boston's rapidly changing environment threatened their health. The post–Civil War decades brought growing recognition of the environmental sources of disease, the identification of specific pathological agents, and greater interest in the public oversight of health hazards.[60] Despite advances in the science of public health, middle-class Bostonians, and even city officials, clung to an old-fashioned model of sanitary problems. They talked not so much about specific germs as about amorphous, invisible hazards lurking in the city's dirty streets, unsafe water, impure air, faulty sewage system, and foul marshes.

To some degree, their alarm was justified. Changes in Boston's landscape during the last quarter of the century both improved and aggravated its sanitary condition.[61] Since colonial times, Bostonians had been forced to improvise ways of expanding their physical space; dotted with marshes and virtually surrounded by water, the city's land mass was limited. During the second half of the nineteenth century, Boston's most ambitious project filled out the western edge of the neck, the thin strip of land connecting the central city to the mainland. The creation of the Back Bay proceeded gradually from the late 1850s until the early 1880s. It helped relieve a long-standing public nuisance and health hazard, since the area tended to collect much of the city's sewage. In 1881, Boston's Board of Health proudly declared that the Back Bay "presents to-day but a fractional part of its original, unfilled, unhealthy, and unsightly condition."[62]

Elsewhere, the physical geography worsened. Since the early 1800s, for example, various projects had enlarged the eastern edge of the neck, creating the new South End and closing much of the South Boston Bay. At the southern end of the bay, where the neck joined the mainland, ran the Roxbury Canal, which was foul enough "to nauseate any decent man" and even to dissuade horses from crossing over its bridge.[63] "The sewage and mire lie, a fathom deep," the Board of Health reported in 1877, "bubbling their gases through the black, putrid water, while the lighter and soluble portions of filth are slowly surging back and forth with the rising and falling of the tide."[64] During the late 1860s and 1870s, the tide also played havoc with streets on the western edge of the neck, close to the new Back Bay. In one section, two hundred brick buildings had to be raised fourteen feet to new foundations, while in a thirty-two-acre area nearby, six hundred buildings were elevated, another one hundred fifty destroyed, and many streets were made over.[65] One trouble spot did disappear when the marshy area just west of the Back Bay was converted into the Fenway, part of landscape designer Frederick Law Olmsted's plan for an "emerald necklace" stretching from Jamaica Plain to the central city. The constant face-lift of Boston gave citizens a new environment in which to live, and new concerns about public health with which to contend.

Sanitary conditions, however, were not the sole issue. For middle-class Bostonians, "environment" signified not only the cleanliness of their city, but also its layout and inhabitants. During the late 1800s, many changes took place in the physical organization of Boston, disrupting the lives of middle-class residents. For one, the separation of residential and commercial districts increased during the late Victorian period.[66] The central city was devoted to business, with only a few residential areas remaining on the perimeter near the ocean. An example is Fort Hill, a once exclusive, but gradually deteriorating residential district near the waterfront, which was leveled for the Back Bay project and converted into business property. Nearby, a section that once housed private homes, businesses, and noncommercial institutions was destroyed in the Great Fire of November 9, 1872. When rebuilt, the area became the site of Boston's major department stores. Among the few residential districts still near the central city were the North and West ends, where a predominantly immigrant population lived in tenements and lodging homes. Meanwhile, land reclamation projects opened new possibilities for other residents. Promising to be a fashionable area, the new South End continued to be settled in the late 1860s and 1870s, becoming the site of elegant homes and various churches, schools, and businesses. (By the end of the century, however, it had reverted to lodging homes and tenements.) Meanwhile, the Back Bay assumed from the outset, and never lost, its appeal as one of the preferred residential districts in the city.

Boston was undergoing suburbanization.[67] Between 1870 and 1900, the middle class settled in areas between 2½ and 6 miles from the central city, enjoying the convenience of the expanding streetcar system and, in some cases, the status of a privately owned home. By 1900, the well-to-do, if not entrenched downtown on Beacon Hill or occupying a new brownstone along the Back Bay, had built country estates five to fifteen miles out, in the more distant suburbs. The size of the metropolitan area (Boston wards plus outlying towns) more than quadrupled between 1850 and 1900. Over the same period, the percentage of residents living in the outer wards of Boston and in commuter towns grew at the expense of the central city. Whereas two-thirds of the metropolitan population lived within a two-mile radius of downtown in 1850, less than half did so in 1900.

By the turn of the century, Boston "was very much a city divided."[68] Except for the Back Bay, "it was an inner city of work and low-income housing, and an outer city of middle- and upper-income residences."[69] By 1900, the related trends of industrial concentration and suburbanization had split Boston into "two functional parts: an industrial, commercial, and communications center packed tight against the port, and an enormous outer suburban ring of residences and industrial and commercial subcenters."[70] Both economic function and social class had cut the city into discrete parcels.

The compartmentalization of Boston upset the lives of middle-class inhabitants. Even minor adjustments seemed momentous. For example, people dashed to catch the morning streetcar, instead of walking to work.[71] Other differences were more profound. The new layout of Boston helped formalize the sexual division of spheres. Literally and figuratively, a greater distance separated the workplace and the home, and the lives of middle-class men and women diverged even further than before. Middle-class men learned the routine of commuting to work, conducting their business, then returning home to the suburbs. Middle-class wives and mothers adapted to a truly residential life, increasingly isolated from the world and work of their husbands. The impact was as much psychological as physical, and middle-class Bostonians found the city's new physical face a source of dis-ease.

They worried too about the city's human face. Between 1850 and 1900, Boston's overall population more than quadrupled, from approximately 137,000 to 561,000.[72] The annexation of five communities between 1868 and 1874 accounted for some of the growth, while most came from in-migration and net births over deaths. More than its absolute size, the fluidity of the city was remarkable. An analysis by Stephan Thernstrom demonstrated that about one-third of the city's population in 1890 had arrived since 1880, "and that the actual number of separate families who lived in Boston at *some* point between 1880 and 1890 was a staggering 296,388, more than three times the total number residing there at any one time in this 10-year period!"[73] At the very least, such high mobility disrupted the continuity of neighborhoods and the sense of community shared by residents.

Even more troubling to native Bostonians was the growth in the city's foreign population. Given their assumption that, at best, ethnic traits receded only slowly, contemporaries usually identified "foreigners" by parentage, rather than birthplace. Thus, the tabulation of Boston's foreign population included foreign-born immigrants and their native-born children, as well as those of "mixed parentage." By that measure, Boston became a predominantly foreign city during the nineteenth century. In 1850, foreigners constituted nearly one-half of the city; they accounted for almost two-thirds of the population in 1880 and close to three-quarters in 1910.[74] Even if one uses birthplace as the criterion, the result is striking. Between 1850 and 1900, foreign-born residents comprised roughly one-third of Boston's population.[75]

In addition, a dramatic shift was underway in the immigrants' point of origin. Whereas nearly three-quarters of the foreign population before mid-century had been Irish, the immigrants of the late 1800s came from eastern and southern Europe. In 1870, the Irish still comprised about two-thirds of the foreign population in Boston, while by 1920, new immigrants outnumbered them two to one.[76]

Those trends alarmed native Bostonians of the middle and upper classes. Decades of interaction had not dispelled their fears about Irish culture and influence; by the mid-1880s, the Irish exerted considerable political power in the city. The new immigrants, such as Italians and Jews, seemed to pose a more insidious problem. Their customs, political philosophies, and religious views challenged the self-proclaimed values of long-time New Englanders. Many native Bostonians held the new immigrants responsible for the prevalence of crime, inadequate public education, and general moral decay in the city. Another concern was the immigrants' apparent detriment to public health. Analysts of Boston's vital statistics did not systematically tabulate deaths by birthplace or ethnicity until the end of the nineteenth century. Uniformly, however, native residents were convinced that foreigners became ill and died in excessive numbers.[77] In addition, they believed that the homes of immigrants bred filth and disease, which then spread throughout the city. The differences between natives and foreigners led some Bostonians to support remedial means (education) or preventive measures (immigration restrictions) for correcting the problem.[78] Only then, it seemed, would long-time Bostonians be safe from the apparent dangers of their new neighbors.

In sum, middle-class Bostonians found many reasons to be anxious about their health. They worried about infectious diseases and chronic conditions, about the vulnerability of women and children, and about the troublesome needs of their own bodies. They regarded their city as a menacing place, one that harbored both physical and human perils; some were clear and present, while others were invisible. Social developments—an erratic economy, the pace of urban life, and a technological revolution in the home and workplace—were equally unsettling. Though diverse, those problems seemed connected: physical ailments and emotional stress were related to the transformation of urban life; public health improved or declined as the city's face was made over; the likelihood of sickness seemed to mirror the inevitability of social change. Biological, personal, and environmental risks looked inseparable. It was no longer clear where individual conditions ended and social context began.

The blending of private experience and social developments is well illustrated by women's lives. In late Victorian Boston, middle-class women worried about health for several, interrelated reasons. Some factors were biological and demographic, while others involved the status of women, both in and out of the home, and the accompanying national debate about women's "proper" place. Those intersecting trends, joining individual experience and social position, made health a focal issue for women in the late nineteenth century.

Women's sense of healthfulness derives, in part, from the pattern of their life cycle. The cycle covers both immediate events and long-term expectations dealing with relationships, fertility, and longevity. It includes biological processes, such as menstruation and sickness, and personal circumstances, such as marital status. In late Victorian times, the average contour of the female life cycle in America was both similar to and different from earlier decades. Together, the continuities and changes affected women's attitudes about their lives. Their well-being seemed at once better and more precarious.

One improvement was the rise in women's life expectancy at birth during the second half of the century. The chances of surviving until age 20 grew significantly for women born in Massachusetts between 1830 and 1870, and even more dramatically after 1870.[79] Thus, young females could expect to pass through adolescence, with all the physical and emotional upheavals it entailed, and to approach adulthood, with its anticipation of marriage.

Patterns of marriage were much the same as before. Women's first marriage usually occurred between the ages of 20 and 23, and between 82 and 90 percent of all females eventually married.[80] Among white women born in Massachusetts between 1830 and 1890, the proportion who remained single rose slightly.[81] Still, the vast majority of women got married at some point during their lives.

In some respects, the life of a married woman in the late 1800s differed significantly from that of her ancestors. One critical change was the steady decline in the birth rate among native-born women. Within the white population, the number of births per 1000 dropped from 50 in 1800 to 28.5 in 1900.[82] Between 1850 and 1900, native-born wives could expect to have three children, down from seven in the eighteenth century.[83] Moreover, compared to earlier generations, a greater number of married women in the late nineteenth century reached their fiftieth birthday without bearing any children.[84] Although women tended to marry in roughly the same proportion as before, they bore fewer and fewer children as the nineteenth century progressed.

That fact had profound implications. It reveals that couples practiced some form of birth control, whether abstinence, a mechanical device, or other measures. There also are indications that the rate of abortions jumped during the nineteenth century, despite the dangers of the procedure.[85] For the woman who carried a pregnancy to term, the risk of complications or maternal death remained high. Accurate historical data about mortality during childbirth are sparse, but evidence suggests that rates did not improve until well into the twentieth century. The involvement of male obstetricians, beginning in the late eighteenth century among well-to-do urban families, did not uniformly increase the safety of childbirth in America compared to the custom of delivery with female midwives and friends in attendance. In fact, doctors' common modes of intervention, such as bloodletting, forceps, and drugs, could introduce additional dangers, and unsanitary physicians often spread infectious diseases, such as puerperal fever, among their patients. Fewer pregnancies meant that women in the late 1800s faced the potential hazards of childbirth, including death, less often.[86]

The birth of fewer children also affected the character of domestic life. The size of the typical household in America (excluding slaves) dropped by 0.4 persons between 1790 and 1860 and by another 0.5 persons between 1860 and 1890.[87] Local data indicate that mean family size in Boston declined slowly from 4.84 in 1870 to 4.53 in 1900.[88] If children were spaced at the same rate as before, then smaller families meant that women devoted a shorter span of their lives to childbirth and child care. There was less time between the birth of one's first child and the departure from home of one's last. In addition, greater life expectancies for both males and females decreased the possibility that a native white woman would be widowed before age 55.[89] Overall, a married woman could anticipate spending fewer years with fewer children, and more years with only her husband.

The growing frequency of divorce, however, had an opposite effect. While divorce was extremely uncommon in the seventeenth through mid-nineteenth century, it occurred more regularly during the late 1800s.[90] Explanations vary, but the fact is undeniable that more marriages than before ended deliberately through divorce, than accidentally by the death of a spouse. Although some factors increased the years a husband and wife spent together, other events may have shortened them.

In any era, the natural processes of female life and the particular demographic trends of the time combine to shape women's private experience in a unique way. During the late nineteenth century, the female life cycle had some familiar features. Puberty, menstruation, and menopause were predictable stages; most women experienced sexual intercourse, pregnancy, and childbirth; acute and chronic illness continued to be commonplace. Meanwhile, patterns of marriage, the shrinking of the family, increases in life expectancy, and other developments formed a new context for the biological phases of womanhood. Some of the most sensitive issues for women involved their physical lives: birth control and abortion, maternal health, and domestic relations (how long and with whom would a woman live?). Not surprisingly, young and old women alike saw health, both physical and psychological, as an urgent matter in the late nineteenth century.

The same questions had significance beyond women's private lives. In Victorian times, conventional opinion held that a woman was imprinted by nature for specific roles, and uniquely situated in the home to carry them out. Dictating certain qualities, while proscribing others, biology appeared to define an ideal female life cycle. The social ideology and institutions of America further supported the model of motherhood and domesticity. Regardless of a woman's aspirations, then, her gender and course of life influenced her social position. Questions about marriage, reproduction, and physical health had a bearing on women's experience in the public, as well as private, sphere.[91]

In Boston and around the country, women were second-class citizens during the nineteenth century. Legislators and other brokers of power claimed that women, who were creatures of the home, should not be troubled with matters of politics. Thus, women's political status in Boston improved only slightly during the last quarter of the century. In the 1870s, they gained the right to be elected to Boston's School Committee and, some years later, to vote in such elections.

The belief in separate spheres also affected the evolution of women's education. Because of their distinct futures, it seemed neither desirable nor necessary to offer the sexes identical education.

Since the organization of Boston's public school system in 1789, the city provided education for young girls, but its duration and content differed from instruction given to boys. Although primary schools were coeducational, grammar classrooms were not integrated on even a limited basis until the late 1830s. Opportunities for girls beyond grammar school were nonexistent before 1852, when the city opened its Normal (later Normal and High) School for girls. Clearly, the original intent was to prepare girls for employment as teachers. College preparatory courses were not available to girls until 1878 when the exclusive Girls' Latin School opened.[92]

In the private sector, possibilities for education from childhood into the late teens were more numerous, but limited to girls whose families could afford the tuition. Many academies hoped merely to put the "finishing" touches on genteel young womanhood, while others emphasized more intellectual programs. Few, however, challenged the notion that education should equip women for their primary roles as wives and mothers. Several colleges for women opened in New England after the Civil War and some universities in the area offered full or token higher education for women. For example, Boston University went coeducational in 1869, and in 1879, through the efforts of a women's organization, Harvard University agreed to offer separate instruction for selected women. The Society for the Collegiate Instruction of Women, known colloquially as "The Harvard Annex," became Radcliffe College in 1894. Many members of the University and the community saw little need, and much bother, in providing higher education for women.[93]

Employment outside the home also depended on one's sex, as well as class and marital status. If a woman was native-born, white, and middle-class, she may have held a paying job before marriage. Perhaps half of all white women worked outside the home prior to marriage.[94] Since the work force in factories, domestic service, and other blue-collar jobs consisted of poor native, immigrant, and black laborers, the native-born middle-class woman found employment in areas considered more "respectable." For example, around one in every five young white women in postbellum Massachusetts was a school teacher at some point in her life.[95] It was the exception, however, for a middle-class woman to continue her job after marriage. On the average, less than 5 percent of all married white women worked outside the home in the late nineteenth century.[96] Correlatively, although data are sketchy, many career women apparently remained single.[97] In academia, for example, the Wellesley College faculty included no married women between 1880 and 1920. The case of female physicians seems to be exceptional; between 25 and 35 percent of women doctors in the nineteenth century married, and 30 to 40 percent did so in the first half of the twentieth century.[98] On the whole, though, American culture viewed work and marriage as incompatible for women, and the structure of jobs and families virtually made them so.

Being married was a commitment to one's husband and children and to domestic responsibilities. While those duties did not confine a middle-class woman to the home, her outside activities too were subject to society's expectations about proper womanhood. Customarily, middle-class women paid social visits, tended sick friends and relatives, participated in church groups or charities, and joined clubs devoted to literature, benevolence, and other pursuits. During the last third of the century, cultural opportunities in Boston, especially women's clubs, flourished. Among the more prominent organizations were the Boston branch of the Young Women's Christian Association (founded in 1867), the New England Women's Club (1868), the Woman's Education Association (1872), and the Women's Educational and Industrial Union (1877). Working in such diverse fields as female employment, dress, housing, health, and moral uplift, those groups attracted middle- and upper-class women interested in reform.

Developments in the social sphere, then, were not far removed from private experience. Women's legal and political status, their opportunities for education and employment, and their extradomestic interests revolved around the same questions that preoccupied women in their personal lives. Was a woman single or married? Did she have children? Was she able-bodied or not? Was her course of life "typical" or not? Only a fine line separated personal and social issues; women's private lives and public status seemed intimately connected. As those two worlds changed and interacted, women's uncertainty about their well-being, physical and otherwise, grew.

If women themselves became uneasy, the issue of female health carried additional weight in the late nineteenth century because of the intensifying national debate about "the Woman Question." What was women's actual condition, and what ideally should it be? As the discussion proceeded, questions about women's place in society became further enmeshed with the private issues of marriage, reproduction, and health. For the country, as for individual women, concern about the personal experiences and social position of women merged.

"The Woman Question" was as much a reassessment of American society as it was an inquiry into women's status. As industrialization and urbanization reshaped the nature of work, the home, and community life, Americans necessarily re-examined the structure of the family, the relationship of the sexes, and the quality of their lives. Whatever commentators concluded about those problems and their solution, female health seemed a crucial element.

Protagonists in "the Woman Question" cannot be neatly classified as conservative or progressive. Still, some clearly defended a traditional division of the sexes. Their belief in separate spheres and their contention that any change invited social disaster often involved biological arguments. For example, some Victorian Americans viewed the declining birth rate among native white women as the first step toward "race suicide." Partly because of women's incapacity or unwillingness to reproduce, they argued, native-born Americans faced extinction. In his 1884 essay on the "Deterioration of the Puritan Stock and Its Causes," for example, Dr. John Ellis examined the "inability to bear, care for and rear children, which is largely the fault, either physically or mentally, of the native women."[99] Tight-dressing, "fashionable idleness,"[100] late marriage, contraception, and other forms of "self-love and love of the world" among women, Ellis complained, promoted "the speedy destruction of the native American population" and ensured that "this country is to be peopled mainly, and at no distant day, by the inflowing immigrants and those who were foreign born less than half a century ago and their descendants."[101] Race suicide was imminent, Ellis and others warned, unless women's physical health and spiritual values were elevated.

The debate over women's higher education produced equally dire forecasts. Opponents argued that advanced learning for women was undoubtedly harmful, and probably unnecessary. At crucial stages in a female's development, especially menarche, studying diverted precious energy from physiological processes to mental work. A likely consequence was the interruption, even cessation, of the female cycle, and a host of other complications.

The classic statement of that opinion was Dr. Edward H. Clarke's monograph called *Sex in Education; or, A Fair Chance for Girls.*[102] As did most of his medical colleagues, Clarke, a Harvard professor, believed that the careful distribution of one's limited vital force was required for the entire body to function smoothly. Given that principle, Clarke reasoned, "the system never does two things well at the same time."[103] A prime example was the incompatibility of "brain-work" and menstruation. As Clarke noted, however, the development of a girl's reproductive system, "this peculiar and marvellous apparatus,"[104] usually coincided with a period of fairly demanding education. "Both muscular and brain labor," he argued, "must be remitted enough to yield sufficient force for the work [of menarche]. If the reproductive machinery is not manufactured then, it will not be later."[105] While acknowledging that certain customs contributed to America's overabundance of sick women, Clarke maintained that "to a large extent, our present system of educating girls is the cause of this palor [sic] and weakness."[106]

As many people condemned Clarke's presentation as applauded it. Twenty years later, however, his views were still popular in medical circles. Addressing the Medical Society of New York in 1891, for example, one physician contended that many a sterile wife or invalid mother was the result of inappropriate education. How can a female fulfill the destiny assigned her anatomy, asked Dr. William Warren Potter, "if her reproductive organs are dwarfed, deformed, weakened, and diseased, by artificial causes imposed upon her during their development?"[107] The improper growth of the sexual system, Potter argued, derived from failures in the nervous system, a "nerve turmoil which begins in the overworked, weary, and anaemic cerebrum."[108] Commentators such as Clarke and Potter believed that the ill effects of education were not confined to a girl's generative system, but also surfaced in minor complaints, such as backaches and headaches, and in prolonged emotional disorders and perhaps invalidism.[109]

Critics of female education proposed various remedies, ranging from school programs that respected the uniqueness of female physiology to abandonment of extensive education for women altogether. Whatever their particular suggestions, Clarke's allies agreed with his pronouncement that the solution to "the problem of woman's sphere" must come "from physiology, not from ethics or metaphysics."[110] "The *quoestio vexata* of woman's sphere," Clarke observed, "will be decided by her organization."[111]

Americans who wanted to bar women from other activities took the same line of attack. "It is every way desirable," wrote Dr. I. P. Davis in *Hygiene for Girls,* "that a woman should be occupied with such employments and recreations as are adapted to her nature and position."[112] Those included raising children, tending the sick and needy, and providing a healthy environment for one's family. "It is only when work is unsuited in character or amount to the conditions

in which the individual is placed," Davis continued, "that it is unnatural and injurious."[113] Although Davis accepted some types of
female employment, most of his peers argued that church and charity
were the only justifiable extensions of female nurturance from the
private to public realm. A woman is ill-equipped, the conservative
position held, to engage in vigorous exercise, to pursue demanding
professions such as medicine, or to inhabit the high-pressure world
of business or politics. Her physiology and her moral sensibilities
could not tolerate such abuse. As Dr. William Goodell of Philadelphia concluded in his text on gynecology in 1879,

> Woman shines best and thrives best, not in the adulation of society,
> not in obtrusive self-assertion, but in the quiet and faithful perfor-
> mance of her home duties. The heat and stir of life is food for man's
> more rugged nature. The wholesomest passages of her life are those
> which, like the thesis of a symphony, are unpercussed and unac-
> cented.[114]

Though less poetically, many of Goodell's colleagues also recommended that women's every activity conform to their natural constitutions and their social roles.

Health and propriety lay at the heart of another problem as well.
Many Americans in the late 1800s regarded the rise in birth control
and abortion as physical and moral sacrilege. No woman who respected God or her body, Victorian moralists concluded, would agree
to such depraved acts. Campaigns to control the practices, including
the Comstock Law of 1873, which banned the distribution of contra-
ceptive information and devices through the mail, prospered with the
support of physicians, religious groups, and certain elements of the
social purity and eugenics movements.[115]

For Americans such as Ellis, Clarke, and Goodell, women's
health was implicated in many social problems during late Victorian
times. They viewed the decline in female health as both cause and
effect of deeper crises in the family structure, social order, and moral
fabric of the nation. Virtue and stability would return, they declared,
when women's health was restored.

The issue of female health was equally important to Americans
who sought to improve women's status after mid-century. Although
women's advocates agreed that female health was in jeopardy, they
believed the causes were more social than personal. They argued that
conventional upbringing and roles endangered female health more

than occasional indiscretions or oversights did. Participating in a symposium on "The Health of American Women" in 1882, Elizabeth Cady Stanton, a pioneer of women's rights, acknowledged that "variable climate," "the excitement of a young civilization," and "improper dress, diet, and general habits of life" adversely affected people's health.[116] Of greater significance for women's health, she continued, "are many social customs and restrictions."[117] Stanton reviewed an average female's life cycle, noting the prejudices that imperiled health at each stage. She cited restrictions on young girls' physical activity; the high demands and low rewards of married life; and the sentiment against employment, mental stimulation, and worthwhile pursuits outside the home for both young and married women. In most cases, Stanton contended, the source of ill-health was not an excess of freedom, but its absence. For example, "a woman of ambition," who pursued unusual roles, broke down not because she had violated nature, but because "to surmount obstacles exhausts the reserve energies of mind and body."[118] Ill-health, Stanton concluded, stemmed from society's denial of women's legitimate needs and abilities.

Sharing Stanton's views, many intellectuals and reformers proceeded to dismantle common misconceptions about women. For example, a new generation of sociologists and psychologists, many of them women, formulated nontraditional theories about the biological and social bases of female life.[119] Likewise, supporters of women's rights and some doctors countered the notion that women's health necessarily suffered during advanced schooling.[120] Several women's organizations and colleges presented data that proved higher education, when properly designed, did not ruin women's health or fertility.[121] Some experts challenged the medical and popular belief that menstruation essentially incapacitated women. Female physicians, such as Dr. Mary Putnam Jacobi in her monograph *The Question of Rest for Women during Menstruation,* found little evidence that physiological changes during the female cycle impinged on women's mental or physical abilities.[122] A wide collection of health reformers, educators, and women's advocates sought to liberalize customs of female exercise and to expand women's opportunities in recreation and sports. Finally, some women's activists defended birth control, under the label of "voluntary motherhood," as both a moral and physical right. Foreshadowing today's feminists, they argued that women's rights must begin with control over their own bodies.[123]

Though Ellis and Stanton stood at opposite ends of "the Woman

Question," they agreed that female health was a crucial problem. Virtually every commentator, in fact, believed that women's health had personal and social value, that women's physical condition seemed deficient, and that educating women about health was a wise investment. Differences of opinion arose over what people regarded as women's natural position, and how that might be achieved. As Americans debated the proper roles of women, they necessarily grappled with the meaning of able-bodied womanhood.

In fact, fear about women's vitality typified Americans' general sense of dis-ease during the last quarter of the nineteenth century. Some difficulties were immediate and tangible: alarming rates of illness and death could not be ignored, nor could the internal processes of one's body. Other conditions were more impersonal, but no less unsettling. Familiar patterns of life began to erode under the weight of industrialization and urbanization. The structure of the home, the workplace, and the community underwent significant change. For men and women alike, the result was a profound uneasiness, a sense that their physical and psychological well-being was at risk.

Late Victorian Americans were less confident than their ancestors had been about finding a cure. The social environment seemed more alien, and everyday life less amenable to control. Even the natural processes of the human body puzzled them. Old ways of managing one's world no longer sufficed, and new approaches were needed.

One source of advice was health reform and popular physiology. A new generation led America's health movement in the late nineteenth century, and their qualifications were diverse. Some were self-proclaimed experts on diet, exercise, and personal hygiene. Horace Fletcher (1849–1919), for example, was an ink manufacturer, silk importer, opera company manager, and dozens of other things before devoting himself to popular health in the mid-1890s. Exuberant, yet well-respected, Fletcher believed that good nutrition was the ultimate source of physical and mental health, and that thorough mastication was the first step to efficient digestion. ("Fletcherizing," or vigorous chewing, became a common word, if not practice, during his lifetime.) Another sensational health advocate at the turn of the century was Bernarr A. Macfadden (1868–1955), who overcame childhood debility with dumbbell workouts and distance walking. Equating health with strength, Macfadden viewed muscle development as the road to vitality (and virility). Perhaps Macfadden's best advertisements for exercise were the revealing pictures, including those of his own admirable physique, that appeared in his many books, magazines, and exhibitions.[124]

The medical profession also produced late Victorian health reformers. A noteworthy example is John Harvey Kellogg, M.D. (1852–1943), who trained at Russell Trall's Hygeio-Therapeutic College and then at two regular schools, the College of Medicine and Surgery of the University of Michigan and the Bellevue Hospital Medical School in New York.[125] In 1876 Kellogg became chief physician at the Western Health Reform Institute in Battle Creek, Michigan, a sanitarium founded by the Seventh-Day Adventists and their leader, Ellen G. White. A zealous supporter of vegetarianism, temperance, natural healing, and sexual purity, Kellogg was a prolific writer and lecturer for popular audiences, and also joined his brother, William, in developing a line of health foods, ranging from peanut butter to dry cereals. Though originally intended for the sanitarium at Battle Creek, the products evolved into the commercial enterprise that still bears the Kellogg name. A host of other doctors, both regular and nonorthodox, from the prominent to the obscure, contributed to the movement as authors of texts and primers about health. While some wrote only occasional guides, others made virtual careers out of popularizing physiology and hygiene.

Finally, many supporters came to health reform by way of physical education, a new field in the late nineteenth century.[126] The very name of the profession indicated its claim on popular health. Across the country, both ordinary and renowned physical educators taught the rules of hygienic living and shaped American attitudes about health. Some of the country's most influential physical educators were among the leading popularizers of physiology and exercise in the late nineteenth and early twentieth century. Dudley Allen Sargent, M.D. (1849–1924), for example, who directed physical training and supervised the men's gymnasium at Harvard for forty years, wrote numerous speeches and articles for the lay public. Another force in the new discipline was William G. Anderson, M.D. (1860–1947), who prepared physical educators at his school in Brooklyn (later at New Haven) and directed the gymnasium at Yale University for nearly forty years. Luther Gulick, M.D. (1865–1918), who made physical activity a focus of the Young Men's Christian Association, advocated "muscular Christianity,"—the attainment of spiritual and physical well-being through calisthenics and athletics.

Together, popular physiologists, doctors, and physical educators assumed responsibility for advising the public about health and disease. Although their specific formulas varied, they agreed that new attitudes about health would help Americans adjust to modern society. The many biological, personal, and external risks in life could be managed, health reformers said, if people adopted new concepts and habits of well-being. They portrayed health as a means of handling both the internal needs of one's body and the demands of one's environment.

The new model of health in the late nineteenth century revolved around the theme of personal control.[127] Physical educators and doctors described health as cooperation between body and mind, as an effective relationship between physical and mental processes. More specifically, health was the neurological direction of physiological functions, or a mind capable of governing and a body willing to obey. People could thereby monitor their own well-being, practicing healthy habits while avoiding ill-conceived or accidental ones.

This definition of health did not replace the old principles of physiology. It merely focused the laws of use and repair and of harmonious interdependence on the mind-body partnership. The law of use and repair stated that activity was necessary for the proper development of any organ. As Dr. J. C. Hutchison observed in his treatise on physiology, "Action is the law of the living body. Every organ demands use to preserve it in full vigor, and to obtain from it its best services."[128] In contrast, another writer pointed out, "an unused organ dwindles away."[129] Without exercise, malfunctioning and perhaps complete atrophy would ensue. The need for rest was a logical corollary. "Every motion that we make, and every thought that we think," explained a physiological text, "destroys some of the minute cells" comprising the body. If replenishment, through digested food in the blood, does not occur, "the parts soon wear out, and the body dies."[130]

Applied to physical tissues, the principle of use and repair was self-evident. Dr. John Harvey Kellogg contrasted the "large and hard" muscles in the arms of blacksmiths and wood-choppers with the "thin and soft" arms of "students, lawyers, editors, and most professional men."[131] According to health writers, the law was equally valid for activities of the mind. "The brain, like the muscles," explained H. Newell Martin, the eminent physiologist from Johns Hopkins University, "is improved and strengthened by exercise and injured by overwork or idleness."[132] Similarly, one's nervous system required appropriate stimuli and sufficient rest. Nerves, wrote Johonnot and Bouton, need exercise "to make their growth vigorous and to secure strength."[133] Without rest, however, "weariness increases, and the nervous system breaks down."[134]

Health consisted of more than individual organs that were properly exercised and rested. It also required harmonious interaction between all systems in the body. In the late nineteenth century, the law of interdependence emphasized relationships between physical and neurological processes, or, more simply, between body and mind. Popular physiologists described the human body as the material vehicle for physical movement, emotional states, and mental activities. In a rudimentary way, the same held true for lower animals. The human body, though, as Dr. A. F. Blaisdell exclaimed in 1885, is "not simply a most perfect and delicate machine, but one endowed with life,—a mind,—a soul."[135] That distinction was momentous. Whereas raw instinct ruled animal life, the human mind, consciously or not, coordinated the activities of the body. Without mental supervision, people's internal processes would lack direction, and mere urges would prevail. The will, explained Jessie H. Bancroft, is a positive force of inhibition and direction. It "controls, defers or suppresses action 'with reference to remoter ends.' It restrains impulse and places action under the espionage of reflection and judgment."[136] The ancient phrase *mens sana in corpore sano* took on new meaning. In a uniquely human way, health was an active body monitored by a discriminating mind.[137]

Popular health literature of the late nineteenth century outlined the many forms that the mind-body relationship took. Obviously, the mind controlled the vital functions of the heart, lungs, and stomach, without people being aware of them. Voluntary actions, such as movements of an arm or hand, were direct responses to a conscious decision and command. Other processes were the result of habitual training, in which mental direction slowly transformed an unfamiliar act into a reflex one through repetition. All of these situations required a disciplined mind and a responsive body.

Popular physiologists argued that feelings were also the product of mind-body interactions. As William G. Anderson, the noted physical educator, explained, "All emotion is expressed by muscular movement: muscular movement is controlled by will."[138] Thus, emotions too could be regulated once the body learned to obey the mind. For Anderson, the achievement of emotional control meant the virtual suppression of feelings:

He who never shows emotion, who is calm and self-contained in the face of danger, who curbs his temper, is not cast down by grief, checks an angry word—in short, who can manage himself—exhibits self-control. . . .

Self-control is the mastery over the restless members of the body. What is the loss of self-control? Visible emotion. How do we express any emotion but by muscular movement? Anger, sadness, joy, fear, jealousy, are all shown in this way. When suddenly confronted with unpleasant news our muscles, like wild horses, at once slip from our control and it is shown by the face, if in no other way, that we are affected.[139]

One ideal of health was the victory of the conscious mind over unruly parts of the body.

For many ordinary feelings, that goal seemed possible. Anger, for example, was readily subject to mental control. If one failed to contain anger, though, Dr. I. P. Davis warned, it could lead to further "vexation," more violent outbursts, and even nervous exhaustion and physical collapse.[140] Other "sensations and desires," however, were more problematic because they were "not within the influence of reason, nor controlled by will."[141] Hunger, explained Dr. Davis, could not be quashed, "when once it is roused, by any effort of will. We can withhold food by an effort of will, and the hunger will remain unsatisfied."[142] In and of itself, the mind could not create or dissipate a feeling such as hunger; one's only choices were to ignore or to gratify the demand.

Even more troublesome were reflex sensations, such as sexual feelings. "There are some appetites," Dr. Davis noted, "that, when fully roused, paralyze the will, and control the whole being, so that, unlike the appetite for food, it is impossible to withhold from them the object of their desire."[143] For Davis and others, the prospect of rampaging sexual passion and complete breakdown of self-restraint was a frightening one. Although people could contain most feelings, their will was powerless against sexual desire. The only recourse, said Dr. Davis, was prevention: people should avoid any situation that might trigger such feelings.

According to popular physiologists, the exercise of self-control would neutralize many threats to personal health. At the very least, health writers assured, Americans would gain power over their mischievous bodies and unpredictable feelings. Health advocates promised that people who achieved self-discipline would be able to make deliberate movements, to monitor their feelings, and to guide their activities and emotions toward rational goals. Biological events would lose their apparent autonomy. Moreover, by learning how to manage the strains of the day-to-day world, people could live more confidently and productively. A successful adjustment to the modern world began with mastering one's own body and mind.

What remained unsolved were larger forces that affected people's sense of well-being. What could be done about economic conditions, technological developments, or other social changes? Health writers advised their audiences to accommodate, rather than to resist; social trends were beyond direct control, but individuals could advance public order through private restraint. In effect, health writers predicted that personal discipline would translate into social stability.

Some physiologists explained that process in metaphoric terms. They described the human body, organizationally and operationally, as a miniature version of American society. H. Newell Martin of Johns Hopkins, for example, developed an elaborate analogy between organic and economic systems, between the physical body and modern industrial capitalism.[144] Martin noted that specialization of function separated advanced and primitive civilizations, just as it distinguished higher from lower animal life. The division of labor, he said, had three consequences: individuals tended to perform their tasks better and their society functioned more smoothly; a society had to devise some means of integrating its specialized industries, especially for conveying essential products and removing waste; finally, "arrangements" were needed "by which, at any given time, the activity of individuals shall be regulated in accordance with the wants of the whole community or of the world at large."[145] Martin identified modern capitalists as the people who coordinated individual activities and supervised the distribution of goods, according to the law of supply and demand and their perception of the common good.

Martin then developed the physical metaphor: specialized structures allowed the human body to operate more efficiently; the heart and circulatory system served as the *"distributing mechanism"*; the nervous system was the *"regulating mechanism."*[146] The body was simply a physical replica of advanced capitalism: individual organs performed small tasks under the supervision of master systems; their physical needs, such as nourishment, were met; efficiency was maximized; the health and strength of the body as a unit were promoted. Martin's scheme was evaluative, not merely heuristic. He believed that a capitalist economy best served human needs; similarly, industrial physiology enhanced one's prospects for health. By justifying as well as interpreting the modern world, Martin taught his readers an important lesson: civilization and nature follow the same rules. The health of American society, as of a human organism, depends on the performance of its constituents; self-discipline would produce both individual happiness and social stability. The last stumbling block to complete control was thereby removed.

While Martin relied on metaphors, other popular physiologists approached the question of control more directly. For example, the connection between self-mastery and social order was a common theme for Dudley Allen Sargent. His background and work are representative of the new generation that promoted health reform at the turn of the century through physical education and medicine.[147] Born in Maine in 1849, Sargent read widely in biology, popular physiology, and philosophy during his high-school years. After abandoning the idea of becoming a minister, Sargent tutored under local doctors, studying the work of Darwin, Spencer, and Huxley in the process. An enthusiastic gymnast, Sargent often performed stunts for his friends and even joined a circus for a while. At the age of twenty, he went to Bowdoin College where he served as director of physical education and devised a system of exercise, while earning his baccalaureate. There, Sargent committed himself to the infant profession of physical education. Convinced that further training in physiology and medicine would be important for his new career, Sargent enrolled at Yale and received his medical diploma in 1877. Unable to find a school that would hire him and adopt his exercise program, Sargent moved to New York City in 1878 and opened his Hygienic Institute and School for Physical Culture. Shortly thereafter, Harvard College invited Sargent to become its first director of physical training and the supervisor of the men's gymnasium, posts he held until 1919, five years before his death. Sargent also operated a private gymnasium in Cambridge, where he taught townspeople and Annex girls (Radcliffe students). He also trained physical education teachers at his gym and ran a famous normal school at Harvard each summer. (His training programs evolved into today's Sargent College of Allied Health Professions at Boston University.) A prolific writer and speaker and a member of numerous health, civic, and education associations, Sargent was a powerful figure in the professionalization of American physical education. He led his field in articulating the new model of health, especially the relationship between individual and social well-being.

Sargent had little use for the old-fashioned image of health as self-fulfillment. He viewed reliable performance as the main objective of health, on a personal and social level. If each organ functioned well, one's entire body ran smoothly; similarly, the diligence of individual workers enabled their society to be efficient and productive. Sargent named this state "fitness." "The great thing to be desired and attained," he explained, "is that prime physical condition called fitness—fitness for work, fitness for play, fitness for anything a man may be called upon to do."[148]

According to Sargent, fitness was the first casualty, as well as prime requisite, of performance. Increased specialization, he explained, forced most people to use their bodies unevenly, overtaxing some parts while neglecting others. Moreover, however useful to society as a whole, work exhausted the individuals who performed it. As Sargent remarked, we have to "shut ourselves up in shops, offices, and warehouses, and assume positions, habits, and customs which are detrimental to us individually, however the results of our efforts may serve to advance the condition of humanity as a whole."[149] Sargent likened modern life to a giant furnace "into which individuals enter . . . and are consumed in order to generate the power that moves the machinery of the world and insures progress."[150] In essence, health was a form of life insurance; it offered some protection against the demands of modern civilization. In turn, physical education might be called a recycling program, which compensated for the adverse effects of work and prepared an individual to re-enter the social furnace.

Sargent regarded this arrangement as inevitable, necessary, and beneficial. Health was no longer an idyllic journey to self-improvement or social perfection; it was a technique of personal adjustment and social management. As Sargent explained so succinctly in 1904, "It is no longer a question of adaptation of the tool and the employment to the man, it is now a question of the adaptation of the man to the tool and the work to be accomplished."[151]

In Sargent's mind, that change did not subjugate the individual to the state. It was a reciprocal, not exploitative, relationship. Training the body and mind facilitated health; health enabled one to work efficiently; productive labor ensured social growth; a vigorous society rewarded its members with wealth and happiness. In the bargain between people and their society, each expenditure of health was repaid with interest. Though Martin's and Sargent's terms differed, their logic brought them to the same conclusion. Accommodation allowed for personal happiness and social progress. What began as an effort to master the processes inside one's body became a means of contending with the world outside. In Martin's terms, to understand the human body is to understand one's world, and to follow the rules of physiology is to survive industrial society.

In this model of health, the problem of motivation dissolved. Some health writers still taught readers the moral calculus of hygiene. As Professor J. D. Steele admonished in 1875, "Every physical sin subtracts from the sum and strength of our years."[152] Others belabored the obligatory nature of health. "It is our duty," declared Professor D. L. Dowd in 1890, "not only to ourselves and the laws of nature, but to our families, our friends, our country, and all that are dependent upon our efforts in every walk of life, to take care of this precious temple in which we live."[153] Though sermons of this kind continued into the late nineteenth century, most writers discussed the inducements for health in less moralistic terms. For Sargent and others, health no longer was an option chosen because of prudence or conscience; it was compensatory and compulsory. As the new paradigm of evolutionary biology made clear, life was a struggle that only the fit would survive. The exigencies of urban industrial life compelled one to be healthy. It was a necessity, not a choice.

The equation between fitness and performance also entailed new ways of measuring personal health. Popular physiologists of the late 1800s still used appearance and behavior as indicators. For an age that valued precision and objectivity, however, those factors seemed ambiguous. Scientific analysis, and quantification in particular, were the most promising tools for standardizing the criteria of health. Believing that numbers revealed the underlying order of human affairs, Americans had always counted and measured. In the late nineteenth and early twentieth century, though, the enthusiasm for numbers spread well beyond vital statisticians and political economists. Quantification helped identify norms, locate weaknesses, and guide intervention in such areas as intelligence testing and worker productivity. Frederick W. Taylor's studies of time expenditure, output, and efficiency in factories helped popularize the concept of scientific management; through quantification of a system's operational steps, one could analyze and improve the overall process. Numbers not only disclosed what was, but also determined what should be.[154]

According to American doctors and physical educators, that held true for personal health as well. Numerical analysis of body size, strength, and symmetry seemed a reliable gauge of health. In Boston, doctors measured the city's school children, and around New England, college officials tested the physical abilities of their students. Advocates of weightlifting and muscle-building eagerly agreed that fitness could be counted and measured. Even competing systems of physical education, from Swedish gymnastics to German calisthenics, found value in quantifying health. Many such efforts were unscientific; supporters gathered numbers without a theoretical model for collating or interpreting the data.

One exception was the work of Dudley Allen Sargent, whose quantification of health achieved at least the appearance of rigor. Sargent based his approach on the concepts and methods of anthropometry, the quantitative study of the human animal. Anthropometry was by no means a new technique in the late 1800s; comparative anatomists and ethnologists had already spent decades using physical measurements to identify supposed qualitative differences between the sexes and races. From the 1860s on, doctors and physical educators such as Henry Pickering Bowditch, Edward Hitchcock, Jr., and Sargent enlisted anthropometry for the purpose of standardizing levels of health. They argued that a statistical analysis of quantifiable physical characteristics, drawn from a broad population, provided a scientific basis for determining individual healthfulness. An anthropometric study of health would reveal the status quo, establish an ideal, indicate deficiencies, and standardize comparisons.[155]

The Sargent system consisted of more than fifty tests of size and strength, conducted with tape measures, spring dynamometers, and other devices. Measurements included girth of head, size of left and right forearm, lung capacity, and strength of the back and legs. In the 1880s and 1890s, Sargent's tests emerged as one of the most common schemes for judging group and individual development. Academies, colleges, and normal schools around New England, and the country as a whole, adopted his plan and instruments. With such wide distribution, Sargent claimed to have gathered, directly or indirectly, data on over 10,000 people, male and female, generally seventeen to thirty years old, during the first twenty years of his career.[156]

From those results, Sargent prepared standardized charts for displaying a person's individual and relative condition. (See figure.) The process involved two basic steps. First, Sargent collated the test results of a reference population, say, young white males. For each of the fifty tests, he determined the "normal" measurement for

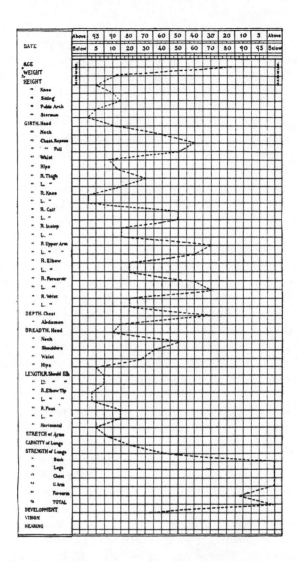

Dudley Allen Sargent's anthropometric chart for a young man of Irish descent, 22½ years old, 117 pounds, 5 feet 4 inches tall. Source: "The Physical Proportions of the Typical Man," *Scribner's Magazine* 2 (July 1887): 13. Courtesy of Charles Scribner's Sons.

the group. Taking the norm in each case to be the fiftieth percentile, he then calculated percentile rankings for other scores on the tests, according to the distribution of measurements within the sample group. For each test, then, Sargent coded the results of the reference population by means of percentile rank from 0 to 100. By gathering all fifty tests on one chart, Sargent had what he considered a numerical standard of human development, from tip to toe.

In order to judge the condition of an individual, Sargent performed the same fifty tests on his subject and plotted the results on the standard chart. For each test, he marked the percentile ranking to which the person's measurement corresponded. A score quite inferior to the reference group's norm fell on the left-hand side of the chart; a superior measurement fell on the right. By connecting the marks for all fifty tests, Sargent generated a zig-zag line, representing the individual's degree of development and strength relative to the reference group.[157]

Such a plot revealed absolute as well as relative fitness. According to Sargent, the ideal graph was a vertical line. If one's scores resulted in a perpendicular line, one had achieved what Sargent called "perfect symmetry."[158] That is, one exhibited the same degree of development, whether thirtieth or eighty-fifth percentile, in every category of measurement. No part was inappropriately too large or too small, too strong or too weak; one's features were perfectly balanced. As Sargent explained, "The straight line is the physical sign of health and longevity, of perfect structure and harmony of function, and a symmetrical development of the whole body."[159]

Sargent searched the country for specimens of genuine symmetry. In 1890, he ran a contest to find America's most symmetrical man and woman, and proudly displayed their charts in a Boston newspaper.[160] Admiring the physical development of two young female swimmers in Boston, Sargent also published their measurements and pictures.[161] Unable to find perfect symmetry in real life, Sargent created it in art. For the 1893 World Exposition in Chicago, Sargent had statues made to represent what his data indicated were the fiftieth-percentile male and female.[162] The figures showed what might be called typically healthy Americans, or the symmetry of perfect normalcy. (See figure.)

With Sargent's approach, the evaluation of health assumed the look of science. Rejecting the inexact standards of earlier times, Sargent and like-minded contemporaries made the measurement of health concrete and precise by quantifying it. Their system was nor-

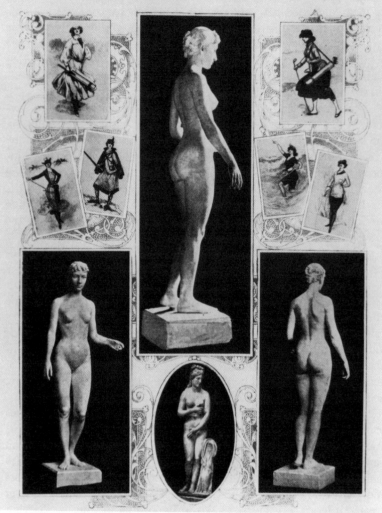

Dudley Allen Sargent's statue of the average American female in the 1890s. Sargent later worried that athletics were masculinizing women by broadening their shoulders, narrowing their hips, and enlarging their hands and necks. Source: *The Sketch* 72 (Dec. 7, 1910): 255. Courtesy of The Illustrated London News Picture Library.

mative as well as descriptive. Sargent used numbers to reveal disparities between individual growth and group standards, and between actual and ideal development. A person's level of health, though, depended more on which group was chosen as the reference than on his or her particular test scores. However quantified and standardized, judgments about health remained subjective in an age of science.

Though flawed, Sargent's techniques suited the new perspective on health in the late nineteenth century. Health was fitness for work or play, and the ability to rebound quickly after performing. Presumably, size and strength measurements helped disclose a person's readiness to function well. Did Americans have the physical vigor to handle modern life? Or, as Sargent had asked, was a man prepared for anything he might be called upon to do?

Was a woman? Toward the close of the nineteenth century, many Americans doubted that women's health was sufficient for the tasks at hand. Sickness, even invalidism, seemed epidemic. More generally, social developments led people to wonder what a fit woman should be and do. Changes in the typical female life cycle raised questions about fertility and the family; industrialization, urbanization, and new technologies restructured women's daily lives; the social status and educational opportunities of some women improved gradually, through the persistent efforts of reformers; around the country, commentators on "the Woman Question" debated the qualities of true womanhood and called attention to the relationship between female health and social conditions; finally, the concept of personal health was being redefined, to fit the temper of late Victorian times. Given those diverse changes, what did able-bodied womanhood now mean?

In Boston, there was no single answer to that question. As issues about health, women, and American society merged, Bostonians held different perceptions of able-bodied womanhood. The following chapters describe how two groups, officials at Wellesley College and female graduates of the Boston Normal School of Gymnastics, addressed the problem of women's health.

Following the Civil War, public and private schools, from the primary to the collegiate ranks, handled an increasing share of health education and physical training in America. By the turn of the century, teaching positions in physical education became more numerous in schools and other institutions, and graduates of the country's new training programs, such as the Boston Normal School of Gymnastics, assumed many of those jobs.

The work of Wellesley College officials and female physical educators was especially crucial to the definition of able-bodied womanhood. As females, they were, willingly or not, both subjects of and participants in "the Woman Question." As teachers, they were responsible for the health and education of other women, and for demonstrating that female exercise and study were compatible. As professionals, they were standard-bearers of new ideas about health and womanhood. There were no precedents, no universal answers to the issues they faced. As the two case studies will illustrate, conflicting expectations of able-bodied womanhood were not easily resolved.

6

"Stronger in Body as well as in Mind":
Physical Education at Wellesley College,
1875–1900

Wellesley College opened in 1875 as a small, private, residential school for girls sixteen years and older.[1] The founders were Henry Fowle Durant, a prominent Boston lawyer and investor, and his wife, Pauline Adeline Fowle Durant.[2] After their two children died (in 1857 and 1863), the Durants devoted themselves to the furtherance of Christianity and education. Leaving his legal practice, Mr. Durant toured eastern Massachusetts as a lay evangelist and became a trustee of Mount Holyoke; Mrs. Durant helped establish the Boston branch of the Young Women's Christian Association. After weighing many possibilities, they decided to use their sizable fortune and country estate for a school dedicated to "the glory of God and the service of the Lord Jesus Christ, in and by the education and culture of women."[3]

Located on three hundred acres of wooded land about fifteen miles from Boston, Wellesley College offered an idyllic setting for the mental and moral development of young ladies. The Durants created a home-like, Christian atmosphere in which honor, obedience, and cooperation were paramount virtues. The early academic program included the classics, modern languages, English literature, composition, history, Biblical studies, mathematics, and natural science. Students represented middle- and upper-class families, primarily from New England. During the late 1870s, the college had about three hundred students and a faculty of around thirty members. By 1900, over six hundred girls studied at Wellesley each year under the tutelage of some eighty faculty and under the protective eyes of administrators, residential matrons, and medical personnel.

From the outset, the question of student health was "of primary importance" at Wellesley.[4] Early catalogues of the college assured parents and their daughters "that everything possible is done to provide for the health, the comfort, and the happiness of the students."[5] Brochures highlighted the school's ample grounds and lake, its well-designed buildings, which supplied "an abundance of light, sunshine, and fresh air to the inmates," and the "large gymnasium" where "the students are instructed in Calisthenics."[6] In addition, Wellesley provided an infirmary and a lady physician, who monitored the girls and counseled them "in the care of their health and the laws of Hygiene."[7] During its first quarter-century, the college also initiated physiology classes, exercise requirements, and physical exams. School officials obviously regarded the supervision, even improvement, of the girls' physical well-being as an institutional trust. Wellesley College, they believed, had an obligation to maintain a safe and clean campus, to protect its students from sickness and contagion, and to supply whatever instruction and recreation were necessary for health.

Why did the college pay so much attention to health? The question has relevance well beyond Wellesley, as virtually every female school of the day expressed similar concern. Private education for women grew dramatically during the 1800s, especially in the Northeast.[8] Before the Civil War, female seminaries and academies multiplied. In Massachusetts alone, some twenty-one private schools for girls were incorporated between 1830 and 1860; many others may have existed without official recognition.[9] During the second half of the century, opportunities for women's higher education emerged.[10] In some cases, men's colleges began to admit female students. More commonly in the Northeast, separate women's colleges were founded, including Elmira (1855), Vassar (1865), Smith (1875), Wellesley (1875), and Bryn Mawr (1884). Academies and colleges for women offered comprehensive programs that addressed the intellectual, moral, and physical development of their students. Graduates were expected to be able-bodied as well as knowledgeable and virtuous.

Beyond those generalities, though, American educators shared no universal model of womanhood, nor did there exist a standard method of inculcating it. The specific goals and program at Wellesley College, therefore, differed from those of other schools. Yet across the country, administrators and teachers did face similar responsibilities and constraints. In particular, some common factors influenced their deliberations about student health and physical education. The approaches chosen at Wellesley illustrate how leaders at one institution defined and promoted healthy womanhood between 1875 and 1900.[11]

In some respects, attention to health was mandatory at female academies and colleges. As Wellesley and other schools opened, the debate over women's health and education raged in America.[12] Could young females, who had just passed through menarche, withstand rigorous intellectual training? Would mental work disturb menstruation and jeopardize a girl's personal and physical maturation? Some observers believed that intense education during such a sensitive stage of development was dangerous. Detractors never tired of reporting instances of promising young women who ruined their charm, health, and prospects for marriage by excessive study. Unconvinced that education necessarily caused sickness or sterility, other Americans proposed that women's schools devise programs, both academic and hygienic, that ensured their students' immediate and long-term health.

At Wellesley, as throughout the East, college officials recognized that their institution was on trial. Catalogues from the 1870s acknowledged that "the prevailing delicacy of health in American girls excites just alarm among thoughtful teachers."[13] Although some observers had charged that "the health of girls is destroyed by hard study in schools and colleges," the administration at Wellesley refused to "submit in silence to this odious injustice."[14] To set the record straight, the school's publications insisted that the frailty of young girls was "in most cases due to continued violation of the plain laws of nature, as to fresh air by night and day; simple and nourishing food at regular hours; daily exercise in the open air; sufficient sleep and suitable dress."[15] Nevertheless, opponents of women's higher education found Wellesley and similar institutions to be convenient scapegoats. When women's colleges admitted girls whose condition was already poor, Wellesley protested, critics mistakenly blamed the schools for the deterioration of female health.

Rhetoric, of course, would not settle the question. Officials at Wellesley hoped to demonstrate the healthfulness of advanced study for women. Their one condition was that the experiment be a fair one. In 1876, the *Calendar* announced that Wellesley would "not be responsible for the health of invalids" and that "hereafter new students who are in delicate health will not be received."[16] To effect that policy, the college required certification of the health of prospective students, and refused to accept any who did not measure up.[17] Starting with a collection of good specimens, Wellesley was determined to show that "healthy girls under proper regulations are usually capable of continued hard study without injury."[18] Four years at Wellesley College, its catalogues declared, could make students "stronger in body as well as in mind."[19] If women's education was on trial, Wellesley resolved not to lose the case.

The controversy over health and education set a context that female institutions could not ignore. The physical condition of their students was under constant scrutiny. Still, critics couched the problem in decidedly negative terms; they offered no model of healthy womanhood, nor strategies whereby schools might promote it. That remained the job of individual educators. Around the country, chief administrators and teachers devised environments and curricula that served their own visions of well-educated, able-bodied womanhood.

At Wellesley, Mr. Durant and a series of five presidents defined the college's mission between 1875 and 1900. During the early years, Mr. Durant's official title was treasurer, but it was he who governed Wellesley. Every important decision, from faculty appointments to landscaping, was his domain, and his ideals pervaded the institution. In Durant's words, "the five great essentials for education at Wellesley College" were God, Health, Usefulness, Thoroughness, and "the supreme development and unfolding of every power and faculty, of the Kingly reason, the beautiful imagination, the sensitive emotional nature, and the religious aspirations."[20] The curriculum balanced literary and classical studies with mathematics and the sciences; students performed much of the college's domestic work, from serving meals to cleaning rooms; twice a day, they devoted twenty minutes of "Silent Time" to private reflection; worship and prayer were frequent and required; courtesy and integrity were expected on all occasions. For Durant, the goal of education was Christian character—best revealed in one's values, conduct, and physical well-being.

From 1875 until Durant died in 1881, Ada L. Howard, a Mount Holyoke graduate with considerable teaching experience, served as Wellesley's president. Given Durant's authority, however, the position was a nominal one. The first independent leader of Wellesley was Howard's successor, Alice Freeman, whose tenure ran from 1882 through 1887.[21] Born to a poor rural family in New York in 1855, Freeman taught school in Wisconsin and Michigan after earning a baccalaureate from the University of Michigan. Bright, strong-willed, and energetic, she attracted the attention of her mentors at Michigan and, through them, Durant. He finally succeeded in luring her to Wellesley in 1879 as head of the history department. Though young and relatively new to Wellesley, Freeman was a charismatic and influential administrator, who rationalized the college's internal structure and raised its academic standards. She relinquished the presidency in 1887 to marry George Herbert Palmer, a professor of philosophy at Harvard. Her impact in academic circles continued through the Woman's Education Association, the Massachusetts State Board of Education, a deanship at the University of Chicago, and the advice that many other college administrators sought from her regarding policies and appointments.

Alice Freeman Palmer believed that ideal womanhood blended grace and virtue with rationality and discipline.[22] Advanced education for women should combine morality and knowledge, feminine sensitivity with human learning. Her recipe for a good life resembled Durant's. "A college course," she wrote, "offers the most attractive, easy, and probable way of securing happiness and health, good friends and high ideals, permanent interests of a noble kind, and large capacity for usefulness in the world."[23] For Durant and Freeman, Wellesley was an institution (or, really, a community) in which young women pursued the learning, values, and health necessary for a life of service.

Three other presidents guided Wellesley in the late nineteenth century. Although their personal styles and administrative projects varied widely, each continued the school's main objectives.[24] Helen A. Shafer, who led the college from 1888 to 1894, was the daughter of a minister, an alumna of Oberlin, and a mathematics teacher. Her primary contribution was a major reform of Wellesley's curriculum. The next president was Julia J. Irvine, a Hicksite Quaker and product of Antioch and Cornell, who joined Wellesley's faculty as a classicist in 1890. During her term of office (1895–99), Irvine oversaw many changes in the academic program and a relaxation of the boarding-school regimen with a blunt (some would have said "masculine") manner. Her successor was Caroline Hazard, a devout and cultivated woman in her early forties from a distinguished Rhode Island family. President from 1899 to 1910, Hazard brought grace and culture, rather than academic training, to her administration. She secured numerous donations to Wellesley's endowment and rescued the school from financial ruin.[25] Despite many differences, each of these leaders believed that scholarship, health, Christianity, and service were the hallmarks of an educated woman.

Of particular interest is their concept of female health. While complete uniformity cannot be presumed, Wellesley's chief administrators and the faculty most responsible for student health shared a general view of able-bodied womanhood. In part, their model was a physical description of health and femininity. Desirable qualities included strong muscles and nerves, capacious lungs, and symmetrical growth; other features, such as agility, grace, and fine carriage, seemed equally important. Applauding Wellesley's exercise requirement, President Helen A. Shafer reported in 1892 that first-year students showed an "increase of physical vigor" as well as "improvement in pose and bearing."[26] Lucille E. Hill, who directed physical training at the college from 1882 to 1909, agreed that a pleasing "physical beauty" resulted from "abounding health, grace of motion, and dignity of bearing."[27]

Another ingredient of health was the mutual discipline of mind and body. Lucille Hill, for example, believed that effective physical education, and sports in particular, conditioned the mind and character, and that exercise programs subordinating neurological development to muscle training were inadequate.[28] Even students at the college appreciated the relationship between mental control and physical fitness. As one undergraduate wrote in 1905, systematic exercise builds "an all-around, healthy body which is in perfect subjection to the mind," and grants "the grace and unconscious ease of a perfectly trained body, the ready tool of the mind."[29] By emphasizing mental and physical cooperation, Wellesley followed the trend in American concepts of health at the turn of the century.

The partnership of mind and body was a natural objective for an educational institution. Wellesley officials were convinced that physical training contributed directly to better scholarship, and that mental work made exercise more welcome and more effective. The cooperation of mind and body seemed to have long-term benefits as well. Members of the Wellesley community hoped that early training would prepare students for vigorous and productive lives. Evelyn B. Sherrard, one of Wellesley's resident health officers in the late 1890s, frequently spoke of fostering " 'a physical conscience: a sense of personal responsibility for every avoidable weakness, indisposition or defect, and a constant desire and effort for the highest physical efficiency and integrity which are attainable.' "[30] Lucille Hill set equally high goals. As a graduate of 1909 recalled,

> Few of us who were put through our course of sprouts in the little old cramped and battered College Hall gymnasium have ever worn unnatural shoes, gone deliberately without sleep, or grown round-

shouldered, without a guilty sense of having fallen below Miss Hill's standard of intelligent living. Her appeal that it was not sportsman-like to be satisfied with less than perfect health was a powerful one to her young hearers.[31]

Apparently, being a good sport meant playing the game of life responsibly.

In a word, health was fitness. College leaders and alumnae of Wellesley echoed America's new definition of health as discipline and preparedness. Able-bodied womanhood represented that degree of fitness necessary to fulfill one's duties in the modern world. As one student reminded her classmates in 1891, "It lies with each student whether the Wellesley women shall be those whom the world needs, women whose physical education goes hand in hand with the moral and intellectual."[32] Graduates of the 1890s saw themselves as a new breed, and as new breeders. Wellesley, said an alumna of 1894, sends forth "women who will make the next generation strong, who are strong themselves and able to cope with the struggles of the workaday world."[33] Mirroring general attitudes about health in late nineteenth-century America, Wellesley's leaders and students had a practical view of fitness. In conjunction with sound morals and a well-trained mind, physical health prepared young women for productive lives in a demanding world.

School officials therefore vowed to watch over the student body as a whole, while improving the health of individual girls by every available means—custodial, medical, and educational. The goal was ambitious, and the right course was hardly self-evident. What evolved at Wellesley between 1875 and 1900 was not so much a coherent, unchanging program in health, as an eclectic and variable one. During its first quarter-century, the college instituted numerous regulations, courses, and activities related to health and physical education. Components changed as school leaders reassessed their aims and accomplishments, and as internal constraints—limited facilities, personnel, and other resources—dictated what they could and could not undertake. As in female schools across the country, physical education at Wellesley College was a compromise between vision and fact.

From its inception, the college established strict regulations about student behavior. During the early years in particular, the school code, which included rules about deportment, studying, and hygiene, was detailed and stringent. Students were advised to air their bed covers for an hour during the morning, to avoid reading in front of a window lest the light hurt their eyes, to monitor the temperature and ventilation in their rooms, to bathe regularly, and to have a wardrobe that was "neat, very simple, and adapted to the season."[34]

Regulations about eating were especially stern. College brochures claimed that ill-health among school girls was often the result of "pernicious habits of eating confectionery, sweetmeats, etc., and of eating at irregular hours. It is absolutely essential to mental and physical vigor that students eat only proper food and at regular hours."[35] Because the college served ample nutritious food, it prohibited snacks, except for fresh fruit, and the receipt of "boxes of eatables."[36] Students were *pledged in honor* neither to buy nor receive in any manner whatsoever any confectionery or eatables of any kind not provided for them by the College."[37] Wellesley had neither patience nor responsibility for girls who violated its rules "by childish self-indulgence and disobedience."[38] Nor would the school tolerate parental interference or subversion. For example, college circulars asked families "not to furnish their daughters with wines or liquors of any kind—to be used as medicines," since a physician at the college would supervise cases of illness.[39] If parents could not "assist . . . in the strict enforcement of these necessary regulations," the college urged them not to send their daughters to Wellesley.[40] If girls were unwilling to follow the rules scrupulously, they were not welcome at the college. Inflexibility seemed necessary. The school's reputation, and the fate of women's higher education, appeared to depend on the safety of the students' health. Wellesley could not afford to admit recalcitrant girls or to permit lax behavior on campus.

Because girls who understood the laws of health were more likely to observe them, instruction complemented coercion. The second feature of Wellesley's program in health was coursework in physiology and gymnastics.[41] Early publications of the college mentioned that a resident female doctor would provide "Lectures on Physiology with special reference to health . . . early in the course," and that she would be available for consultation about all matters of health and hygiene.[42] The college catalogue for 1883–84 included the first reference to an academic requirement in the subject. As part of Wellesley's general curriculum reform during that period, a course in human anatomy and physiology, with an emphasis on hygiene, was required of all freshmen during their first term.[43] By the late 1880s, juniors and seniors were permitted to elect a course in anatomy, physiology, and hygiene.[44] During the 1890s, the physiology program tended to change every few years: in 1890–91, the requirement was dropped, but freshmen and juniors could elect a course in physiology and hygiene; in 1893–94, sophomores were required to take the elementary course, unless they had passed an entrance exam in the subject; in 1896–97, the required course was switched from the sophomore to freshman year.[45] The teacher of physiology, a female, varied from year to year. During the 1870s and 1880s, the instructor was the college physician. Beginning in 1892, different members of the Zoology Department taught the course. One of the college's resident health officers covered it during the late 1890s.

Little is known about the content of the physiology course. College catalogues suggest that useful, not merely theoretical, knowledge was emphasized. According to the *Calendar* for 1887–88, first-year students learned about food, heat, ventilation, and other practical matters.[46] The catalogue for 1899–1900 announced that the class considered "the proper care of the body" and was "designed to give a practical knowledge of its structure and an understanding of the laws of life and health. An outline is also given of the general principles of public hygiene."[47] The college supplemented the required course with public lectures on health and hygiene. In 1883, for example, a physician delivered a series of talks about "Practical Physiology," and Dr. Dudley Allen Sargent spoke on "Physical Culture."[48] In 1890, a guest lecturer discussed "Dress Reform, or Dress Improvement."[49] Without further details, one cannot judge the full significance of the classes in physiology or the public lectures on health. Obviously, the college did believe that a well-educated young woman should understand the human body and the rules for maintaining health. Thus, the study of practical hygiene took its place in the curriculum alongside language, literature, and natural science.

Without application, though, knowledge was not apt to endure. From the outset, Wellesley believed that some form of physical training should support the girls' classroom work in physiology and hygiene. Between 1875 and 1900, the college's various presidents, teachers, and health officers set several objectives for physical education at Wellesley: the participation of most, if not all, of the college's students; reliable monitoring of each girl's development and deficiencies; attention to the needs of frail students; effective use of the school's facilities and grounds; and trustworthy evidence of undergraduate health, to counter allegations about the adverse effects of female education.

Certain circumstances made those goals difficult to realize. The school's resources in physical education—facilities, time, and staff—were restricted. The most glaring problem was the gym, a small room in the college's main building. Until 1909, when new facilities were ready, the entire Wellesley community bemoaned the inadequacy of the old recreation hall. Successive presidents stressed the need for larger quarters.[50] Students also grew weary of the situation. The 1894 yearbook included the sketch of a skeleton dressed in cap and gown, alongside a humorous, but plaintive verse:

> O Thou Foolish Freshman who nibblest much of Huyler's;
> O Thou heedless Sophomore who takest not thy daily walk;
> O Thou reckless junior who sittest up late o'nights,—
> See to what a pass thou wilt come if thou turnest not from thy evil way!
> O Thou poor senior who hast committed all these sinful deeds, and who hast no saving training of the gymnasium sort, see what thou art!
> O Thou pitying reader, who hast gold, please die and give us a gymnasium.[51]

Generally regarded as "a very serious embarrassment,"[52] the small gym precluded supervised exercise for all students.

Wellesley's dilemma was neither unique nor simple. Faced with significant limitations, how could the college pursue its broad objectives in physical education? The answer emerged gradually between 1875 and 1900. The college experimented with different exercise systems to facilitate both individual and group development; instituted anthropometric exams to evaluate the condition and progress of each girl; and featured outdoor activities on the school's grounds and lake, to make recreation widely accessible.

Physical training was the first component to arrive. From the outset, Wellesley tried to insure that its students had daily exercise. One of the college's earliest brochures noted that "a gymnasium has been provided, and calisthenics will be taught by skillful instructors."[53] The *Regulations* for 1877–78 required students to "exercise *not less than one hour daily* in the open air, unless excused by the Physician."[54] During the winter, when attendance at gymnastic classes was mandatory, outdoor exercise was reduced to half an hour a day.[55] Those rules remained in effect through the late 1880s.[56] Around 1890, the requirement in physical education changed. The college catalogue for 1890–91 stated that "the Ling system of educational gymnastics is prescribed for the Freshman Class, and this exercise is required three times weekly, unless the student is excused by the [college's] Board of Health. Physical training is elective in the upper classes."[57] That arrangement held until 1902, when sophomores joined the freshmen in required classes of gymnastics.[58]

Of greater interest than the actual requirement is the changing character of the training. Physical educators at Wellesley (usually a staff of one to three people, mostly women) wanted to combine group instruction for diverse students with corrective or developmental work for individual girls. They puzzled over which form of training would best serve those needs. During the late nineteenth century, many schemes of supervised exercise competed for favor among the country's schools and gymnasia.[59] Among the most popular were: Ling gymnastics, a system devised in Sweden during the early 1800s involving free movements and some work with light apparatus, often following the beat of music; Swedish gymnastics, a systematic progression of free movements and exercise on equipment, done in response to a leader's commands; German gymnastics, which consisted of workouts on heavy apparatus, such as horizontal bars, parallel bars, and stationary horses; military drill, a sequence of movements, frequently with mock guns, that resembled routines performed by military units; and Sargent exercises, a program of strength development using Dudley Allen Sargent's machines. Between 1875 and 1900, Wellesley experimented with most of these systems, in search of one that was well adapted for both group and individual training.

During the college's early years, Wellesley students exercised according to the program devised by Dio Lewis in the 1860s. An offshoot of the Ling system, Lewis gymnastics, often called light calisthenics, consisted of free movements and exercises performed by individuals or pairs, with simple apparatus, such as wands, dumbbells, and rings.[60] (See figure.) Other women's colleges, including Rockford, Elmira, Vassar, Smith, Mills, and Mount Holyoke, also adopted the Lewis program.[61] At Wellesley and most other women's schools, however, the Sargent system soon replaced Lewis gymnastics.[62] When Lucille Hill arrived as Wellesley's director of physical training in 1882, she introduced Sargent apparatus. A native New Englander, Hill apparently had trained under Dudley Allen Sargent and taught gymnastics at a private girls' academy in western Massachusetts before going to Wellesley.[63] She initially favored the Sargent system because it allowed for personalized diagnosis and correction

A class in Lewis gymnastics at Wellesley College, ca. 1875–82. Source: Wellesley College Archives.

of weaknesses, a primary concern at Wellesley. The *Calendar* for 1882–83 explained the advantages of the college's new system of physical education:

> The gymnasium has been improved and fitted up under the direction of Dr. D. A. Sargent, director of Harvard Gymnasium, and, by the use of his system of physical training, is conducted on a strictly scientific basis, the amount and manner of exercise being carefully prescribed, and directed, according to the needs of each individual. The apparatus includes chest-weights, clubs, horizontal and parallel bars, rowing-machines, flying-rings, inclined planes, and a great variety of mechanical arrangements for special work.[64]

Students were also welcome to arrange for "special training, in addition to the work required by the College."[65] Subsequent literature continued to emphasize the individual attention afforded by the Sargent program. Gradually, however, Hill became disenchanted with the system. Along with other physical educators, she came to recognize its limitations for group instruction.[66]

By the late 1880s, physical education at Wellesley had incorporated other forms of exercise. They included Delsarte exercise, which involved rhythmic or dance-like movements, and some Swedish free gymnastics and apparatus work.[67] The variety reflected Hill's conclusion that no one system of physical exercise was complete, physiologically or pedagogically. At a conference on physical training in Boston in November 1889, she challenged the partisanship of other speakers, and proclaimed, "I hate the word 'system,'—don't you? I mean the running-in-one-track part of it, and being satisfied with one's own ideas without recognizing the good in all methods."[68] Hill went on to describe the eclectic program at Wellesley:

> I am sure Dr. Sargent would feel at home in the Wellesley Gymnasium, because we have the statistics of over a thousand women, and we use his system of measurements and strength-tests. Dr. Hitchcock would feel at home with us because the *minimum* amount of exercise in the gymnasium is compulsory, and we march very well indeed. Dr. Anderson would be at home because we could not swing Indian clubs as remarkably as we do *without* music, and Dr. Posse would be gratified if he knew that there are just as many exercises that he could not possibly perform with music! To General Moore we owe our enthusiasm for the "setting up" drill, and we have a real drum.[69]

By 1889, Wellesley had sampled many of the era's most prominent systems of physical education.

During the 1890s, Wellesley's program remained diverse, but emphasized Swedish gymnastics for most classroom instruction. The college catalogue for 1890–91 announced the arrival of more Swedish equipment and the requirement of "the Ling system of educational gymnastics" for freshmen.[70] The following year, the appointment of Hartvig Nissen, an expert in the Swedish system, confirmed the college's decision.[71] Students were quick to notice the change. Besides a "new coat of paint," the gym in 1891 had "strange looking apparatus," which, according to one upperclassman, "promises an interesting course to those who have just entered."[72]

Swedish exercises were a systematic and progressive scheme of physical training.[73] Each session followed a plan called "the day's order," specifying the sequence in which different muscle groups would be exercised. Workouts on successive days increased the complexity and vigor of the exercises, resulting in a "gymnastic progression" over time. Routines involved both free movements and work on ropes, ladders, and portable floor apparatus. All exercises were done

in response to vocal commands. One physical educator called it the
" 'I yell, you jump' method" of exercise.[74]

For educators at Wellesley and other women's colleges, Swedish
gymnastics appeared to have several advantages. They afforded instruction in small or large classes; "the day's order" and "gymnastic
progression" represented a scientific method of thorough exercise,
both preventive and therapeutic; finally, Swedish gymnastics combined muscular and neurological development. As Theodore Hough,
a biologist, explained, the sequence and repetition of exercises in a
given "day's order" involved every muscle group in "its appropriate
functional activity."[75] With habitual practice, "the various neuromuscular mechanisms become more perfect machines, capable of doing the work demanded of them at any time."[76] The system also
trained "the power of nervous co-ordination of movements."[77] As its
many parts learned to cooperate, the body became less awkward and
more efficient. Finally, Hough noted, "The carrying out of definite
movements with accuracy and precision is a training in volitional
control."[78] Such mastery over physical activities made a person more
efficient and more adaptable; people gained confidence in their ability
to control their neuromuscular systems and to learn new skills when
necessary.[79] In keeping with contemporary attitudes about health,
Wellesley chose a form of physical education that disciplined the
body and the mind, as separate and interdependent systems. Because
it seemed superior both theoretically and practically, Swedish gymnastics became the most common type of physical training in wom-
en's colleges, and many other institutions, by the end of the nineteenth century.[80]

During the 1890s, Swedish gymnastics was the nucleus of Wellesley's eclectic program in physical education. A spoof published in
the 1890 yearbook accurately conveyed the situation. Trying to imagine the faculty performing the varied routines that students learned,
the yearbook writers conjured up the following scene:

> Accordingly for twelve nights they [the faculty] arrayed themselves
> in suitable garments, and repaired to the gymnasium. In order to
> serve as a complete example, they courageously took upon them-
> selves the work of all four classes. For the sake of the Freshman,
> with heads erect and sternums high, they wearily marched around
> and around the great black circle. Exhorted by the leader, they
> struggled bravely with Indian clubs, thinking tenderly, meanwhile,
> of the Juniors and Sophomores, in whose interests they were labor-
> ing. In their ardor and zeal, disregarding the dust upon the floor,

they willingly laid themselves down and reflected upon the exceeding heaviness of their heads, and of all the members of their bodies.[81]

The diversity of physical training at Wellesley was a natural outcome of the school's commitment to exercising the student body, in groups and as individuals, and of considerations of space and pedagogy. Throughout the 1890s and into the twentieth century, college literature stressed that physical education at Wellesley was a scientific and thorough process, which attended to each student's needs.[82]

Whatever its form, however, group gymnastics precluded much personalized instruction. To complement its exercise classes, Wellesley instituted anthropometric exams, modeled after the work of Dudley Allen Sargent.[83] Quantified tests of physical development would fulfill the school's promise to monitor the weaknesses and progress of individual girls. In addition, Sargent exams would enable the college to compile scientific evidence about the physical effects of higher education. In a single step, the college could meet two important responsibilities.

Wellesley conducted anthropometric exams with remarkable fervor. The practice of testing the students' physical condition probably began in 1882, with the arrival of Lucille Hill. College literature first mentioned the exams in 1883. In her annual report for that year, President Alice E. Freeman noted that the appointment of an additional staff member in physical education would enable Hill to examine Wellesley's students more carefully.[84] In 1885, M. Anna Wood was hired as an assistant in the gym and, by 1888, was the college's chief physical examiner.[85]

Within six years, the program was well enough established to highlight the exams and results in college publications. The catalogue of 1888–89 informed candidates that "all students receive a thorough physical examination, including Dr. D. A. Sargent's measurements and strength tests."[86] A subsequent catalogue noted that each incoming student was tested for "physical development, strength of heart and lungs, and hereditary tendencies."[87] By 1890, Hill and Wood had collected data on 1100 students and were able to prepare a graph of physical development for each girl at the college.[88] Appearing in the school's literature, Hill and Wood's "average anthropometric table" became a promotional tool for Wellesley.[89] Shortly thereafter, it seems, the college developed a genuine Sargent chart, based on the results of 1500 students and standardized according to percentile rankings. Each student, announced the catalogue for 1892–93, was "given an Anthropometrical Table, compiled from the measurements of fifteen hundred Wellesley students, upon which her individual condition is plotted."[90]

Wellesley officials soon realized that comparisons over time were even more valuable than isolated tests. Periodic exams would reveal the progress, or continuing deficiencies, of each student. Such data would also carry more force in the debate over women's health and education. As testimony of Wellesley's positive influence on health, the college produced before-and-after statistics, indicating individual or group improvement after a term or more of physical training. For example, Hill and Wood published a study of the class of 1891, comparing the girls' overall health and habits as freshmen and as seniors.[91] The annual report of Wellesley's president often included tables or graphs demonstrating progress in the students' well-being over the college course. In 1889, for example, President Helen A. Shafer presented data on two girls who arrived at Wellesley in poor condition, but improved dramatically after daily workouts in the gym for six months.[92] The report from Lake Waban, where students rowed, was equally impressive. Wellesley literature proudly displayed graphs of size and strength tests conducted on the college boating teams. The scores of regular students who exercised in the gym and of crews who trained both in the gym and on the lake improved, whereas measurements for a control group of twenty students (who had received no training) showed no change, or even declined.[93] The benefits of exercise were self-evident.

In 1895, Wellesley felt confident enough to suspend its program of physical exams. According to President Julia J. Irvine, accumulated results "proved conclusively the value of the present course in Swedish Gymnastics."[94] Five years later, however, the college reinstituted the exams, and, for instructional and research purposes, continued them in some form through the 1920s.[95]

Except for a brief interruption, then, anthropometric exams were a ritual of undergraduate life at Wellesley. Unfortunately, student attitudes about the tests were rarely recorded. One surviving clue is an entry in the 1895 Wellesley yearbook, which suggests that physical training and exams were regular enough to inspire dreams:

> "Heads up; heels together; chins in," dreamed the athletic Freshman, while ropes, chest weights, parallel bars, rowing machines, and blue-bloused maidens are hopelessly confused in her dream-consciousness. She turns uneasily. Ah! it is her commencement day; the President is delivering a Latin address; she holds in

her hand a parchment,—and her degree, at last! Proudly she unrolls
it. *An-An-Anthro-Anthropometric Table.* And she is but a Freshman after all, of whom is required three hours weekly practice in
Swedish Gymnastics.[96]

Beyond the Wellesley campus, too, people took notice of the college's
efforts. By the mid-1890s, popular magazines, as well as journals in
medicine and physical education, reviewed Wellesley's program and
anthropometric data. As the school's leaders had hoped, the assessments were often favorable.[97]

Complementing group exercise, anthropometric exams served a
major role in Wellesley's supervision of student health. By evaluating
individual development, the tests satisfied Wellesley's commitment to
the personal, not merely collective, well-being of its girls. The exams
also had considerable value in public relations. Administrators at
Wellesley and other colleges recognized that the debate over women's
health and education would be uninformed, and perhaps lost, without concrete evidence. The more substantial and quantitative the
proof was, the better. Armed with volumes of anthropometric data,
Wellesley joined other colleges and organizations in arguing that
women could be well educated *and* able-bodied.[98]

One nagging problem remained. With such a small gym, Wellesley could not offer supervised exercise to all students; larger facilities did not arrive until 1909. In the meantime, the college discovered
a way out, literally, by taking advantage of the campus's spacious
grounds and lake. College brochures from the late 1870s highlighted
the "ample opportunities for exercise and recreation" on the school's
three hundred acres, including summer boating and winter skating on
Lake Waban.[99] Outdoor exercise quickly became a part of physical
education at the college, and soon prospered in the form of organized
athletics.[100]

Not surprisingly, the first sport to be established was boating.
By the late 1870s, a rowing club had been founded, and by the
1890s, each class had its own crew and crew song. (Members were
chosen, the president advised in 1893, for their overall "physical fitness," not their "vocal talent."[101]) From the mid-1880s through 1890s,
clubs for other activities followed, including tennis, bicycling, walking, basketball, golf, lacrosse, archery, and baseball.[102] Athletic facilities grew concurrently.[103] While continuing to limp along with its
old gym during the 1890s, the college constructed a boathouse and
purchased additional boats, and created a playstead, with a running
track and fixtures for tennis and basketball. Dr. Walter Channing of

Wellesley College students playing tennis, early 1890s. Source: Wellesley College Archives.

Brookline, who served on the college's Board of Visitors for physical training during the 1890s, arranged for Wellesley students to use his town's swimming pool, and also conducted weekly classes on the college's golf course.

Without question, athletics inspired great enthusiasm and pride on Wellesley's campus. Administrators and faculty underscored the contribution that sports made to students' physical conditioning, skills, and spirit. Lucille Hill, for example, believed that the program in rowing had " 'laid up a store of health and energy that made [the Wellesley classes] better women and better students.' "[104] Organized sports fostered personal qualities as well. As Hill explained,

> The necessary submission to strict discipline, the unquestioning obedience demanded by the officers, the perfect control of the temper and sensitiveness under coaching, together with the fact that she [the athlete] must be absolutely unselfish in order to become a loyal and valued member of her organization, develops a young girl's character while she develops her muscles.[105]

A Wellesley student prepares for a bicycle ride, ca. 1890s. Source: Wellesley College Archives.

The young participants were equally fervent. When an athletic association was formed in 1896 to oversee all sports clubs on campus, perhaps one-third of the approximately six hundred undergraduates paid the required fifty cents and became members.[106] By the turn of the century, Wellesley had earned a reputation as a sports school, and at least some students enjoyed the tag. In the 1900 yearbook, they offered "The Baby's ABC Book," which included the following lessons for the letters A and I:

> *A* is for Athletics,
>   And you must all agree,
> If it were not for this,
>   Where would our Wellesley be?
>
>   . . .
>
> *I* is for the Idlers,
>   Who don't go out at all,

> But sit and grind, or else make Fudge,
> When they could play at Ball.[107]

For some students, there was no embarrassment in being athletic.

Was that the same as being able-bodied? Wellesley's plunge into sports raised questions for which the college was not prepared. The people responsible for student health at Wellesley had organized physiology courses, physical training, and anthropometric exams without doubting that healthy womanhood would follow. They believed implicitly in both the means and the end. As sports grew, however, the school's leaders had to re-examine what "able-bodied" meant. Would athletics promote competitiveness and muscularity, while eroding grace and refinement? Along with physical educators around the country, Wellesley officials puzzled over the relationship between womanhood, femininity, and athleticism.

The national debate over female sports did not coalesce until the first decades of the twentieth century, but skirmishes were underway before 1900. The issue of competition illustrates well the early discussions. As a step beyond play, organized athletics required more intensive training, developed more specialized skills, and often fostered a desire to display one's prowess. Frequently, the result was a contest in which opposing teams played not "for play's sake," but to win. During the 1890s, the administration and physical education staff at Wellesley believed that sports should remain relatively noncompetitive. While supporting athletics as a source of exercise, fun, and character-building, they frowned on intramural games, and adamantly opposed interscholastic sports.

Their primary concern was the physical and emotional hazards of competition. Leaders at Wellesley regarded intense rivalry in sports as both unhealthy and unbecoming for women. Thus, the college did not permit its boating crews to race, lest the girls "overstrain" themselves and defeat the goal of health, "skill and grace."[108] Even Lucille Hill tried to avoid " 'any rivalry whatever among the students or the crews.' " She continued, " 'I believe that Wellesley is delightful free from any such sentiment. Feats of athletic skill and exhibitions of strength are also out side our object. What we do aim at is to keep the girls' physical beings on a par with their intellectual beings. . . .' "[109] As recreational exercise, boating and other sports contributed to health. Competition, on the other hand, might damage the students' physical and emotional well-being.

A second objection was more philosophical. For Hill and others at Wellesley, the principle that physical education should be available to everyone was sacrosanct. By requiring high standards of skill and training and by excluding average players, competitive athletics, especially interscholastic sports, threatened the democratic nature of physical education. Hill was unwilling to accept intercollegiate games as the norm unless certain issues were resolved: Would competitive athletics increase or decrease the number of students involved in recreation? Were such activities conducive to health? And, would they be consistent with the goals and structure of an institution's academic program?[110] Wary of interscholastic sports, Hill preferred the " 'New Athletics,' " activities that trained "a great many girls somewhat, instead of a few girls a great deal."[111]

The debate over competitive sports was hardly confined to Wellesley. By 1900, health advocates around the country, particularly in schools and colleges, had begun taking sides on the matter.[112] In large measure, both male and female physical educators in America opposed intensive athletics among women, for the same reasons as did Hill and her colleagues. First, they asked, was competition healthy? Many observers, such as Dudley Allen Sargent, regarded it as a natural and useful instinct in men.[113] Sargent, however, did fear that interscholastic games would turn male undergraduates into specialists, rather than symmetrically developed young men. Virtually every physical educator believed that the potential risks for women were even higher. Competition might encourage aggressiveness and other unfeminine traits in women, a prospect that displeased physical educators of both sexes. They agreed that athletic games should be modified to suit the refined sensibilities and unique physiology of women. Female physical educators, in fact, led the campaign to devise "women's basketball."[114]

The other concern was the exclusive nature of competitive sports. In an era when "the greatest good for the greatest number" was becoming a slogan throughout American education, intensive athletics seemed blatantly undemocratic. As Sargent protested, physical education would become the province of highly skilled students, thereby depriving average ones of a chance for training. No one suggested that schools and colleges abandon sports altogether. Instead, physical educators in America tried to resolve the controversy over competition without slowing the momentum of the athletics movement. Without a ready answer to the problem, Lucille Hill could only urge more discussion. "The approaching warm debates on the subject of *how much* and *how keen* competition is desirable to attain the true object of athletics," she remarked in 1902, deserved consideration by everyone involved in health and education.[115]

Wellesley's students, however, were not interested in theoretical arguments. Never doubting the advantages of competition, they dismissed the college's reservations about sports. They enjoyed, and even mocked, the athletic image, with its hint of diminished femininity. The yearbook of 1898, for example, took stock of the participants after a basketball game:

> The grimy and generally disheveled appearance of the players, as they emerge from the fray, fills our athletic souls with pride, although we cannot but echo, somewhat sadly, the words of the poet:—
>
> > "Had she no hairpins?
> > Had she no comb?"[116]

Nor did students believe that sports would deter either participation or health. In 1891, for example, a student publication asserted that the boating club would attract more interest if it sponsored races; in addition, they said, "we would hear less of overwork and ruined health among our students."[117] A decade later, students reprimanded the administration for approving interscholastic "mental athletics," namely, a debate between Wellesley and Vassar, while rejecting Radcliffe's challenge to play Wellesley in basketball.[118] The undergraduates, at least, were convinced that competitive athletics were a part of educated, healthy womanhood. For a quarter-century, Wellesley's administration and staff had tried to settle the question of female health, only to find it reopened.

Since 1875, the school's objective had been to promote able-bodied womanhood by as many means and for as many girls as possible. Lectures in practical physiology, supervised exercise, anthropometric exams, and organized recreation had enabled the college to guard the health of the student body, individually and collectively. In the process, Wellesley had gathered substantial evidence about the compatibility, even symbiosis, of mental education and physical health for women. College officials believed that, despite limited facilities and staff, Wellesley had fulfilled its responsibilities toward its students, and toward women's higher education in America. Over the years, President Julia J. Irvine declared in 1897, Wellesley's program had produced a "steady gain in strength, cheerfulness, and buoyancy" among the college's students.[119] In 1900, her successor, Caroline Hazard, agreed that "girls who entered somewhat anaemic, with poor color and flabby tissue, have grown stronger, and improved in health with regular exercise and the routine of College discipline."[120] After twenty-five years of experimentation, the college had shown that higher education could indeed make women "stronger in body as well as in mind."[121]

Competitive athletics, however, changed the terms of discourse about able-bodied womanhood. In 1900, few Americans still doubted that college women could be sound in body and mind. But was *any* level of female health acceptable? Could there be too much of a good thing? After all their efforts, the leaders of Wellesley discovered that the definition of healthy womanhood was still subject to debate, and that the best means of attaining it remained uncertain as well.

That realization was perhaps most disturbing for women such as Lucille Hill, who became professional physical educators. They were both teachers and models of able-bodied womanhood during a time when female health was under intense scrutiny. Personally and professionally, Hill and her colleagues found themselves in the middle of a storm. What qualities of health and character should they embody and convey to their students? The next chapter examines America's first generation of female physical educators, the women who taught and exemplified health at the turn of the century.

7

"Veritable Crusaders": The Early Graduates of the Boston Normal School of Gymnastics, 1889–1900

> The graduates of the old Boston Normal School of Gymnastics, now the Department of Hygiene of Wellesley College, were veritable Crusaders. . . . When they went into the field, women in Physical Education were quite looked down upon either as Physical Culturists or as acrobatic performers. Not until those early graduates began to make their way into educational groups, and take their stand with the best of them, did the professional respect, which the young teacher to-day finds waiting for her, become possible.
>
> ETHEL PERRIN, in 1930

As one of those "veritable crusaders," Ethel Perrin (1871–1962) understood firsthand the transformation of physical education in America between the late 1800s and early 1900s.[1] Perrin graduated from the Boston Normal School of Gymnastics in 1892, when physical education was a relatively new vocation for both men and women. Her career included the directorship of physical training in the public schools of Detroit and an administrative position with the American Child Health Association. When Perrin retired in 1936, she had witnessed the half-century during which physical education was established as a profession.[2]

In the mid-nineteenth century, few Americans would have identified themselves as physical educators. Moreover, journals, organizations, and training programs in the field tended to be local and short-lived. During the 1880s and 1890s, the professional apparatus of physical education became more stable. Among the new, often partisan, journals were *The Triangle* (published by the Young Men's Christian Association), the *Posse Gymnasium Journal* (founded in 1892 by an advocate of Swedish exercise), and *Mind and Body* (sponsored by the *Turnerbund,* the central committee of gymnastics clubs for German immigrants). In 1885, a common forum for promoters of physical education was founded. The *Proceedings of the American Association for the Advancement of Physical Education* was the official organ of America's first national society in the discipline. An eclectic group, the AAAPE complemented the more partisan societies around the country. Its direct descendant is today's American Alliance for Health, Physical Education, Recreation and Dance.

Normal (or training) schools for physical educators also appeared in more substantial numbers during the 1880s and 1890s.[3] The most notable private operations included the Normal School of the North American Gymnastic Union, whose first branch opened in 1871; Dudley Allen Sargent's program in Cambridge, founded in 1881; William G. Anderson's school, which originated in Brooklyn in 1885 and became the New Haven Normal School of Gymnastics; the Springfield International Training School, organized by the Young Men's Christian Association in 1886; the Boston Normal School of Gymnastics, founded in 1889; the Posse Gymnasium, established in Boston in 1890; and the Savage School of Physical Education, begun in New York in 1898. Simultaneously, teacher training programs appeared in city and state schools around the country, as did summer courses in both private and public institutions. By 1903, at least 1400 men and women had graduated from such programs, and summer sessions enrolled roughly 800 students per year.[4] At the turn of the century, then, physical education had all the trappings of a mature profession.

From the outset, a large proportion of the discipline's rank and file was female. For example, a 1903 survey of the country's major training schools in physical education showed that close to 80 percent of currently enrolled students and nearly 75 percent of all graduates were women.[5] Other studies revealed a large number of women among active physical educators. A report for the United States Commissioner of Education in 1891–92 concluded that women comprised almost 53 percent of the physical education specialists in the public schools of eighty-three cities from coast to coast.[6] In 1905,

Dr. J. H. McCurdy found that 65 percent of physical training staff members in 128 public school systems were female.[7] Finally, women joined professional associations in significant numbers. When the AAAPE was founded in 1885, only about 12 percent of its members were female.[8] Within a year, the figure exceeded 25 percent; on the tenth and twentieth anniversaries of the organization, women's representation was slightly more than 50 percent.[9] The Boston Physical Education Society, founded in 1896 as a local affiliate of the AAAPE, had 193 members in 1900, of whom 59 percent were women.[10] Clearly, women's access to training, employment, and organizations in the new profession was considerable.

At the same time, female physical educators had separate and unequal status. For example, impressionistic data (such as the institutional affiliations of AAAPE members) suggest that jobs in the field were sex-segregated: females usually supervised exercise among girls and women, while men trained other males. In institutions serving students of both sexes, men were more likely than women to be directors of the program in physical training.[11] In addition, the salaries of female physical educators were often lower than men's.[12] Finally, women held few leadership positions in the chief professional societies. For example, a small fraction of the early officers and council members of the AAAPE were female, although women constituted a majority of the organization. The society elected its first female president in 1932.[13] Although women found the door to physical education wide open, they apparently had second-class status once inside the profession.

That pattern deserves more study. We do not understand fully the significance of women's participation during the formative years of physical education, nor the extent of sexual equality or bias in the field.[14] Descriptive accounts of individual leaders, organizations, and institutions are plentiful.[15] Sociological studies and disciplinary textbooks about women in contemporary physical education and sports are also numerous.[16] At present, however, analytical histories of the professionalization of American physical education are scarce, and the fortunes of women in the field have not been researched systematically.

Such a job is too large for the book at hand. The lives of America's earliest female physical educators can be only sketched here. How did women such as Ethel Perrin perceive themselves and their role in the late nineteenth and early twentieth century? No ready-made model awaited them. As the nation debated women's duties and attributes, Perrin and many of her colleagues spurned marriage and chose careers; as the myth of female invalidism gave way, they helped define able-bodied womanhood; as popular views about health changed, they were responsible for physical education in America; as a new profession evolved, they faced unexpected opportunities and difficulties as women. What did health, womanhood, and work signify to Perrin and her cohorts? The 212 women who graduated in the first ten classes (1891–1900) of the Boston Normal School of Gymnastics (BNSG) provide a case study. As females and as physical educators, the alumnae of the BNSG grappled every day with the meaning of able-bodied womanhood.[17]

Opened in the fall of 1889, the BNSG was the creation of Mary Porter Tileston Hemenway, a local philanthropist, and her assistant, Amy Morris Homans.[18] The widow of a wealthy shipping merchant, Hemenway supported a variety of projects, from anthropological research in the Southwest to an orphanage outside Boston. Her primary bequests, however, went to educational ventures, including work among southern blacks and poor whites, and sewing classes, manual training, and a cooking school in the Boston area. Physical education soon became Hemenway's special interest.[19] As Homans explained many years later,

> From the outset we saw the need of something which would lift the life of the masses to a higher level of health and vigor, to a more sane and wholesome outlook, a more rational, self-controlled way of living. The comparatively new field of hygiene and physical education seemed more promising in these directions than anything else.[20]

In 1888, as an initial experiment in physical education, Hemenway enabled the Boston public schools to train some of its teachers in Swedish gymnastics and to hire an expert in the system for the city's normal school. The BNSG was an outgrowth of those efforts.[21] The school's first brochure announced that the BNSG would teach Swedish gymnastics to men and women "who desire to make themselves competent to direct gymnasia or to conduct physical training with an educational and hygienic aim on scientific principles and by safe and effective methods."[22] Through its two-year course of study, the BNSG hoped to provide "the best instruction to be found this side of Sweden."[23]

The BNSG became one of the most productive and respected training programs in physical education in the country. During its first ten years of operation, the BNSG awarded diplomas to 212 women and 6 men.[24] Those graduates comprised the rank and file of America's first generation of physical educators, and some became leading figures in the profession. At the turn of the century, the BNSG had the largest number of female graduates among the nation's top physical training schools.[25] By roughly the same time, BNSG alumnae accounted for over half the female directors of physical education programs in public normal schools and a substantial share of physical education specialists in public school systems.[26] In 1909, the BNSG merged with the Department of Hygiene and Physical Education at Wellesley College. It became a graduate department of the college in 1917, admitting only students with a bachelor's degree. When the program began its thirtieth year in 1918, it could claim more than 700 graduates; the total reached nearly 1000 on the fiftieth anniversary.[27] The department graduated its last class in 1953, when Wellesley College closed its master's curriculum in physical education. For nearly sixty-five years, a program that began as the BNSG had prepared young women for careers as physical educators.

Who were those women, and what attracted them to the BNSG? The earliest graduates, those who comprised the first ten classes (1891–1900), are the focus of this study. In order to discover any changes in the students' backgrounds, the classes were divided into two five-year cohorts. Information about the first 104 female graduates (classes 1891–95) and about the next 108 (classes 1896–1900) was obtained through various records of the BNSG and Wellesley College.[28] Of greatest value for the analysis were the women's physical examination cards, prepared during their enrollment at the school. On the front of each girl's 4″ x 7″ card, a BNSG staff member recorded such data as birthdate and birthplace, nationality of parents and grandparents, father's occupation, causes of parental death, general level of health, hereditary diseases, and previous ailments (a checklist of twenty-nine disorders, ranging from colds and headaches to dysentery and heart conditions). Results from anthropometric tests (following Sargent's basic categories) and other physical data were noted on the back. Based primarily on those cards, the following profiles of BNSG graduates emerged.

The typical member of classes 1891–95 was a native, white, middle-class, urban Northeasterner in her early twenties, who claimed to be in good health. (See Table 1 in the Appendix.) Both of her parents and most of her grandparents were apt to be American-born.

Her immediate family was likely to be intact (neither parent deceased). Compared to the general female population in America in 1890, the BNSG student was of median age, but was more likely to have native-born parents and to reside in the urban Northeast. While the male labor force in 1890 worked chiefly in manual, service, and farm-related jobs, a majority of the fathers of BNSG graduates had white-collar occupations. (See Table 1 for these comparisons.) Forty other women entered the BNSG during its early years, but failed to complete either a one- or two-year program. Compared to those unsuccessful students, the graduates of 1891–95 were somewhat younger, more likely to be a native New Englander and to reside in the Northeast, more apt to come from a family that was middle-class and intact, and, by self-report, healthier.[29]

Data on the classes of 1896–1900 reveal some interesting changes over a short span of time. (See Table 2.) Compared to their predecessors, graduates in the second cohort were somewhat younger and more diverse, ethnically and geographically. The second group of classes included more foreign students and one black, and the women represented regions of the United States other than the Northeast. The nationalities of their parents and grandparents were also more varied than previous students'. More women in the second cohort came from urban communities, from middle-class backgrounds, and from complete families. While claiming to be in very good health, graduates between 1896 and 1900 actually reported more illnesses than did earlier students.

Those differences, however, did not alter the basic make-up of BNSG classes. During the 1890s, the school attracted young, single, middle-class, urban women. If the students were at all similar to their peers in late Victorian America, they were concerned about their health, education, and futures. How could they avoid the ailments that so frequently plagued women? What steps would ensure them of a secure and respectable life? A closer look at BNSG graduates suggests why physical education was their answer.

Born and raised in the last third of the nineteenth century, BNSG students lived in a culture that delivered conflicting messages about female health. On the one hand, concern about the nation's vigor, and of women in particular, was growing. Medical and popular literature often portrayed females as delicate, even invalid, creatures. On the other hand, marriage and motherhood required considerable fitness. A host of publications and institutions offered to guide American women toward genuine health. Faced with that paradox, many young females regarded their physical condition as tenuous, or at least in need of improvement.

BNSG students were no exception. Their physical exam cards presented a curious mix of claims to health and reports of serious ailments. While the average number of illnesses disclosed per student was low, what is striking is the frequency with which chronic or severe disorders were mentioned. Obviously, students would not jeopardize being admitted to the BNSG by confessing to poor health; at the same time, past infirmities were too real to ignore. When surveying the students' cards, one naturally wonders how much credence to give medical self-histories; the women may have misrepresented their condition. The relationship between "real" and "perceived" sickness, however, is complex. The data on the women's cards are significant if only because they indicate that ill-health distressed many applicants to the BNSG.

Other sources also suggest that health was an important issue for BNSG students. Several of the program's most successful early graduates were quite fragile during childhood. One example is Senda Berenson (BNSG 1892/1895), who directed physical training at Smith College between 1892 and 1911.[30] In 1875, when Senda was seven years old, her family emigrated from Lithuania and settled in Boston. (The children also included Bernard Berenson, who became a renowned art critic.) Because of ill-health as a youngster, Senda rarely completed a full year at school; enrollment at the Boston Conservatory of Music was also cut short because Senda's sore back prevented her from practicing. J. Anna Norris (BNSG 1895), head of women's physical education at the University of Minnesota for twenty-nine years, had a spinal curvature, which her high school physical education teacher discovered.[31] Mabel Lee (BNSG 1910) directed women's physical education at the University of Nebraska for many years and was the first female president of the American Physical Education Association (the immediate descendant of the AAAPE). Lee recalled that she had been "hollow chested and round shouldered and sadly underweight" as a child, "a veritable beanpole with two scrawny pigtails" and frequent ailments.[32] For these young women and others, physical education promised some relief from acute and chronic problems. As a road to health, physiological instruction and systematic exercise were an intriguing alternative to medical treatment.

Some, however, regarded physical activity as more distasteful than medicine. Reportedly, young Senda Berenson " 'hated all forms of exercise,' " and found her first months at the BNSG to be excruciating.[33] Other young women, though, gravitated toward the BNSG because of their love of exercise and sports. Mabel Lee recalled the wonderful hours that she spent playing with neighborhood pals, and her random, but memorable encounters with formal gymnastics in school. As she entered high school, Lee's career was already taking shape:

> With my love of swinging Indian clubs, jumping and running, marching and leading a company of Lancers [a girls' military drill team], and now with rumors reaching my town about a game called basketball taking intent possession of me, quite certainly, although completely unrecognized by myself as yet, my future life's work was beginning to take form in the deep recesses of my mind in spite of my all-too-frequent illnesses and constant serious underweight condition.[34]

Physical education allowed Lee and other BNSG alumnae to disguise youthful play as adult work.

A playful spirit characterized much of what BNSG graduates did. They often turned simple activities into games or tests of physical prowess. Lucy Pratt (BNSG 1895), for example, once reminisced about catching the train for Boston each morning to attend classes at the BNSG. To walk from her home to the station "seemed both inappropriate and slothful," so Pratt assumed the gait of a true Swedish gymnast, "a swift and easy 'quick time, march.' "[35] She soon mastered the game:

> By the first of June I had things so well in hand that when, at the breakfast table, I heard the train whistle as it drew into the station a mile or so away, I took my last swallow of coffee, and immediately left the house. By the time the incoming passengers had descended from the train, and the slow ones had climbed aboard, I was there ready to swing on. . . .[36]

On the thirtieth anniversary of her graduation, Pratt admitted that she recently had *waited* for a train. She recalled, "I never made a mistake of that nature in 1895."[37] Similarly, a graduate of 1893 confessed at the age of ninety-one to being " 'ashamed of myself nowadays.' "[38] Plagued by arthritis, Edith Hill Brown could no longer undertake her "six laps around the garden daily, 'running up and down the stairs,' or exercising in her room."[39] From their youthful to elderly years, most BNSG graduates enjoyed, and believed in, physical activity. That affinity led them, as young women, to consider formal training in gymnastics.

The BNSG program, however, involved more than cultivating one's own health and avocations. Its main purpose was to prepare physical educators, men and women who would teach exercise in schools and other institutions around the country. Employment as a teacher, either short- or long-term, was the natural step after training at the BNSG. Although physical education was a new specialty at the turn of the century, teaching in general was becoming a common job for women. Formerly the province of men, teaching, especially at the elementary and secondary levels, was "feminized" in America during the nineteenth and early twentieth centuries. One historian has estimated that women comprised 59 percent of the country's teaching force in 1870, 70 percent in 1900, and 86 percent in 1920.[40] Between 1870 and 1940, teaching never ranked lower than fifth on the list of women's occupations outside the home.[41] For a young, single, middle-class woman in particular, teaching was a popular means of supplementing her family's income and/or of supporting herself, for a brief or extended time. It also had social sanction as a respectable, if not instinctive, job for women. Given their personal backgrounds, BNSG students were prototypic candidates for normal schools and for teaching positions.

Today, a combined interest in fitness and teaching spells physical education. That logic was less automatic in the late nineteenth century. The infrastructure of the new profession, including training programs, was still being built; jobs for physical education specialists had just begun to proliferate. In rare cases, young aspirants in the field recognized its potential. Jessie H. Bancroft, who gained prominence in the discipline, later reflected, "Its possibilities, rather than its immediate opportunities, doubtless drew me to physical training as a profession."[42] Few women or men were as prescient as Bancroft was in the late nineteenth century.

Instead, early physical educators entered the field by following the example and advice of other teachers. That certainly held true for many applicants to the BNSG. One example is Ethel Perrin, who attended a preparatory school in West Bridgewater, Massachusetts, where a graduate of Sargent's school directed exercise twice a week. Much to the "horror" of Perrin's classmates, physical exams were also conducted, "from top to toe."[43] Perrin, on the other hand, enjoyed the challenge of becoming "absolutely symmetrical," by means of the "exciting pieces of apparatus" that adorned the walls of the makeshift gym in the school's attic.[44] The academy's principal, a friend of Amy Morris Homans, suggested that Perrin pursue her interest in gymnastics by attending the BNSG. Role models also influenced the decisions of J. Anna Norris (BNSG 1895), Helen McKinstry (BNSG 1900), Mabel Lee (BNSG 1910), and Josephine Rathbone (BNSG 1923).[45] In the first two cases, their teachers were BNSG alumnae. Throughout the history of the BNSG, a national network of female physical educators enabled the school to recruit students and to place its graduates.

Several factors guided early applicants toward the BNSG. As products of late Victorian society, the young candidates were both anxious about their health and determined to improve it. Since most of the women probably enjoyed exercise, physical training promised to be instructive and therapeutic, while not too onerous. Single and middle-class, the young women also worried about their futures. Education and employment were sensible options, especially as intermediate stops on the road to marriage. Few jobs were as available or as acceptable as teaching. Physical education was a natural way to satisfy the women's concerns about health and security. If that solution did not emerge on its own, teachers already in the field recommended that young prospects consider becoming physical educators. As normal schools grew in number, the friends and alumnae of the BNSG directed promising candidates to the program of Hemenway and Homans in Boston.

The BNSG was a congenial place for young women to train in physical education. The school was determined to attract students with a respectable degree of health, education, and character. During its early years, the BNSG required that applicants have the equivalent of a high-school education, the endorsement of "at least two well-known persons," and no "organic disease or serious functional disorder."[46] In the early 1900s, the school added that pupils should have *"the ability to speak and write good English"* and have "a keen sense of rhythm."[47] Furthermore, the student body was virtually all female. Although the BNSG invited both male and female applicants, only a handful of men matriculated, and fewer still graduated. In 1903–4, when the school catalogue no longer encouraged male applicants, the BNSG became, officially, a female-only institution.[48] Finally, the program was not cheap. In 1890, the yearly fee for the basic course was $100. Tuition rose to $150 in 1891, and remained so for many years. Students also incurred the expense of room and board in Boston (estimated to be $7 to $8 per week in 1900) and of books, shoes, gym suits, and other items (totaling about $40 for the two-year program).[49] The average working-class family could not

The Boston Normal School of Gymnastics gymnasium, with apparatus for Swedish exercises, late 1890s. Source: Wellesley College Archives.

afford such expenses; even the resources of a middle-class family might be strained. Its entrance requirements, student body, and cost defined the BNSG as an institution for reputable young women from comfortable circumstances.

In some respects, the school began as a humble operation. The first home of the BNSG was a modest hall on Park Street. In 1890 it moved to more spacious quarters in Paine Hall at 9 Appleton Street. As of 1897 it occupied part of the Massachusetts Charitable Mechanic Association Building on Huntington Avenue.[50] Despite cramped facilities, the BNSG had a full complement of portable Swedish gymnastic apparatus, including suspended ropes and ladders, "the boom" (a swinging, gate-like structure attached to the wall), vaulting horses, inclined planes, and other equipment. (See figure.[51]) The BNSG also maintained a library and a collection of scientific instruments and aids, such as microscopes, tissue preparations, skeletons, and anatomical charts.[52] At times, instructors had to invent their own teaching devices. A graduate of 1893, for instance, recalled that the woman doctor who lectured on physiology " 'made organs of the body for demonstration out of cloth.' "[53] The BNSG also owned anthropometric equipment, which it used to test the students and teach them the techniques of physical examination.[54]

Anthropometric testing at the BNSG was legendary. One of the students' first, and most unforgettable, experiences at the school was their physical exam. The adventure was still vivid years later, as Lucy Pratt recalled:

> [W]e went through the varying forms of initiation without serious trepidation. We ascended the stairs to the little third story room [at 9 Appleton Street] for our physical tests and measurements, feeling brave and strong, and we undoubtedly would have descended in the same spirit but for one trifling set-back which sent us down both hushed and awed. We had silently viewed Miss Margaret Wallace— to our undoing. [Wallace was the physical examiner.] We felt shrunken, mean, crooked, under-fed, hollow-chested, "stoop-shoul- dered," bilaterally unsymmetrical [sic], everything that we ought not to have been. Conceit was gone from us. Vanished. A thing of the past. We asked questions of Seniors. How long had she been in the school—this perfect looking person on the third floor? How long was it necessary to remain *in order to look like that?* They were vague. Apparently some must remain longer than others. But there was one point which they impressed upon us in kind and elderly fashion. It was whispered about among us. She had achieved it and still looked like that without the aid of corsets![55]

Dreaming about health was one matter. Meeting a live paragon was another.

Miss Wallace on the third floor exemplified what the BNSG re- garded as able-bodied womanhood. A graduate of the program's first class (1891), Wallace was physically fit and professionally compe- tent. She supervised anthropometry at the BNSG for five years (in- timidating new students in the process) and, simultaneously, directed physical training at Radcliffe College. The BNSG curriculum was de- signed to replicate Miss Wallace—to develop the students' own level of fitness and to prepare capable teachers of physical education.

On the premise that "theoretical and practical instruction go hand in hand," the two-year program at the BNSG combined intel- lectual and physical training.[56] During the school's early years, ju- niors studied anatomy, physiology, and hygiene as theoretical and ap- plied sciences, especially in relation to exercise and gymnastics. The first-year curriculum also covered anthropometry, emergency training (first aid), drills in pedagogical gymnastics and games, and voice les- sons.[57] In 1893 junior-level science courses expanded to include physics, chemistry, and biology.[58] Over the next ten years, dance, gymnastic games, swimming, and athletics were added.[59] The senior year originally included histology, pathology, psychology, pedagogy, the theory of gymnastics, drills in educational and medical gymnastics, and practice teaching.[60] Beginning in 1892, second-year work also covered sanitary science, fencing, and applied anthropometry.[61] By the early 1900s, seniors also studied symptomatology, swimming, athletics, dancing, games, corrective gymnastics, and the history of education.[62]

As the curriculum grew, so did the faculty.[63] When the BNSG opened in 1889, its staff consisted of Amy Morris Homans, the director, and Baron Nils Posse, the sole instructor. An expert in Swedish gymnastics, Posse first became associated with Mary Hemenway when she engaged him to train teachers in Boston's public schools. Their once-friendly relationship soon soured; in 1890, Posse left the BNSG to establish his own gymnasium and training program. His replacement was Claes J. Enebuske, a fellow advocate of the Swedish system. Another early addition was Dr. Emma L. Call, a physician at the New England Hospital for Women and Children, who taught anatomy and physiology at the BNSG. In 1891–92, six new instructors arrived, including several part-time lecturers from Harvard (Josiah Royce, who taught psychology and pedagogy; Dr. Henry P. Bowditch, anthropometry; and Dr. W. M. Conant, emergency instruction). Students soon began to take some of their natural science courses at the Massachusetts Institute of Technology, where, for example, William T. Sedgwick taught biology, and Theodore Hough, physiology. By the opening of its tenth year, the school's staff (full- and part-time) numbered fifteen, ranging from eminent doctors and academicians in the Boston area to recent graduates of the BNSG.[64]

The intellectual studies and physical training made for a rigorous program. The most difficult academic subjects were anatomy and physiology, which the students learned inside and out. Assigned a dead cat in dissection class, Lucy Pratt never forgot the many weeks she "observed and poked at that poor embalmed animal."[65] Pratt also recalled how she and her classmates went "staggering among the intricacies of genuine physiology" at MIT at a pace that, fortunately, "was not too rapid for our own good."[66] Another graduate remembered the schedule to be so demanding that students often had " 'a bone in one hand and a sandwich in the other at lunch.' "[67]

Vigorous physical training complemented the regimen of intellectual work. The already-converted had no complaints about the classes in gymnastics. Ethel Perrin experienced "a satisfied feeling of exhilaration and well-being" after a day's order of Swedish exercise.[68] Even students who resolutely hated exercise came to appreciate it. Senda Berenson, the once fragile female, was a striking example:

> "Gymnastic work did not interest me and the simplest exercises made me ache all over. I heard that my case was quoted for years by Dr. Enebuska [sic] as encouragement of students who were not strong. But I persevered. . . . After five minutes of standing erect [doing Swedish gymnastics] I had to lie flat on three stools. After three months, however, I began to feel that I was better and at the end of the year was doing all the gymnastics required."[69]

As their skills developed, the students took great pride in being competent gymnasts and athletes. Lucy Pratt remembered the final demonstration and basketball game of her senior year. At the conclusion, she and her classmates "felt that all the work had been worth while, that everything paid, and that life was worth while, after all." Pratt continued, "We had showed what speed we could, what skill we had. . . . We had even won the game."[70]

A curriculum in science and pedagogy had prepared the students to be teachers. A full course of sports and Swedish exercise had rendered them fit. What remained was to make them womanly. A trained mind and body were necessary but not sufficient marks of able-bodied womanhood. Decorum, appearance, and other personal qualities were equally important. In their reminiscences, BNSG graduates often mentioned the school's high standard of propriety. The comments of Helen McKinstry are typical:

> Particular attention was paid to the manners, dress and behavior of the young women in training. Through the dressing rooms, and in other conspicuous places in the school, were posted neatly printed and framed copies of the following quotation from "King Lear"— "Her voice was ever soft, gentle and low. An excellent thing in woman."[71]

Amy Morris Homans, who directed the BNSG for twenty-nine years, was responsible for the signs and for maintaining grace and civility among the students. She reinforced the good habits of well-bred students, such as Ethel Perrin. Raised in Wellesley and versed in many "Boston idiosyncrasies," Perrin believed that gum chewing in the gym was unladylike and that, when seated, one should plant both of her feet firmly on the floor.[72] With other students, though, Homans's job was more difficult. Upon observing Helen McKinstry and learning that she hailed from Minnesota, Homans declared, " 'You are doing satisfactory work, my dear, but you need a great deal of toning down, and I shall see that you get it.' "[73] Unkempt students were asked when they last polished their shoes or cleaned their gym suits; others were informed that their stockings were not straight or were too transparent.[74] Nor would Homans tolerate arrogance among the young women. When the class of 1895 basketball team became over-confident prior to a big game, a patient "gentle-voiced lady" emerged from the director's office to remind the girls that they "belonged, with little doubt, to the *Animal* Kingdom!"[75] So Pratt and her classmates learned to play, and to win, "without showing our teeth too."[76] However smart and however fit, able-bodied women had to be ladies too. The program at the BNSG developed physical skills, prepared teachers, and cultivated decorum. With that training, a young woman was ready for a job in physical education.

For some graduates, their education at the BNSG was almost a religious experience, and their approaching work was a crusade. Senda Berenson, for example, underwent a virtual conversion at the school:

> "It is impossible to tell how my life had altered. I had changed an aching body to a free and strong mechanism, ready and eager for whatever might come. My indifference had changed to deep conviction and I wanted to work only in physical education so that I might help others as I had been helped."[77]

Ethel Perrin considered herself "an apostle going forth to redeem the world," armed with the gospel of Swedish gymnastics.[78] Physical education was a "mission,"[79] and its teachers were witnesses for health.

The workaday world, however, was not a sanctuary, and physical educators did not lead a blessed existence. As graduates of the BNSG entered the work force, they faced challenges and decisions that were unexpected. Three issues in particular awaited them. First, what was the relationship between career and marriage? Consciously or not, BNSG alumnae had to resolve the tension between work and domesticity. Second, they found out that physical education often resembled a military campaign more than a holy crusade. Could teachers with ladylike demeanor survive, much less succeed, in the battlefields of education and administration? Finally, health was the focal point of a physical educator's personal and professional identity. What ideals of female health should a woman teacher espouse, in her own life and through her work? Each of these three problems forced BNSG graduates to reflect on their values as women. However complete their training had been, the first generation of female physical educators had to re-examine the meaning of health, womanhood, and work during their careers. They discovered that practicing able-bodied womanhood was even more difficult than learning about it.

To understand that process among BNSG graduates, one needs some basic information about their lives as working women. The following profile of the careers of the school's first ten classes is based on biographical data maintained by the BNSG, the Mary Hemenway Alumnae Association, and the Department of Hygiene and Physical Education at Wellesley and its section of the college's Alumnae Association.[80]

A great majority of BNSG students took a job in physical education immediately after graduation. (Information about 198 of the first 212 alumnae was found.) In the first five classes, almost 92 percent went directly into the field; about the same proportion of the graduates between 1896 and 1900 did so as well. Most of the women who did not enter physical education upon graduating chose some other line of work or got married.

The tenures of early BNSG graduates in physical education ranged from zero to nearly fifty years. Among members of the first five classes, about one-third worked in the field from one to five years, 30 percent from six to fifteen years, and 28 percent sixteen years or more. The pattern among the next five classes was similar: 31 percent from one to five years, 29 percent from six to fifteen years, and 31 percent sixteen years or more. Altogether, the data reveal a fairly even split between short, medium, and extended careers. The longevity of many women in the two cohorts is especially noteworthy; nearly 30 percent of the first ten classes spent sixteen or more years in the profession.

Their degree of mobility is also interesting. Many graduates moved from job to job early in their careers. Those who stayed in the field more than five years, however, eventually settled into stable, even permanent, positions. That pattern became visible in an analysis of the career tracks for both cohorts, focusing on positions that BNSG alumnae held for five or more years. (See Tables 3 and 4 in the Appendix.) Among the graduates of 1891–95, forty-seven held a particular job or were employed by the same institution continuously for five or more years. (Because some women had that experience more than once in their careers, the total number of five-year positions (seventy-one) exceeds the number of women in the sample.) The most frequent sources of stable employment were public schools and teacher-training schools. Among BNSG alumnae from 1896 through 1900, fifty-five had a tenure of five or more years in one or more specific jobs or institutions (for a total of seventy-seven such positions). The second cohort held long-term jobs primarily at private secondary schools, public schools, and normal schools.

BNSG graduates constituted a pool of both temporary and long-term employees. While some of the women changed jobs frequently, during either short or extended careers, many occupied one or more positions for a considerable period of time. In addition, opportunities for steady work were available in both public and private institutions, and became more diverse as the discipline matured. By the turn of the century, America's first female physical educators, trained at the BNSG and elsewhere, had begun to establish themselves in the new profession.

What happened to the women who left physical education? The lives of early BNSG graduates, organized by the number of years spent in physical education, were examined to determine why class members terminated their careers. (See Tables 5 and 6.) Among the alumnae of 1891–95, three-quarters of the women who did not enter physical education directly after the BNSG opted for another area of work. More than two-fifths of their classmates who spent one to five years in the field left because of marriage. The graduates who remained in physical education for six or more years (the last three columns in Table 5) moved on for different reasons, notably, further education, other types of work, or retirement. (Still, nearly a fifth of those women also gave up work for marriage.) Among graduates between 1896 and 1900, marriage had greater allure. About three-fifths of the women who never worked in physical education and over three-fifths of those who did so for only a short time left because of marriage. More than a third of the graduates who taught physical education for six to ten years also quit to become married. For those with longer tenures, however, their career in physical education more likely concluded with a change in profession or retirement. The overall pattern is clear: marriage led BNSG alumnae to terminate their careers in the early stages; among women who remained in physical education for a longer period, other job opportunities or retirement, more than marriage, drew them away.

Those observations do not necessarily imply that work and marriage were mutually exclusive. For example, graduates who married early in their careers may still have worked, though not in physical education; similarly, graduates who pursued long careers in the field may have gotten married without leaving their jobs. Further analysis, however, shows that neither conjecture is true. Of the more than two hundred women in the first ten classes of the BNSG, only a few worked outside the home for pay in any field after they married. Nearly 58 percent of the members of classes 1891–95 never married; in virtually every case, single graduates were precisely the women who had long careers in physical education. About 45 percent of the next five classes never married; they too represented the career women within their cohort. Comparisons with other women put those figures in perspective. BNSG graduates married at a far lower rate than did the general female population in America at the turn of the century, but roughly in the same proportion as alumnae of various colleges.[81] The separation of work and marriage, though, may have been more pronounced among BNSG graduates than for other professional women in America during the early twentieth century.[82]

Perhaps the first crossroads that BNSG graduates faced was the choice between marriage and career. For young, single, middle-class females, employment was both acceptable and common in America at the time. The expectation stood, however, that eventually a woman would become a wife and mother, maintaining a home, not a job. About half of the early graduates of the BNSG picked marriage over work. The other half remained single and pursued careers. An intriguing question is how and why they made those choices. What did their decisions reveal about their perceptions of work and womanhood?

The answer is elusive. Few of the single career women left comments about their personal lives. Only some secondhand anecdotes remain. For example, Mabel Lee once disclosed, by way of Ethel Perrin, that William Skarstrom (BNSG 1895) "fell deeply in love with J. Anna Norris and begged her to marry him. He finally had to accept her determined refusal in favor of a career."[83] Information is too scarce to ascertain if other BNSG graduates had similar opportunities and made equally conscious decisions. Nor is it known what feelings—of contentment, regret, or ambivalence—such women may have experienced as single professionals.

The private lives of married alumnae are more accessible to the historian. The annual registers of graduates prepared by the Mary Hemenway Alumnae Association after 1915 included news about members of various classes. Entries from married graduates convey their obvious satisfaction with family life. As her report for 1921 indicated, for example, one alumna of 1896 achieved more than the average American dream:

> "As I am the happy possessor of a fine husband, five children, a good-sized house and yard with our own tennis court and boat slip, to say nothing of vegetable garden and poultry yard, all in an interesting and flourishing city . . . , my days are very busy and interesting. . . ."[84]

Though happy and secure with their families, BNSG alumnae were anything but homebodies. Along with great numbers of middle- and upper-class American women in the early twentieth century, married graduates joined voluntary associations devoted to charitable and civic causes. As one graduate exclaimed in 1917, " 'Of course all women belong to a club these days!' "[85] Activities in the public sphere held significance for them as women and as BNSG graduates. One alumna of 1898 echoed Jane Addams's belief that women's community work was housekeeping on a social scale:

> "I am just an ordinary housekeeper with 2 children and an auto manufacturer for a husband. However, I find time for larger house keeping interests such as child welfare and anti-tuberculosis work. I often thank the fates for my B.N.S.G. training, which trains for social service, whether one uses it in teaching, physical training or just living."[86]

Married alumnae regarded voluntarism as a natural service for women and a logical application of their BNSG degree.

At times, however, married graduates seemed defensive about their choice of domesticity over career. Did their alma mater approve of students who had forsaken physical education for family life? The representative for the graduates of 1900 tried to reassure her classmates:

> "You will note the expression of tranquil domesticity which pervades the letters of the girls who have married. Doesn't it sound as if 1900 had a goodly showing of A 1 wives and mothers,—don't you think success in that line is just as praiseworthy as success in the line of teaching?"[87]

As wives and mothers, married alumnae had fulfilled one model of able-bodied womanhood. Without regretting that course, some still dreamt about the alternative they had not chosen. What had they missed? Similarly, career-minded alumnae had been able-bodied women by carrying the message of female health across the country, even around the world. Did they have any second thoughts? Unfortunately, their reminiscences do not shed much light on that question.

Instead, professional issues dominate the accounts of working alumnae. As women and as representatives of a new discipline, BNSG graduates faced situations that stretched their abilities. Trained as teachers of gymnastics and games, few perhaps anticipated the practical demands of getting a job and performing it well in bureaucratic environments. As their careers progressed, female physical educators developed new qualities as able-bodied women.

The first step, finding a job, was not always easy. In some areas of the country, positions in physical education were scarce or already filled. Jessie H. Bancroft, for instance, spent a couple of years on the road in the Midwest as a lecturer in schools, private homes, and church parlors. Even after training under Dudley Allen Sargent, Bancroft had to solicit virtually every private girls' school in New York City before securing a teaching position.[88] Other women found openings more readily, but had to convince employers of their competence. When Ethel Perrin applied for a job in Detroit in 1908, she already had more than fifteen years' experience in physical education. Nonetheless, she anxiously prepared for her interview by boning up on her sciences and buying a new pair of gloves. The content and brevity of the event startled her:

> The Superintendent, the Principal, and I sat solemnly looking at each other, my mind a blank, when the Superintendent burst out with "Can you swim?" Aghast, for I had never even heard of a high school with a pool, I said "Yes, I can swim" and thereupon they hired me. If they had asked me to describe my method of teaching swimming, I might not have been hired.[89]

Matching a school's needs and a teacher's skills could be difficult; for both employers and practitioners, physical education was a new, often ambiguous, specialty.

Once on the job, early physical trainers rarely had adequate facilities or staff. That was especially true among women teachers, who usually supervised programs for female students. For example, when J. Anna Norris arrived at the University of Minnesota in 1912 to direct women's physical education, she discovered that the so-called women's gym was one end of the Armory, available only occasionally when male students were not using the area. Accommodations included "a woman's office (a little nook) set up in a small room off a balcony, and a small dressing room in the basement which boasted of two showers and a bath tub. For a staff she had one instructor and a combination clerk-accompanist."[90] One of Norris's first priorities was to gain separate and equal facilities for women's physical education at the institution, a goal she achieved within a few years.

Another common frustration among early physical educators was the disrespect they encountered. Because physical training was a new field, one BNSG graduate recalled, " 'you had to explain its purpose in those days.' "[91] For example, BNSG alumnae faced unenlightened and uncooperative students. One of her successors at Smith College noted the "abysmal and blissful ignorance of the real value of physical education"[92] that Senda Berenson found among undergraduates.

> Many a girl got an excuse from required work from a doctor as ignorant as she, and juniors and seniors scarcely exercised at all. A few were fond of tennis and croquet, a few walked, and baseball of a sort was an after-supper fad. It was played, of course, in long dresses and on one occasion at least the pitcher wore a ruffled white muslin with a train for good measure.[93]

Even more "formidable," Berenson's colleague continued, were uninformed parents, who feared for the safety of their delicate daughters.[94] Finally, early physical educators had to deal with skeptical faculty members and administrators, who wondered about the legitimacy of physical training in an intellectual curriculum.[95] Moreover, the question arose of whether physical educators deserved the same status and privileges as enjoyed by the academic staffs of schools.[96] Gaining recognition for physical education and for its practitioners, Senda Berenson once observed, " 'was like punching a pillow—if you made a dent in one place a bulge came out in another.' "[97] According to Berenson, physical education was primarily " 'moral suasion.' "[98]

Ethel Perrin would have called her work administrative suasion. As did many of her former classmates, Perrin held jobs that taught her about effective leadership. Both her Boston upbringing and BNSG training had made Perrin a "strict formalist," dedicated to Swedish gymnastics and feminine decorum.[99] Penned in 1938, Perrin's "confessions" described the principles of administration that she discovered and applied during her fourteen years as director of physical education in Detroit's public schools. One rule was to *"separate essentials from nonessentials."*[100] For instance, Perrin advocated a deep breathing technique, called West Point Breathing, which involved "rolling our hands and arms backward and puffing out our chests like soldiers."[101] One teacher misinterpreted the instructions. In that classroom, Perrin recalled, "I saw the children in perfect unison and with great pride turn and point to the west, but the breaths were very deep and the teacher had no sense of humor so I praised them and let it go—a case of relative importance—of essentials versus nonessentials."[102] A leader's role, Perrin learned, was to achieve results while maintaining some degree of order and happiness, through innovation and conservation, through persuasion and accommodation. The strict formalist and fussy Bostonian became a flexible administrator. That transformation may have surprised her, but Perrin came to regard the tools of leadership as part of able-bodied womanhood.

Other BNSG graduates underwent the same evolution, as women and as professionals. Raised during late Victorian times, they were familiar with the female virtues of dignity and service. While reinforcing those traditional qualities, their training at the BNSG also fostered new ones. Independence and determination became as important as grace and propriety. If BNSG students failed to learn those habits under Amy Morris Homans, they developed them on the job. Their concept of able-bodied womanhood came to include the skills and values necessary for professional success.

One wonders how the experiences of BNSG alumnae compared with those of male physical educators. Were jobs, facilities, and respect equally hard to attain for both sexes? Did women and men perceive their careers and the role of physical education in similar terms? In light of recent scholarship about such fields as medicine and science, one would expect to find significant differences in the lives and attitudes of America's earliest male and female physical trainers.[103] Although some work on those questions is underway, complete answers await a more comprehensive study of the professionalization of physical education in America.

Whatever BNSG alumnae learned about themselves and about work was related to their identity as female teachers. Decisions about marriage, lessons as professionals, and other issues were refracted through the women's responsibilities as educators. Along with other physical trainers, they inculcated the values and habits of personal health. In particular, they taught exercise and hygiene to other women, of all ages and backgrounds, and they served as exemplars of health for their students. What model of able-bodied womanhood did they project? No single answer fits all graduates of the BNSG. Nor can one assume that their ideas remained static throughout their careers. Nevertheless, a survey of the published speeches and articles of early BNSG alumnae reveals certain common themes and questions.[104]

Their general views on health were typical of their background and era. Born primarily during the 1860s and 1870s and trained at a school representative of the period, graduates of the first BNSG classes adopted the concept of health that became popular during the late nineteenth century. As did other observers of American society, BNSG graduates believed that urban, industrial life limited physical exercise and heightened mental stress, thereby jeopardizing people's health. Writing in 1926, for example, Lillian C. Drew (BNSG 1893) regretted that mechanical devices, automobiles, and other modern conveniences were eliminating "many of the natural opportunities for exercise."[105] Particularly in cities, she continued, "habits of life become more sedentary, the tax upon nervous energy is increased, while physical activity is lessened."[106] Consequently, " 'standing' and 'sitting' inactivities are replacing 'running around' activities."[107] Not wishing to return "to the life of primitive man," Drew recommended "some artificial means" to protect physical and mental well-being.[108] Lest health become a casualty of modernization, Drew and others advocated systematic physical education.

What Drew and her BNSG classmates hoped to teach was physical fitness, mental discipline, and personal integrity. Their vision of health included such familiar physical traits as "good posture, agility, vigor, grace and poise, strength, speed, endurance."[109] Mental and spiritual development were also essential to health. As Drew explained in old-fashioned terms, "Man is a being whose mental and physical processes are so closely related that we cannot minister to either alone. 'Health is the wholeness of mind, body and soul.' "[110] Most alumnae found the vocabulary of contemporary neurophysiology and psychology more instructive when describing the "wholeness" of human life. According to Elizabeth R. Stoner (BNSG 1899), one purpose of physical training was "the development of motor control, nervous conservation, the education of fine neuromuscular adjustments, training of sense of direction and balance."[111] Youngsters, concurred Helen McKinstry, should prepare for "a life of 'willed action,' " which depended on muscles and nerves becoming "responsive servants of mind and will."[112] Health required a well-conditioned body under the direction of an orderly mind.

Finally, BNSG graduates believed that physical training developed certain personal attributes, which were diagnostic of good health. Exercise and athletics, observed Elizabeth Stoner, fostered "promptness of decision, courage, initiative and judgment; and the training of moral qualities."[113] Ethel Perrin added the "ability to respond to commands" and "originality, poise, resourcefulness, self-appraisal" to the list.[114] The pursuit of health also improved one's social relations. Physical training, and games in particular, Stoner noted, promoted "good sportsmanship, fairness, enthusiasm, leadership and the sense of responsibility."[115] In short, health was the emblem of physical vigor, mental control, moral rectitude, and social responsibility. Physical education, as the means to those ends, was nothing less than "excellent training in good citizenship."[116]

The word "fitness" summarized the ideal of control and service, of a comfortable and productive life. That simple definition of health became commonplace among BNSG graduates, as for other Americans. J. Anna Norris elaborated on the theme in a discussion of "The Moral Obligation To Be Physically Fit":

> The ideal now is to be fit for work, to do a fine piece of work, and yet have surplus energy to enjoy our leisure time in some kind of satisfying recreation. When we have the vitality that this implies, coupled with disciplined emotions, we find that work is a joy and life a tremendously worth while experience.[117]

Elizabeth Stoner believed that the purpose of physical education was

> To make girls fit to be mothers and boys fit to be fathers.
>
> To make students fit to be citizens.
>
> To make them fit for professional life.
>
> To make them fit for social life.
>
> To make them fit for industrial life.[118]

Stoner's agenda was a paradigmatic model of health as America entered the twentieth century.

If health was the ability to perform, then it was an observable and perhaps quantifiable state. As America's fascination for scientific analysis grew, physical educators assumed that human fitness, much as intelligence or worker efficiency, was a measurable phenomenon. The program at the BNSG led its graduates to the same conviction. Students at the school had biannual physical exams and took classes in the theory and application of anthropometric testing. Many graduates applied anthropometric techniques during their own careers, and some also incorporated evaluations of physiologic functions, medical check-ups, and other information. J. Anna Norris and Helen McKinstry, in particular, featured medical and physical examinations in their work.[119] They believed that such procedures yielded reliable evidence about a person's status, deficiencies, and progress.[120] Health had become a quantifiable parameter of human life.

Altogether, BNSG alumnae taught and measured thousands of children and adults during their careers. Because of the division of labor in physical education, most of their students were female, and many of their publications dealt with female health. Convinced that women could and should be fit, BNSG graduates proclaimed that the cult of female invalidism was dead. Only cultural myths and misguided customs, they insisted, perpetuated the notion that women were inherently fragile. Fortunately, Helen McKinstry cheered in 1931, the American woman had been "freed from the physical imprisonment of dress exemplified by 'stays' and 'crinoline,' exercise and out-of-door recreation broadened her wasp waist, deepened her tubercular chest and substituted muscle for 'softness and curves.' "[121] Lillian Drew also welcomed women's freedom from burdensome clothing—"corsets, heavy skirts, high collars and tight neck bands"— and the demise of the belief that "healthy activities were 'unladylike.' "[122] Although "emancipation from the high heel and pointed toe shoe is still to be accomplished," Drew added, many "foolish traditions of the past" were gone and women could no longer be called " 'the weaker sex.' "[123] In fact, Drew concluded, people now understood that "strength and weakness both physical and mental" were not "definite attributes" of either men or women, but applied to both sexes.[124] Physical educators often noted that more than one-third of America's draftees during World War I were declared physically unfit. As the myth that all women were weak collapsed, so did the fiction that all men were strong.

That of course did not mean that the two sexes were physically equal. Obviously, menstruation, childbearing, and menopause distinguished women's biological lives. No discussion about female health could proceed without attention to those unique functions. At the turn of the century, doctors, physical educators, social reformers, and other Americans debated the implications of women's physiological cycle for health. In particular, they asked, what types of exercise, games, and athletics were advisable for females?[125]

That question was especially germane to BNSG graduates and

other female physical educators. Overall, their opinions were neither the most conservative nor the most progressive in the debate. On the one hand, they insisted, the female cycle was a natural, not pathological, process, which need not interfere with a woman's normal schedule.[126] "Most happily," Helen McKinstry reported in 1917, "actual facts and statistics are absolutely disproving previous theories of woman's physical and mental inferiority and particularly this antiquated temporary shelving of woman for the menstrual period and permanent retirement to caps and knitting at 50."[127] Compare menstruation to "other normal physiologic functions," McKinstry suggested.[128] How much would a person accomplish if she faced digestion, for example, "with apprehension and exaggerated care, and considered [herself] ill for an hour or two after each meal"?[129] In particular, McKinstry argued, girls and young women may continue exercising, with some adjustments, during their periods; physical activity could even be therapeutic, by helping to relieve menstrual discomfort and related disorders. Likewise, activity would enable the older woman to pass safely through menopause. "The mentally and physically active woman of today," McKinstry observed, "may have little fear of premature death or permanent incapacity and suffering at the change of life."[130]

At the same time, BNSG graduates cautioned that physiological changes during menstruation, though temporary, were consequential. While not incapacitated during her period, a girl was not likely to perform, mentally or physically, up to her highest ability. "Do not plan or expect to do your most taxing mental work during at least the first day of the period, no matter how well you feel," advised Helen McKinstry.[131] Because physical limitations were harder to gauge than mental ones, BNSG alumnae were less sure what level of exercise young women could sustain without peril during menstruation. Noting that "strain or displacement" of the uterus was more likely at such times, McKinstry suggested that young women moderate their physical activities while menstruating.[132] The potential risks of vigorous sports were the most troubling to BNSG graduates. Augusta L. Patrick (BNSG 1894), for example, attributed "irregularities" in girls' cycles to "the excitement" of athletic contests.[133] The game of basketball under boys' rules seemed especially hazardous to girls, whether they were menstruating or not. According to J. Anna Norris, the game placed "such heavy demands on organic vitality" that it "was ill-adapted to the rank and file of girls."[134] Moreover, "the dangers from collision, violent contact and falling were more serious for the girl than for the boy."[135] Another alumna, Ethel Perrin, was less certain about the effects of athletics, because scientific information on the subject was so scarce.[136] She did believe, however, that menstruation limited a girl's abilities, much as nearsightedness would prevent a boy from succeeding as a jumper. "All we can say at present is that this is a girl's handicap," Perrin concluded, "and it does not seem sensible to train her to do something into which she may never be able to put her maximum effort when the opportunity comes."[137]

Neither Perrin nor any of her colleagues recommended that girls' athletics be abolished. Instead, Perrin suggested that women's training merely exclude those skills designed only for "highly specialized meets."[138] J. Anna Norris advised girls not to join basketball practice or gymnastics class for the first few days of their periods.[139] The solution most commonly proposed was the modification of athletic games to suit what trainers regarded as girls' physical peculiarities. For example, Senda Berenson took the lead in devising so-called girls' basketball. Berenson formulated special rules, including the division of the court into two or more zones, to make the game less tiring and less violent. After some revision, Berenson's guidelines became the official regulations for girls' basketball.[140] If sports were physically dangerous, the answer was prudence, not prohibition.

BNSG alumnae also worried about the psychological consequences of athletics. Competitive games, they argued, bred undesirable traits in both the participants and spectators. J. Anna Norris, for example, disliked the "fighting features" of basketball because they encouraged "aggressive characteristics that added nothing of charm and usefulness, and were not in harmony with the best traditions of the [female] sex."[141] Other features of sports events only aggravated the problem.[142] Athletic contests made spectators boorish, communities exploitative, and the local press greedy. Driven by an obsession to win, by the enthusiasm of partisan crowds, and by the lure of individual publicity and glory, young girls learned that nothing short of excellence and victory was acceptable. Contestants no longer played a game for its own sake; winners became cocky and selfish; losers often suffered nervous breakdowns. No worthy graduate of the BNSG would endorse those as qualities of able-bodied womanhood. "I may be old-fashioned," admitted Augusta Patrick, "in wanting to keep my girls simple, wholesome and girlish, yet abounding in natural enthusiasm and vivacity. Give me the bright eyes, red cheeks and happy smiles of the many, rather than the names of a few experts in the newspapers."[143]

Patrick's image highlighted another weakness of competitive athletics. As did many of their colleagues, BNSG graduates opposed exclusionary sports on philosophic grounds. A preoccupation with expertise and victory, they observed, confined physical training to a select group of qualified athletes. Repeating a familiar slogan of the early twentieth century, Patrick invited physical educators to "seek the greatest good to the greatest number."[144] Another advocate of *"democracy in recreation,"* Ethel Perrin also sought to "provide interesting activity for *everybody* and not only for the specialized athlete."[145] While accepting intramural and interscholastic contests during her career in Detroit's public schools, Perrin also introduced recreational games and playdays that served the many, not just the few.[146] One priority of physical education, Perrin declared, must be to ensure "equal opportunities for health and joy to all girls."[147]

The concerns of BNSG graduates were typical of America's first generation of physical educators. Professional literature at the turn of the century often addressed such subjects as health for girls and women, the effects of competitive sports, and the philosophy of recreation. The positions of BNSG alumnae did not deviate much from the norm. Most of their colleagues, including female teachers, also feared the physical and emotional damage of athletics among girls and women; similarly, many objected to training and events that were exclusionary.[148] Charged with organizing physical education in America and committed to the development of their discipline, most professional leaders and rank-and-file teachers avoided radical opinions. Their conservatism contrasted sharply with the liberal views of many students and athletes.[149]

The debate over recreation and athletics involved the values of physical education more than the structure of the discipline. The heated discussions about competition, specialization, and equal opportunity served to define the purpose of physical education and, only secondarily, its organization. What role should physical activity play in the development of America's young men and women? Once the destination was known, a route could be charted.

For the early alumnae of the BNSG, the goal of physical education was to instill the ideals and practices of health. Their model of personal health was representative of popular opinion in America at the close of the nineteenth century. Combining physical, mental, and personal attributes, health was essentially a partnership between the mind and the body, through which the will directed neuromuscular activity. BNSG graduates adopted the operational definition of health as fitness, a state conducive to performance and efficiency. Sharing the country's enthusiasm for scientific analysis, they believed that a person's well-being could be tested and quantified.

The job of physical educators was to apply those general principles to the particular students in their classes. What if those bodies and minds were female? The question had double relevance for graduates of the BNSG. First, they were themselves women, whose careers mandated activity and fitness. Second, because of the structure of physical education, most of their students were female. The meaning of able-bodied womanhood was integral to the personal lives and professional roles of BNSG alumnae. Their views about female health were a product of several factors—their upbringing in late Victorian America, their training at the BNSG, and their experiences as working women. The result was a mixture of unorthodox and conventional ideas, laced with some ambivalence.

Among the country's popularizers of health at the turn of the century, BNSG alumnae and other female physical educators were champions of women's health. Challenging medical and popular opinion, they regarded menstruation and menopause as natural, nondebilitating processes. Cheering women's emancipation from delicate exercise and restrictive clothing, they increased women's opportunities for recreation, physical training, and athletics. BNSG alumnae affirmed that women of all ages were capable of full health and active living. In fact, BNSG graduates themselves were visible testimony against the myth of female invalidism.

During their careers, however, several issues emerged that puzzled BNSG alumnae. Some questions derived from their personal experiences as working women. Did able-bodied womanhood necessarily involve marriage? About half of the early graduates decided that the answer was no. Did female propriety include the practical skills and assertive behavior that success seemed to require? Professional leaders such as Ethel Perrin somehow reconciled their model of femininity with the demands of the workaday world. Still other problems arose as BNSG graduates tried to guide girls and women to health. As did most of their professional colleagues, both male and female, BNSG alumnae wondered if there were limits to able-bodied womanhood. Was every activity consistent with the physiology and temperament of the female sex? In particular, would competitive athletics overtax the female body and violate feminine decorum? As young students at the BNSG, the women did not have to reckon with such questions; they absorbed their studies and enjoyed their physical training. As architects of physical education, however, the graduates of the BNSG helped define able-bodied womanhood in America.

That some answers about female health eluded them is not surprising. The careers of BNSG alumnae spanned the end of the nineteenth century and the first third of the twentieth. As American culture and women's lives changed, the boundaries of female health continued to shift as well. Neither the theory nor the practice of able-bodied womanhood was simple, then or now.

Conclusion

Every day, people go through the ritual of asking each other how they are. Answers are usually short and simple: "fine," "okay," "not so good." Friends might volunteer some details about their problem—a sniffle, a headache, fatigue. Within moments, the conversation naturally drifts to other matters—a family crisis, work-related stress, a broken relationship. Our sense of well-being derives as much from personal difficulties and feelings as from biological conditions. In 1946, the World Health Organization, an agency of the United Nations, described health as "a state of complete physical, mental and social well-being and not merely the absence of disease or infirmity."[1] Whatever its flaws, that definition properly conveys the scope of "health."

The concept of health is such a powerful one precisely because it is so comprehensive. As illustrated by the case of nineteenth-century Boston, the ideals and routines of health serve many functions in people's lives. First, middle-class Bostonians learned the rules of health in order to improve their physical welfare. Between 1830 and 1900, residents of the city worried about health in part because it seemed precarious. Certainly by modern standards, morbidity and mortality rates were high, life expectancy was low, nutrition and hygiene were inadequate, and medical knowledge and therapeutics were limited. Physiological reform gave hope of better lives. If nothing else, a sensible regimen organized one's daily habits.

Those practical benefits were especially important to women. Various disorders seemed pandemic among girls and women; medical care for female ills was ineffective, even harmful; popular and scientific literature fostered a cult of female delicacy. Portrayed as sick, yet required to be well, women looked for sources of information and advice about health. Throughout its first half-century, the Ladies' Physiological Institute of Boston and Vicinity provided instruction in practical physiology, domestic medicine, and female health. Armed with scientific knowledge, members faced their domestic responsibilities with more confidence. Similarly, students at the Boston Normal School of Gymnastics sought to better their own welfare while preparing to teach others about health. The staff at Wellesley College, the alumnae of the BNSG, and other female physical educators believed in the direct value of health, for themselves and for other women. In their minds, able-bodied womanhood was not only possible but essential.

The lessons of health were more than practical tools. They helped people manage external as well as internal disorders. Social conditions in Boston changed considerably between 1830 and 1900. The city's population grew and diversified. Residents moved frequently. Landfill projects and suburbanization altered the city's physical layout. Fluctuations in the local economy made success possible but uncertain for middle-class families. Technological innovations transformed many activities in the home and at the workplace. The result was a sense of apprehension, of dis-ease.

Nineteenth-century Bostonians used models of health and sickness to interpret the changes in their lives. Biological processes became metaphors for external events; physical diagnosis served as social analysis. In antebellum times, for example, members of the Ladies' Physiological Institute believed that ill-health, social discord, and immorality were related, and that personal negligence was their common source. During the last third of the century, such moralism gave way to more pragmatic views. For graduates of the Boston Normal School of Gymnastics, the problem was not social change per se, but ill-adaptation to the demands of industrial life. The lack of neuromuscular discipline made a body dysfunctional; similarly, irresponsible citizens made a society unproductive. From 1830 to 1900, concepts of health and sickness helped Bostonians evaluate their social, not merely physical, circumstances. What was good or bad, what was desirable, what was troublesome?

Treatment follows diagnosis. By prescribing standards of behavior, models of health chart a course of improvement. In the mid-nineteenth century, for example, Bostonians believed that morality underlay health and, conversely, that hygienic living encouraged goodness. Moderation and persistence in all habits would produce ideal citizens—independent men, unselfish women, and dutiful children. Health literature in the late 1800s also advised temperance, vigilance, and self-governance. Increasingly, though, popular physiologists stressed the importance of mind-body cooperation. The new mark of health was the ability of the rational mind to regulate physical activity and emotional impulses. A self-controlled person was ready for any task that modern society posed.

Nineteenth-century Bostonians hoped that personal health would translate into social stability. During the 1840s and 1850s, for example, the Ladies' Physiological Institute regarded health reform as a panacea. If members were unable to correct social problems directly, they could nurture health and virtue in their families. Self-improvement, they believed, led naturally to social progress. In late Victorian times, health advocates taught accommodation, not reform. Industrial America required the physical efforts of many citizens; in return, people would enjoy the fruits of a prosperous society. Wellesley College and the Boston Normal School of Gymnastics promoted fitness so that women could lead comfortable and responsible lives in the modern world. However much ideas about health changed between 1830 and 1900, they remained ideological and political. Popular concepts of health set behavioral norms and defined people's relationship to society.

Those expectations varied according to one's class, sex, race, and age. To discuss personal health was to specify what qualities and roles were appropriate given an individual's station in life. To consider female health was to explore the meaning of womanhood. Middle-class Bostonians in 1830 and in 1900 would have agreed that women must be knowledgeable and able-bodied. They construed those words differently, however. When women attended public lectures about health in antebellum Boston, some reportedly veiled their faces; feminine modesty did not mix easily with physiology. Fifty years later, the BNSG prepared respectable young women to teach health and exercise to other females. At mid-century, recreation for young ladies consisted of light calisthenics and walking. By 1880, the students at Wellesley College were rowing on Lake Waban; by 1900, they were playing basketball and lacrosse. As the nineteenth century ended, the cult of female delicacy had begun to recede, and the boundaries of able-bodied womanhood were growing.

Though prescriptive, concepts of health are not monolithic. Their interpretation and uses vary; their impact can be conservative or progressive. For instance, the Ladies' Physiological Institute served more than one model of healthy womanhood during its first half-century. Some members applied their studies to domestic responsibilities; others were public lecturers, nurses, and social reformers. In large measure, the Institute survived because its functions as a women's club devoted to physiology were so diverse. Similarly, alumnae of the Boston Normal School of Gymnastics explored different versions of womanhood. Each graduate had to find a satisfactory relationship between marriage, work, health, and femininity. Those who chose careers were obligated to teach and to exemplify the qualities of able-bodied womanhood. As their work evolved, so did their perceptions of women's health. At Wellesley College and other institutions, for example, female physical educators wondered if competitive athletics were compatible with female physiology and decorum. There was no fixed or universal standard of able-bodied womanhood.

For all their power to explain and guide, ideas about health are also flexible. As social conditions change, so do popular images of fitness. As different people search for health, they redefine its attributes and rules. Advice literature in the nineteenth century often depicted health as a predetermined goal that could be reached systematically. As middle-class Bostonians discovered, however, health was more an experiment than a blueprint. The Ladies' Physiological Institute, Wellesley College, and the Boston Normal School of Gymnastics enabled women to change, as well as to learn, what able-bodied womanhood meant.

Since that process did not end in 1900, this study concludes at the turn of the century for other reasons. First, the date reflects the historical development of the institutions being examined here. By 1900, the Institute, Wellesley College, and the Boston Normal School of Gymnastics had each undergone one or more stages of evolution, and were about to enter new ones. The leadership of the Institute passed from Dr. Helen O'Leary and Dr. Salome Merritt to other hands; the physical education program at Wellesley, having quieted its detractors, faced new issues; the BNSG, now an established school with over two hundred graduates, would help delineate the purpose of a burgeoning young profession. The groups' narratives did not finish in 1900, but merely assumed different directions.

More generally, the early twentieth century marked a new period in American attitudes about health.[2] Between the 1890s and 1930s, the changes signaled in the latter half of this book became well-articulated and dominant themes in popular culture. Increasingly, the effects of modern civilization seemed both welcome and alarming, and that ambivalence shaped the nation's concepts of health.

On the one hand, industrial society provided the central metaphors and goals of health. The body resembled a machine; scientific study revealed how to maintain and improve it; the main objective was efficient operation. On the other hand, twentieth-century life posed considerable dangers. Among the most worrisome was nervous depletion, the loss of energy through stress, overwork, or laziness. Moreover, bacteriological discoveries heightened people's concern about sanitation and public health; the environment apparently teemed with germs and pollutants. How could one protect against the internal and external perils of the modern world?

Several answers were common in the early 1900s. Some Americans looked to proper nutrition as a means to invigorate and cleanse their bodies. For others, "the strenuous life," epitomized by Teddy Roosevelt, seemed the road to health. Recreation and sports would tone the mind and body, while rehearsing such patriotic values as discipline and success. The movements for physical and mental hygiene also intensified, as social reformers sought ways of preserving the national character while assimilating new immigrants. Many of those concerns, of course, were already evident by 1900. In the early decades of the twentieth century, they became more fully elaborated and widespread as Americans devised an image of health that suited industrial and bureaucratic society.

Throughout the Progressive era, female health remained a prominent issue.[3] There were many lingering fears: women's predisposition to nervous complaints, the continued decline in the native birth rate, and the impact of physical activity on female physiology and decency. On the whole, though, the fragile female became an outmoded picture. Compared to her weak, consumptive sister of the 1800s, the "new woman" of the early twentieth century had a robust figure, wore sensible clothes, exercised outdoors, and exuded health. Advertisements for nutritious foods and hygienic products featured glowing, active young women. Vigorous recreation, such as bicycling and swimming, became more customary. Collegiate sports in female and coed institutions grew, although interscholastic competition remained rare. Women gained their own sports heroines, including champion swimmers and walkers. In both image and fact, a new model of able-bodied womanhood had emerged.

Since the early twentieth century, the limits of women's health have stretched even further. One dramatic example is the range of activities in which women of all ages now participate. We are accustomed to soccer leagues for girls, female executives striding to work in their running shoes, housewives training for marathons, and grandmothers out jogging or biking. As recreation and athletics became more popular in the 1970s and 1980s, women campaigned for opportunities and facilities that were comparable to men's. The results are readily apparent in professional sports, the Olympics, and Title IX of the 1972 Higher Education Act, which prohibited sex discrimination at schools receiving federal funds. (Following Title IX, female athletics increased markedly at all levels of education in the country.)

Despite that progress, though, America is still contending with the implications of able-bodied womanhood. The dilemma is an old one: where do "health" and "femininity" meet? Our culture seems to prefer the wholesome look of a female ice skater to the lean form of a long-distance runner, the cool grace (and grit) of Chris Evert to the pronounced athleticism of Martina Navratilova. We wonder if female bodybuilders are fit, sexy, or grotesque. A chic, tight-fitting leotard is considered more appropriate than a baggy sweatsuit for aerobics class at the health club. Deodorant companies remind us that, while both sexes do sweat, women require a product that "protects you like a man, [but] treats you like a woman." A photo in a news magazine shows a roller skater in Boston pausing to redo her lipstick.[4] Women's journals print recipes for lavish meals alongside ads for clothes and diet food featuring noticeably thin models. The Marilyn Monroe ideal of the 1950s was replaced by the Twiggy look in the 1960s; today, the "accepted" female figure lies somewhere in between, yet girls and women take extreme measures to beat the weight charts and be slender. What *is* an able-bodied woman?

The current confusion about female health has many sources. The women's rights movement has broadened our view of female character and identity; the sexual revolution allowed women to perceive and express themselves in new ways; women's activists focused attention on birth control, abortion, and medical care; the health consumers' movement has encouraged women to learn about and even treat their own bodies; increased access to education, athletics, and employment has challenged old conventions about female roles. Each of those developments raises questions about the physical well-being of women.

For example, how will new patterns of work among women affect their health? On the average, women experience more acute illnesses than men, and also outlive them. Some observers fear that women's morbidity rates, especially from chronic disorders such as heart ailments, will rise as more of them take jobs outside the home. Recent data, however, refute that popular belief. Research indicates that employed, married women (with or without children) enjoy better health than women who do not have multiple roles.[5] There also is no consensus about the type or amount of exercise that is healthy for women. While weight-bearing activities such as running may forestall osteoporosis, high-level training can reduce body fat beyond the point needed to sustain menstruation. Could new opportunities also bring new risks? Today, as in earlier times, social and biological issues are prodding Americans to reconsider the nature of able-bodied womanhood.

In fact, a general interest in health has pervaded American culture during the 1980s. The popularity of health books, fitness centers, and natural foods indicates that a "wellness revolution" is underway. At first glance, this preoccupation with health seems paradoxical. After all, life expectancy in America has never been higher, nor mortality rates lower. Better nutrition, hygiene, and medicine have virtually eradicated certain diseases that once plagued this country. We are, ironically, "doing better and feeling worse."[6] Despite significant gains, Americans still worry—because old age frightens us, because cancer and other degenerative illnesses abound, and because doctors seem unable to protect us. As physical conditions improve and as medicine becomes more sophisticated, expectations rise. We demand more of ourselves and of our doctors.

Social developments, too, have contributed to this fixation upon health. The events of the past twenty years frustrated many young and middle-aged Americans. The Vietnam War, Watergate, the arms race, and economic crises made responsible involvement in the world seem increasingly futile. Finding their private concerns more tangible, many Americans turned inward.[7] Personal comfort became more satisfying than social activism; physical health seemed more accessible than political change. "Living in a world which seems dangerously out of our control," observed columnist Ellen Goodman, "we have become obsessed with defending our own bodily turf. When we can't do anything about the big hazardous wastes out there, we worry about the hazardous waist around our middle."[8] After surveying American attitudes about health, a cover story in *Psychology Today* drew the same conclusion:

> A 33-year-old postal clerk from Ohio confides, "Health is the only thing left in my life that I can control." While most Americans have little influence over events in Lebanon, unemployment or interest rates, urban crime, or the threat of nuclear annihilation, they can grasp the reins of control of their health.[9]

For the generation that came of age during the 1960s and 1970s, in particular, health promises more than physical well-being; it restores order and control. Few investments reap such benefits.

The language of finance seems appropriate. Increasingly, fitness has become a commodity, sold by entrepreneurs and purchased by the well-to-do. The most conspicuous consumers of health are young, well-educated, affluent men and women. For them, "having it all" includes being physically fit. Since few can afford it, the upscale version of health may remain an emblem of prosperous Americans.

Is today's fitness craze just a fad? One can only speculate how long it will last. Better health and better medicine will continue to raise our expectations; economic and social conditions may create further dis-ease. On the other hand, technological change could make us complacent about our physical lives, and some issue other than health may capture our attention. Whether interest waxes or wanes, health will remain a tantalizing, if problematic, ideal. Because the notion is relative, one can neither define nor achieve perfect health. Because its criteria are cultural, female health will always be subject to debate. At least, able-bodied womanhood is no longer a contradiction in terms.

Notes

Introduction

1. For example, see John C. Burnham, "Change in the Popularization of Health in the United States," *Bulletin of the History of Medicine* 58 (Summer 1984): 183–97; Anita Clair Fellman and Michael Fellman, *Making Sense of Self: Medical Advice Literature in Late Nineteenth-Century America* (Philadelphia: Univ. of Pennsylvania Press, 1981); Harvey Green, *Fit for America: Health, Fitness, Sport and American Society* (New York: Pantheon, 1986); George Rosen, "Political Order and Human Health in Jeffersonian Thought," *Bulletin of the History of Medicine* 26 (Jan.–Feb. 1952): 32–44; and James C. Whorton, *Crusaders for Fitness: The History of American Health Reformers* (Princeton: Princeton Univ. Press, 1982).

2. The following discussion draws primarily on Arthur L. Caplan, H. Tristram Engelhardt, Jr., and James J. McCartney, eds., *Concepts of Health and Disease: Interdisciplinary Perspectives* (Reading, Mass.: Addison-Wesley, 1981), 1–142. Of particular value is the essay by Lester S. King, "What Is Disease?," 107–18. Equally provocative is Susan Sontag, *Illness as Metaphor* (New York: Vintage, 1979), which describes the mythology of tuberculosis in the nineteenth century and of cancer in the twentieth century.

3. For example, see Charles E. Rosenberg, *The Cholera Years: The United States in 1832, 1849, and 1866* (Chicago: Univ. of Chicago Press, 1962).

4. William A. Alcott, *The Young Woman's Book of Health* (New York and Auburn: Miller, Orton & Mulligan, 1855), 2 (emphasis in original).

1. The Etiology of Dis-ease

1. Orson Squire Fowler, *Physiology, Animal and Mental: Applied to the Preservation and Restoration of Health of Body, and Power of Mind*, 6th ed. (New York: Fowlers and Wells, 1853), 21.

2. Catharine E. Beecher, *Letters to the People on Health and Happiness* (New York: Harper & Brothers, 1855; reprint ed., New York: Arno Press and the *New York Times*, 1972), 9.

3. Edward Jarvis, M.D., *Practical Physiology; For the Use of Schools and Families* (Philadelphia: Thomas, Cowperthwait, 1848), 363.

4. "Education of Females," *American Journal of Education* 2 (June 1827): 339.

5. *Ibid.*, 340.

6. "Influence of Woman on Society," *Ladies' Magazine* 4 (June 1831): 262.

7. *Ibid.*

8. Dio Lewis, M.D., "New Gymnastics," [*Barnard's*] *American Journal of Education* 11 (June 1862): 531.

9. "One Great Secret of Health and Happiness," *Dio Lewis's Monthly* 1 (Sept. 1883): 198, and 197–98 in general.

10. Maris A. Vinovskis, "Mortality Rates and Trends in Massachusetts before 1860," *Journal of Economic History* 32 (1972): 206; also, Maris A. Vinovskis, *Fertility in Massachusetts from the Revolution to the Civil War* (New York: Academic, 1981), 33.

11. Secondary sources include John B. Blake, *Public Health in the Town of Boston, 1630–1822* (Cambridge, Mass.: Harvard Univ. Press, 1959), 217–19, 247–57; Vinovskis, "Mortality Rates and Trends," 196, 199, 203–4, 212; and Vinovskis, *Fertility in Massachusetts*, 32. Among primary documents containing mortality and related data for the first half of the nineteenth century are Lemuel Shattuck, "On the Vital Statistics of Boston," *American Journal of Medical Sciences* n.s. 1 (April 1841): 369–401; Lemuel Shattuck, *Report to the Committee of the City Council Appointed To Obtain the Census of Boston for the Year 1845, Embracing Collateral Facts and Statistical Researches, Illustrating the History and Condition of the Population, and Their Means of Progress and Prosperity* (Boston: John H. Eastburn, 1846), 132, and 131–33, 136–77, and appendices 00–UU in general; *Report of the Committee Appointed by the City Council; and also a Comparative View of the Population of Boston in 1850, with the Births, Marriages, and Deaths, in 1849 and 1850, by Jesse Chickering, M.D.,* (1851, City Document #60), 28; and *Report of the Joint Special Committee on the Census of Boston, May, 1855, Including the Report of the Censors, with Analytical and Sanitary Observations,* (1855, City Document #69), 43. (The chief author of the latter report was Dr. Josiah Curtis.)

12. Shattuck, "On the Vital Statistics of Boston," 395, 400, and 388–400 in general. See also Curtis, *Report . . . on the Census of Boston, May, 1855,* pp. 64–104.

13. *Report by the City Registrar of the Births, Marriages, and Deaths, in the City of Boston, for the Year 1849,* (1850, City Doc. #4), 10.

14. Shattuck, "On the Vital Statistics of Boston," 393 (emphasis in original); also, Shattuck, *Report . . . Census of Boston for the Year 1845,* p. 146.

15. Shattuck, *Report . . . Census of Boston for the Year 1845,* p. 146.

16. See Charles E. Rosenberg, "The Bitter Fruit: Heredity, Disease, and Social Thought in Nineteenth-Century America," *Perspectives in American History* 8 (1974): 189–235.

17. The following secondary sources describe population growth, public health, and other physical developments in Boston from colonial times to the mid-1800s: Blake, *Public Health in the Town of Boston,* 117–228; Oscar Handlin, *Boston's Immigrants: A Study in Acculturation,* rev. ed. (Cambridge, Mass.: Belknap Press of Harvard Univ. Press, 1959), 88–123; Peter R. Knights, *The Plain People of Boston, 1830–1860: A Study in City Growth* (New York: Oxford Univ. Press, 1971), 11–77, 120–23; and Walter Muir Whitehill, *Boston: A Topographical History,* 2d ed. (Cambridge, Mass.: Belknap Press of Harvard

Univ. Press, 1968), 1–173. For contemporary accounts, see Shattuck, "On the Vital Statistics of Boston," 373–77, and Shattuck, *Report . . . Census of Boston for the Year 1845,* pp. 2–7, 26–57.

18. *Journal of Health* 3 (June 27, 1832): 307–8.

19. Shattuck, *Report . . . Census of Boston for the Year 1845,* p. 157.

20. Shattuck, "On the Vital Statistics of Boston," 378–82, and Shattuck, *Report . . . Census of Boston for the Year 1845,* pp. 153–54.

21. Curtis, *Report . . . on the Census of Boston, May, 1855,* p. 48, and 47–55 in general.

22. Shattuck, *Report . . . Census of Boston for the Year 1845,* pp. 162–64.

23. Mary S. Gove, *Lectures to Ladies on Anatomy and Physiology* (Boston: Saxton & Peirce, 1842), 12.

24. *Ibid.*

25. *Ibid.,* and 11–17 in general.

26. Superintendent of Burials, quoted in Shattuck, *Report . . . Census of Boston for the Year 1845,* p. 156.

27. Knights, *The Plain People of Boston,* 47, and 33–47 in general.

28. Shattuck, *Report . . . Census of Boston for the Year 1845,* pp. 129, 155–58.

29. *Ibid.,* 156, and Chickering, *Report . . . ; and also a Comparative View of the Population of Boston in 1850,* pp. 9–11, 28–32. Much of Chickering's analysis (pp. 9–45) focuses on the comparative birth and death rates among Boston's native and foreign populations. See also Curtis, *Report . . . on the Census of Boston, May, 1855,* pp. 44–46, 55–58, and *Report of the Committee of Internal Health on the Asiatic Cholera, Together with a Report of the City Physician on the Cholera Hospital,* (1849, City Doc. #66).

30. Curtis, *Report . . . on the Census of Boston, May, 1855,* p. 69.

31. According to Dr. Josiah Curtis, for example, environmental conditions eroded both moral and physical well-being; see *Report . . . on the Census of Boston, May, 1855,* pp. 64–104. In contrast, Dr. Jesse Chickering argued that high morbidity and mortality among both natives and foreigners resulted from their misguided behavior and values; see *Report . . . ; and also a Comparative View of the Population of Boston in 1850,* pp. 50–58.

32. For example, see Amariah Brigham, M.D., *Remarks on the Influence of Mental Cultivation and Mental Excitement upon Health,* 2d ed. (Boston: Marsh, Capen & Lyon, 1833), viii–ix.

33. Beecher, *Letters to the People on Health and Happiness,* 129 (emphasis in original). Pages 121–33 cover Beecher's survey of women's health in America during the 1840s and 1850s, and pp. 112–20 give an account of Beecher's "personal experience" with ill-health and her long search for effective treatment.

34. Shattuck, "On the Vital Statistics of Boston," 384; also, Shattuck, *Report . . . Census of Boston for the Year 1845,* pp. 149–50.

35. Shattuck, *Report . . . Census of Boston for the Year 1845,* p. 150.

36. Shattuck, "On the Vital Statistics of Boston," 385.

37. Using Shattuck's information, I calculated percent of all mortality and percent of population for males and females in various age groups (in five- and ten-year increments from ages 0 to 100). The raw data came from Shattuck, *Report . . . Census of Boston for the Year 1845,* appendices F and UU.

38. Among the more important discussions are Carroll Smith-Rosenberg, "Puberty to Menopause: The Cycle of Femininity in Nineteenth-Century America," *Feminist Studies* 1 (Winter–Spring 1973): 58–72; Carroll Smith-Rosenberg and Charles E. Rosenberg, "The Female Animal: Medical and Biological Views of Woman and Her Role in Nineteenth-Century America," *Journal of American History* 60 (Sept. 1973): 332–56; and Ann Douglas Wood, "'The Fashionable Diseases': Women's Complaints and Their Treatment in Nineteenth-Century America," *Journal of Interdisciplinary History* 4 (Summer 1973): 25–52.

39. John Duffy, "Mental Strain and 'Overpressure' in the Schools: A Nineteenth-Century Viewpoint," *Journal of the History of Medicine and Allied Sciences* 23 (Jan. 1968): 63–79.

40. "Dr. Grigg's Lecture," *Ladies' Magazine* 4 (Nov. 1831): 517.

41. *Ibid.* See also "Physical Education of Girls," *Journal of Health* 1 (Sept. 9, 1829): 14–16.

42. Abel L. Peirson, M.D., "On Physical Education," in *The Introductory Discourse, and the Lectures Delivered before the American Institute of Instruction, at Springfield, (Mass.) August, 1839. Including the Journal of Proceedings, and a List of the Officers* (Boston: Marsh, Capen, Lyon and Webb, 1840), 220.

43. *Ibid.*

44. Beecher, *Letters to the People on Health and Happiness,* 108.

45. *Ibid.,* 107 (emphasis in original).

46. Mary S. Gove, *Lectures to Women on Anatomy and Physiology. With an Appendix on Water Cure* (New York: Harper & Brothers, 1846), 245.

47. Gove, *Lectures to Ladies,* (1st ed., 1842), 27. See 27–28, 53–54, 61–63, 91–109 in general.

48. Jerome V. C. Smith, M.D., *The Class Book of Anatomy, Explanatory of the First Principles of Human Organization, as the Basis of Physical Education. Designed for Schools and Families,* 6th improved stereotype ed. (Boston: Robert S. Davis; Philadelphia: Hogan and Thompson, 1841), 42. For historical studies about the controversy over women's dress, see John S. Haller, Jr., and Robin M. Haller, *The Physician and Sexuality in Victorian America* (Urbana: Univ. of Illinois Press, 1974), 146–74; David Kunzle, *Fashion and Fetishism: A Social History of the Corset, Tight-Lacing and Other Forms of Body Sculpture in the West* (Totowa, N.J.: Rowman and Littlefield, 1982); Robert Riegel, "Women's Clothes and Women's Rights," *American Quarterly* 15 (Fall 1963): 390–401; and Helene E. Roberts, "The Exquisite Slave: The Role of Clothes in the Making of the Victorian Woman," *Signs* 2 (1976–77): 554–69.

49. "Nervous Disorders of Females," *Journal of Health* 2 (March 23, 1831): 223.

50. *Ibid.,* 223, 224. See also "Health of Women," *Library of Health and Teacher on the Human Constitution* 2 (March 1838): 97–98, and "Pains of Indolence," *Journal of Health* 1 (March 10, 1830): 202–3.

51. Beecher, *Letters to the People on Health and Happiness,* 121.

52. Useful, albeit partisan, accounts of Boston's economic growth are found in Justin Winsor, ed., *The Memorial History of Boston, Including Suffolk County, Massachusetts, 1630–1880,* 4 vols. (Boston: J. R. Osgood, 1880–81), IV: 69–234, and Albert Bushnell Hart, ed., *Commonwealth History of Massa-*

chusetts: Colony, Province, and State, 5 vols. (New York: States History Company, 1927–30), IV: 372–433. The experiences of different classes in the city are described in Handlin, *Boston's Immigrants,* rev. ed., 54–87; Knights, *The Plain People of Boston,* 78–102, 119–26; and Ronald Story, *The Forging of an Aristocracy: Harvard and the Boston Upper Class, 1800–1870* (Middletown, Conn.: Wesleyan Univ. Press, 1980).

53. Shattuck, *Report . . . Census of Boston for the Year 1845,* pp. 51, 84, and 82–85 in general. Shattuck reported that Boston's white population included 34,059 males over age 20 and 33,916 females over age 20. (In 1845, the black population totaled only 1,842; *ibid.,* 43.) Shattuck's tabulation of workers over age 20, which apparently excluded blacks as well, showed 24,887 males and 5,842 females.

54. Calculated from data in *ibid.,* 84.

55. On the pattern of employment among single and married women in nineteenth-century America, see Carl N. Degler, *At Odds: Women and the Family in America from the Revolution to the Present* (New York: Oxford Univ. Press, 1980), 374–75, 384–85, and 362–94 in general.

56. Vinovskis, *Fertility in Massachusetts,* 48–49. See also Robert V. Wells, "Women's Lives Transformed: Demographic and Family Patterns in America, 1600–1970," in *Women of America: A History,* Carol Ruth Berkin and Mary Beth Norton, eds. (Boston: Houghton Mifflin, 1979), 20.

57. Peter R. Uhlenberg, "A Study of Cohort Life Cycles: Cohorts of Native Born Massachusetts Women, 1830–1920," *Population Studies* 23 (Nov. 1969): 411. See also Wells, "Women's Lives Transformed," 20.

58. The following sources describe women's experiences during childbirth and their attitudes about changing modes of delivery from the eighteenth to twentieth century: Judith Walzer Leavitt, " 'Science' Enters the Birthing Room: Obstetrics in America since the Eighteenth Century," *Journal of American History* 70 (Sept. 1983): 281–304; Judith Walzer Leavitt and Whitney Walton, " 'Down to Death's Door': Women's Perceptions of Childbirth in America," in *Women and Health in America: Historical Readings,* Judith Walzer Leavitt, ed. (Madison: Univ. of Wisconsin Press, 1984), 155–65; Catherine M. Scholten, " 'On the Importance of the Obstetrick Art': Changing Customs of Childbirth in America, 1760–1825," in *ibid.,* 142–54; and Richard W. Wertz and Dorothy C. Wertz, *Lying-In: A History of Childbirth in America* (New York: Free Press, 1977).

59. Ruth Schwartz Cowan, *More Work for Mother: The Ironies of Household Technology from the Open Hearth to the Microwave* (New York: Basic Books, 1983), 40–68.

60. Vinovskis, *Fertility in Massachusetts,* 18, and 11–23 in general. See also Wells, "Women's Lives Transformed," 18–19.

61. Mary P. Ryan, *Womanhood in America: From Colonial Times to the Present* (New York: New Viewpoints, 1975), 57, 162, and Wells, "Women's Lives Transformed," 18.

62. For a discussion of birth control in nineteenth-century America, see Linda G. Gordon, *Woman's Body, Woman's Right: A Social History of Birth Control in America* (New York: Penguin Books, 1977), especially 3–71, and James Reed, *From Private Vice to Public Virtue: The Birth Control Movement and American Society since 1830* (New York: Basic Books, 1978), 3–45. See

Vinovskis, *Fertility in Massachusetts,* 73–154, for an analysis of factors that may have contributed to the declining birthrate. Little precise information is available concerning maternal death rates, or the relative risk at each successive birth, in the nineteenth century. Some estimates for earlier and later periods have been made. For example, see Leavitt, " 'Science' Enters the Birthing Room," and Wertz and Wertz, *Lying-In.* For discussions of the implications of the changing family profile for women's lives, see Uhlenberg, "A Study of Cohort Life Cycles," 415–19, and Wells, "Women's Lives Transformed," 25–27.

63. Overviews of that transformation include Donald Meyer, "The Dissolution of Calvinism," in *Paths of American Thought,* Arthur M. Schlesinger, Jr., and Morton White, eds. (Boston: Houghton Mifflin, 1970), 71–85, and Timothy L. Smith, *Revivalism and Social Reform: American Protestantism on the Eve of the Civil War,* reprint ed. (Baltimore: Johns Hopkins Univ. Press, 1980).

64. Informative studies about antebellum social reform include David Brion Davis, ed., *Ante-Bellum Reform* (New York: Harper & Row, 1967); Clifford S. Griffin, *The Ferment of Reform, 1830–1860,* Crowell American History Series (New York: Thomas Y. Crowell, 1967); and Ronald G. Walters, *American Reformers, 1815–1860,* American Century Series (New York: Hill and Wang, 1978).

65. The general state of orthodox medicine and public misgivings about doctors are examined in Joseph F. Kett, *The Formation of the American Medical Profession: The Role of Institutions, 1780–1860* (New Haven: Yale Univ. Press, 1968); William G. Rothstein, *American Physicians in the Nineteenth Century: From Sects to Science* (Baltimore: Johns Hopkins Univ. Press, 1972); and Paul Starr, *The Social Transformation of American Medicine* (New York: Basic Books, 1982). Secondary literature about nonorthodox medicine and health reform in the mid-nineteenth century is diverse. General surveys include John B. Blake, "Health Reform," in *The Rise of Adventism: Religion and Society in Mid-Nineteenth-Century America,* Edwin S. Gaustad, ed. (New York: Harper & Row, 1974), 30–49; Harvey Green, *Fit for America: Health, Fitness, Sport and American Society* (New York: Pantheon, 1986), 1–100; Guenter B. Risse, Ronald L. Numbers, and Judith Walzer Leavitt, eds., *Medicine without Doctors: Home Health Care in American History* (New York: Science History Publications/USA, 1977); William B. Walker, "The Health Reform Movement in the United States, 1830–1870" (Ph.D. dissertation, Johns Hopkins Univ., 1955); and James C. Whorton, *Crusaders for Fitness: The History of American Health Reformers* (Princeton: Princeton Univ. Press, 1982), 3–131. Among the studies about individual health crusaders or medical alternatives in the 1800s are John B. Blake, "Mary Gove Nichols, Prophetess of Health," *Proceedings of the American Philosophical Society* 106 (June 1962): 219–34; Martin Kaufman, *Homeopathy in America: The Rise and Fall of a Medical Heresy* (Baltimore: Johns Hopkins Univ. Press, 1971); Stephen Nissenbaum, *Sex, Diet, and Debility in Jacksonian America: Sylvester Graham and Health Reform* (Westport, Conn.: Greenwood Press, 1980); Ronald L. Numbers, *Prophetess of Health: A Study of Ellen G. White* (New York: Harper and Row, 1976); Harry B. Weiss and Howard R. Kemble, *The Great American Water-Cure Craze* (Trenton, N.J.: Past Times Press, 1967); and James Harvey Young, *The Toadstool Millionaires: A Social History of Patent Medicines in America be-*

fore Federal Regulation (Princeton: Princeton Univ. Press, 1961). Additional sources are cited in later notes and in the Selected Bibliography.

66. The phrase comes from William A. Alcott, *Forty Years in the Wilderness of Pills and Powders* (Boston: John P. Jewett, 1859).

67. "The Middle Classes," *Journal of Health* 1 (Aug. 11, 1830): 358. See also Henry H. Porter, *The Catechism of Health; or, Plain and Simple Rules for the Preservation of the Health and Vigour of the Constitution from Infancy to Old Age. For the Use of Schools,* 5th ed. (Philadelphia: Office of the Journal of Health, Journal of Law, and Family Library of Health, 1836), 14–15, 194–95, and Horace Mann, *Sixth Annual Report of the [Massachusetts] Board of Education, Together with the Sixth Annual Report of the Secretary of the Board* (Boston: Dutton and Wentworth, 1843), 77–79. Another example of good health as a middle-class emblem is found in eighteenth-century France; see William Coleman, "Health and Hygiene in the *Encyclopédie:* A Medical Doctrine for the Bourgeoisie," *Journal of the History of Medicine and Allied Sciences* 29 (Oct. 1974): 399–421.

2. *Moral Physiology and the Habits of a Healthy Life*

1. Catharine E. Beecher, *Physiology and Calisthenics. For Schools and Families* (New York: Harper & Brothers, 1856), v (emphasis in original). See also p. 172.

2. A. A. Livermore, "Gymnastics," *North American Review* 81 (July 1855): 51–52.

3. Beecher, *Physiology and Calisthenics,* v (emphasis in original).

4. "Remarks on Dress—No. II," *Moral Reformer and Teacher on the Human Constitution* 1 (Feb. 1835): 55. See also M. S. G., "Thoughts For Those Who Will Read Them," *Graham Journal of Health and Longevity* 2 (June 23, 1838): 199. (In all likelihood, the author was Mary S. Gove.)

5. The following discussion is based on a survey of literature about health and hygiene between 1830 and 1865. Sources included popular physiology books for schools and families; health magazines, pamphlets, and essays; and journals for women, teachers, and the general populace. (See the Selected Bibliography for a partial listing.) The sample emphasized materials that were representative of antebellum health reform and were available to middle-class Bostonians. In particular, the library of the Ladies' Physiological Institute of Boston and Vicinity included most of the items in the survey (see Chapter 3).

6. For example, Richard D. Brown, *Modernization: The Transformation of American Life, 1600–1865* (New York: Hill and Wang, 1976), especially 3–22, 94–121.

7. The intellectual context of the Northeast, and of New England in particular, during the mid-nineteenth century is discussed in Theodore Dwight Bozeman, *Protestants in an Age of Science: The Baconian Ideal and Antebellum American Religious Thought* (Chapel Hill: Univ. of North Carolina Press, 1977); George H. Daniels, *American Science in the Age of Jackson* (New York: Columbia Univ. Press, 1968); Daniel Walker Howe, *The Unitarian Conscience: Harvard Moral Philosophy, 1805–1861* (Cambridge, Mass.: Harvard

Univ. Press, 1970); and Charles E. Rosenberg, *No Other Gods: On Science & American Social Thought* (Baltimore: Johns Hopkins Univ. Press, 1976), 1–21.

8. Andrew Combe, M.D., *The Principles of Physiology Applied to the Preservation of Health, and to the Improvement of Physical and Mental Education* (New York: Harper & Brothers, 1839), 15–16. The works of Andrew Combe, a physiologist and phrenologist, and those of his brother George, a phrenologist, were popular in antebellum America.

9. For general background on physiology and medicine in the eighteenth and nineteenth centuries, see William Coleman, *Biology in the Nineteenth Century: Problems of Form, Function, and Transformation* (New York: John Wiley & Sons, 1971), 118–59; G. J. Goodfield, *The Growth of Scientific Physiology* (London: Hutchinson, 1960; New York: Arno Press, 1975); Lester S. King, *The Medical World of the Eighteenth Century* (Chicago: Univ. of Chicago Press, 1958), 59–226, 263–96; and Lester S. King, *The Philosophy of Medicine: The Early Eighteenth Century* (Cambridge, Mass.: Harvard Univ. Press, 1978).

10. See Stephen Nissenbaum, *Sex, Diet, and Debility in Jacksonian America: Sylvester Graham and Health Reform* (Westport, Conn.: Greenwood Press, 1980).

11. See James C. Whorton, *Crusaders for Fitness: The History of American Health Reformers* (Princeton: Princeton Univ. Press, 1982), 62–91.

12. For other discussions of popular physiology in mid-century America, see Gerald N. Grob, *Edward Jarvis and the Medical World of Nineteenth-Century America* (Knoxville: Univ. of Tennessee Press, 1978); Charles E. Rosenberg, "The Bitter Fruit: Heredity, Disease, and Social Thought in Nineteenth-Century America," *Perspectives in American History* 8 (1974): 189–235; Charles E. Rosenberg, "The Therapeutic Revolution: Medicine, Meaning, and Social Change in Nineteenth-Century America," in *The Therapeutic Revolution: Essays in the Social History of American Medicine,* Morris J. Vogel and Charles E. Rosenberg, eds. (Philadelphia: Univ. of Pennsylvania Press, 1979), 3–25; and Whorton, *Crusaders for Fitness,* 3–131. Two articles by John Rickards Betts are rather descriptive, but still useful: "Mind and Body in Early American Medical Thought," *Journal of American History* 54 (1967–68): 787–805, and "American Medical Thought on Exercise as the Road to Health, 1820–1860," *Bulletin of the History of Medicine* 45 (March–April 1971): 138–52.

13. John C. Warren, M.D., *Physical Education and the Preservation of Health,* 2d ed. (Boston: William D. Ticknor, 1846), 10.

14. Dio Lewis, *Weak Lungs, and How To Make Them Strong. Or Diseases of the Organs of the Chest, with Their Home Treatment by the Movement Cure* (Boston: Ticknor and Fields, 1863), 232.

15. For discussions of the concept of excitability, see Mary A. B. Brazier, "Historical Development of Neurophysiology," in *Handbook of Physiology, Section I: Neurophysiology,* John Field, ed. (Washington, D.C.: American Physiological Society, 1959), I: 1–58, and King, *The Medical World of the Eighteenth Century,* 123–55.

16. Charles Caldwell, M.D., *Thoughts on Physical Education: Being a Discourse Delivered to a Convention of Teachers in Lexington, Ky., on the 6th & 7th of Nov., 1833* (Boston: Marsh, Capen & Lyon, 1834), 36.

17. For example, see William A. Alcott, M.D., *The House I Live In; or*

The Human Body. For the Use of Families and Schools, 2d ed. (Boston: Light and Stearns, 1837), and Jerome V. C. Smith, M.D., *The Class Book of Anatomy, Explanatory of the First Principles of Human Organization, as the Basis of Physical Education. Designed for Schools and Families,* 6th improved stereotype ed. (Boston: Robert S. Davis; Philadelphia: Hogan and Thompson, 1841).

18. Sylvester Graham, *Lectures on the Science of Human Life,* 2 vols. (Boston: Marsh, Capen, Lyon and Webb, 1839), II: 93–95 (which summarizes Graham's general theory of depletion and replenishment) and II: 178–81 (which deals with muscle functioning).

19. *Ibid.,* I: 489.

20. *Ibid.,* I: 123.

21. Dio Lewis, *Our Girls* (New York: Harper & Brothers, 1871; reprint ed., New York: Arno Press and the *New York Times,* 1974), 233 (emphasis in original).

22. T. S. Lambert, M.D., *Hygienic Physiology* (Portland, Maine: Sanborn and Carter, 1852), 135.

23. B. N. Comings, M.D., *Class-Book of Physiology; For the Use of Schools and Families. Comprising the Structure and Functions of the Organs of Man, Illustrated by Comparative Reference to Those of Inferior Animals* (New York: D. Appleton, 1853), 150.

24. Elisha Bartlett, M.D., *Obedience to the Laws of Health, a Moral Duty. A Lecture, Delivered before the American Physiological Society, January 30, 1838* (Boston: Julius A. Noble, 1838), 16–17.

25. Edward Jarvis, M.D., *Primary Physiology, for Schools* (Philadelphia: Thomas, Cowperthwait, 1848), 7–8.

26. For a sample of nineteenth-century advice about sexual behavior, see Ronald G. Walters, *Primers for Prudery: Sexual Advice to Victorian America* (Englewood Cliffs, N.J.: Prentice-Hall, 1974).

27. Caldwell, *Thoughts on Physical Education,* 63.

28. *Ibid.* (emphasis in original).

29. "Health and Education," *Massachusetts Teacher* 9 (Dec. 1856): 560.

30. Catharine E. Beecher, *Letters to the People on Health and Happiness* (New York: Harper & Brothers, 1855; reprint ed., New York: Arno Press and the *New York Times,* 1972), 172 (emphasis in original).

31. *Ibid.*

32. Charles Lane, "Inward and Outward Life," *American Vegetarian and Health Journal* 2 (April 1852): 55.

33. *Ibid.*

34. *Ibid.*

35. *Ibid.,* 53.

36. "Quackery," *Teacher of Health and the Laws of the Human Constitution* 1 (Nov. 1843): 346.

37. For an overview of those philosophies, see Bozeman, *Protestants in an Age of Science,* and Howe, *The Unitarian Conscience,* especially 53–68.

38. "Address of Cyrus M. Burleigh, Esq.," *American Vegetarian and Health Journal* 1 (Oct. 1851): 172 (emphasis in original).

39. J. W. Colburn, "An Obstinate Case of Dyspepsy, with Its Train of Horrors," *Graham Journal of Health and Longevity* 2 (June 9, 1838): 191.

40. *Ibid.*

41. Abel L. Peirson, M.D., "On Physical Education," in *The Introductory Discourse, and the Lectures Delivered before the American Institute of Instruction, at Springfield, (Mass.) August, 1839. Including the Journal of Proceedings, and a List of the Officers* (Boston: Marsh, Capen, Lyon and Webb, 1840), 227.

42. Edward Jarvis, M.D., *Practical Physiology; For the Use of Schools and Families* (Philadelphia: Thomas, Cowperthwait, 1848), 362–63.

43. Bartlett, *Obedience to the Laws of Health, a Moral Duty*, 5–6.

44. D., " 'Every Man Makes His Own Health,' " *Graham Journal of Health and Longevity* 2 (Feb. 17, 1838): 61 (emphasis in original).

45. For a historical account, see Charles E. Rosenberg, "The Bitter Fruit." Two interesting examples of nature-nurture themes in antebellum health literature are Caldwell, *Thoughts on Physical Education*, and Frederick W. Bird, *Physiological Reform. An Address, Delivered before the American Physiological Society, at Their First Annual Meeting, June 1, 1837* (Boston: Marsh, Capen & Lyon, 1837), 36–39.

46. Dio Lewis, *Talks about People's Stomachs* (Boston: Fields, Osgood, 1870), 22, and 20–25 in general. See also *Dio Lewis's Monthly* 1 (Aug. 1883): 94–95.

47. Dio Lewis, M.D., "Physical Culture," *Massachusetts Teacher* 13 (Nov. 1860): 404. See also Larkin B. Coles, M.D., *Philosophy of Health: Natural Principles of Health and Cure; or, Health and Cure without Drugs. Also, the Moral Bearings of Erroneous Appetites*, revised and enlarged (Boston: Ticknor, Reed, & Fields, 1853), chap. 8.

48. Bartlett, *Obedience to the Laws of Health, a Moral Duty*, 20.

49. William A. Alcott, in *Second Annual Report of the American Physiological Society. June 1, 1838* (Boston: George W. Light, 1838), 35.

50. William A. Alcott, *The Young Woman's Book of Health* (New York and Auburn: Miller, Orton & Mulligan, 1855), 18.

51. T. W. Higginson, "Gymnastics," *Atlantic Monthly* 7 (March 1861): 301.

52. *Ibid.*

53. Dio Lewis, "Physical Culture—What Is It?," *Lewis' New Gymnastics for Ladies, Gentlemen, & Children, and Boston Journal of Physical Culture* 1 (March 1861): 73 (emphasis in original).

54. For historical background, see Stephen Kern, *Anatomy and Destiny: A Cultural History of the Human Body* (Indianapolis and New York: Bobbs-Merrill, 1975), and Anne Hollander, *Seeing Through Clothes* (New York: Viking, 1978).

55. "Training for Ladies," *Journal of Health* 3 (June 27, 1832): 315, and 315–16 in general.

56. Dio Lewis, *Five-Minute Chats with Young Women, and Certain Other Parties* (New York: Harper & Brothers, 1874), 49.

57. *Ibid.*

58. "Henry Ward Beecher on Physical Health," *Lewis' New Gymnastics for Ladies, Gentlemen, & Children, and Boston Journal of Physical Culture* 1 (Nov. 1860): 13.

59. Senex, "Female Education—No. II," *Annals of Education* 5 (July 1835): 314.

60. See Mary P. Ryan, *Womanhood in America: From Colonial Times to the Present* (New York: New Viewpoints, 1975), 137–91, and Barbara Welter, "The Cult of True Womanhood, 1820–1860," *American Quarterly* 18 (Summer 1966): 151–74.

61. William A. Alcott, *The Young Woman's Guide to Excellence,* 13th ed. (Boston: Charles H. Peirce, 1847), 93 (emphasis in original).

62. Caldwell, *Thoughts on Physical Education,* 60.

63. *Ibid.*

64. See sources in n. 60, and Kathryn Kish Sklar, *Catharine Beecher: A Study in American Domesticity* (New York: W. W. Norton, 1976).

65. "A Chapter To Be Read," *Ladies' Magazine* 5 (Nov. 1832): 518.

66. Beecher, *Letters to the People on Health and Happiness,* 123.

67. Lewis, "Recreation *vs.* Propriety," in *Our Girls,* 337. The following quotations all come from *ibid.,* 337–38 (emphasis in original). See also "Physical Education of Girls," *Journal of Health* 1 (Sept. 9, 1829): 14–16.

68. Lewis, *Five-Minute Chats,* 185.

69. *Ibid.*

70. Lewis, "Employments for Women," in *Our Girls,* 131–72.

71. "The Din of Pots and Kettles," *Moral Reformer and Teacher on the Human Constitution* 2 (July 1836): 212.

72. *Ibid.,* 214.

73. Anne Denton, "The Rights of Woman," *American Vegetarian and Health Journal* 2 (Dec. 1852): 187.

74. "The Din of Pots and Kettles," 213.

75. Lewis, "The Language of Dress," in *Our Girls,* 50.

76. Lewis, "Large vs. Small Women," in *Our Girls,* 86, and 85–92 in general.

77. Dio Lewis, *The Dio Lewis Treasury* (New York: Canfield, 1887), 686–87.

78. Lewis, "The Language of Dress," in *Our Girls,* 50. See also *Dio Lewis Treasury,* 687.

79. Feminist authors have made a similar point about contemporary ideals of slimness. They argue that norms about the size and shape of the female body are tied to women's social position and, therefore, vary over time and by culture. For example, see Kim Chernin, *The Obsession: Reflections on the Tyranny of Slenderness* (New York: Harper & Row, 1981).

3. "Know Thyself"

1. Alexis de Tocqueville, *Democracy in America,* Henry Reeve text, revised by Francis Bowen, notes by Phillips Bradley (New York: Alfred A. Knopf, 1945), II: 106.

2. *Ibid.*

3. Popular health journals of the period enthusiastically reported the establishment and activities of such organizations. See *Graham Journal of Health and Longevity* (1837–39) and the series edited by William A. Alcott, including *Library of Health and Teacher on the Human Constitution* 4 (Jan. 1840): 39–40.

4. See Hebbel E. Hoff and John F. Fulton, "The Centenary of the First American Physiological Society Founded at Boston by William A. Alcott and Sylvester Graham," *Bulletin of the History of Medicine* 5 (Oct. 1937): 687–734, and Stephen Nissenbaum, *Sex, Diet, and Debility in Jacksonian America: Sylvester Graham and Health Reform* (Westport, Conn.: Greenwood Press, 1980), 143–45.

5. *Second Annual Report of the American Physiological Society. June 1, 1838* (Boston: George W. Light, 1838), 6. Notices and reports of the women's meetings were published in the *Graham Journal,* for example, 3 (March 2, 1839): 88.

6. References to such groups are scattered throughout popular health journals of the 1830s and 1840s; for example, see *Library of Health and Teacher on the Human Constitution* 4 (Jan. 1840): 39–40, and 5 (Jan. 1841): 40. The memoirs of physiological reformers contain similar citations; for example, see Harriot K. Hunt, *Glances and Glimpses; or Fifty Years Social, Including Twenty Years Professional Life* (Boston: John P. Jewett, 1856), 170–71, 177–80, 247–48. See also Richard H. Shryock, "Sylvester Graham and the Popular Health Movement, 1830–1870," *Mississippi Valley Historical Review* 18 (Sept. 1931): 176, and 172–83 in general.

7. The surviving records and memorabilia of the Institute are housed at the Arthur M. and Elizabeth Schlesinger Library on the History of Women in America, Radcliffe College, Cambridge, Mass. The collection, hereafter designated LPI, includes record books from 1850–57, 1881–86, and 1937–44, and assorted other materials.

8. The memoirs of Mrs. Eunice Hale Waite Cobb (1803–80), a founder, officer, and guiding spirit of the group, consist of a five-volume set of details and reflections about her life. The diaries are housed in the Rare Book Department, Boston Public Library, Boston, Mass. Hereafter, the collection will be designated E. H. W. Cobb diary, BPL.

9. The following account is based primarily on the Institute's manuscript records, LPI. The sources include books of minutes (volume I: Jan. 1850 to Jan. 1851; volume II: Jan. 1851 to May 1854; and volume III: May 1854 to May 1857); a volume covering board of directors' meetings (IV: Jan. 1851 to April 1857); and a treasurer's book (volume V). Yearly reports in those records will be referred to as "Second Ann. Report," "Third Ann. Report," and so on. Citations will follow the format of each volume: page numbers in I and II, dates in III and IV.

10. From the Institute's report of 1848, quoted in "The Secretary's Review of Fifty Years, 1898," in *Ladies' Physiological Institute. Semi-Centennial Report. In Memoriam—Salome Merritt, M.D.* (Boston: n.p., 1900?), 20 (hereafter cited as *Semi-Centennial Report*). Other accounts appear in "Second Ann. Report," I: 45, LPI; "Sixth Ann. Report," II: 247–48, LPI; and *Synopsis of the Proceedings of the Second Annual Meeting of the Ladies' Physiological Institute of Boston and Vicinity. With the Secretary's Report, and the Constitution and By-laws of the Society, with Catalogue of Library* (Boston: Alfred Mudge, 1851), 4 (hereafter designated *Second Annual Meeting*). Notices and accounts of the organizational meetings also appeared in the *Boston Daily Evening Transcript* during April and May 1848. It should be noted that $1,000 was a

considerable sum of money in 1848, leading one to wonder about Bronson's motives.

11. The Boston city directory listed Bronson as a "physician and oculist." He explained the principles of his elocutionary system in *Elocution; or, Mental and Vocal Philosophy: Involving the Principles of Reading and Speaking; and Designed for the Development and Cultivation of Both Body and Mind; in Accordance with the Nature, Uses, and Destiny of Man,* 5th ed. (Boston: Otis Clapp, and Crosby, Nichols, 1845). In 1856, Bronson and his wife, a noted elocutionist and social activist, moved to New York, where he died in 1868 and she in 1885. (See obituary in *New York Daily Tribune,* Sept. 26, 1885.)

12. Area doctors debated Bronson's work through the pages of the *Boston Medical and Surgical Journal:* "Prof. Bronson's Lectures on Oratory," 22 (July 1, 1840): 336–37; "New School of Elocution—Prof. Bronson," 22 (July 29, 1840): 396–98; and "Respiratory Apparatus—Mr. Bronson, &c.," 23 (Aug. 26, 1840): 49–51.

13. "Second Ann. Report," I: 45, and "Sixth Ann. Report," II: 248–49, LPI, and *Second Annual Meeting,* 4.

14. Printed in *Second Annual Meeting,* 13 (emphasis in original).

15. IV: Nov. 25, 1853, LPI; also, "Sixth Ann. Report," II: 254, and III: May 3, 1855, LPI.

16. Invariably, annual reports commented on the size and condition of the library. Summaries of progress during the early years are found in "Sixth Ann. Report," II: 249–55, LPI.

17. "Third Ann. Report," II: 42, LPI.

18. The entire contents were listed in *Second Annual Meeting,* 12 and in *Constitution and By-laws of the Ladies' Physiological Institute, of Boston and Vicinity* (Boston: Alfred Mudge & Son, 1857), 2.

19. The following examples were drawn from the minute books, I–III, LPI. In most cases, only the lecturer's name and topic were listed. Occasionally, a synopsis or the secretary's personal reflections were included.

20. I: 109, LPI.

21. Information about the Institute during the 1860s and 1870s is based primarily on E. H. W. Cobb diary, BPL.

22. "Second Ann. Report," I: 51, LPI, and *Second Annual Meeting,* 9.

23. "Seventh Ann. Report," III: May 3, 1855, LPI.

24. "Third Ann. Report," II: 46, LPI; also, "Seventh Ann. Report," III: May 3, 1855, LPI.

25. *Ninth Annual Meeting of the Ladies' Physiological Institute, May Sixth, 1857* (Boston: Alfred Mudge & Son, 1857), 11 (hereafter cited as *Ninth Annual Meeting*). This statement was a virtual repeat of "Fourth Ann. Report," II: 132–33, LPI.

26. *Ninth Annual Meeting,* 11.

27. E. H. W. Cobb diary, V: 60 (Dec. 9, 1877), BPL (emphasis in original).

28. "Fourth Ann. Report," II: 138, LPI.

29. "Third Ann. Report," II: 46–47, LPI.

30. *Ibid.,* 47.

31. "Fourth Ann. Report," II: 137–37 [sic], LPI.

32. "Third Ann. Report," II: 34, LPI.

33. "Second Ann. Report," I: 52, LPI; also, *Second Annual Meeting,* 9.

34. "Third Ann. Report," II: 47, LPI (emphasis in original).

35. I: 123, LPI.

36. E. H. W. Cobb diary, V: 79 (Feb. 28, 1878), BPL (emphasis in original).

37. III: June 10, 1856, LPI.

38. III: June 18, June 25, July 2, and July 16, 1856, LPI.

39. The speakers listed in Institute records were identified through various primary and secondary sources. The former included general medical registers, medical society catalogues, city directories, and obituaries from the nineteenth century. Secondary materials included standard references such as the *Dictionary of American Biography,* Allen Johnson and Dumas Malone, eds., 20 vols. (New York: C. Scribner's Sons, 1928–36), and *American Medical Biographies,* Howard A. Kelly and Walter L. Burrage, eds. (Baltimore: Norman, Remington, 1920), and historical accounts of various nineteenth-century medical sects and health reform groups.

40. Based on entries in E. H. W. Cobb diary, II–V, BPL.

41. Histories of those struggles include Joseph F. Kett, *The Formation of the American Medical Profession: The Role of Institutions, 1780–1860* (New Haven: Yale Univ. Press, 1968); William G. Rothstein, *American Physicians in the Nineteenth Century: From Sects to Science* (Baltimore: Johns Hopkins Univ. Press, 1972); and Paul Starr, *The Social Transformation of American Medicine* (New York: Basic Books, 1982).

42. II: 22–23, LPI.

43. *Ibid.*

44. The only exception was a discussion in 1850 over petitioning Congress for "the repeal of certain Laws, whereby certain privileges now enjoyed by Medical Colleges, may be secured to similar institutions with our own, including schools" (I: 27, LPI). Because of incomplete records, the exact nature of the complaint and its eventual disposition are not known.

45. M. A. Sawin, "Physiological Instruction to Women," *Boston Medical and Surgical Journal* 41 (Oct. 10, 1849): 201. (Hereafter designated *BMSJ.*)

46. "Physiological Lectures for Ladies," *BMSJ* 41 (Oct. 10, 1849): 206.

47. *Ibid.*

48. *Ibid.*

49. "Ladies' Physiological Institute," *BMSJ* 48 (June 29, 1853): 443.

50. *Ibid.,* 444.

51. The following analysis is based on a survey of the *BMSJ* from its inception in 1828 to 1870. Two qualifications are required. First, the discussion considers regular doctors' views about popular instruction in the form of public courses, lyceums, voluntary associations, and sectarian and popular health books. Their opinions about instruction in other settings, such as schools and similar institutions, often differed from those related here. Second, public rhetoric did not necessarily correspond to private behavior. Frequently, regular doctors' social and professional relations with sectarian practitioners were cordial and open. Distinctions and dangers that seemed so important in principle were often overlooked in practice.

52. Medicus, " 'Popular Physiology,' " *BMSJ* 43 (Sept. 25, 1850): 152.

53. "Popular Anatomy," *BMSJ* 34 (May 6, 1846): 285.

54. "Anatomical Museum," *BMSJ* 35 (Nov. 4, 1846): 283. Also, "Popular Instruction in Anatomy and Medicine," *BMSJ* 15 (Aug. 10, 1836): 19; "Popular Lectures on Anatomy," *BMSJ* 27 (Oct. 26, 1842): 208; and "Travelling Manakins [sic]," *BMSJ* 30 (March 13, 1844): 124–25.

55. "Lectures to Ladies on Anatomy and Physiology," *BMSJ* 26 (March 16, 1842): 97, and 97–98 in general. Also, "Popular Lectures on Tight Lacing," *BMSJ* 12 (July 1, 1835): 336–37; " 'Lectures to Ladies on Anatomy and Physiology,' by Mary S. Gove," *BMSJ* 25 (Jan. 12, 1842): 374; and "Female Hygiene," *BMSJ* 48 (April 20, 1853): 244.

56. J. D. Mansfield, "Dr. Lambert's Popular Anatomy and Physiology—Quackery, &c.," *BMSJ* 42 (April 24, 1850): 249.

57. Medicus, " 'Popular Physiology,' " *BMSJ* 43 (Sept. 25, 1850): 152.

58. Wm. W. Finch, M.D., "Popular Physiology," *BMSJ* 43 (Sept. 18, 1850): 133–34 (emphasis in original).

59. *Ibid.,* 133 (emphasis in original).

60. Mansfield, "Dr. Lambert's Popular Anatomy and Physiology," *BMSJ* 42 (April 24, 1850): 249.

61. Finch, "Popular Physiology," *BMSJ* 43 (Sept. 18, 1850): 134. Also, *BMSJ* 21 (Sept. 11, 1839): 85, and Mansfield, "Dr. Lambert's Popular Anatomy and Physiology," *BMSJ* 42 (April 24, 1850): 250.

62. M. L. North, "On the Expediency of Popular Lectures on Health by Physicians," *BMSJ* 12 (July 15, 1835): 370, and 365–70 in general.

63. "Theory of Respiration," *BMSJ* 45 (Dec. 3, 1851): 376.

64. From "Man's Physical Being and Disorders," *BMSJ* 38 (Feb. 23, 1848): 84; "Large Profits on a Small Capital," *BMSJ* 30 (June 12, 1844): 384 (emphasis in original); I. F. Galloupe, "Popular Physiology," *BMSJ* 43 (Aug. 21, 1850): 59; and "Clairvoyancy," *BMSJ* 45 (Aug. 20, 1851): 65. See also N. H. Allen, "Ultraism," *BMSJ* 21 (Dec. 4, 1839): 270–73.

65. "Lectures on Mesmerism," *BMSJ* 29 (Jan. 10, 1844): 466. Similar points are developed in "American Physiological Society," *BMSJ* 20 (July 31, 1839): 398–99; "Medical Miscellany," *BMSJ* 22 (April 22, 1840): 179; "Water Curing," *BMSJ* 29 (Jan. 3, 1844): 444; and J. D. Mansfield, "Dr. Lambert's Second Book on Anatomy and Physiology," *BMSJ* 44 (Feb. 12, 1851): 36.

66. Galloupe, "Popular Physiology," *BMSJ* 43 (Aug. 21, 1850): 60.

67. "Itinerant Lecturers on Anatomy and Physiology," *BMSJ* 71 (Dec. 29, 1864): 444; also, Galloupe, "Popular Physiology," *BMSJ* 43 (Aug. 21, 1850): 60–62.

68. "Travelling Manakins," *BMSJ* 30 (March 13, 1844): 124. Also, "Practical Schools of Anatomy," *BMSJ* 39 (Sept. 27, 1848): 185; "Popular Anatomical Lectures," *BMSJ* 40 (March 7, 1849): 104; "Itinerant Lecturers on Anatomy and Physiology," *BMSJ* 71 (Dec. 29, 1864): 443–44; and "The Present Position of the Medical Profession," *BMSJ* 78 (Feb. 27, 1868): 60–62.

69. "Anatomical Museum," *BMSJ* 35 (Nov. 4, 1846): 283. Also, "Itinerant Lecturers on Anatomy and Physiology," *BMSJ* 71 (Dec. 29, 1864): 443–44.

70. "Popular Lectures on Tight Lacing," *BMSJ* 12 (July 1, 1835): 336 (emphasis in original).

71. "Itinerant Lecturers on Anatomy and Physiology," *BMSJ* 71 (Dec. 29, 1864): 444.

72. "Large Profits on a Small Capital," *BMSJ* 30 (June 12, 1844): 385.

73. "Practical Schools of Anatomy," *BMSJ* 39 (Sept. 27, 1848): 185.

74. "Fourth Ann. Report," II: 134, LPI. Also in *Ninth Annual Meeting,* 12.

75. For example, "Third Ann. Report," II: 39–40, and "Seventh Ann. Report," III: May 3, 1855, LPI.

76. I: 27, and "Third Ann. Report," II: 40, LPI.

77. *Second Annual Meeting,* 13 (emphasis in original). The only discussions of such a possibility are recorded in "Sixth Ann. Report," II: 253–54, and IV: April 29, 1854, LPI.

78. Methodological problems associated with these sources, especially directories, have been discussed by several scholars, including those who pioneered the techniques. For example, see Peter R. Knights, "Using City Directories in Ante-Bellum Urban Historical Research," *Historical Methods Newsletter* 2 (Sept. 1969): 1–10 (and reprinted as Appendix A in *The Plain People of Boston, 1830–1860: A Study in City Growth* (New York: Oxford Univ. Press, 1971)); Stephan Thernstrom and Peter R. Knights, "Men in Motion: Some Data and Speculations about Urban Population Mobility in Nineteenth-Century America," in *Anonymous Americans: Explorations in Nineteenth-Century Social History,* Tamara K. Hareven, ed. (Englewood Cliffs, N.J.: Prentice-Hall, 1971), 17–47; and Stephan Thernstrom, *The Other Bostonians: Poverty and Progress in the American Metropolis, 1880–1970* (Cambridge, Mass.: Harvard Univ. Press, 1973), Appendix A.

79. Peter R. Uhlenberg, "A Study of Cohort Life Cycles: Cohorts of Native Born Massachusetts Women, 1830–1920," *Population Studies* 23 (Nov. 1969): 410–11. See also Robert V. Wells, "Women's Lives Transformed: Demographic and Family Patterns in America, 1600–1970," in *Women of America: A History,* Carol Ruth Berkin and Mary Beth Norton, eds. (Boston: Houghton Mifflin, 1979), 20–23.

80. Carl N. Degler, *At Odds: Women and the Family in America from the Revolution to the Present* (New York: Oxford Univ. Press, 1980), 155–56, 374–75, 383–84, and 362–94 in general.

81. Comparative figures were calculated from Knights, *The Plain People of Boston,* Table V–1, p. 84 (1850 census).

82. *List of Persons, Copartnerships, and Corporations, Who Were Taxed Twenty Five Dollars and Upwards, in the City of Boston, in the Year 1842,* (1843, City Document #9); *List of Persons, . . . Taxed Twenty-five Dollars and Upward, . . . in the Year 1847,* (1848, City Document #12); and *List of Persons, . . . Taxed on Six Thousand Dollars and Upwards, . . . in the Year 1855,* (1856, City Document #22). See also Knights, *The Plain People of Boston,* 89–90.

83. The geographical divisions of Boston and their character are described in Knights, *The Plain People of Boston,* 11–18; Sam Bass Warner, Jr., *Streetcar Suburbs: The Process of Growth in Boston, 1870–1900,* 2d ed. (Cambridge, Mass.: Harvard Univ. Press, 1978); and Walter Muir Whitehill, *Boston: A Topographical History,* 2d ed. (Cambridge, Mass.: Belknap Press of Harvard Univ. Press, 1968).

84. No information was found on Mrs. F. A. M. Baldwin, recording secretary, 1848–50 and president, 1851–52.

85. See "Sylvanus Cobb (1798–1866)," *Dictionary of American Biography*

4: 245–46; E. H. W. Cobb diary, BPL; an obituary about her in the *Boston Advertiser,* May 4, 1880; and an entry in *Sketches of Representative Women of New England,* Julia Ward Howe, ed. (Boston: New England Historical Publishing, 1904), 136–40.

86. See Hunt's autobiography, *Glances and Glimpses,* and a biographical sketch in *Notable American Women, 1607–1950,* Edward T. James, ed., 3 vols. (Cambridge, Mass.: Belknap Press of Harvard Univ. Press, 1971), 2: 235–37.

87. See Frederick C. Waite, "Dr. Martha A. (Hayden) Sawin: The First Woman Graduate in Medicine to Practice in Boston," *New England Journal of Medicine* 205 (Nov. 26, 1931): 1053–55.

88. See *Notable American Women, 1607–1950* 1: 428–29.

89. See *Notable American Women, 1607–1950* 3: 265–68.

90. E. H. W. Cobb diary, II: 17 (Sept. 6, 1864), BPL.

91. "Sixth Ann. Report," II: 251, LPI. Membership figures were noted in the recording secretary's annual reports. The fluctuations become more apparent when yearly changes in membership are calculated for 1849 to 1857: $-34\%, +7\%, -26\%, -27\%, -24\%, +18\%, +14\%,$ and $+70\%$.

92. The second figure comes from a news clipping found in E. H. W. Cobb diary, II, BPL. Cobb recorded the last tally after attending a special Institute meeting in 1871; see E. H. W. Cobb diary, IV: 91 (Jan. 5, 1871), BPL.

93. Turnover rates were calculated from information in the annual reports about total and new membership, and double-checked through tabulations of new admissions reported in weekly minutes.

94. *Ninth Annual Meeting,* 9.

95. *Second Annual Meeting,* 7; "Fourth Ann. Report," II: 120, LPI; and *Ninth Annual Meeting,* 9–11.

96. "Third Ann. Report," II: 44–45, LPI.

97. Anne Firor Scott, "On Seeing and Not Seeing: A Case of Historical Invisibility," *Journal of American History* 71 (June 1984): 7–21.

98. Barbara J. Berg, *The Remembered Gate: Origins of American Feminism—The Woman & the City, 1800–1860,* Urban Life in America Series (New York: Oxford Univ. Press, 1978), 145, 158.

99. For example, see Estelle Freedman, "Separatism as Strategy: Female Institution Building and American Feminism, 1870–1930," *Feminist Studies* 5 (Fall 1979): 512–29, and Mary P. Ryan, "The Power of Women's Networks: A Case Study of Female Moral Reform in Antebellum America," *Feminist Studies* 5 (Spring 1979): 66–85.

100. Nancy F. Cott, *The Bonds of Womanhood: "Woman's Sphere" in New England, 1780–1835* (New Haven: Yale Univ. Press, 1977).

101. Kathryn Kish Sklar, *Catharine Beecher: A Study in American Domesticity* (New York: W. W. Norton, 1976).

102. Karen J. Blair, *The Clubwoman as Feminist: True Womanhood Redefined, 1868–1914* (New York: Holmes & Meier, 1980), 4.

103. *Ibid.*

104. See Berg, *The Remembered Gate*; Barbara Leslie Epstein, *The Politics of Domesticity: Women, Evangelism, and Temperance in Nineteenth-Century America* (Middletown, Conn.: Wesleyan Univ. Press, 1981); Keith E. Melder, *Beginnings of Sisterhood: The American Woman's Rights Movement, 1800–1850* (New York: Schocken Books, 1977); Ryan, "The Power of

Women's Networks"; and Carroll Smith-Rosenberg, "Beauty, the Beast and the Militant Woman: A Case Study in Sex Roles and Social Stress in Jacksonian America," *American Quarterly* 23 (Oct. 1971): 562–84.

105. Ryan, "The Power of Women's Networks," 82.

106. Epstein, *The Politics of Domesticity,* 1–9, 84–87, 128–37, 147–51.

107. Ryan, "The Power of Women's Networks," and Smith-Rosenberg, "Beauty, the Beast and the Militant Woman."

108. Examples are found in Melder, *Beginnings of Sisterhood.*

109. For example, see Shryock, "Sylvester Graham and the Popular Health Movement, 1830–1870," and Barbara Ehrenreich and Deirdre English, *For Her Own Good: 150 Years of the Experts' Advice to Women* (Garden City, N.Y.: Anchor Books, 1979), 48–58.

110. For example, Regina Markell Morantz-Sanchez has argued that health reform offered both a platform for feminists and reassuring advice for more conventional women. See Morantz, "Nineteenth Century Health Reform and Women: A Program of Self-Help," in *Medicine without Doctors: Home Health Care in American History,* Guenter B. Risse, Ronald L. Numbers, and Judith Walzer Leavitt, eds. (New York: Science History Publications/USA, 1977), 73–93; Morantz, "Making Women Modern: Middle Class Women and Health Reform in 19th Century America," *Journal of Social History* 10 (Summer 1977): 490–507; and Morantz-Sanchez, *Sympathy and Science: Women Physicians in American Medicine* (New York: Oxford Univ. Press, 1985), 28–46. That position is also developed in a previous version of this chapter; see Martha H. Verbrugge, "The Social Meaning of Personal Health: The Ladies' Physiological Institute of Boston and Vicinity in the 1850s," in *Health Care in America: Essays in Social History,* Susan Reverby and David Rosner, eds. (Philadelphia: Temple Univ. Press, 1979), 45–66.

111. Among the important studies are Cott, *The Bonds of Womanhood,* and Carroll Smith-Rosenberg, "The Female World of Love and Ritual: Relations between Women in Nineteenth-Century America," *Signs* 1 (Autumn 1975): 1–29.

112. "Third Ann. Report," II: 38, LPI.

113. *Ibid.*

114. E. H. W. Cobb diary, IV: 137 (April 28, 1871), BPL.

115. *Ibid.,* IV: Jan. 24, 1872.

116. *Ibid.,* II: 128–29 (Oct. 12, 1865).

117. *Second Annual Meeting,* 4.

118. Although Bronson continued lecturing before the Institute, the once-friendly relationship seemed to sour. In the spring of 1851, the Institute voted against "making our former President a Professor" because it was "inexpedient" ("Third Ann. Report," II: 36, LPI). A month later, the group invited Bronson to come and "defend himself against the charges made against him" (II: 58, LPI). Further details about those incidents are not known.

119. IV: 4–5, and II: 5, LPI.

120. "Third Ann. Report," II: 42, LPI.

121. *Ibid.,* and "Fourth Ann. Report," II: 126, LPI.

122. Cott, *The Bonds of Womanhood,* 187 (emphasis in original), and 187–88 in general.

123. For example, see the studies cited above in notes 98–104, and Susan Porter Benson, "Business Heads and Sympathizing Hearts: The Women of the Providence Employment Society, 1837–1858," *Journal of Social History* 12 (Winter 1978): 302–12.

124. The groups included the Boston Female Anti-Slavery Society, Boston Children's Friend Society, City Missionary Society, Boston Fatherless and Widows' Society, the Massachusetts Home Missionary Society, and the Ladies' American Home Education and Temperance Union. (Since the survey covered only a limited number of groups and years, it may have missed Institute women who joined those organizations at other times and those who were members of societies outside the survey, such as ladies' groups in local churches.)

125. III: May 9, 1855, LPI (emphasis in original).

126. I: 109, LPI.

127. I: 95 (Oct. 9, 1850), and II: 151 (Sept. 15, 1852), LPI.

128. E. H. W. Cobb diary, II: 202 (May 31, 1866), and IV: 219 (Dec. 28, 1871), BPL.

129. I: 71–72 and 74, LPI.

130. I: 118–19, LPI.

131. "Second Ann. Report," I: 52, LPI. Also printed in *Second Annual Meeting,* 9.

132. "Second Ann. Report," I: 54, LPI.

133. E. H. W. Cobb diary, II: 95 (July 14, 1865), BPL (emphasis in original).

134. For example, *ibid.,* II: 73 (March 18, 1865), II: 192–93 (May 8–10, 1866), II: 222–23 (Aug. 2–5, 1866), and IV: 203 (Nov. 17, 1871).

135. *Ibid.,* V: 159 (Nov. 16, 1878), and IV: 117 (March 14, 1871).

136. *Ibid.,* II: 153–56 (Jan. 13, 1866), V: 38–40, 42–43 (Sept. 26, Sept. 30, and Oct. 5, 1877), and V: 160 (Nov. 18, 1878).

137. *Ibid.,* IV: 100–101 (Jan. 25, 1871).

138. The practical and psychological value of physiological knowledge for women has also been discussed by Regina Markell Morantz-Sanchez. See Morantz, "Nineteenth Century Health Reform and Women: A Program of Self-Help"; Morantz, "Making Women Modern: Middle Class Women and Health Reform in 19th Century America"; and Morantz-Sanchez, *Sympathy and Science,* 28–46.

139. More information about these women is found in "Signor Sarti's Anatomical, Physiological and Pathological Collection," *BMSJ* 42 (July 17, 1850): 498, and "Medical Miscellany," *BMSJ* 43 (Oct. 9, 1850): 207; Frederick C. Waite, "Dr. Nancy E. (Talbot) Clarke: The Second Woman Graduate in Medicine to Practice in Boston," *New England Journal of Medicine* 205 (Dec. 17, 1931): 1195–98; "Lydia Folger Fowler," *Notable American Women, 1607–1950* 1: 654–55; and "Paulina Kellogg Wright Davis," *Notable American Women, 1607–1950* 1: 444–45.

140. IV: 9, 11 (board meetings, March 28 and April 25, 1851), and II: 69–70 (weekly minutes, Sept. 3, 1851), LPI.

141. "Fourth Ann. Report," II: 125, LPI.

142. "Third Ann. Report," II: 41, LPI.

143. "Fourth Ann. Report," II: 131, LPI.

144. I: 102, and "Third Ann. Report," II: 38–39, LPI.

145. See Morantz-Sanchez, *Sympathy and Science,* and Mary Roth Walsh, *"Doctors Wanted: No Women Need Apply": Sexual Barriers in the Medical Profession, 1835–1975* (New Haven: Yale Univ. Press, 1977).

146. Morantz-Sanchez, *Sympathy and Science,* 49, 81–84; Walsh, *"Doctors Wanted: No Women Need Apply,"* chaps. 1 and 2; and Frederick C. Waite, *History of the New England Female Medical College, 1848–1874* (Boston: Boston Univ. School of Medicine, 1950).

147. *Second Annual Meeting,* 15.

148. I: 127–28 (board meeting, Dec. 27, 1850), LPI.

149. Walsh, *"Doctors Wanted: No Women Need Apply,"* 76–83.

150. III: Oct. 15, 1856, LPI.

151. III: Dec. 10 and Dec. 24, 1856, LPI, and *Ninth Annual Meeting,* 7–8.

152. E. H. W. Cobb diary, V: [208] (June 1, 1879), BPL (emphasis in original).

153. *Ibid.,* IV: 88 (Dec. 30, 1870). A remark opposing women ministers is found in *ibid.,* II: 2 (July 24, 1864).

154. *Ibid.,* IV: 36 (July 15, 1870).

155. I have borrowed the classifications of woman-oriented, woman-defined, and man-defined from Gerda Lerner, *The Majority Finds Its Past: Placing Women in History* (New York: Oxford Univ. Press, 1979), 146.

156. Printed in *Semi-Centennial Report,* 28 (emphasis in original).

4. *In Private and In Public*

1. Henry James, *The Bostonians* (New York: Macmillan, 1886). Citations refer to the 1966 Penguin edition (reprint ed., 1973).

2. *Ibid.,* 25.

3. *Ibid.,* 154.

4. *Ibid.,* 154.

5. *Ibid.,* 223.

6. The following discussion is based on the only surviving manuscript records from this period, "Secretary's Reports. May 1881–1886," in the Papers of the Ladies' Physiological Institute of Boston and Vicinity, Arthur M. and Elizabeth Schlesinger Library on the History of Women in America, Radcliffe College, Cambridge, Mass. (hereafter designated VI, LPI). Though it covers only a brief span of time, the volume is especially valuable for its summaries of lectures (whereas the minutes from the 1850s listed only titles and speakers). The volume, however, is equally cryptic regarding business affairs and controversies within the Institute.

7. Background information about speakers was ascertained through standard biographical dictionaries and various primary sources, such as medical registers, obituaries, and city directories.

8. Data on circulation came from several annual reports of the recording secretary, including VI: May 12, 1881, May 10, 1883, and May 8, 1884, LPI.

9. From the annual reports of the secretary, VI, LPI; my own tally of memberships taken, as recorded in weekly minutes, VI, LPI; and a list in *Ladies' Physiological Institute. Semi-Centennial Report. In Memoriam—Salome*

Merritt, M.D. (Boston: n.p., 1900?), 29–33 (hereafter cited *Semi-Centennial Report*).

10. Based on the recording secretary's annual reports about total membership and number of new members, in VI, LPI. For 1881–85, the renewal rates were 70, 78, 82, and 86 percent.

11. From obituaries in the *Boston Evening Transcript,* Jan. 7, 1884, p. 3, and Jan. 9, 1884, p. 8.

12. VI: April 17, April 24, and May 1, 1884, LPI. (During the previous three elections, an average of 35 percent had voted, according to information in VI: May 5, 1881, May 4, 1882, and May 3, 1883, LPI.)

13. The following sketch derives from an obituary in the *Boston Evening Transcript,* Nov. 8, 1900, p. 10; memorial addresses in *Semi-Centennial Report,* 37–65; an entry in *Sketches of Representative Women of New England,* Julia Ward Howe, ed. (Boston: New England Historical Publishing, 1904), 299–301; and private correspondence with Mrs. C. L. Gardner, a current member of the Institute and a grandniece of Dr. Merritt.

14. *Semi-Centennial Report,* 43–46.

15. *Boston Evening Transcript,* Nov. 8, 1900, p. 10.

16. Information about O'Leary is limited to Institute records and an obituary in the *Boston Evening Transcript,* March 8, 1916, p. 23.

17. "President's Inaugural Address," VI: May 8, 1884, LPI.

18. "President's Address," VI: May 14, 1885, LPI.

19. *Ibid.*

20. *Ibid.*

21. "President's Inaugural Address," VI: May 8, 1884, LPI.

22. *Ibid.*

23. *Ibid.;* also, "President's Address," VI: May 14, 1885, LPI.

24. "President's Address," VI: May 14, 1885, LPI.

25. *Semi-Centennial Report,* 29–33.

26. I have assumed that this cohort in 1898 is representative of the general membership for the 1880s and 1890s. Included were members from Allston, Boston proper, Charlestown, Dorchester, East Boston, Hyde Park, Jamaica Plain, Neponset, Roslindale, Roxbury, and South Boston. City directories and newspaper obituaries were the main sources of information. Successful traces were made on seventy-two of the eighty-nine women. Obituaries for fourteen members or their husbands were found.

27. At least five women were designated in city directories as Miss for between twenty and fifty years.

28. National data and local studies suggest that around 10 percent of all adult white women worked outside the home in 1860 and that the number of native white married women who were employed was less than 5 percent between 1880 and 1900. (See Carl N. Degler, *At Odds: Women and the Family in America from the Revolution to the Present* (New York: Oxford Univ. Press, 1980), 374, 384, and 362–94 passim.)

29. Forty of the forty-eight married women were successfully traced. Their husbands' occupations were classified according to the scheme described in Stephan Thernstrom, *The Other Bostonians: Poverty and Progress in the American Metropolis, 1880–1970* (Cambridge, Mass.: Harvard Univ. Press, 1973), 289–302.

30. *Ibid.,* 50, 115.

31. Thernstrom discovered a high degree of occupational continuity among high and low white-collar male workers beginning during their second decade in the city and extending throughout their careers. (See *The Other Bostonians,* chap. 4.)

32. The best guides to Boston's neighborhoods in the late nineteenth century are Sam Bass Warner, Jr., *Streetcar Suburbs: The Process of Growth in Boston, 1870–1900,* 2d ed. (Cambridge, Mass.: Harvard Univ. Press, 1978), and Walter Muir Whitehill, *Boston: A Topographical History,* 2d ed. (Cambridge, Mass.: Belknap Press of Harvard Univ. Press, 1968).

33. Thernstrom, *The Other Bostonians,* 40.

34. *Ibid.,* 21.

35. Gleaned from Boston city directories (1880–1911) and an obituary of Mrs. Spaulding, *Boston Evening Transcript,* April 15, 1930, p. 17.

36. From Boston city directories (1850–1900).

37. From Boston city directories (1876–1900) and an obituary of Benjamin Pope, *Boston Evening Transcript,* Sept. 25, 1879, p. 1.

38. From an obituary, *Boston Evening Transcript,* Dec. 18, 1930, p. 28.

39. Lecture by Reverend A. A. Wright on "Wise or Otherwise," VI: May 19, 1881, LPI.

40. Lecture by Miss Fannie Morris on "The Women of Zulu," VI: Feb. 9, 1882, LPI.

41. Lecture by Dr. Salome Merritt on "The Labor Question," VI: April 29, 1886, LPI.

42. Obituary, *Boston Evening Transcript,* Nov. 7, 1923, p. 11.

43. Overlapping membership was checked for the following organizations and years: Moral Education Association (1887); New England Female Moral Reform Society (1892–96, 1899–1901, 1903); New England Woman's Club (1898–1901); Woman's Education Association (1886–90, 1897–1900); Women's Christian Temperance Union of Boston (1882, 1884, 1886–89); Women's Educational and Industrial Union (1879, 1881–85, 1890–92, 1898–1902). While a few Institute members joined some of those organizations at some time, the only active women, besides Mrs. Frink, were Mrs. Oliver (Sibylla) Crane and Mrs. Micah (Julia K.) Dyer, Jr. (See entries for the two women, respectively, in Howe, *Sketches of Representative Women of New England,* 348–49 and 126–28, and obituaries for their husbands, respectively, in *Boston Evening Transcript,* Nov. 30, 1896, p. 5 and Nov. 26, 1897, p. 5.)

44. According to the entry of a member in Howe, *Sketches of Representative Women of New England,* 228.

45. The manuscript records of the early 1880s and the *Semi-Centennial Report* generated a list of medical members and of the lay and medical women who served as officers or on the board of directors between 1875 and 1900. The list included twelve medical members or officers and forty-six lay officers and/or directors. Information about those fifty-eight women was obtained from city directories, obituaries, Howe's *Sketches of Representative Women of New England,* and other local sources. (Obituaries for twenty of the members or their husbands were located.)

46. Marital status during time of service was determined for twenty-eight

of the forty-six lay women. The other eighteen were referred to as "Mrs." in the records and, therefore, were either married or widowed.

47. One of the single women was an artist and teacher in Boston for nearly thirty years, and one of the widows was an author and public reader.

48. Husbands for fourteen of the married women were traced via city directories and/or obituaries; the occupations of seven of the ten widows' husbands were also identified.

49. Memberships of several organizations during the period were compared to the Institute's; see n. 43 above.

50. See entry in Howe, *Sketches of Representative Women of New England*, 227–29.

51. When she died in 1892 at the age of eighty-five, Mrs. Hobbs was the oldest surviving charter member of the Institute. See her obituary in *Boston Evening Transcript*, July 25, 1892, p. 5.

52. Medical members were traced via obituaries (six were located), city directories, medical registers and medical society directories, LPI records, and other local sources.

53. Regina Markell Morantz-Sanchez, *Sympathy and Science: Women Physicians in American Medicine* (New York: Oxford Univ. Press, 1985), and Mary Roth Walsh, *"Doctors Wanted: No Women Need Apply": Sexual Barriers in the Medical Profession, 1835–1975* (New Haven: Yale Univ. Press, 1977).

54. Morantz-Sanchez, *Sympathy and Science*, 64–89.

55. Walsh, *"Doctors Wanted: No Women Need Apply,"* 104, 105, 216, 264; Margaret Noyes Kleinert, "Medical Women in New England: History of the New England Women's Medical Society," *Journal of the American Medical Women's Association* 11 (1956): 63–64, 67; and Virginia G. Drachman, *Hospital with a Heart: Women Doctors and the Paradox of Separatism at the New England Hospital, 1862–1969* (Ithaca: Cornell Univ. Press, 1984), 125–32.

56. Morantz-Sanchez, *Sympathy and Science*, 49.

57. Walsh, *"Doctors Wanted: No Women Need Apply,"* 181–82, 185–86.

58. For some statistics on women's declining representation in medicine, see Morantz-Sanchez, *Sympathy and Science*, 234.

59. "President's Inaugural Address," VI: May 8, 1884, LPI.

60. Morantz-Sanchez, *Sympathy and Science*, 47–63.

61. *Ibid.*, 203–31. After studying obstetrical cases at two Boston hospitals, Morantz-Sanchez concluded that male and female doctors viewed childbirth and handled parturient women in similar ways, except for drug prescriptions. Gender, though, had a marked effect on doctors' perceptions of and relationships with their patients. Women doctors regarded medicine as supportive therapy and "continued to cling to traditional holistic orientations," while "men embraced a more 'modern,' technocratic approach to their patients" (p. 230). A longer discussion of those points is found in Regina Markell Morantz and Sue Zschoche, "Professionalism, Feminism, and Gender Roles: A Comparative Study of Nineteenth-Century Medical Therapeutics," *Journal of American History* 67 (Dec. 1980): 568–88. For another analysis of the issue, see Drachman, *Hospital with a Heart*.

62. Morantz-Sanchez, *Sympathy and Science*, 28–46, 266–311 (especially 286–89).

5. *Fitness of Body and Mind*

1. Surveys of popular health, mental hygiene, and domestic medicine in the late nineteenth century include Anita Clair Fellman and Michael Fellman, *Making Sense of Self: Medical Advice Literature in Late Nineteenth-Century America* (Philadelphia: Univ. of Pennsylvania Press, 1981); Harvey Green, *Fit for America: Health, Fitness, Sport and American Society* (New York: Pantheon, 1986), 101–215; Barbara Sicherman, "The Quest for Mental Health in America, 1880–1917" (Ph.D. dissertation, Columbia Univ., 1967), 12–280; James C. Whorton, *Crusaders for Fitness: The History of American Health Reformers* (Princeton: Princeton Univ. Press, 1982), 132–330; and James Harvey Young, *The Toadstool Millionaires: A Social History of Patent Medicines in America before Federal Regulation* (Princeton: Princeton Univ. Press, 1961). William B. Walker discusses the denouement of antebellum crusades in "The Health Reform Movement in the United States, 1830–1870" (Ph.D. dissertation, Johns Hopkins Univ., 1955). Donald J. Mrozek analyzes the rise of games and athletics in *Sport and American Mentality, 1880–1910* (Knoxville: Univ. of Tennessee Press, 1983).

2. For example, see Stephen Hardy, *How Boston Played: Sport, Recreation, and Community, 1865–1915* (Boston: Northeastern Univ. Press, 1982). For further information about physical education in Boston's public schools and private gymnasia in the city, see Martha H. Verbrugge, "Fitness for Life: Female Health and Education in Nineteenth-Century Boston" (Ph.D. dissertation, Harvard Univ., 1978), 264–382, 452–511.

3. The following summary comes from an initial brochure, *Massachusetts Emergency and Hygiene Association. June, 1884* (Boston: Cochrane & Sampson, 1884); the annual reports of the MEHA (1885–1906); and two volumes of "Scrapbooks Relating to the Massachusetts Emergency and Hygiene Association, compiled by James J. Minot," Francis A. Countway Library of Medicine, Harvard Univ. Medical School, Boston, Mass.

4. Hope W. Narey, "Physical Training for Women," *The Bostonian* 1 (Oct. 1894): 101. (Narey was director of the Durant Gymnasium at Boston's YWCA.)

5. From early annual reports of the WEIU (1877–1903).

6. For example, see *Second Annual Report of the Boston Association of Working Girls' Clubs, 1890* (Boston: Morning Star, 1890).

7. "Physical Training. The Normal Schools for Teachers Around Boston," *Providence [Rhode Island] Journal*, March 5, 1892, p. 14.

8. William Blaikie, *How To Get Strong, and How To Stay So* (New York: Harper & Brothers, 1879), 9.

9. "Running To Catch the Train," *Boston Journal of Health* n.s. 1 (March 1888): 89.

10. Edward H. Clarke, M.D., *Sex in Education; or, A Fair Chance for Girls* (Boston: James R. Osgood, 1874), 62.

11. *Ibid.*, 27–28.

12. *Ibid.*, 21–22.

13. Local figures are not available, but state-wide data indicate that life expectancy at birth for males rose from 38.3 in 1850 to 41.7 between 1878 and

1882, and to 44.1 between 1893 and 1897. The comparable figures for females were 40.5, 43.5, and 46.6. See Bureau of the Census, U.S. Department of Commerce, *Historical Statistics of the United States: Colonial Times to 1970,* 2 vols. (Washington, D.C.: Government Printing Office, 1975), I: Series B 126–135, p. 56. (Hereafter designated *Historical Statistics.*)

14. From 1872 to 1876, the mortality rate in Boston fluctuated between roughly 26 and 30 deaths per 1000 in the population, due primarily to outbreaks of smallpox and other contagious diseases. Between 1877 and 1900, it tended to remain between 22 and 25. Yearly crude death rates from 1872 on were noted in the annual reports of the Boston Board of Health. For cumulative data from twenty years, see John S. Billings, M.D., *Vital Statistics of Boston and Philadelphia Covering a Period of Six Years Ending May 31, 1890* (Washington, D.C.: Government Printing Office, 1895), 3. For data covering over two hundred years, see John B. Blake, *Public Health in the Town of Boston, 1630– 1822* (Cambridge, Mass.: Harvard Univ. Press, 1959), 252. Not surprisingly, cities that were substantially larger than Boston had higher death rates; New York City, with three times the population of Boston, had an average mortality rate of 26.82 between 1880 and 1889. (See John Duffy, *A History of Public Health in New York City, 1866–1966* (New York: Russell Sage Foundation, 1974), 643.) The unexpected news was that Philadelphia, Baltimore, and Pittsburgh, each a northeastern city of size comparable to Boston's, were healthier. (Billings, *Vital Statistics,* 2, reports mortality rates for other cities in the Northeast.) Boston's Board of Health attempted to explain away such unfavorable comparisons; see *Sixteenth Annual Report of the Board of Health of the City of Boston,* (1888, City Document #21), 3–4.

15. To analyze causes of death in the city, the Board of Health used an outmoded taxonomy of diseases, which included four groups: zymotic ("diseases which are due to contagion, filth, or miasma, and are known as preventable by, or amenable to, sanitary force," such as smallpox and diphtheria); constitutional (cancer, tuberculosis, and other conditions that "are largely inherited," or so contemporaries thought); local (diseases that affected particular organs or systems, such as pneumonia and peritonitis); and developmental (conditions associated with childhood or old age). This taxonomy is described in Board of Health, *Fourth Annual Report,* (1876, City Doc. #53), 25. The most important category for the board was zymotic diseases, whose contribution to deaths in the city seemed the best indicator of the residents' health and Boston's sanitary efficiency. Typical figures for the distribution of cause of death appear in Board of Health, *Fifth Annual Report,* (1877, City Doc. #67), 39–40; *Ninth Annual Report,* (1881, City Doc. #87), 10; *Fourteenth Annual Report,* (1886, City Doc. #31), 2–4; and *Twenty-fifth Annual Report,* (1897, City Doc. #12), 3.

Both contemporaries and medical historians have debated the reasons for the changing pattern among causes of death during the 1800s. Since specific preventive and remedial agents were not available for many contagious diseases until the turn of the century or later, other factors, such as sanitary measures and personal hygiene, would appear to have been the most consequential. (For a controversial discussion of the issue, see Thomas McKeown, *The Role of Medicine: Dream, Mirage, or Nemesis?* (Princeton: Princeton Univ. Press, 1979).) While recognizing its own deficiencies, Boston's Board of Health insisted that credit was due for the reduction of zymotic diseases. Despite Boston's "many and serious short-comings in its sanitary appliances," the board contended in 1882, its citizens had "good reason to congratulate themselves on the comparative healthfulness of the city." (See Board of Health, *Tenth Annual Report,* (1882, City Doc. #87), 5 and 5–6, 24–27 in general.)

16. See Board of Health, *Twenty-second Annual Report,* (1894, City Doc. #13), 5–6, and *Twenty-fifth Annual Report,* (1897, City Doc. #12), chart between pp. 16–17.

17. Board of Health, *Thirteenth Annual Report,* (1885, City Doc. #89), 7.

18. For a twenty-five-year survey, see Board of Health, *Twenty-fifth Annual Report,* (1897, City Doc. #12), 4. The Board of Health maintained that infant death rates were far worse in comparable cities throughout America and Europe. See Board of Health, *Tenth Annual Report,* (1882, City Doc. #87), 24–27; *Thirteenth Annual Report,* (1885, City Doc. #89), 7; and *Sixteenth Annual Report,* (1888, City Doc. #21), 3.

19. As did other vital statisticians, the board itself recognized that limitation. See Board of Health, *Fifth Annual Report,* (1877, City Doc. #67), 37; also, Charles E. Buckingham, M.D. et al., *The Sanitary Condition of Boston. The Report of a Medical Commission . . .* (Boston: Rockwell and Churchill, 1875), 46–58.

20. According to the Buckingham report, Boston's infant mortality in 1870 was 276.9, a figure similar to the alarming rates at mid-century. See Buckingham et al., *The Sanitary Condition of Boston,* 47. Dr. John S. Billings, deputy-surgeon general of the United States Army, calculated the rate to be 225.05 in 1880 and 261.34 in 1890. See Billings, *Vital Statistics,* 7. State-wide figures for infant deaths increased between the 1850s and the 1870s and declined slowly in the 1890s, but to a level still exceeding that of mid-century. See *Historical Statistics,* I: Series B 148, p. 57. The death rate among children under 5 years of age was no more encouraging. In a special report to the city's Board of Health, Boston physician W. L. Richardson stated that mortality for the year ending on April 30, 1876 was 94.84 deaths per 1000 residents age 5 and under, compared to only 16.73 for those over age 5. See W. L. Richardson, M.D., "Infant Mortality," in Board of Health, *Fourth Annual Report,* (1876, City Doc. #53), 50. See also *Fifth Annual Report,* (1877, City Doc. #67), 37.

21. One attempt to determine historical patterns in differential sickness and death is H. B. M. Murphy, "Historic Changes in the Sex Ratios for Different Disorders," *Social Science and Medicine* 12B (1978): 143–49. For studies of sex differences in morbidity, mortality, and health care in present times, see Lois M. Verbrugge, "Females and Illness: Recent Trends in Sex Differences in the United States," *Journal of Health and Social Behavior* 17 (Dec. 1976): 387–403; Lois M. Verbrugge, "Sex Differentials in Health," *Public Health Reports* 97 (Sept.–Oct. 1982): 417–37; and Ingrid Waldron, "An Analysis of Causes of Sex Differences in Mortality and Morbidity," in *The Fundamental Connection Between Nature and Nurture,* Walter R. Gove and G. Russell Carpenter, eds. (Lexington, Mass.: LexingtonBooks, D. C. Heath, 1982), 69–116. Two essays focusing on mental health are Ihsan Al-Issa, "Gender and Adult Psychopathology," in *Gender and Psychopathology,* Ihsan Al-Issa, ed. (New York: Academic, 1982), 83–101, and Bruce P. Dohrenwend

and Barbara Snell Dohrenwend, "Sex Differences and Psychiatric Disorders," *American Journal of Sociology* 81 (May 1976): 1447–54.

22. Calculated from Lemuel Shattuck, *Report to the Committee of the City Council Appointed To Obtain the Census of Boston for the Year 1845, Embracing Collateral Facts and Statistical Researches, Illustrating the History and Condition of the Population, and Their Means of Progress and Prosperity* (Boston: John H. Eastburn, 1846), 11, 13, 15, 18, 19, 73 in the appendices. Shattuck provided tables showing the total number of females in Boston (white and "colored") in various years and the annual number of deaths among males and females. (The calculation for 1810 used the national census figure for white females, an estimate for "colored" females, and the death registration for 1811.)

23. Billings, *Vital Statistics*, 5. Because Billings's figure included all Boston females, regardless of race or nationality, it is comparable to the calculations based on Shattuck's data.

24. *Ibid.* As the figures demonstrate, the difference between aggregate and group-specific rates is important. The significant increase in the immigrant population in the city (including all women born, either in America or abroad, of foreign parents) may have accounted for the rise in the overall female death rate. No definite conclusion can be reached about long-term trends in mortality rates among women born to American parents, since earlier data, such as Shattuck's, did not specify birthplaces for the white population.

25. Calculated from Shattuck, *Report . . . Census of Boston for the Year 1845*, pp. 18, 95 in the appendices.

26. Billings, *Vital Statistics*, 5.

27. Calculated from data about male population and deaths in Boston, in Shattuck, *Report . . . Census of Boston for the Year 1845*, pp. 13, 15, 19, 73 in the appendices.

28. Billings, *Vital Statistics*, 5.

29. *Ibid.*

30. *Ibid.*

31. All of the above figures were calculated from data about the distribution of Boston's white population by age and sex and of deaths among whites by age and sex, in Billings, *Vital Statistics*, 4, 7, 27 (tables 4, 9, 31).

32. For example, see *The Diary of Alice James,* edited with an introduction by Leon Edel (New York: Penguin American Library, 1982). A discussion of James's life follows shortly.

33. For descriptions of childbirth practices and women's attitudes about pregnancy and delivery, see Judith Walzer Leavitt, " 'Science' Enters the Birthing Room: Obstetrics in America since the Eighteenth Century," *Journal of American History* 70 (Sept. 1983): 281–304; Judith Walzer Leavitt and Whitney Walton, " 'Down to Death's Door': Women's Perceptions of Childbirth in America," in *Women and Health in America: Historical Readings,* Judith Walzer Leavitt, ed. (Madison: Univ. of Wisconsin Press, 1984), 155–65; Catherine M. Scholten, " 'On the Importance of the Obstetrick Art': Changing Customs of Childbirth in America, 1760–1825," in *ibid.,* 142–54; and Richard W. Wertz and Dorothy C. Wertz, *Lying-In: A History of Childbirth in America* (New York: Free Press, 1977).

34. A typical example is Lucy A. Smith, "Let Invalid Women Take Cour-

age," *Laws of Life and Journal of Health* 22 (Dec. 1879): 358–60. Smith related that she recovered her health only after abandoning orthodox treatment and dressing and eating more sensibly.

35. See Sarah Stage, *Female Complaints: Lydia Pinkham and the Business of Women's Medicine* (New York: W. W. Norton, 1979), 103, 105–6, 119–20. The company claimed that it received hundreds, even thousands, of letters seeking help and comfort. Apparently, only a couple of the original letters have survived.

36. Historians' indictments of nineteenth-century gynecology include G. J. Barker-Benfield, *The Horrors of the Half-Known Life: Male Attitudes Toward Women and Sexuality in Nineteenth-Century America* (New York: Harper Colophon, 1976); Barbara Ehrenreich and Deirdre English, *Complaints and Disorders: The Sexual Politics of Sickness* (Old Westbury, N.Y.: Feminist Press, 1973), 32–38; and Ann Douglas Wood, " 'The Fashionable Diseases': Women's Complaints and Their Treatment in Nineteenth-Century America," *Journal of Interdisciplinary History* 4 (Summer 1973): 25–52. Several scholars have cautioned against the villain-victim model of women's medical care, however inadequate the treatments were. For example, see Regina Morantz, "The Lady and Her Physician," in *Clio's Consciousness Raised: New Perspectives on the History of Women,* Mary S. Hartman and Lois W. Banner, eds. (New York: Harper Torchbooks, 1974), 38–53.

37. For a philosophical and historical discussion, see Lester S. King, "What Is Disease?," in *Concepts of Health and Disease: Interdisciplinary Perspectives,* Arthur L. Caplan, H. Tristram Engelhardt, Jr., and James J. McCartney, eds. (Reading, Mass.: Addison-Wesley, 1981), 107–18.

38. Jean Strouse, *Alice James: A Biography* (New York: Bantam Books, 1982).

39. *Ibid.,* 129.

40. *Ibid.,* 136.

41. The following discussion draws on such studies as Joan Jacobs Brumberg, "Chlorotic Girls, 1870–1920: A Historical Perspective on Female Adolescence," *Child Development* 53 (1982): 1468–77; Barbara Sicherman, "The Uses of a Diagnosis: Doctors, Patients, and Neurasthenia," *Journal of the History of Medicine and Allied Sciences* 32 (Jan. 1977): 33–54; Carroll Smith-Rosenberg, "Puberty to Menopause: The Cycle of Femininity in Nineteenth-Century America," *Feminist Studies* 1 (Winter–Spring 1973): 58–72; and Carroll Smith-Rosenberg, "The Hysterical Woman: Sex Roles and Role Conflict in 19th-Century America," *Social Research* 39 (Winter 1972): 652–78. Sociologists have also studied the meaning of illness for the individual and its implications for the doctor-patient relationship. The classic analysis of the sick role is Talcott Parsons, *The Social System* (Glencoe, Ill.: Free Press, 1951), 428–79.

42. The four historical studies cited in the previous note also discuss the psychological, professional, and social implications that female illness had for male physicians in the late nineteenth century. For a general analysis of the significance that diagnosis and care held for doctors, see Charles E. Rosenberg, "The Therapeutic Revolution: Medicine, Meaning, and Social Change in Nineteenth-Century America," in *The Therapeutic Revolution: Essays in the Social History of American Medicine,* Morris J. Vogel and Charles E. Rosenberg, eds. (Philadelphia: Univ. of Pennsylvania Press, 1979), 3–25.

43. For a general overview, see Charles E. Rosenberg, "The Bitter Fruit: Heredity, Disease, and Social Thought in Nineteenth-Century America," *Perspectives in American History* 8 (1974): 189–235.

44. Analyses of nineteenth-century medical opinion about women's health include John S. Haller, Jr., and Robin M. Haller, *The Physician and Sexuality in Victorian America* (Urbana: Univ. of Illinois Press, 1974), 45–87; Smith-Rosenberg, "Puberty to Menopause"; Carroll Smith-Rosenberg and Charles E. Rosenberg, "The Female Animal: Medical and Biological Views of Woman and Her Role in Nineteenth-Century America," *Journal of American History* 60 (Sept. 1973): 332–56; and Wood, " 'The Fashionable Diseases.' " The belief in women's innate inferiority gained further support from theories in evolutionary biology and anthropology. See Jill Conway, "Stereotypes of Femininity in a Theory of Sexual Evolution," *Victorian Studies* 14 (Sept. 1970): 47–62; Lorna Duffin, "Prisoners of Progress: Women and Evolution," in *The Nineteenth-Century Woman: Her Cultural and Physical World,* Sara Delamont and Lorna Duffin, eds. (London: Croom Helm, 1978; New York: Barnes & Noble, 1978), 57–91; and Elizabeth Fee, "The Sexual Politics of Victorian Social Anthropology," *Feminist Studies* 1 (Winter–Spring 1973): 23–39.

45. For typical misgivings, see Irenaeus P. Davis, M.D., *Hygiene for Girls* (New York: D. Appleton, 1883), 22–26, 208–10.

46. Charles H. Stowell, M.D., *The Essentials of Health: A Text-Book on Anatomy, Physiology, Hygiene, Alcohol, and Narcotics* (New York: Silver, Burdett, 1896), 36.

47. George H. Taylor, M.D., *Health by Exercise. What Exercises To Take and How To Take Them, To Remove Special Physical Weakness. Embracing an Account of the Swedish Methods, and a Summary of the Principles of Hygiene* (New York: American Book Exchange, 1881), 255 (emphasis in original).

48. Blanche A. Phillips, "Reform in Living," *Mind and Body* 4 (March 1897): 23.

49. Dr. Luther Gulick, "Physical Health, Education, Recreation," *The Triangle* 1 (May 15, 1891): 56.

50. Conditions in Boston around 1880 are described in *Fifty Years of Boston: A Memorial Volume,* Elisabeth M. Herlihy, ed. Compiled by the Subcommittee on Memorial History of the Boston Tercentenary Committee (Boston: n.p., 1932), 200, 441–42, and Sam Bass Warner, Jr., *Streetcar Suburbs: The Process of Growth in Boston, 1870–1900,* 2d ed. (Cambridge, Mass.: Harvard Univ. Press, 1978), 21–31.

51. Ruth Schwartz Cowan, *More Work for Mother: The Ironies of Household Technology from the Open Hearth to the Microwave* (New York: Basic Books, 1983), 40–68.

52. For a general survey of the city's economic history in the late 1800s, see Herlihy, *Fifty Years of Boston,* 157–300.

53. On the distribution of the male work force, see Peter R. Knights, *The Plain People of Boston, 1830–1860: A Study in City Growth* (New York: Oxford Univ. Press, 1971), 84, and Stephan Thernstrom, *The Other Bostonians: Poverty and Progress in the American Metropolis, 1880–1970* (Cambridge, Mass.: Harvard Univ. Press, 1973), 50.

54. Thernstrom, *The Other Bostonians,* chaps. 4–8.

55. *Ibid.,* 45–75.

56. *Ibid.*, 111–44.

57. *Ibid.*, 142.

58. *Ibid.*, 176–219.

59. "Ruinous Habits and Wasted Lives," *Boston Journal of Health* n.s. 4 (1890–91): 25.

60. Studies about these developments include Charles E. Rosenberg, *The Cholera Years: The United States in 1832, 1849, and 1866* (Chicago: Univ. of Chicago Press, 1962); Barbara Gutmann Rosenkrantz, *Public Health and the State: Changing Views in Massachusetts, 1842–1936* (Cambridge, Mass.: Harvard Univ. Press, 1972); and William G. Rothstein, *American Physicians in the Nineteenth Century: From Sects to Science* (Baltimore: Johns Hopkins Univ. Press, 1972), 249–81.

61. For a general overview, see Walter Muir Whitehill, *Boston: A Topographical History*, 2d ed. (Cambridge, Mass.: Belknap Press of Harvard Univ. Press, 1968), 119–99. Marjorie Drake Ross, *The Book of Boston: The Victorian Period, 1837 to 1901* (New York: Hastings House, 1964), uses architecture to trace the city's ongoing face-lift.

62. Board of Health, *Ninth Annual Report*, (1881, City Doc. #87), 44.

63. Board of Health, *Fifth Annual Report*, (1877, City Doc. #67), 4.

64. *Ibid.*

65. Whitehill, *Boston: A Topographical History*, 138–39.

66. On the changing organization of the city, see Ross, *The Book of Boston: The Victorian Period*, 86–94, 99–103, 131–49; Warner, *Streetcar Suburbs*, 1–3, 15–21; and Whitehill, *Boston: A Topographical History*, 119–99.

67. Warner, *Streetcar Suburbs*, 1–3, 46–66, 179–80; Thernstrom, *The Other Bostonians*, 10–11.

68. Warner, *Streetcar Suburbs*, 2.

69. *Ibid.*

70. *Ibid.*, 153.

71. On the stresses of commuting, see "Running To Catch the Train," 89–90.

72. Knights, *The Plain People of Boston*, 20; Thernstrom, *The Other Bostonians*, 11.

73. Thernstrom, *The Other Bostonians*, 16 (emphasis in original), and 15–21 in general.

74. *Ibid.*, 113.

75. *Ibid.*, 112.

76. *Ibid.*, and Buckingham et al., *The Sanitary Condition of Boston*, 68.

77. For sample figures, see Billings, *Vital Statistics*, 5. For a discussion of the immigrants' plight, see Buckingham et al., *The Sanitary Condition of Boston*, 58–78.

78. See Barbara Miller Solomon, *Ancestors and Immigrants: A Changing New England Tradition* (Cambridge, Mass.: Harvard Univ. Press, 1956), and John Higham, *Strangers in the Land: Patterns of American Nativism 1860–1925*, rev. ed. (New York: Atheneum, 1970).

79. Peter R. Uhlenberg, "A Study of Cohort Life Cycles: Cohorts of Native Born Massachusetts Women, 1830–1920," *Population Studies* 23 (Nov. 1969): 419.

80. Robert V. Wells, "Women's Lives Transformed: Demographic and

Family Patterns in America, 1600–1970," in *Women of America: A History,*
Carol Ruth Berkin and Mary Beth Norton, eds. (Boston: Houghton Mifflin,
1979), 20; Uhlenberg, "A Study of Cohort Life Cycles," 410.

81. Uhlenberg, "A Study of Cohort Life Cycles," 410–11, 420. The fact
that the increase resulted from the number of women who were single at age
50 and beyond, rather than of single women who died between ages 20 and
50, is significant. It indicates that singlehood may have been a deliberate choice,
not merely the accident of a short life. Another factor may have been the unusually high imbalance between the numbers of adult men and women, because
of casualties during the Civil War.

82. Wells, "Women's Lives Transformed," 18. See also Uhlenberg, "A
Study of Cohort Life Cycles," 413, and Carl N. Degler, *At Odds: Women and
the Family in America from the Revolution to the Present* (New York: Oxford
Univ. Press, 1980), 178–81.

83. Wells, "Women's Lives Transformed," 18.

84. Uhlenberg, "A Study of Cohort Life Cycles," 412.

85. On the history of birth control and abortion in the 1800s, see Degler,
At Odds, 178–248, and Linda Gordon, *Woman's Body, Woman's Right: A Social History of Birth Control in America* (New York: Penguin Books, 1977),
26–71.

86. For discussions about childbirth practices and the impact of male
physicians, see Leavitt, " 'Science' Enters the Birthing Room"; Leavitt and
Walton, " 'Down to Death's Door' "; Scholten, " 'On the Importance of the
Obstetrick Art' "; and Wertz and Wertz, *Lying-In.* Maternal death rates in En-
gland are examined in B. M. Willmott Dobbie, "An Attempt To Estimate the
True Rate of Maternal Mortality, Sixteenth to Eighteenth Centuries," *Medical
History* 26 (Jan. 1982): 79–90. Figures for twentieth-century America are
found in Leavitt, " 'Science' Enters the Birthing Room," 299–301.

87. Wells, "Women's Lives Transformed," 28.

88. Warner, *Streetcar Suburbs,* 181.

89. Uhlenberg, "A Study of Cohort Life Cycles," 414.

90. See Elaine Tyler May, *Great Expectations: Marriage and Divorce in
Post-Victorian America* (Chicago: Univ. of Chicago Press, 1980), and Degler,
At Odds, 165–77.

91. For overviews of the female experience in the late nineteenth and
early twentieth century, see Lois W. Banner, *Women in Modern America: A
Brief History* (New York: Harcourt Brace Jovanovich, 1974), 1–130, and
Mary P. Ryan, *Womanhood in America: From Colonial Times to the Present*
(New York: New Viewpoints, 1975), 193–249. For contemporary accounts of
the status of women in Massachusetts and Boston, see Ednah Dow Cheney,
"The Women of Boston," in *The Memorial History of Boston, Including
Suffolk County, Massachusetts, 1630–1880,* Justin Winsor, ed., 4 vols. (Boston:
J. R. Osgood, 1880–81), IV: 331–56, and Frances G. Curtis, "Woman's Widen-
ing Sphere," in Herlihy, *Fifty Years of Boston,* 626–35.

92. On public education for girls in Boston, see Cheney, "The Women of
Boston," 343–45, and Stanley K. Schultz, *The Culture Factory: Boston Public
Schools, 1789–1860* (New York: Oxford Univ. Press, 1973), 14–15, 117–25.

93. For a history of private academies and colleges that educated women,
see Thomas Woody, *A History of Women's Education in the United States,* 2

vols. (New York: Science Press, 1929; reprint ed., New York: Octagon Books, 1966), I: 329–459, II: 137–223, and Barbara Miller Solomon, *In the Company of Educated Women: A History of Women and Higher Education in America* (New Haven: Yale Univ. Press, 1985).

94. Degler, *At Odds,* 155.

95. Carl F. Kaestle and Maris A. Vinovskis, *Education and Social Change in Nineteenth-Century Massachusetts* (London and New York: Cambridge Univ. Press, 1980), 203–6. For a general survey of the distribution of women in the work force over time, see Janet M. Hooks, *Women's Occupations Through Seven Decades,* Women's Bureau Bulletin, no. 218 (Washington, D.C.: Government Printing Office, 1947).

96. Degler, *At Odds,* 375, 384. (That estimate may be low. Recent scholarship suggests that middle-class women workers may have lied about being married for fear of jeopardizing their jobs.)

97. See Joan Jacobs Brumberg and Nancy Tomes, "Women in the Professions: A Research Agenda for American Historians," *Reviews in American History* 10 (June 1982): 280–81.

98. Regina Markell Morantz-Sanchez, *Sympathy and Science: Women Physicians in American Medicine* (New York: Oxford Univ. Press, 1985), 136 and 129–42 in general.

99. John Ellis, M.D., *Deterioration of the Puritan Stock and Its Causes* (New York: Published by the Author, 1884), 3.

100. *Ibid.,* 7.

101. *Ibid.,* 4.

102. See n. 10 above. For historical studies about the debate over education and women's health in America and England, see Vern Bullough and Martha Voght, "Women, Menstruation, and Nineteenth-Century Medicine," *Bulletin of the History of Medicine* 47 (Jan.–Feb. 1973): 66–82; Joan N. Burstyn, *Victorian Education and the Ideal of Womanhood* (New Brunswick, N.J.: Rutgers Univ. Press, 1984); and Elaine and English Showalter, "Victorian Women and Menstruation," *Victorian Studies* 14 (1970–71): 83–89.

103. Clarke, *Sex in Education,* 40.

104. *Ibid.,* 37.

105. *Ibid.,* 42.

106. *Ibid.,* 22.

107. William Warren Potter, M.D., "How Should Girls Be Educated? A Public Health Problem for Mothers, Educators, and Physicians," *Transactions of the Medical Society of the State of New York* (1891), 48.

108. *Ibid.,* 50.

109. Other examples of the persistence of Clarke's views include "Coeducation and the Higher Education of Women: A Symposium," *Medical News* (Philadelphia) 55 (Dec. 14, 1889): 667–73, and G. J. Engelmann, M.D., "Causes Which Imperil the Health of the American Girl, and the Necessity of Female Hygiene," *Medical News* (Philadelphia) 57 (Dec. 6, 1890): 599–605.

110. Clarke, *Sex in Education,* 12.

111. *Ibid.,* 12–13.

112. Davis, *Hygiene for Girls,* 119.

113. *Ibid.,* 119–20, and 114–32 in general.

114. William Goodell, M.D., *Lessons in Gynecology* (Philadelphia: D. G. Brinton, 1879), 353.

115. See David J. Pivar, *Purity Crusade: Sexual Morality and Social Control, 1868–1900* (Westport, Conn.: Greenwood Press, 1973), and Gordon, *Woman's Body, Woman's Right,* 116–85.

116. Elizabeth Cady Stanton, "The Health of American Women," *North American Review* 135 (Dec. 1882): 510.

117. *Ibid.*

118. *Ibid.,* 513. Modern studies continue to confirm Stanton's observation about stress among women in atypical roles.

119. See Rosalind Rosenberg, *Beyond Separate Spheres: Intellectual Roots of Modern Feminism* (New Haven: Yale Univ. Press, 1982).

120. Clarke's essay, for example, inspired many critical responses, including Anna C. Brackett, ed., *The Education of American Girls Considered in a Series of Essays* (New York: G. P. Putnam's Sons, 1874); Mrs. E. B. Duffy, *No Sex in Education; or, An Equal Chance for Both Girls and Boys. Being a Review of Dr. E. H. Clarke's "Sex in Education"* (Philadelphia: J. M. Stoddart, 1874); T. A. Foster, M.D., "Coeducation of the Sexes," *Transactions of the Maine Medical Association* 5 (1874): 130–46; and *Sex and Education. A Reply to Dr. E. H. Clarke's "Sex in Education,"* edited, with an introduction, by Mrs. Julia Ward Howe (Boston: Roberts Brothers, 1874).

121. For example, see *Health Statistics of Women College Graduates. Report of a Special Committee of the Association of Collegiate Alumnae* (Boston: Wright & Potter, 1885), and Grace A. Preston, M.D., "Influence of College Life on the Health of Women," *Medical Communications of the Massachusetts Medical Society* 16 (1893): 167–90.

122. Mary Putnam Jacobi, M.D., *The Question of Rest for Women during Menstruation* (New York: G. P. Putnam's Sons, 1877).

123. For historical studies of birth control advocates, see Gordon, *Woman's Body, Woman's Right,* 95–115, 162–70, 186–245, and James Reed, *From Private Vice to Public Virtue: The Birth Control Movement and American Society since 1830* (New York: Basic Books, 1978), especially 65–139.

124. The careers of Fletcher and Macfadden are described in Green, *Fit for America,* 242–54, 294–302, and Whorton, *Crusaders for Fitness,* 168–200, 296–303.

125. See Ronald L. Numbers, *Prophetess of Health: A Study of Ellen G. White* (New York: Harper and Row, 1976), 123–28, 188–98, and passim, and Whorton, *Crusaders for Fitness,* 201–38.

126. The development of professional physical education in the United States will be discussed in more detail in Chapter 7.

127. The following analysis of popular concepts of health is based on a sample of the vast literature about fitness in late nineteenth-century America. Sources included physiology textbooks for schools and homes, exercise manuals, practical guides about hygiene and medicine, health magazines and physical education journals, and articles from women's and general magazines. Another useful survey of such material is Fellman and Fellman, *Making Sense of Self.* See also Green, *Fit for America,* 101–317, and Whorton, *Crusaders for Fitness,* 132–330. For a discussion of British views during the same period, see Bruce

Haley, *The Healthy Body and Victorian Culture* (Cambridge, Mass.: Harvard Univ. Press, 1978).

128. Joseph C. Hutchison, M.D., *A Treatise on Physiology and Hygiene for Educational Institutions and General Readers* (New York: Clark & Maynard, 1871), 30.

129. J. H. Kellogg, M.D., *Second Book in Physiology and Hygiene* (New York: American Book Company, 1894), 198.

130. James Johonnot and Eugene Bouton, Ph.D., *How We Live: or, the Human Body, and How To Take Care of It* (New York: D. Appleton, 1884), 21.

131. Kellogg, *Second Book in Physiology and Hygiene,* 198.

132. H. Newell Martin, M.D., *The Human Body. An Elementary Text-Book of Anatomy, Physiology and Hygiene,* 2d ed. (New York: Henry Holt, 1885), 311.

133. Johonnot and Bouton, *How We Live,* 115.

134. *Ibid.,* 116.

135. Albert F. Blaisdell, M.D., *Our Bodies and How We Live. An Elementary Text-Book of Physiology and Hygiene for Use in the Common Schools, with Special Reference to the Effects of Stimulants and Narcotics on the Human System* (Boston: Lee and Shepard, 1885), 3.

136. Jessie H. Bancroft, *School Gymnastics—Free Hand. A System of Physical Exercises for Schools* (New York and Chicago: E. L. Kellogg, 1896), 9. A prominent physical educator in Brooklyn's and New York's public schools during the Progressive era, Bancroft (1867–1952) was a pioneering woman in the new profession.

137. The mind-body relationship seemed as crucial to mental hygiene as to physical health. For a discussion of late nineteenth-century ideas about mental health, including the importance of a disciplined will, see Sicherman, "The Quest for Mental Health in America, 1880–1917," 78–152.

138. William Gilbert Anderson, *Anderson's Physical Education. Health and Strength, Grace and Symmetry* (New York: A. D. Dana, 1897), 12.

139. *Ibid.*

140. Davis, *Hygiene for Girls,* 22–26.

141. *Ibid.,* 208.

142. *Ibid.,* 208–9.

143. *Ibid.,* 209.

144. Martin, *The Human Body,* 17–19.

145. *Ibid.,* 18.

146. *Ibid.,* 19 (emphasis in original).

147. See *Dudley Allen Sargent: An Autobiography,* edited by Ledyard W. Sargent, with an introduction by R. Tait McKenzie, M.D. (Philadelphia: Lea & Febiger, 1927), and "Dudley Allen Sargent," *Dictionary of American Biography,* Dumas Malone, ed. (New York: Charles Scribner's Sons, 1935), 16: 355–56.

148. Dudley Allen Sargent, *Physical Education* (Boston: Ginn, 1906), 297.

149. Dudley Allen Sargent, *Health, Strength and Power* (New York and Boston: H. M. Caldwell, 1904), 78. See also Sargent, *Physical Education,* 55.

150. Sargent, *Physical Education,* 38 and 19–48 in general (essay on "The Physical State of the American People").

151. Sargent, *Health, Strength and Power*, 21.

152. J. Dorman Steele, Ph.D., *Fourteen Weeks in Human Physiology* (New York: A. S. Barnes, 1875), xvi; see xv–xvi in general.

153. Prof. D. L. Dowd, *Physical Culture for Home and School. Scientific and Practical* (New York: Fowler & Wells, 1890), 5.

154. On the early uses of number-gathering in America, see James H. Cassedy, *Demography in Early America: Beginnings of the Statistical Mind, 1600–1800* (Cambridge, Mass.: Harvard Univ. Press, 1969), and *American Medicine and Statistical Thinking, 1800–1860* (Cambridge, Mass.: Harvard Univ. Press, 1984). On the growth of the bureaucratic mentality in the late nineteenth and early twentieth century, see Robert H. Wiebe, *The Search for Order, 1877–1920* (New York: Hill and Wang, 1967), 133–63. The fallacies of intelligence testing are discussed in Stephen Jay Gould, *The Mismeasure of Man* (New York: W. W. Norton, 1981). For an overview of Taylorism, see Samuel Haber, *Efficiency and Uplift: Scientific Management in the Progressive Era, 1890–1920* (Chicago: Univ. of Chicago Press, 1964).

155. Examples of anthropometry and other physical tests applied to health are found in John Freeman Bovard and Frederick W. Cozens, *Tests and Measurements in Physical Education, 1861–1925. A Treatment of the Original Sources with Critical Comment*, Univ. of Oregon Publication, Physical Education Series, vol. I, no. 1 (Eugene: Univ. of Oregon Press, 1926).

156. For descriptions of the tests and examples of results, see Dudley Allen Sargent, "The Physical Proportions of the Typical Man," *Scribner's Magazine* 2 (July 1887): 3–17; Sargent, "The Physical Characteristics of the Athlete," *Scribner's Magazine* 2 (Nov. 1887): 541–61; Sargent, "The Physical Development of Women," *Scribner's Magazine* 5 (Feb. 1889): 172–85; Sargent, "The Physical Test of a Man," *Proceedings of the American Association for the Advancement of Physical Education* 5 (1890): 36–56; "The Human Form Divine. Prizes for Symmetry Awarded by Dr. Sargent of Harvard," *Boston Herald*, Sept. 7, 1890, p. 22; Sargent, "Strength Tests and the Strong Men of Harvard," *Harvard Graduates' Magazine* 5 (June 1897): 513–25; and Sargent, *Universal Test for Strength, Speed, and Endurance of the Human Body* (Cambridge, Mass.: Powell Press, 1902). Concerning Sargent's exercise equipment and recommended workouts, see *Handbook of Developing Exercises* (Boston: Rand, Avery, 1882; revised and enlarged edition, Cambridge, Mass., 1889), and *Dr. Sargent's System of Developing Appliances and Gymnastic Apparatus* (Cambridge, Mass.: John Ford & Son, 1882).

157. That was all deceptively simple. There are a couple hidden complications. First, a person's line and relative standing changed dramatically according to the reference population used. Imagine the result if the scores of an elderly person were plotted against those of young adults, instead of his or her own peer group. Second, Sargent's definition and calculation of the "normal" result, the 50th percentile, for each test were ambiguous. He treated it like a true median. Occasionally, though, he called it the "typical" or "average" result, suggesting that it represented the mean. Yet he also described it as the mode. (The best examples of this confusion appear in Sargent's articles "Strength Tests and the Strong Men of Harvard" and "The Physical Test of Man," and in the newspaper article on "The Human Form Divine.") Even when one has an opportunity to work through Sargent's actual data and analy-

sis, it is hard to decipher his intent or to reproduce his results. In "Strength Tests and the Strong Men of Harvard," for instance, Sargent's determinations of the 50/50 markers for various groups did not consistently match my own calculations of the mean, median, or mode for the data. Obviously, the real meaning of the "norm" is important. The scores represented by each percentile ranking differ if the mean, the median, or the mode constitutes the 50/50 marker; an individual's plot against the standard would likewise vary. It appears that Sargent's understanding of the vocabulary and techniques of elementary statistics was deficient.

158. Sargent, "The Physical Proportions of the Typical Man," 16.

159. *Ibid.*

160. "The Human Form Divine. Prizes for Symmetry Awarded by Dr. Sargent of Harvard."

161. "The Most Symmetrical Woman in America—The Strongest Woman in America," newspaper item in Clipping File, Dudley Allen Sargent Papers, Harvard Univ. Archives, Pusey Library, Harvard Univ., Cambridge, Mass.

162. See "The American Woman before Athletics 'Mannified' Her," *The Sketch* 72 (Dec. 7, 1910): 255.

6. *"Stronger in Body as well as in Mind"*

1. Standard histories of the college include Florence Converse, *Wellesley College: A Chronicle of the Years 1875–1938* (Wellesley, Mass.: Hathaway House Bookshop, 1939); Jean Glasscock, ed., *Wellesley College, 1875–1975: A Century of Women* (Wellesley, Mass.: Wellesley College, 1975); and Alice Payne Hackett, *Wellesley: Part of the American Story* (New York: E. P. Dutton, 1949). A more analytical study is Patricia Ann Palmieri, "In Adamless Eden: A Social Portrait of the Academic Community at Wellesley College, 1875–1920" (Ed.D. dissertation, Harvard Univ., 1981). For nineteenth-century accounts, see Edward Abbott, "Wellesley College," *Harper's Magazine* 53 (Aug. 1876): 321–32, and A. C. Goodloe, "Undergraduate Life at Wellesley," *Scribner's Magazine* 23 (May 1898): 515–38.

2. See "Henry Fowle Durant," *Dictionary of American Biography,* Allen Johnson and Dumas Malone, eds. (New York: C. Scribner's Sons, 1930), 5: 541–42, and Florence Morse Kingsley, *The Life of Henry Fowle Durant: Founder of Wellesley College* (New York and London: Century, 1924).

3. From the original statutes of the college, quoted in Hackett, *Wellesley: Part of the American Story,* 31.

4. *Wellesley College Calendar,* 1876–77, p. 16. The *Calendar* served as the college catalogue, with summaries of the school's facilities, requirements, and program. (Hereafter cited as *Calendar,* with year.) It should be noted that, until his death in 1881, Mr. Durant oversaw every detail of the college's operation, including the content of its brochures.

5. *Calendar,* 1876–77, p. 18.

6. *Ibid.,* 16, 18; also, *Calendar,* 1877–78, pp. 45–46.

7. *Calendar,* 1877–78, p. 46.

8. A classic survey is Thomas Woody, *A History of Women's Education in the United States*, 2 vols. (New York: Science Press, 1929; reprint ed., New York: Octagon Books, 1966).

9. *Ibid.*, I: 364.

10. *Ibid.*, II: 137–320; Mabel Newcomer, *A Century of Higher Education for American Women* (New York: Harper & Brothers, 1959); and Barbara Miller Solomon, *In the Company of Educated Women: A History of Women and Higher Education in America* (New Haven: Yale Univ. Press, 1985).

11. The chapter is based primarily on published and manuscript records located in the Wellesley College Archives, Margaret Clapp Library, Wellesley College, Wellesley, Mass. (hereafter designated WCA). The archival collection for the Department of Hygiene and Physical Education will be cited as Papers, Dept. of HPE, WCA.

12. Secondary sources about the controversy in America and England include Vern Bullough and Martha Voght, "Women, Menstruation, and Nineteenth-Century Medicine," *Bulletin of the History of Medicine* 47 (Jan.–Feb. 1973): 66–82; Joan N. Burstyn, *Victorian Education and the Ideal of Womanhood* (New Brunswick, N.J.: Rutgers Univ. Press, 1984); and Elaine and English Showalter, "Victorian Women and Menstruation," *Victorian Studies* 14 (1970–71): 83–89.

13. *Calendar*, 1877–78, p. 49.

14. *Ibid.*, 50.

15. *Ibid.*, 49.

16. *Calendar*, 1876–77, p. 24.

17. Shortly after its inception, Wellesley began to request that applicants submit a certificate of health from their family physicians. Finding such reports to be inadequate, even misleading, the college established its own board of health in 1891 in order, among other tasks, to screen the students' certificates. (See the *President's Report to the Board of Trustees, for the Year Ending in 1891*, p. 3. Hereafter cited as *President's Report*, with year.) The undertaking seemed useful. In 1891–92, for example, the board uncovered two girls who "proved candidates for the sanitarium rather than for the college." (See *President's Report*, 1892, p. 7.) In 1896, as a temporary replacement for anthropometric exams, the college instituted medical exams for the students. (See *President's Report*, 1896, p. 8.) In 1900, the college decided to send health questionnaires to the students' mothers, hoping to gather further information and to prepare for girls with special needs. (See *President's Report*, 1900, p. 13.) For a later, and quite adamant, statement on documentation about health, see the college brochure titled *To Parents Whose Daughters Are Candidates for Wellesley College*, 1913, p. 1. Health certification was a different process from anthropometric and physical exams, which will be discussed later.

18. *Calendar*, 1877–78, p. 49.

19. *Ibid.*, 1876–77, p. 24.

20. From one of Durant's sermons at the college, quoted in Converse, *Wellesley College: A Chronicle of the Years 1875–1938*, p. 34.

21. See George Herbert Palmer, *The Life of Alice Freeman Palmer* (Boston and New York: Houghton Mifflin, 1908); Roberta Frankfort, *Collegiate Women: Domesticity and Career in Turn-of-the-Century America* (New York:

New York Univ. Press, 1977), 17–25, 41–48, 59–71; and "Alice Elvira Freeman Palmer," in *Notable American Women, 1607–1950,* Edward T. James, ed., 3 vols. (Cambridge, Mass.: Belknap Press of Harvard Univ. Press, 1971), 3: 4–8.

22. A good explication is found in Palmer's essay "Why Go to College?," printed in George Herbert Palmer and Alice Freeman Palmer, *The Teacher: Essays and Addresses on Education* (Boston and New York: Houghton Mifflin, 1908), 364–95. For an analysis of Palmer's concept of womanhood, and her reconciliation of its domestic and intellectual elements, see Frankfort, *Collegiate Women.*

23. Palmer, "Why Go to College?," 394.

24. For information about the following three women, see the histories by Converse, Glasscock, Hackett, and Palmieri.

25. See "Caroline Hazard," in *Notable American Women, 1607–1950* 2: 169–70.

26. *President's Report,* 1892, p. 8. For similar comments by Shafer, see her annual reports of 1889, p. 8; 1890, p. 8; and 1893, p. 12.

27. Lucille Eaton Hill, ed., *Athletics and Out-Door Sports for Women. Each Subject Being Separately Treated by a Special Writer* (New York: Macmillan, 1903), 13. See also Hill's comments in "Physical Training," [*Wellesley*] *Prelude* 3 (Jan. 23, 1892): 178–79, and "Wellesley College Bloomer Crew," *The* [*Boston*] *Journal,* April 19, 1896 (copy located in History files, Papers, Dept. of HPE, WCA). Students expressed similar views. See F. S. R., Class of 1893, "A Word on Physical Culture," [*Wellesley*] *Prelude* 3 (Oct. 3, 1891): 5, and *L'egenda,* 1889, p. 111. The *Prelude* and *L'egenda,* the college yearbook, were student publications.

28. See Hill, *Athletics and Out-Door Sports for Women,* 13, and Hill, "Physical Training," 179. (In the latter, Hill clarifies her views through a long quotation from Dr. Edward M. Hartwell, a prominent physical educator, an advocate of mind-body development, and, at the time, the director of physical training in Boston's public schools.)

29. "The Work and Purpose of the Department of Physical Training," [*Wellesley*] *College News* 4 (May 3, 1905): 1.

30. Quoted in "Wellesley College—Current Affairs—'Physical Education at Wellesley,'" *Boston Evening Transcript,* Oct. 8, 1901, p. 10 (an article reprinted from *Our Town,* a community newspaper in Wellesley, Mass.). See also Palmer, "Why Go to College?," 371.

31. Ruth C. Hanford, Class of 1909, "Lucille Eaton Hill: An Appreciation," *The Wellesley Alumnae Magazine* 9 (April 1925): 317–18.

32. F. S. R., "A Word on Physical Culture," 5.

33. Millicent Peirce Potter, Class of 1894, "Athletics at Wellesley," *The American Athlete* 1 (April 1897): 3; also p. 1. (Copy found in History files, Papers, Dept. of HPE, WCA.) See also Palmer, "Why Go to College?," 372–73.

34. For example, see Wellesley College *Regulations,* Sept. 6, 1876, pp. 4–5; *Regulations,* 1877–78, pp. 4–7; *Regulations,* 1885–86, p. 2; *Circular to Parents,* 1877, p. 2; and *Circular to Parents,* 1879, p. 3 (which included the quotation about dress).

35. *Circular to Parents,* 1876, p. 2.

36. *Regulations,* 1887–88, p. 2.

37. *Regulations,* 1877–78, p. 5 (emphasis in original); also, *Circular to Parents,* 1878, pp. 1–2.
38. *Circular to Parents,* 1876, p. 2.
39. *Ibid.,* 1877, p. 2.
40. *Ibid.,* 1876, p. 2.
41. Other surveys of instruction in these areas include Victoria Frances Summers, "The Historical Development of the Undergraduate Program in Health and Physical Education at Wellesley College" (Master's thesis, Wellesley College, 1939), and "Gymnastics in Wellesley College, 1876–1946," a twenty-two-page typescript, in History files, Papers, Dept. HPE, WCA. For studies about similar work at other women's colleges, see Mary Taylor Bissell, M.D., "The Physical Training of Women," *Proceedings of the American Association for the Advancement of Physical Education* 4 (1889): 8–17; Dorothy S. Ainsworth, *The History of Physical Education in Colleges for Women. As Illustrated by Barnard, Bryn Mawr, Elmira, Goucher, Mills, Mount Holyoke, Radcliffe, Rockford, Smith, Vassar, Wellesley and Wells* (New York: A. S. Barnes, 1930); and Woody, *A History of Women's Education in the United States,* II: 98–136.
42. From a four-page brochure titled *Wellesley College, Lake Waban,* Dec. 1874, p. 3; see also *Circular for 1876,* 1876, p. 11, and *Calendar, 1877–78,* p. 46.
43. *Calendar, 1883–84,* pp. 25, 46. The requirement applied to girls in both of the college's courses of study, the classical and the scientific. Beginning in 1884–85, "an elective course in practical hygiene and sanitary science" was offered during the second and third terms (*Calendar, 1884–85,* p. 45).
44. *Calendar, 1887–88,* p. 48; *President's Report,* 1888, pp. 9–10.
45. *Calendar,* 1890–91, pp. 22, 36; 1892–93, pp. 22–23, 52; 1894–95, p. 20; 1896–97, pp. 16, 62.
46. *Calendar, 1887–88,* p. 48. The texts were Foster's *Practical Physiology* and H. Newell Martin's *The Human Body.*
47. *Calendar, 1899–1900,* p. 66. See also *President's Report,* 1897, p. 9.
48. *President's Report,* 1883, pp. 8, 15.
49. *Ibid.,* 1890, p. 29.
50. For example, see the following issues of the *President's Report:* 1883 (Alice E. Freeman), pp. 7–8; 1888 (Helen A. Shafer), p. 7; 1889 (Shafer), p. 8; 1890 (Shafer), pp. 7–8; 1892 (Shafer), p. 18; 1897 (Julia J. Irvine), p. 9; and 1899 (Caroline Hazard), p. 7.
51. *L'egenda,* 1894, p. 156.
52. *President's Report,* 1888, p. 7.
53. *Wellesley College, Lake Waban,* Dec. 1874, p. 3. A similar announcement appeared in the *Calendar* from the mid-1870s to the early 1880s.
54. *Regulations,* 1877–78, p. 5 (emphasis in original).
55. *Ibid.*
56. Slight additions or revisions were made along the way. In 1879, for example, the requirement for outdoor exercise was dropped on Sundays and on days with inclement weather; in the latter case, however, students were expected to use the gym. (See *Regulations, 1879–80,* p. 5.) In 1880, the college advised students to take part of their exercise early in the day, and not to leave the campus in the evening. (See *Regulations, 1880–81,* p. 6.)

57. *Calendar,* 1890–91, p. 38; also p. 22.

58. *Calendar,* 1902–3, p. 116.

59. For brief descriptions of the systems, and the so-called "Battle of the Systems" in the late nineteenth century, see C. W. Hackensmith, *History of Physical Education* (New York: Harper & Row, 1966), 352–57, and Emmett A. Rice, John L. Hutchinson, and Mabel Lee, *A Brief History of Physical Education,* 5th ed. (New York: Ronald Press, 1969), 177–82, 203–8. A useful, though biased, contemporary review is Luther H. Gulick, M.D., *Physical Education by Muscular Exercise* (Philadelphia: P. Blakiston's Son, 1904), 54–63.

60. See figure on p. 150. There is no other definitive record of the type of gymnastic instruction followed at Wellesley during the 1870s. For Lewis's own description of the method, see Dio Lewis, *The New Gymnastics for Men, Women, and Children. With a Translation of Prof. Kloss's Dumb-bell Instructor and Prof. Schreber's Pangymnastikon* (Boston: Ticknor and Fields, 1862).

61. Ainsworth, *The History of Physical Education in Colleges for Women,* 27; also, Woody, *A History of Women's Education in the United States,* II: 117–22.

62. Ainsworth, *The History of Physical Education in Colleges for Women,* 16–18, 25, 27, 40, notes the adoption of Sargent exercises at Radcliffe, Bryn Mawr, Vassar, Rockford, Mount Holyoke, and Wellesley.

63. Biographical information about Hill is quite limited. The best sources are Hanford, "Lucille Eaton Hill: An Appreciation"; Marie Warren Potter, Class of 1907, *Wellesley Magazine* (Feb. 1942): 168; and "Lucille Eaton Hill," *Newsletter of the Department of Hygiene and Physical Education* (May 1942): 1, in Department files, Papers, Dept. of HPE, WCA. Although Hill apparently studied under Sargent (*Calendar,* 1888–89, p. 50), it is not known when or where. After twenty-seven years at Wellesley, Hill devoted her time to social service in the fields of health and physical education. She died on Nov. 4, 1941.

64. *Calendar,* 1882–83, pp. 59–60.

65. *Ibid.,* 60.

66. For example, see Hill, "Physical Training," 178–79. In this article, Hill quotes favorably Dr. Edward M. Hartwell's objections to Sargent exercises. (See n. 28 above.)

67. One sign of the additions was an entry in *L'egenda,* 1889, p. 111, which listed the types of exercise performed by each class in the college.

68. Hill's remarks, which followed a speech by Dudley Allen Sargent, were published in *Physical Training. A Full Report of the Papers and Discussions of the Conference Held in Boston in November, 1889,* Isabel C. Barrows, reporter and editor (Boston: George H. Ellis, 1890), 79.

69. *Ibid.* (emphasis in original).

70. *Calendar,* 1890–91, p. 38. As did other people, the staff at Wellesley tended to equate the Swedish and Ling systems, despite their significant differences. See also *Calendar,* 1892–93, p. 56, and 1894–95, p. 62.

71. Arriving in Washington, D.C., in 1883 as vice-counsul for Norway and Sweden, Nissen (1856–1924) promoted Swedish gymnastics among local doctors and schools. In 1891, he became the assistant to Edward M. Hartwell, Boston's new director of physical training. See Mabel Lee, *A History of Physical Education and Sports in the U.S.A.* (New York: John Wiley & Sons, 1983), 84–85.

72. F. S. R., "A Word on Physical Culture," 4. See also an editorial on gymnastics, *Prelude* 3 (Oct. 17, 1891): 51.

73. For a general discussion of the system, and its advantages, see Theodore Hough, *A Review of Swedish Gymnastics* (Boston: George H. Ellis, 1899). For an instructional guide written by a leading advocate and Wellesley staff member, see Hartvig Nissen, *ABC of the Swedish System of Educational Gymnastics. A Practical Hand-Book for School Teachers and the Home* (Boston: Educational Publishing, 1892). A similar work is Baron Nils Posse, *Handbook of School-Gymnastics of the Swedish System* (Boston: Lee and Shepard, 1894).

74. Ethel Perrin, "The Confessions of a Once Strict Formalist," *Journal of Health and Physical Education* 9 (Nov. 1938): 533.

75. Hough, *A Review of Swedish Gymnastics,* 19. At the time, Hough was an assistant professor of biology at the Massachusetts Institute of Technology and an instructor in physiology and hygiene at the Boston Normal School of Gymnastics.

76. *Ibid.*

77. *Ibid.,* 21.

78. *Ibid.,* 25.

79. *Ibid.,* 25–26.

80. Beginning in the 1890s, Swedish gymnastics overtook the Sargent system at most women's colleges, except for Vassar. (See Ainsworth, *The History of Physical Education in Colleges for Women,* 18–19, 25, 27.) Swedish exercises remained popular at female schools well into the 1930s and 1940s.

81. "The Faculty in the Gymnasium—A Remarkable Instance of the Devotion of the Wellesley Faculty to the Students," *L'egenda,* 1890, p. 149. The relaxation routine, done on behalf of the seniors, probably imitated the breathing exercises that accompanied most classwork in the gym (see *L'egenda,* 1889, p. 111).

82. For descriptions of the program in the early 1900s, see *Calendar,* 1902–3, p. 116, and *Calendar,* 1903–4, pp. 126–27.

83. Other women's colleges that adopted Sargent's tests included Vassar, Bryn Mawr, and Rockford. (See Ainsworth, *The History of Physical Education in Colleges for Women,* 16–18, 25, 64–66.)

84. *President's Report,* 1883, p. 11.

85. M. Anna Wood worked at Wellesley from 1885 to 1895. She then attended medical school at Tufts University, receiving her degree in 1898 and being admitted to the Massachusetts Medical Society in 1899. Little else is known about her life prior to or after her years at Wellesley.

86. *Calendar,* 1888–89, p. 50.

87. *Ibid.,* 1890–91, p. 38.

88. A considerable number of charts and records from those early years have been preserved in the Archives at Wellesley College (WCA). The Wellesley method of anthropometric testing is best represented in Lucille Eaton Hill and M. Anna Wood, *The Average Anthropometric Table—Used in Recording an Examination—Wellesley College Gymnasium,* Files on Anthropometry, Papers, Dept. of HPE, WCA. Hill and Wood calculated the mean results of 1100 Wellesley students in 55 tests of size and strength (comparable to Sargent's). Their standardized graph consisted of three columns: "below the average,"

"average of 1100 measurements," and "at or above the average." Instead of dealing with percentile rankings, as Sargent did, Hill and Wood simply recorded whether the results of an individual girl fell below, at, or above the statistical mean for the reference group in each test. It is not clear if any consideration was given to differences in age, height, or weight. (In 1890, however, President Helen A. Shafer indicated that a student could judge her results against "the averaged measurements of all girls of her height, also with those of her college class and of the average Wellesley student." See *President's Report,* 1890, p. 9. Further reports of charts standardized by height and class were not found.)

89. For example, see *President's Report,* 1890, pp. 8–9, 32.

90. *Calendar,* 1892–93, p. 56; see also 1894–95, p. 62.

91. L. E. Hill and M. A. Wood, *Statistical Tables—Wellesley College Gymnasium—1891,* Files on Anthropometry, Papers, Dept. of HPE, WCA. The study did not consist of full-fledged anthropometric exams; instead, it was an assessment of changes in the students' general well-being, patterns of exercise and sleep, level of nervousness, and other conditions during their four years at Wellesley. (Not all of the trends were flattering.)

92. *President's Report,* 1889, p. 8; see also 1890, p. 8.

93. For example, see *President's Report,* 1893, pp. 35–40, and *L'egenda,* 1894, pp. 149–50.

94. *President's Report,* 1896, p. 8 and 8–9 in general. Medical exams replaced the anthropometric tests.

95. See *Calendar,* 1900–1901, p. 17, and 1901–2, p. 23. The Papers of the Dept. of HPE, WCA, contain anthropometric data and studies covering the first third of the twentieth century. See also Ainsworth, *The History of Physical Education in Colleges for Women,* 64–69.

96. *L'egenda,* 1895, p. 130 (emphasis in original).

97. For example, see Albert Shaw, "Physical Culture at Wellesley," *Review of Reviews* (American edition) 6 (Dec. 1892): 545–49. An advocate of physical education at women's colleges, Shaw complimented Wellesley's attention to student health, especially its anthropometric studies. Newspaper articles about the exams and physical education at Wellesley and other women's colleges at the turn of the century included "Wellesley College—Current Affairs— 'Physical Education at Wellesley,' " *Boston Evening Transcript,* Oct. 8, 1901, p. 10; Walter Channing, M.D., "Physical Training at Wellesley College" (newspaper clipping, ca. 1896), History files, Papers, Dept. of HPE, WCA; and in the scrapbooks of the Boston Normal School of Gymnastics (BNSG), Papers, Dept. of HPE, WCA: "The Listener," *Boston Transcript,* Dec. 6, 1892, and Mary Taylor Bissell, "Physical Culture for Women" (newspaper clipping, n.d.). A more extensive review of programs at various women's colleges, including Wellesley, is found in Bissell, "The Physical Training of Women." A strong supporter of women's health and education, Bissell asserted that "the institutions which the public has criticized as enemies to the health of women prove, upon investigation, to be the only ones . . . where their physical training is conducted on any thorough and scientific basis" (pp. 8–9). For another doctor's opinion, see C. H. Cook, M.D., "The Effect of College Life at Wellesley," *Medical Communications of the Massachusetts Medical Society* 16 (1893): 191–95. In his rather haphazard article, Cook found aspects of Wellesley's pro-

gram to praise and to question. Finally, doctors and physical educators used Wellesley's anthropometric data to develop comparisons with other female populations, both in and out of college. For example, see Alice B. Foster, M.D., "A Few Figures on Occupation and Exercise," *Proceedings of the American Association for the Advancement of Physical Education* 9 (1894): 72–81. Compared to young working women and coeds in the Midwest, Foster concluded, "New England shows greater heights, longer bones, large head, small chest, small hips, little adipose, firm flesh, good nervous system, but low chest capacity and poor forearms" (p. 79).

98. See also *Health Statistics of Women College Graduates. Report of a Special Committee of the Association of Collegiate Alumnae* (Boston: Wright & Potter, 1885), and Grace A. Preston, M.D., "The Influence of College Life on the Health of Women," *Medical Communications of the Massachusetts Medical Society* 16 (1893): 167–90.

99. *Calendar, 1877–78*, p. 46.

100. For a brief summary of sports at the college, see Summers, "The Historical Development of the Undergraduate Program in Health and Physical Education at Wellesley College," 75.

101. *President's Report*, 1893, p. 12.

102. Contemporary articles provide the best record of how sports developed at Wellesley. The scrapbooks of the BNSG and the History files in the Papers of the Dept. of HPE, WCA, are filled with magazine and newspaper clippings about athletics at the school. For example, Channing, "Physical Training at Wellesley College," and Potter, "Athletics at Wellesley."

103. For a brief overview, see Summers, "The Historical Development of the Undergraduate Program in Health and Physical Education at Wellesley College," 71. Also, "Girls with Sound Bodies. Aiding Physical Culture at Wellesley College" (newspaper clipping, ca. 1894), and "Playing Golf and Basketball. Students at Wellesley Devoting Much Attention to Physical Training" (newspaper clipping, ca. 1894), in the Scrapbooks of the BNSG, Papers, Dept. of HPE, WCA, and an article from the *New York Tri-Weekly Tribune*, May 8, 1901, History files, Papers, Dept. of HPE, WCA.

104. Quoted in "Girls with Sound Bodies. Aiding Physical Culture at Wellesley College."

105. Hill, *Athletics and Out-Door Sports for Women*, 13.

106. Potter, "Athletics at Wellesley," 1, noted that two hundred girls joined. (A later article claimed that the association had roughly four hundred members. See news clipping from the *New York Tri-Weekly Tribune*, May 8, 1901, History files, Papers, Dept. of HPE, WCA.) The fee was mentioned in *President's Report*, 1897, p. 11.

107. *L'egenda*, 1900, pp. 155, 156.

108. *President's Report*, 1893, p. 12.

109. From interview with Hill in "Wellesley College Bloomer Crew," *The [Boston] Journal*, April 19, 1896, in the History files, Papers, Dept. of HPE, WCA.

110. L. E. Hill, "The New Athletics," *College News* 2 (Oct. 29, 1902): 1.

111. *Ibid.*

112. Historical works about women and competitive athletics include Ellen W. Gerber, "The Controlled Development of Collegiate Sport for Women,

1923–1936," *Journal of Sport History* 2 (Spring 1975): 1–28; Mary Lou Remley, "Women and Competitive Athletics," *Maryland Historian* 4 (Fall 1973): 88–94; Stephanie Lee Twin, *Jock and Jill: Aspects of Women's Sports History in America, 1870–1940* (Ann Arbor: Univ. Microfilms International, 1981), 129–275; and Doris Paige Watts, "Changing Conceptions of Competitive Sports for Girls and Women in the United States from 1880 to 1960" (Ed.D. dissertation, Univ. of California, Los Angeles, 1960). A study about competitive sports for undergraduate men is Bruce Leslie, "The Response of Four Colleges to the Rise of Intercollegiate Athletics, 1865–1915," *Journal of Sport History* 3 (Winter 1976): 213–22. See also Donald J. Mrozek, *Sport and American Mentality, 1880–1910* (Knoxville: Univ. of Tennessee Press, 1983), 28–102.

113. For representative remarks by Dudley Allen Sargent, see his following works: *Health, Strength and Power* (New York and Boston: H. M. Caldwell, 1904), 58–76; *Physical Education* (Boston: Ginn, 1906), 66–125, 152–210, 247–76; "What Athletic Games, If Any, Are Injurious for Women in the Form in Which They Are Played by Men?," *American Physical Education Review* 11 (Sept. 1906): 174–81; "Competition in College Athletics," *American Physical Education Review* 15 (Feb. 1910): 98–110; "Competition and Culture," *American Physical Education Review* 15 (Nov. 1910): 579–85; and, from Articles and Speeches, Dudley Allen Sargent Papers, Harvard Univ. Archives, Pusey Library, Harvard Univ., Cambridge, Mass.: "Dedication of Gymnasium at Wheaton College, February 4, 1903"; "Lowell Address, Rogers Hall, Tuesday, October 22, 1912"; and "Physical Training and Athletics for Girls" (n.d.).

114. Ronald A. Smith, "The Rise of Basketball for Women in Colleges," *Canadian Journal of the History of Sport and Physical Education* 1 (Dec. 1970): 18–36.

115. Hill, "The New Athletics," 1 (emphasis in original).

116. *L'egenda,* 1898, p. 91. Invoking the new paradigms of biology, the yearbook also noted that the boat crew "has evolved from its former feeble and tub-like state to its present muscular form, encased in a shell" (*ibid.,* 90). The remark probably signaled the change from wide boats to narrow ones, in which the girls sat in single file.

117. Editorial on physical training, *Prelude* 3 (Oct. 17, 1891): 52.

118. Editorial, *College News* 2 (Oct. 29, 1902): 2.

119. *President's Report,* 1897, p. 9.

120. *President's Report,* 1900, p. 11.

121. *Calendar,* 1876–77, p. 24.

7. *"Veritable Crusaders"*

1. See Ethel Perrin, "Ethel Perrin—An Autobiography," *Research Quarterly of the American Association for Health, Physical Education, and Recreation* 12, supplement (Oct. 1941): 682–85, and an entry in *Notable American Women: The Modern Period,* Barbara Sicherman and Carol Hurd Green, eds. (Cambridge, Mass.: Belknap Press of Harvard Univ. Press, 1980), 539–41. (The opening quotation appeared in a speech by Perrin at a memorial for

another graduate of the BNSG, a copy of which was located in the Wellesley College Archives.)

2. Standard sources include Ellen W. Gerber, *Innovators and Institutions in Physical Education* (Philadelphia: Lea & Febiger, 1971), 245–416; C. W. Hackensmith, *History of Physical Education* (New York: Harper & Row, 1966), 348–516; Mabel Lee, *A History of Physical Education and Sports in the U.S.A.* (New York: John Wiley & Sons, 1983); Frederick E. Leonard, *Pioneers of Modern Physical Training* (New York: Physical Directors' Society of the Young Men's Christian Association of North America, 1910); and Norma Schwendener, *A History of Physical Education in the United States* (New York: A. S. Barnes, 1942). Two useful compilations of primary sources are Aileene S. Lockhart and Betty Spears, eds., *Chronicle of American Physical Education: Selected Readings, 1855–1930* (Dubuque, Iowa: Wm. C. Brown, 1972), and Arthur Weston, *The Making of American Physical Education* (New York: Appleton-Century-Crofts, 1962).

3. Historical studies include Ruth Elliott, *The Organization of Professional Training in Physical Education in State Universities,* Teachers College, Columbia University, Contributions to Education, no. 268 (New York: Bureau of Publications, Teachers College, Columbia Univ., 1927), and Earle F. Zeigler, "A History of Professional Preparation for Physical Education in the United States, 1861–1948" (Ph.D. dissertation, Yale Univ., 1950).

4. Dr. Delphine Hanna, "Present Status of Physical Training in Normal Schools," *American Physical Education Review* 8 (Dec. 1903): 294–97. (Hereafter, journal designated *APER.*)

5. Calculated from *ibid.*, 296–97.

6. James C. Boykin, "Physical Training," in *Report of the [United States] Commissioner of Education for 1891–92* (Washington, D.C.: Government Printing Office, 1894), I: 580.

7. J. H. McCurdy, M.D., "A Study of the Characteristics of Physical Training in the Public Schools of the United States," *APER* 10 (Sept. 1905): 204, 205.

8. Calculated from a membership list in *Proceedings of the American Association for the Advancement of Physical Education* 1 (1885): 2. (Hereafter, journal cited as *Proc. AAAPE.*)

9. Estimated from membership lists in *Proc. AAAPE* 2 (1886): 34–35; 10 (1895): 212–24; and *APER* 10 (1905): 344–64. The calculations included individuals with distinctly female first names, when full names were given, and those with female titles (e.g., Miss), when only initials were cited.

10. From information reported in *APER* 5 (1900): 85.

11. For example, see G. S. Lowman, "The Regulation and Control of Competitive Sport in Secondary Schools of the United States," *APER* 12 (June 1907): 244. Lowman's article revealed that women comprised only 26 percent of the physical directors in public schools around the country.

12. See McCurdy, "A Study of the Characteristics of Physical Training in the Public Schools of the United States," 205. McCurdy reported that the income of male physical education teachers in public schools ranged from $500 to $4,000, while women's ranged from $360 to $2,500. Among teachers in major cities, the "most common" salary for men was $1,200, compared to $1,050 for women. The same disparity surfaced in a 1906 study of salaries

among the directors of physical training programs at public normal schools; the average salary for male directors was $1,166 and for females $959 (and only $862 if one woman's income "at the upper extreme" was omitted). See G. B. Affleck, "The Status of Physical Training in Public Normal Schools in the United States," *APER* 11 (Dec. 1906): 266.

13. According to lists in *Proc. AAAPE* and *APER,* women held between one-tenth and one-quarter of the AAAPE's executive posts during its first twenty years. The first female president of the AAAPE was Mabel Lee, a 1910 graduate of the BNSG. The situation was quite different, of course, in organizations founded and run by female physical educators.

14. A review of historical literature about women in the profession is June A. Kennard, "The History of Physical Education," *Signs* 2 (Summer 1977): 835–42.

15. For example, see the references cited in n. 2.

16. For example, see M. Gladys Scott and Mary J. Hoferek, eds., *Women as Leaders in Physical Education and Sports* (Iowa City: Univ. of Iowa Press, 1979), and Elizabeth Halsey, *Women in Physical Education: Their Role in Work, Home, and History* (New York: G. P. Putnam's Sons, 1961). Both volumes include some historical material.

17. The major sources for this chapter are published and manuscript materials relating to the BNSG in the Wellesley College Archives, Margaret Clapp Library, Wellesley College, Wellesley, Mass. (hereafter designated WCA). Of particular importance are the Papers of the Department of Hygiene and Physical Education, WCA, and the Papers of the Wellesley College Alumnae Association: Hygiene and Physical Education Section, WCA (hereafter designated, respectively, Papers, Dept. of HPE, WCA, and Papers, Alumnae Assn.: HPE, WCA). A secondary source about the BNSG is Margery Fitzstephen Taylor, "A Historical Study of Professional Training in Hygiene and Physical Education in the Boston Normal School of Gymnastics and at Wellesley College" (Master's thesis, Wellesley College, 1939). Briefer accounts include Gerber, *Innovators and Institutions in Physical Education,* 308–13, and Schwendener, *A History of Physical Education in the United States,* 116–18, 120–22.

18. See "Mary Porter Tileston Hemenway," in *Notable American Women, 1607–1950,* Edward T. James, ed., 3 vols. (Cambridge, Mass.: Belknap Press of Harvard Univ. Press, 1971), 2: 179–81; *Memorial Service Held in the Church of the Disciples, March 11, 1894, with a Sermon by Charles Gordon Ames* (Boston: n.p., 1894); and *A Memorial to the Life and Benefactions of Mary Hemenway, 1820–1894* (Boston: privately printed, 1927). On Homans, see William Skarstrom, "Life and Work of Amy Morris Homans: Pioneer and Leader in the Field of Hygiene and Physical Education," *Research Quarterly of the American Association for Health, Physical Education, and Recreation* 12, supplement (Oct. 1941): 615–27; Betty Spears, "The Influential Miss Homans," in *Her Story in Sport: A Historical Anthology of Women in Sports,* Reet Howell, ed. (West Point, N.Y.: Leisure Press, 1982), 391–404; and Betty Spears, *Leading the Way: Amy Morris Homans and the Beginnings of Professional Education for Women,* Contributions in Women's Studies, no. 64 (New York and Westport, Conn.: Greenwood Press, 1986).

19. For a discussion of Hemenway's interest in and contributions to physical education, see Betty Spears, " 'The Building Up of Character Has Been My

Aim': A Glimpse of the Life of Mary Hemenway," *Journal of Health, Physical Education and Recreation* 42 (March 1971): 93–94, and Betty Spears, "The Philanthropist and the Physical Educator," *New England Quarterly* 47 (Dec. 1974): 594–602. (The latter article contrasts Hemenway and Dudley Allen Sargent.)

20. "A Message from Miss Homans," *Mary Hemenway Alumnae Association Bulletin* (Sept. 1929): 3. (Hereafter, source designated *MHAA Bulletin.*)

21. Accounts of the origin and early years of the BNSG include "A School of Gymnastics: Public School Teachers Instructed in the Swedish System of Gymnastics," *Boston Transcript,* Jan. 16, 1889, p. 4; newspaper clippings in Scrapbook (vol. I) of the BNSG, Papers, Dept. of HPE, WCA; and William Skarstrom, "The Early Years of the Boston Normal School of Gymnastics," *MHAA Bulletin* (1934–35): 10–15. A graduate of the BNSG, Skarstrom was an instructor at the school for nearly twenty-five years.

22. *Boston Normal School of Gymnastics. 1890–1891* (n.p., n.d.), 2. (Despite the brochure's wording, admission was not confined to active teachers.)

23. *Ibid.*

24. In addition, there were forty-six certificate holders (who finished a one-year program) and special students, along with seventy-nine nongraduates. The figures in the text and note come from my examination of student admission cards, student registers (published in the BNSG's annual catalogues), and alumnae records for the classes of 1891–1900.

25. Hanna, "Present Status of Physical Training in Normal Schools," 296–97.

26. Affleck, "The Status of Physical Training in Public Normal Schools in the United States," 267, and McCurdy, "A Study of the Characteristics of Physical Training in the Public Schools of the United States," 209. (Less than 40 percent of the respondents in McCurdy's survey identified the means by which their physical education staff members were trained. The available data showed that graduates of the BNSG and the Milwaukee Normal School for the Turners accounted for half of those who had prepared through a recognized program.)

27. From "Alumnae News–Statistics," *MHAA Bulletin* (1918–19): 38, and Taylor, "A Historical Study of Professional Training in Hygiene and Physical Education in the Boston Normal School of Gymnastics and at Wellesley College," 207 and 207–10 in general.

28. The following group profiles are based on the student and graduate registers published in the annual catalogues of the BNSG, WCA; the student records in the Papers of the Dept. of HPE, WCA (consisting of physical examination cards with personal information, a medical history, and data from anthropometric tests); and Biographical Data: Classes 1891–1900, in the records of the Alumnae Assn.: HPE, WCA. Additional information was gleaned from various biographical and autobiographical sources, which will be cited in the notes. The analysis covers *only* the 212 women who received two-year diplomas and excludes certificate holders, special students, nongraduates, and male graduates (a total of roughly 131 people).

29. For purposes of comparison, data on the forty women who did not complete their course of study were compiled. Physical examination cards for

thirty-four of them were located. (The sample did not include one-year certificate holders or women who entered in 1889 but did not return for their second year.)

30. Edith Naomi Hill, "Senda Berenson: Director of Physical Education at Smith College, 1892–1911," *Research Quarterly of the American Association for Health, Physical Education, and Recreation* 12, supplement (Oct. 1941): 658–65; see 659 on her delicacy as a child. As will subsequent references to BNSG graduates, a parenthetical note gives Berenson's class year. A member of the class of 1892, Berenson (1868–1954) interrupted her senior year to teach at Smith College; she officially completed the BNSG program in 1895. (The source cited in this note was a special edition of the *Research Quarterly*, entitled "Pioneer Women in Physical Education." Several articles in the issue focused on women associated with the BNSG. Hereafter designated *Research Quarterly*.)

31. Betty Spears, "Success, Women, and Physical Education," in *Women as Leaders in Physical Education and Sports,* 9. (Spears's article examines eight prominent BNSG graduates.) Another account of the background and contributions of Norris (1874–1958) is Mabel Lee, "A Tribute to J. Anna Norris," a speech presented at a conference of the Midwest Association of Physical Education for College Women, Oct. 1979 (typescript obtained from the Dept. of Physical Education, Univ. of Minnesota, Minneapolis).

32. Mabel Lee, *Memories of a Bloomer Girl (1894–1924)* (Washington, D.C.: American Alliance for Health, Physical Education, and Recreation, 1977), 26; see 26–28 in general. A 1910 graduate of the BNSG, Lee (1886–1985) technically is outside the scope of this chapter. As the account of an early physical educator, however, her book is too special to omit.

33. Quoted in Hill, "Senda Berenson," 659.

34. Lee, *Memories of a Bloomer Girl (1894–1924),* 38 and 28–38 in general. See also Spears, "Success, Women, and Physical Education," 9, on Lee's and other BNSG graduates' enjoyment of exercise.

35. Letter of Lucy Pratt, June 11, 1925, p. 1, in Biographical Data: Class of 1895, Papers, Alumnae Assn.: HPE, WCA.

36. *Ibid.* When the train conductor suggested that Pratt allow more time for her run, her reply was that she did not need "to *start* earlier," but "only . . . to increase my speed a bit" (emphasis in original).

37. *Ibid.* (emphasis in original).

38. "Phys-Ed Pioneer Now 91," *The [Providence, Rhode Island] Evening Bulletin,* Aug. 26, 1963 (an interview with Mrs. Edith Hill Brown), in Biographical Data: Class of 1893, Papers, Alumnae Assn.: HPE, WCA.

39. *Ibid.*

40. David B. Tyack, *The One Best System: A History of American Urban Education* (Cambridge, Mass.: Harvard Univ. Press, 1976), 61 and 59–65 in general. See also Redding S. Sugg, Jr., *Motherteacher: The Feminization of American Education* (Charlottesville: Univ. Press of Virginia, 1978). The two authors agree that the process involved substantial disparities between the salaries, rank, and power of female and male educators.

41. Janet M. Hooks, *Women's Occupations Through Seven Decades,* Women's Bureau Bulletin, no. 218 (Washington, D.C.: Government Printing

Office, 1947), 52, 59, 157–61, and Joseph A. Hill, *Women in Gainful Occupations, 1870 to 1920*, Census Monographs IX (Washington, D.C.: Government Printing Office, 1929; reprint ed., New York: Johnson Reprint, 1972), 32–45.

42. Jessie H. Bancroft, "Pioneering in Physical Training–An Autobiography," *Research Quarterly* 12, supplement (Oct. 1941): 666; also 667. Bancroft (1867–1952) was not a BNSG graduate; she attended the Minneapolis School of Physical Education and Sargent's summer school at Harvard. Her main position was the director of physical training in the public schools of Brooklyn, New York. See biographical sketch in *Notable American Women: The Modern Period*, 46–47.

43. Perrin, "Ethel Perrin–An Autobiography," 682.

44. *Ibid.*

45. Spears, "Success, Women, and Physical Education," 9–10. McKinstry (1878–1949) was best known for her work at the Pratt Institute, the Dept. of Physical Education at New York's central branch of the YWCA, and the Central School of Hygiene and Physical Education, which she founded, and for her service to several professional organizations. See Grace Lecomte, "Biography of Dr. Helen McKinstry," *The Reflector* 8 (Oct. 1949): 1, 4–5. (The journal was the official publication of the Association of Women in Physical Education in New York State.) Josephine Rathbone (b. 1899; married name Karpovich) was a specialist in corrective physical education on the faculty of the Teachers College, Columbia Univ., New York.

46. *Boston Normal School of Gymnastics. First Annual Catalogue of the Instructors, Students, and Graduates, with a Statement of the Course of Instruction and Examinations, 1891–1892* (Boston: Geo. H. Ellis, 1892), 9. (Hereafter the school's annual catalogues will be designated *Ann. Cat.*, with number and year.)

47. *Eleventh Ann. Cat.*, 1901–2, p. 24 (emphasis in original), and *Sixteenth Ann. Cat.*, 1906–7, p. 28. The stipulation about language skills was not a blatant attempt to discourage foreign applicants; even before 1902, English was the native tongue of most students. The school simply believed that effective communication was essential to good teaching.

48. For the restatement of the catalogue's introduction, see *Thirteenth Ann. Cat.*, 1903–4, p. 5.

49. On tuition and other costs, see *Boston Normal School of Gymnastics. 1890–1891*, p. 4; *First Ann. Cat.*, 1891–92, p. 9; and *Tenth Ann. Cat.*, 1900–1901, p. 21.

50. For descriptions, see *Boston Normal School of Gymnastics. 1890–1891*, p. 2, and *Seventh Ann. Cat.*, 1897–98, p. 16. When Wellesley College absorbed the BNSG in 1909, the two institutions cooperated in building the college's long-awaited new gym, and named it after Mary Hemenway.

51. Also see *Third Ann. Cat.*, 1893–94, p. 15. For a description of the apparatus, see "Our Gymnastic SchoolMa'ams" (newspaper clipping, ca. 1890), in Scrapbook (vol. III) of the BNSG, Papers, Dept. of HPE, WCA.

52. See *First Ann. Cat.*, 1891–92, p. 10.

53. "Phys-Ed Pioneer Now 91."

54. See *First Ann. Cat.*, 1891–92, p. 10.

55. Lucy Pratt, "A Brief Soliloquy of a Ninety-fiver," June 1920, p. 1, in

Biographical Data: Class of 1895, Papers, Alumnae Assn.: HPE, WCA (emphasis in original). See also Helen McKinstry, "Vignettes," *MHAA Bulletin* (1934–35): 16, #3.

56. *Boston Normal School of Gymnastics. 1890–1891*, p. 2.

57. For a listing of topics covered in the junior year, see *First Ann. Cat.*, 1891–92, pp. 8, 17–21. Some lecture notes from first-year courses are extant; see "Synopsis of Lectures To Be Held before the Normal Class in Educational Gymnastics, by Claes J. Enebuske," and "Synopsis of Lectures To Be Given to the Normal Class in Educational Gymnastics, session of 1890–91, by Emma L. Call, M.D.," in folders of BNSG, Papers, Dept. of HPE, WCA.

58. *Third Ann. Cat.*, 1893–94, p. 9.

59. For a typical junior-year schedule in the early 1900s, see *Twelfth Ann. Cat.*, 1902–3, pp. 10, 12–13, 16–19.

60. *First Ann. Cat.*, 1891–92, pp. 8, 21–23.

61. *Second Ann. Cat.*, 1892–93, p. 9.

62. For a typical senior schedule, see *Twelfth Ann. Cat.*, 1902–3, pp. 10–11, 14–15, 19–25.

63. On original staffing, see Skarstrom, "The Early Years of the Boston Normal School of Gymnastics," 11–12, and *Boston Normal School of Gymnastics. 1890–1891*, p. 2. Concerning the later growth and composition of the faculty, see *First Ann. Cat.*, 1891–92, p. 7; *Second Ann. Cat.*, 1892–93, pp. 7–8; and *Third Ann. Cat.*, 1893–94, pp. 7–8.

64. *Eighth Ann. Cat.*, 1898–99, pp. 6–7.

65. Pratt, "A Brief Soliloquy of a Ninety-fiver," 3.

66. *Ibid.*

67. "Phys-Ed Pioneer Now 91."

68. Ethel Perrin, "The Confessions of a Once Strict Formalist," *Journal of Health and Physical Education* 9 (Nov. 1938): 533. See also McKinstry, "Vignettes," 16, #4.

69. Quoted in Hill, "Senda Berenson," 659.

70. Pratt, "A Brief Soliloquy of a Ninety-fiver," 3–4.

71. Helen McKinstry, "Woman Climbs," *MHAA Bulletin* (March 1931): 12. See also McKinstry, "Vignettes," 17, #9.

72. Perrin, "The Confessions of a Once Strict Formalist," 534.

73. McKinstry, "Vignettes," 17, #6.

74. *Ibid.*, 18, #16.

75. Pratt, "A Brief Soliloquy of a Ninety-fiver," 2 (emphasis in original).

76. *Ibid.*, 3.

77. Quoted in Hill, "Senda Berenson," 659.

78. Perrin, "Ethel Perrin—An Autobiography," 682.

79. Perrin, "The Confessions of a Once Strict Formalist," 533.

80. The following analysis is based primarily on published and manuscript materials found in the Wellesley College Archives. Until 1910, the annual catalogues of the BNSG included registers of its graduates by class year, listing the women's locations and occupations, if any. From 1915 to 1937, the Mary Hemenway Alumnae Association published an annual bulletin (*MHAA Bulletin*), which contained similar information. When that group became a division of Wellesley College's general alumnae association in 1937, class notes appeared in the *Wellesley Magazine*. (Earlier editions of that publication had

included some items about BNSG alumnae.) In some instances, reports about graduates also appeared in the *Newsletter* of the Dept. of Hygiene and Physical Education and in the *Newsletter* of the Hygiene and Physical Education section of the Alumnae Association. The BNSG and, subsequently, the Dept. of Hygiene and Physical Education at Wellesley also kept files on their graduates; those are designated as Biographical Data: Class of [year], Papers, Alumnae Assn.: HPE, WCA. In some cases, additional information about graduates appeared in other sources, which will be cited in the notes.

81. Barbara Miller Solomon, *In the Company of Educated Women: A History of Women and Higher Education in America* (New Haven: Yale Univ. Press, 1985), 119–22.

82. For comparative data, see Joan Jacobs Brumberg and Nancy Tomes, "Women in the Professions: A Research Agenda for American Historians," *Reviews in American History* 10 (June 1982): 280–81.

83. Lee, "A Tribute to J. Anna Norris," 6–7.

84. Margaret Davis Fisher, (Class Note for 1920–21), in Biographical Data: Class of 1896, Papers, Alumnae Assn.: HPE, WCA.

85. Ursula Margaret Willard, (Class Note for 1916–17), in Biographical Data: Class of 1893, Papers, Alumnae Assn.: HPE, WCA.

86. Florence D'Auby Durand, (Class Note for 1921–22), in Biographical Data: Class of 1898, Papers, Alumnae Assn.: HPE, WCA.

87. Josephine Turck Buxton, (Class Note for 1923–24), in Biographical Data: Class of 1900, Papers, Alumnae Assn.: HPE, WCA.

88. Bancroft, "Pioneering in Physical Training—An Autobiography," 667–72.

89. Perrin, "The Confessions of a Once Strict Formalist," 534. See also Perrin, "Ethel Perrin—An Autobiography," 683.

90. Lee, "A Tribute to J. Anna Norris," 10. See also Gertrude M. Baker, "Portrait of a Pioneer," 4–5, reminiscences of a colleague at the University of Minnesota (typescript obtained from the Dept. of Physical Education, Univ. of Minnesota, Minneapolis).

91. "Phys-Ed Pioneer Now 91."

92. Hill, "Senda Berenson," 660.

93. *Ibid.*

94. *Ibid.*

95. See *ibid.,* 660–61; also, Helen McKinstry, "Organization of Work for Women, with Special Consideration of the Type of Work for Which Colleges Might Reasonably Be Expected To Give Credit," *APER* 22 (June 1917): 344–50.

96. On the quest for equal status, see Hill, "Senda Berenson," 661, and M. L. King, "Harriet Isabel Ballintine—Pioneer Veteran," *Research Quarterly* 12, supplement (Oct. 1941): 657.

97. Quoted in Hill, "Senda Berenson," 660.

98. Quoted in *ibid.*

99. See Perrin, "The Confessions of a Once Strict Formalist," 533–36, 589–90.

100. *Ibid.,* 536 (emphasis in original).

101. *Ibid.*

102. *Ibid.*

103. For a general overview, see Brumberg and Tomes, "Women in the Professions: A Research Agenda for American Historians," 275–96, and Cynthia Fuchs Epstein, *Woman's Place: Options and Limits in Professional Careers* (Berkeley: Univ. of California Press, 1970). Historical studies include Regina Markell Morantz, Cynthia Stokola Pomerleau, and Carol Hansen Fenichel, eds., *In Her Own Words: Oral Histories of Women Physicians* (Westport, Conn.: Greenwood Press, 1982); Regina Markell Morantz-Sanchez, *Sympathy and Science: Women Physicians in American Medicine* (New York: Oxford Univ. Press, 1985); Margaret W. Rossiter, *Women Scientists in America: Struggles and Strategies to 1940* (Baltimore: Johns Hopkins Univ. Press, 1982); and Mary Roth Walsh, *"Doctors Wanted: No Women Need Apply": Sexual Barriers in the Medical Profession, 1835–1975* (New Haven: Yale Univ. Press, 1977).

104. The following discussion is based on roughly sixty articles by graduates of BNSG classes 1891–1900, published in professional journals and other sources between 1900 and 1940. Naturally, prominent alumnae tended to be the most prolific authors. Five women (Lillian C. Drew, 1893; Helen May McKinstry, 1900; J. Anna Norris, 1895; Ethel Perrin, 1892; and E. Blanche Sterling, 1900) wrote almost two-thirds of the items in the survey. Nine other graduates authored the remaining twenty articles.

105. Lillian C. Drew, "Corrective Gymnastics in a Physical Education Program," *APER* 31 (March 1926): 723. An expert in corrective gymnastics, Drew (1867–1930) spent her career in a Boston orthopedics office, at the Teachers College of Columbia University, and with the Central School of Hygiene and Physical Education (founded by Helen McKinstry). Drew was an author and technical consultant on the subject of individualized exercise. See Isabel Sutherland Cooper, "Lillian Curtis Drew," *Research Quarterly* 12, supplement (Oct. 1941): 686–95.

106. Drew, "Corrective Gymnastics in a Physical Education Program," 723.

107. *Ibid.*

108. *Ibid.*

109. Elizabeth R. Stoner, "The Practical and Educational Value of Physical Education," *APER* 26 (Dec. 1921): 415. An 1899 graduate of the BNSG, Stoner (1874–1930) supervised physical education at several public schools and colleges, including Mills College, during a career that spanned nearly twenty-five years. See also Ethel Perrin, "Outdoor Recreation as a Factor in Child Welfare," *Playground* 18 (July 1924): 240.

110. Lillian Curtis Drew, "Work for the Weaker Woman," *APER* 26 (June 1921): 280; also 282.

111. Stoner, "The Practical and Educational Value of Physical Education," 415.

112. McKinstry, "Organization of Work for Women, with Special Consideration of the Type of Work for Which Colleges Might Reasonably Be Expected To Give Credit," 345. See also Helen McKinstry, "Taking a Man's Measure," *APER* 27 (Nov. 1922): 418.

113. Stoner, "The Practical and Educational Value of Physical Education," 415.

114. Perrin, "Outdoor Recreation as a Factor in Child Welfare," 240. See also Ethel Perrin, "Physical Education: One Important Factor in Health Education," *Education* 54 (Dec. 1933): 218–22.

115. Stoner, "The Practical and Educational Value of Physical Education," 415. See also Perrin, "Outdoor Recreation as a Factor in Child Welfare," 240, 241.

116. Perrin, "Outdoor Recreation as a Factor in Child Welfare," 241.

117. J. Anna Norris, "The Moral Obligation To Be Physically Fit—Abstract," *Journal of the Proceedings and Addresses of the National Education Association* 63 (1925): 596; see also 593.

118. Stoner, "The Practical and Educational Value of Physical Education," 416.

119. For example, see J. Anna Norris, "Medical and Physical Examination for Women," *APER* 19 (June 1914): 435–44, and Helen McKinstry, "Physical Examinations: Why, What and How," *MHAA Bulletin* (1920–21): 9–13.

120. See McKinstry, "Physical Examinations: Why, What and How." McKinstry favored many uses for physical testing, including the screening of prospective employees in industry and other workplaces. (See McKinstry, "Taking a Man's Measure," 415–18.)

121. McKinstry, "Woman Climbs," 6; also 17.

122. Drew, "Work for the Weaker Woman," 280.

123. *Ibid.*

124. *Ibid.*

125. For historical background on ideas about menstruation, see Vern Bullough and Martha Voght, "Women, Menstruation, and Nineteenth-Century Medicine," *Bulletin of the History of Medicine* 47 (Jan.–Feb. 1973): 66–82; Janice Delaney, Mary Jane Lupton, and Emily Toth, *The Curse: A Cultural History of Menstruation* (New York: E. P. Dutton, 1976); and Paula Weideger, *Menstruation and Menopause: The Physiology and Psychology, the Myth and the Reality* (New York: Alfred A. Knopf, 1976), 85–113. General discussions of American attitudes about women's health in relation to exercise and athletics include Donald J. Mrozek, *Sport and American Mentality, 1880–1910* (Knoxville: Univ. of Tennessee Press, 1983), 136–60, and Stephanie Lee Twin, *Jock and Jill: Aspects of Women's Sports History in America, 1870–1940* (Ann Arbor: Univ. Microfilms International, 1981), 129–275.

126. For example, see J. Anna Norris, "The College A Potential Laboratory for Developing Exercise Ideals," *MHAA Bulletin* (1919–20): 7; Ethel Perrin, "Health Safeguards in Athletics for Girls and Women," *Research Quarterly* 3 (Oct. 1932): 93–94; and Helen McKinstry, "The Hygiene of Menstruation," *MHAA Bulletin* (1916–17): 15–27.

127. McKinstry, "The Hygiene of Menstruation," 22.

128. *Ibid.*, 25.

129. *Ibid.*

130. *Ibid.*, 22 and 22–26 in general.

131. *Ibid.*, 25.

132. *Ibid.*, 26.

133. Augusta L. Patrick, "Athletics for Girls and Its Problems in the High

School," *APER* 22 (Oct. 1917): 429. An 1894 graduate of the BNSG, Patrick (1869–1947) taught in public schools and normal schools in New Jersey for at least twenty-five years.

134. J. Anna Norris, "Dangers in Basket Ball—Popular Sport Should Be Made Safe for Girls," *Child Health* 5 (Dec. 1924): 512.

135. *Ibid.*

136. Ethel Perrin, "Athletics for Women and Girls," *Playground* 17 (March 1924): 659.

137. *Ibid.*

138. *Ibid.*

139. See Norris, "Dangers in Basket Ball—Popular Sport Should Be Made Safe for Girls," 512, and Norris, "The College A Potential Laboratory for Developing Exercise Ideals," 7.

140. See Senda Berenson, ed., *Basket Ball for Women, as Adopted by the Conference on Physical Training, Held in June, 1899, at Springfield, Mass.* (New York: American Sports Publishing, 1903). The publisher was a division of the Spalding Company, which originally asked Berenson to undertake the project. For a general overview, see Ronald A. Smith, "The Rise of Basketball for Women in Colleges," *Canadian Journal of the History of Sport and Physical Education* 1 (Dec. 1970): 18–36.

141. Norris, "Dangers of Basket Ball—Popular Sport Should Be Made Safe for Girls," 512.

142. For example, see *ibid.*, 513–14; Patrick, "Athletics for Girls and Its Problems in the High School," 427–29; Perrin, "The Confessions of a Once Strict Formalist," 535.

143. Patrick, "Athletics for Girls and Its Problems in the High School," 429.

144. *Ibid.*, 428.

145. Perrin, "Outdoor Recreation as a Factor in Child Welfare," 241 (emphasis in original).

146. See Perrin, "Athletics for Women and Girls," 660–61; Ethel Perrin, "Health-Educating Detroit Children," *The Nation's Health* 6 (March 1924): 177–78, 222; and Ethel Perrin, "When Sport Takes on a New Significance," *Sportswoman* 7 (Feb. 1931): 7–8, 29.

147. Ethel Perrin, "More Competitive Athletics for Girls—But of the Right Kind," *APER* 34 (Oct. 1929): 476.

148. The best summaries of these issues written by BNSG graduates include Perrin, "Athletics for Women and Girls," 658–61, and Mabel Lee, "The Case For and Against Intercollegiate Athletics for Women and the Situation as It Stands Today," *APER* 29 (Jan. 1924): 13–19. For historical studies of views among early physical educators about athletics and competition, see Ellen W. Gerber, "The Controlled Development of Collegiate Sport for Women, 1923–1936," *Journal of Sport History* 2 (Spring 1975): 1–28; Mary Lou Remley, "Women and Competitive Athletics," *Maryland Historian* 4 (Fall 1973): 88–94; Twin, *Jock and Jill: Aspects of Women's Sports History in America, 1870–1940,* pp. 129–74, 221–75; and Doris Paige Watts, "Changing Conceptions of Competitive Sports for Girls and Women in the United States from 1880 to 1960" (Ed.D. dissertation, Univ. of California, Los Angeles, 1960).

149. Chapter 6 of this book noted the disagreement between the faculty

and students at Wellesley College about athletic competition. Twin, *Jock and Jill: Aspects of Women's Sports History in America, 1870–1940,* pp. 175–275, contrasts the attitudes of sportswomen and female physical educators.

Conclusion

1. "Constitution of the World Health Organization," in *Concepts of Health and Disease: Interdisciplinary Perspectives,* Arthur L. Caplan, H. Tristram Engelhardt, Jr., and James J. McCartney, eds. (Reading, Mass.: Addison-Wesley, 1981), 83.

2. See Harvey Green, *Fit for America: Health, Fitness, Sport and American Society* (New York: Pantheon, 1986), 217–317; Donald J. Mrozek, *Sport and American Mentality, 1880–1910* (Knoxville: Univ. of Tennessee Press, 1983); and James C. Whorton, *Crusaders for Fitness: The History of American Health Reformers* (Princeton: Princeton Univ. Press, 1982), 168–330.

3. For example, see Lois W. Banner, *American Beauty: A Social History Through Two Centuries of the American Idea, Ideal, and Image of the Beautiful Woman* (New York: Alfred A. Knopf, 1983), 154–225; Green, *Fit for America,* 219–58 passim; and Mrozek, *Sport and American Mentality,* 136–60.

4. "America Shapes Up," *Time* 118 (Nov. 2, 1981): 104.

5. See Lois M. Verbrugge, "Multiple Roles and Physical Health of Women and Men," *Journal of Health and Social Behavior* 24 (1983): 16–30, and Lois M. Verbrugge and Jennifer H. Madans, "Social Roles and Health Trends of American Women," *Milbank Memorial Fund Quarterly/Health and Society* 63 (Fall 1985): 691–735. As the authors of the latter article note, "This does not mean that combining job and childbearing responsibilities is easy; the health benefits may be hard-won for some of the triple-role women [job, spouse, and mother]" (p. 724).

6. The phrase is borrowed from John H. Knowles, M.D., ed., *Doing Better and Feeling Worse: Health in the United States* (New York: W. W. Norton, 1977).

7. For example, see Christopher Lasch, *The Culture of Narcissism: American Life in an Age of Diminishing Expectations* (New York: W. W. Norton, 1978).

8. Ellen Goodman, "Eating: Enjoy, Enjoy," *Boston Globe* (n.d.).

9. Carin Rubenstein, "Wellness Is All: A Report on *Psychology Today's* Survey of Beliefs about Health," *Psychology Today* 16 (Oct. 1982): 36–37.

Appendix

Table 1. Personal and Medical Backgrounds of Female BNSG Graduates, 1891–95

	BNSG N =	BNSG Women	National Data, 1890[a]
Median Age (at admission)	96	22	22.1[b]
Nationality	89		
American		98%	85%[c]
Foreign		2	15
Birthplace (by region)	89		
New England		80% ⎫	
Mid-Atlantic		7 ⎬ 87% Northeast	
South		2	
Midwest		8	
West		0	
Foreign		2	
At sea		1 ⎭	
Residence (at admission, by region)	97		
New England		88% ⎫	29% Northeast[d]
Mid-Atlantic		5 ⎬ 93% Northeast	
South		2 ⎭	32
Midwest		4	35
West		1	4

258

Size of Residence				
Urban	92	85% [e]	35% [f]	39% [g]
1,000,000 or more		1	6	
500,000–999,999		0	1	
250,000–499,999		10	4	
100,000–249,999		9	4	
50,000– 99,999		12	3	
25,000– 49,999		6	4	
10,000– 24,999		33	5	
5,000– 9,999		3	4	
2,500– 4,999		9	4	
unknown		2		
Rural		15%	65%	61%
1,000–2,499		7.5	4	
under 1,000		7.5	4	
other rural			57	
Parents' Nationality	86 (native-born students only)			
Both American		90% [h]	75% [i]	
Mixed		8 ⎫ 10%	25	
Both Foreign		2 ⎭		
Grandparents' Nationality	87			
Four American		79% [j]		
Three American		5		
Two American		10		
One American		0		
None American		6		

Table 1 cont'd

	BNSG N =	BNSG Women	National Data, 1890[a]
Occupation of Father	78		
White-collar		69%	17% [k]
Manual, Service		17	41
Farm		14	42
Parents' Status	85		
Both alive		58%	
One deceased		34	
Both deceased		8	
General Health	67		
Very good		1%	
Good		81	
Fair		3	
Delicate		15	
Previous Ailments	58[l]		
Average number of conditions cited per student		1.8	
Nature of illness (with number of students reporting the condition)		Pneumonia (10) Rheumatism (9) Dyspepsia (9)	

Neuralgia (8)
Skin Eruptions (8)
Colds in Head or Throat (8)
Boils (7)
Bronchitis (7)

---

a Unless otherwise stated, all data are from 1890. See other notes for source of information and reference group.

b *Historical Statistics of the United States: Colonial Times to 1970* (Washington, D.C.: Government Printing Office, 1975), I: Series A 143–157, p. 19. Reference group: white females. (Hereafter designated *Historical Statistics.*)

c *The Compendium of the Eleventh Census of the United States: 1890* (Washington, D.C.: Government Printing Office, 1892), Part I, p. lxxxvi. Reference group: total United States population. (Hereafter designated *Eleventh Census.*)

d *Historical Statistics*, I: Series A 172–194, p. 22. Reference group: all females.

e The size of a student's community at the time of admission was determined through the *Eleventh Census*, Part I, Tables 3, 4a, 5, 6.

f *Historical Statistics*, I: Series A 57–72, p. 12. Reference group: total United States population.

g *Historical Statistics*, I: Series A 73–81, p. 12. Reference group: white females.

h Of the parents born in a foreign country, one-third were English; 13% each from Ireland, Sweden, Canada, and Lithuania; and about 7% each from Scotland and Denmark.

i *Historical Statistics*, I: Series A 135–142, p. 19. Reference group: native-born white females.

j Of the grandparents born in a foreign country, over a third were English; about 17% Irish; 14% Scottish; 10% each from Sweden, Denmark, and Canada; and 5% were German.

k *Historical Statistics*, I: Series D 182–232, p. 139. Year: 1900. Reference group: all males, 14 years and older. (See *ibid.*, I: Series D 233–682 for a detailed listing of occupations in each category.)

l The cards of 39 students listed either insufficient health data or no previous conditions. Ailments for 58 students were recorded.

Table 2. Personal and Medical Backgrounds of Female BNSG Graduates, 1896–1900

	BNSG N =	*BNSG Women*	
Median Age (at admission)	107	21.0	
Nationality	106		
American		93%[a]	
Foreign		7	
Birthplace (by region)	106		
New England		49%	⎫
Mid-Atlantic		23	⎬ 72% Northeast
South		4	⎭
Midwest		16	
West		2	
Foreign		7	
Residence (at admission, by region)	108		
New England		62%	⎫
Mid-Atlantic		15	⎬ 77% Northeast
South		6	⎭
Midwest		10	
West		5	
Foreign		3	
Size of Residence	98		
Urban		*91%*	
1,000,000 or more		2	
500,000–999,999		3	
250,000–499,999		16	
100,000–249,999		11	
50,000– 99,999		8	
25,000– 49,999		5	
10,000– 24,999		25	
5,000– 9,999		12	
2,500– 4,999		7	
Rural		*9%*	
1,000–2,499		6	
under 1,000		3	
Parents' Nationality	99		
Both American	(native-born	81%	
Mixed	students only)	9	
Both Foreign		10	

	BNSG N =	*BNSG Women*
Parents' Nationality	106	
Both American	(all students)	76%[b]
Mixed		9
Both Foreign		14
Grandparents' Nationality	106	
Four American		69%[c]
Three American		2
Two American		12
One American		0
None American		17
Occupation of Father	85	
White-collar		83%
Manual, Service		11
Farm		6
Parents' Status	105	
Both alive		65%
One deceased		30
Both deceased		5
General Health	74	
Very good		13%
Good		80
Fair		7
Delicate		0
Previous Ailments	83[d]	
Average number of conditions cited per student		2.6
Nature of illness (with number of students reporting the condition)		Colds in Head or Throat (48)
		Skin Eruptions (18)
		Rheumatism (14)
		Neuralgia (13)
		Dizziness (12)
		Bilious Attacks (11)
		Dyspepsia (10)
		Habitual Constipation (10)

Notes to table 2 at top of following page.

Notes to table 2:

[a] Seven women in the sample were foreign-born. Their nationalities were English (3) and Canadian (4).

[b] Among the parents of both native- and foreign-born students, 40 were foreign. Their nationalities were English (32.5%), Irish (20%), Canadian (17.5%), Scottish (12.5%), German (5%), Russian (5%), French (5%), and Norwegian (2.5%).

[c] The nationalities of foreign-born grandparents included: English (30%), Scottish (24%), Irish (17%), Canadian (11%), German (6%), French (5%), Russian (4%), Norwegian (1%), Dutch (1%), and unknown (1%).

[d] The cards of 23 students listed minimal information or no previous ailments. Eighty-three students reported earlier conditions.

Table 3. Positions Held for Five or More Years by Female BNSG Graduates, Classes 1891–95

Position	Percentage (N = 71)[a]
Public School	38
Normal School	22
Private Work	10
Private Secondary School	9
Women's College	9
Coed College[b]	6
Doctor's Office	3
Private Gymnasium	3
Young Women's Christian Association	1

[a] The analysis included women who were physical educators for five or more years (56). Of those, 47 held the same position or were employed by the same institution for five or more years. Each position that a woman held for five or more years counted in the tabulation, for a total of 71 such jobs.

[b] Instructor or Director of Physical Training for Women.

Table 4. Positions Held for Five or More Years by Female BNSG Graduates, Classes 1896–1900

Position	Percentage $(N = 77)$[a]
Private Secondary School	23
Public School	14
Normal School	14
Coed College[b]	12
Women's College	10
Doctor's Office or Hospital	9
Private Work	7
Young Women's Christian Association	7
Gymnasium	4

[a]The analysis included women who were physical educators for five or more years (66). Of those, 55 held the same position or were employed by the same institution for five or more years. Each position that a woman held for five or more years counted in the tabulation, for a total of 77 such jobs.

[b] Instructor or Director of Physical Training for Women.

Table 5. Reasons for Leaving Physical Education, Female BNSG Graduates, 1891–95

	Length of Employment in the Field				
	0 Years $(N = 8)$	1–5 Years $(N = 32)$	6–10 Years $(N = 14)$	11–15 Years $(N = 15)$	16 Years or More $(N = 27)$
Other Work	75%	25%	29%	47%	7%
Marriage	12.5	44	29	27	7
Further Education	0	6	14	0	0
Travel	0	3	14	7	0
Retirement	0	0	0	7	41
Death	0	9	7	0	11
Unknown	12.5	13	7	13	33[a]

[a] Many of these were probably cases of retirement.

Table 6. Reasons for Leaving Physical Education, Female BNSG Graduates, 1896–1900

	Length of Employment in the Field				
	0 Years (N = 8)	1–5 Years (N = 32)	6–10 Years (N = 21)	11–15 Years (N = 9)	16 Years or More (N = 32)
Other Work	0%	3%	14%	33%	38%
Marriage	63	66	38	22	0
Further Education	25	6	5	0	6
Travel	0	6	5	11	0
Personal	13	0	0	0	3
Retirement	0	0	0	11	50
Death	0	0	5	0	0
Unknown	0	19	33	22	3

Selected Bibliography

I. Archival and Manuscript Sources

Boston Public Library, Boston, Mass. Rare Book Department. Journal of Eunice Hale (Waite) Cobb. 5 vols. (1821–77).

Harvard University, Cambridge, Mass. Pusey Library. Harvard University Archives. Papers of Dudley Allen Sargent. Papers of the Physical Education Department.

Radcliffe College, Cambridge, Mass. Arthur M. and Elizabeth Schlesinger Library on the History of Women in America. Papers of the Ladies' Physiological Institute of Boston and Vicinity.

Wellesley College, Wellesley, Mass. Margaret Clapp Library. Wellesley College Archives. Papers of the Department of Hygiene and Physical Education, including the Papers of the Boston Normal School of Gymnastics. Papers of the Wellesley College Alumnae Association: Hygiene and Physical Education Section.

II. Primary Sources—Books and Essays

The following is a representative listing of the books and essays about health examined for this study. Most were published between 1830 and 1900; some items, especially those written by BNSG alumnae, appeared in the early twentieth century.

Alcott, William A., M.D. *An Address Delivered before the American Physiological Society, March 8, 1837*. Boston: Light and Stearns, 1837.

———. *The House I Live In; or The Human Body. For the Use of Families and Schools*. 2d ed. Boston: Light and Stearns, 1837.

———. *The Young Woman's Book of Health*. New York and Auburn: Miller, Orton & Mulligan, 1855.

———. *The Young Woman's Guide to Excellence*. 13th ed. Boston: Charles H. Peirce, 1847.

Anderson, William Gilbert. *Anderson's Physical Education. Health and Strength, Grace and Symmetry.* New York: A. D. Dana, 1897.

Bancroft, Jessie H. *School Gymnastics—Free Hand. A System of Physical Exercises for Schools.* New York and Chicago: E. L. Kellogg, 1896.

Bartlett, Elisha, M.D. *Obedience to the Laws of Health, a Moral Duty. A Lecture, Delivered before the American Physiological Society, January 30, 1838.* Boston: Julius A. Noble, 1838.

Beecher, Catharine E. *Letters to the People on Health and Happiness.* New York: Harper & Brothers, 1855; reprint ed., New York: Arno Press and the *New York Times*, 1972.

————. *Physiology and Calisthenics. For Schools and Families.* New York: Harper & Brothers, 1856.

Bell, John, M.D. *Health and Beauty. An Explanation of the Laws of Growth and Exercise; Through Which a Pleasing Contour, Symmetry of Form, and Graceful Carriage of the Body Are Acquired: and the Common Deformities of the Spine and Chest Prevented.* Philadelphia: E. L. Carey & A. Hart, 1838.

Bird, Frederick W. *Physiological Reform. An Address, Delivered before the American Physiological Society, at Their First Annual Meeting, June 1, 1837.* Boston: Marsh, Capen & Lyon, 1837.

Bissell, Mary Taylor, M.D. "The Physical Training of Women." *Proceedings of the American Association for the Advancement of Physical Education* 4 (1889): 8–17.

Blackwell, Elizabeth, M.D. *The Laws of Life, with Special Reference to the Physical Education of Girls.* New York: Geo. P. Putnam, 1852.

Blaikie, William. *How To Get Strong, and How To Stay So.* New York: Harper & Brothers, 1879.

————. *Sound Bodies for Our Boys and Girls.* New York: Harper & Brothers, 1892.

Blaisdell, Albert F., M.D. *Our Bodies and How We Live. An Elementary Text-Book of Physiology and Hygiene for Use in the Common Schools, with Special Reference to the Effects of Stimulants and Narcotics on the Human System.* Boston: Lee and Shepard, 1885.

Brigham, Amariah, M.D. *Remarks on the Influence of Mental Cultivation and Mental Excitement upon Health.* 2d ed. Boston: Marsh, Capen & Lyon, 1833.

Caldwell, Charles, M.D. *Thoughts on Physical Education: Being a Discourse Delivered to a Convention of Teachers in Lexington, Ky., on the 6th & 7th of Nov., 1833.* Boston: Marsh, Capen & Lyon, 1834.

Clarke, Edward H., M.D. *Sex in Education; or, A Fair Chance for Girls.* Boston: James R. Osgood, 1874.

Coates, Reynell, M.D. *Physiology for Schools*. Philadelphia: Marshall, Williams and Butler, 1840.

Coles, Larkin B., M.D. *Philosophy of Health: Natural Principles of Health and Cure; or, Health and Cure without Drugs. Also, the Moral Bearings of Erroneous Appetites*. Revised ed. Boston: Ticknor, Reed, & Fields, 1853.

Combe, Andrew, M.D. *The Principles of Physiology Applied to the Preservation of Health, and to the Improvement of Physical and Mental Education*. New York: Harper & Brothers, 1839.

Combe, George. *The Constitution of Man Considered in Relation to External Objects*. 10th American ed. Boston: William D. Ticknor, 1840.

Comings, B. N., M.D. *Class-Book of Physiology; For the Use of Schools and Families. Comprising the Structure and Functions of the Organs of Man, Illustrated by Comparative Reference to Those of Inferior Animals*. New York: D. Appleton, 1853.

Cook, C. H., M.D. "The Effect of College Life at Wellesley." *Medical Communications of the Massachusetts Medical Society* 16 (1893): 191–95.

Cutter, Calvin, M.D. *Anatomy and Physiology: Designed for Schools and Families*. Boston: S. N. Dickinson, 1845.

Davis, Irenaeus P., M.D. *Hygiene for Girls*. New York: D. Appleton, 1883.

Dowd, D. L., Prof. *Physical Culture for Home and School. Scientific and Practical*. New York: Fowler & Wells, 1890.

Drew, Lillian Curtis. "Corrective Gymnastics in a Physical Education Program." *American Physical Education Review* 31 (March 1926): 723–26.

———. "Work for the Weaker Woman." *American Physical Education Review* 26 (June 1921): 280–82.

Duncan, Abel G., Rev. *Evils of Violating the Laws of Health, and the Remedy. An Address, Delivered before the American Physiological Society, at Their Monthly Meeting, February 7, 1838*. Boston: Marsh, Capen & Lyon, 1838.

Foster, Alice B., M.D. "A Few Figures on Occupation and Exercise." *Proceedings of the American Association for the Advancement of Physical Education* 9 (1894): 72–81.

Fowler, Orson Squire. *Physiology, Animal and Mental: Applied to the Preservation and Restoration of Health of Body, and Power of Mind*. 6th ed. New York: Fowlers and Wells, 1853.

Gove, Mary S. *Lectures to Ladies on Anatomy and Physiology*. Boston: Saxton & Peirce, 1842. Revised ed., under title *Lectures to Women on Anatomy and Physiology. With an Appendix on Water Cure*. New York: Harper & Brothers, 1846.

Graham, Sylvester. *Lectures on the Science of Human Life.* 2 vols. Boston: Marsh, Capen, Lyon and Webb, 1839.

Griscom, John H., M.D. *Animal Mechanism and Physiology; Being a Plain and Familiar Exposition of the Structure and Functions of the Human System. Designed for the Use of Families and Schools.* New York: Harper & Brothers, 1839.

Gulick, Luther H., M.D. *Physical Education by Muscular Exercise.* Philadelphia: P. Blakiston's Son, 1904.

Haskell, Benjamin, M.D. *A Lecture, Introductory to the First Course of Lectures on Popular Physiology, Instituted by the American Physiological Society, October 10, 1837.* Boston: Office of the Graham Journal, 1838.

Hill, Lucille Eaton, ed. *Athletics and Out-Door Sports for Women. Each Subject Being Separately Treated by a Special Writer.* New York: Macmillan, 1903.

Holbrook, M. L., M.D. *Hygiene of the Brain and Nerves, and Cure of Nervousness.* New York: M. L. Holbrook, 1878.

Hooker, Worthington, M.D. *A First Book in Physiology, for the Use of Schools (An Introduction to the Larger Work by the Same Author).* New York and Chicago: Sheldon, 1884.

Hough, Theodore. *A Review of Swedish Gymnastics.* Boston: George H. Ellis, 1899.

Hunt, Harriot K. *Glances and Glimpses; or Fifty Years Social, Including Twenty Years Professional Life.* Boston: John P. Jewett, 1856.

Hutchison, Joseph C., M.D. *A Treatise on Physiology and Hygiene for Educational Institutions and General Readers.* New York: Clark & Maynard, 1871.

Jacobi, Mary Putnam, M.D. *The Question of Rest for Women during Menstruation.* New York: G. P. Putnam's Sons, 1877.

Jarvis, Edward, M.D. *Practical Physiology; For the Use of Schools and Families.* Philadelphia: Thomas, Cowperthwait, 1848.

————. *Primary Physiology, for Schools.* Philadelphia: Thomas, Cowperthwait, 1848.

Johonnot, James, and Eugene Bouton, Ph.D. *How We Live: or, the Human Body, and How To Take Care of It.* New York: D. Appleton, 1884.

Kellogg, J. H., M.D. *Second Book in Physiology and Hygiene.* New York: American Book Company, 1894.

Lambert, T. S., M.D. *Hygienic Physiology.* Portland, Maine: Sanborn and Carter, 1852.

Lee, Charles A., M.D. *Human Physiology, for the Use of Elementary Schools.* 2d ed. New York: American Common School Union, 1839.

Lee, Mabel. "The Case For and Against Intercollegiate Athletics for

Women and the Situation as It Stands Today." *American Physical Education Review* 29 (Jan. 1924): 13–19.

———. *Memories of a Bloomer Girl (1894–1924)*. Washington, D.C.: American Alliance for Health, Physical Education, and Recreation, 1977.

Lewis, Dio. *The Dio Lewis Treasury*. New York: Canfield, 1887.

———. *Five-Minute Chats with Young Women, and Certain Other Parties*. New York: Harper & Brothers, 1874.

———. *The New Gymnastics for Men, Women, and Children. With a Translation of Prof. Kloss's Dumb-bell Instructor and Prof. Schreber's Pangymnastikon*. Boston: Ticknor and Fields, 1862.

———. *Our Girls*. New York: Harper & Brothers, 1871; reprint ed., New York: Arno Press and the *New York Times*, 1974.

———. "Physical Culture." *Massachusetts Teacher* 13 (1860): 375–77, 401–6.

———. *Talks about People's Stomachs*. Boston: Fields, Osgood, 1870.

———. *Weak Lungs, and How To Make Them Strong. Or Diseases of the Organs of the Chest, with Their Home Treatment by the Movement Cure*. Boston: Ticknor and Fields, 1863.

Lewis, Dio, Elizabeth Cady Stanton, and James Read Chadwick, M.D. "The Health of American Women." *North American Review* 135 (Dec. 1882): 503–24.

McKinstry, Helen May. "Administration of Physical Education for Girls and Women." *American Physical Education Review* 16 (June 1911): 364–79.

———. "The Hygiene of Menstruation." *Mary Hemenway Alumnae Association Bulletin* (1916–17): 15–27.

———. "Organization of Work for Women, with Special Consideration of the Type of Work for Which Colleges Might Reasonably Be Expected To Give Credit." *American Physical Education Review* 22 (June 1917): 344–50.

———. "Physical Examinations: Why, What and How." *Mary Hemenway Alumnae Association Bulletin* (1920–21): 9–13.

———. "Taking a Man's Measure." *American Physical Education Review* 27 (Nov. 1922): 415–18.

———. "Vignettes." *Mary Hemenway Alumnae Association Bulletin* (1934–35): 16–20.

———. "Woman Climbs." *Mary Hemenway Alumnae Association Bulletin* (March 1931): 6–18.

Martin, H. Newell, M.D. *The Human Body. An Elementary Text-Book of Anatomy, Physiology and Hygiene*. 2d ed. New York: Henry Holt, 1885.

Martindale, Joseph C., M.D. *Human Anatomy, Physiology, and Hygiene. A Text-Book for Schools, Academies, Colleges and Families*. Philadelphia: Eldredge & Brother, 1872.

Mitchell, S. Weir, M.D. *Wear and Tear, or Hints for the Overworked.* Philadelphia: J. B. Lippincott, 1871.

Narey, Hope W. "Physical Training for Women." *The Bostonian* 1 (Oct. 1894): 98–106.

Nissen, Hartvig. *ABC of the Swedish System of Educational Gymnastics. A Practical Hand-Book for School Teachers and the Home.* Boston: Educational Publishing, 1892.

Norris, J. Anna, M.D. "The College A Potential Laboratory for Developing Exercise Ideals." *Mary Hemenway Alumnae Association Bulletin* (1919–20): 1–8.

———. "Dangers in Basket Ball–Popular Sport Should Be Made Safe for Girls." *Child Health* 5 (Dec. 1924): 512–14.

———. "Medical and Physical Examination for Women." *American Physical Education Review* 19 (June 1914): 435–44.

———. "The Moral Obligation To Be Physically Fit–Abstract." *Journal of the Proceedings and Addresses of the National Education Association* 63 (1925): 592–96.

Palmer, George Herbert, and Alice Freeman Palmer. *The Teacher: Essays and Addresses on Education.* Boston and New York: Houghton Mifflin, 1908.

Patrick, Augusta L. "Athletics for Girls and Its Problems in the High School." *American Physical Education Review* 22 (Oct. 1917): 427–31.

Peirson, Abel L., M.D. "On Physical Education." In *The Introductory Discourse, and the Lectures Delivered before the American Institute of Instruction, at Springfield, (Mass.) August, 1839. Including the Journal of Proceedings, and a List of the Officers.* Boston: Marsh, Capen, Lyon and Webb, 1840.

Perrin, Ethel. "Athletics for Women and Girls." *Playground* 17 (March 1924): 658–61.

———. "The Confessions of a Once Strict Formalist." *Journal of Health and Physical Education* 9 (Nov. 1938): 533–36, 589–90.

———. "Health-Educating Detroit Children." *The Nation's Health* 6 (March 1924): 177–78, 222.

———. "Health Safeguards in Athletics for Girls and Women." *Research Quarterly of the American Physical Education Association* 3 (Oct. 1932): 93–94.

———. "More Competitive Athletics for Girls–But of the Right Kind." *American Physical Education Review* 34 (Oct. 1929): 473, 476.

———. "Outdoor Recreation as a Factor in Child Welfare." *Playground* 18 (July 1924): 240–42, 246, 266.

———. "Physical Education: One Important Factor in Health Education." *Education* 54 (Dec. 1933): 218–22.

———. "When Sport Takes on a New Significance." *Sportswoman* 7 (Feb. 1931): 7–8, 29.

Porter, Henry H. *The Catechism of Health; or, Plain and Simple Rules for the Preservation of the Health and Vigour of the Constitution from Infancy to Old Age. For the Use of Schools.* 5th ed. Philadelphia: Office of the Journal of Health, Journal of Law, and Family Library of Health, 1836.

Potter, William Warren, M.D. "How Should Girls Be Educated? A Public Health Problem for Mothers, Educators, and Physicians." *Transactions of the Medical Society of the State of New York* (1891): 42–56.

Preston, Grace A., M.D. "The Influence of College Life on the Health of Women." *Medical Communications of the Massachusetts Medical Society* 16 (1893): 167–90.

Safford, Mary J., M.D., and Mary E. Allen. *Health and Strength for Girls.* Boston: D. Lothrop, 1884.

Sargent, Dudley Allen. "Competition and Culture." *American Physical Education Review* 15 (Nov. 1910): 579–85.

———. "Competition in College Athletics." *American Physical Education Review* 15 (Feb. 1910): 98–110.

———. *Dudley Allen Sargent: An Autobiography.* Ledyard W. Sargent, ed. Introduction by R. Tait McKenzie, M.D. Philadelphia: Lea & Febiger, 1927.

———. *Health, Strength and Power.* New York and Boston: H. M. Caldwell, 1904.

———. "The Physical Characteristics of the Athlete." *Scribner's Magazine* 2 (Nov. 1887): 541–61.

———. "The Physical Development of Women." *Scribner's Magazine* 5 (Feb. 1889): 172–85.

———. *Physical Education.* Boston: Ginn, 1906.

———. "The Physical Proportions of the Typical Man." *Scribner's Magazine* 2 (July 1887): 3–17.

———. "The Physical Test of a Man." *Proceedings of the American Association for the Advancement of Physical Education* 5 (1890): 36–56.

———. "Strength Tests and the Strong Men of Harvard." *Harvard Graduates' Magazine* 5 (June 1897): 513–25.

Shaw, Albert. "Physical Culture at Wellesley." *[American] Review of Reviews* 6 (Dec. 1892): 545–49.

Smith, Jerome V. C., M.D. *The Class Book of Anatomy, Explanatory of the First Principles of Human Organization, as the Basis of Physical Education. Designed for Schools and Families.* 6th improved stereotype ed. Boston: Robert S. Davis; Philadelphia: Hogan and Thompson, 1841.

Smith, William Thayer, M.D. *The Human Body and Its Health. A Text-Book for Schools, Having Special Reference to the Effects of Stim-*

ulants and Narcotics on the Human System. New York and Chicago: Ivison, Blakeman, 1884.

Steele, J. Dorman, Ph.D. *Fourteen Weeks in Human Physiology.* New York: A. S. Barnes, 1875.

Stevenson, Sarah Hackett, M.D. *The Physiology of Woman, Embracing Girlhood, Maternity, and Mature Age.* 3d ed. Chicago: Fairbanks, Palmer, 1882.

Stoner, Elizabeth R. "The Practical and Educational Value of Physical Education." *American Physical Education Review* 26 (Dec. 1921): 414–16.

Stowell, Charles H., M.D. *The Essentials of Health: A Text-Book on Anatomy, Physiology, Hygiene, Alcohol, and Narcotics.* New York: Silver, Burdett, 1896.

Sunderland, Laroy. *Book of Health for the Million, with Practical Remarks on Bathing, Diet, Exercise, Disease, and the Water Cure.* Boston: White & Potter, 1847.

Tarbell, John A., M.D. *The Sources of Health, and the Prevention of Disease; or, Mental and Physical Hygiene.* Boston: Otis Clapp, 1850.

Taylor, George, H., M.D. *Health by Exercise. What Exercises To Take and How To Take Them, To Remove Special Physical Weakness. Embracing an Account of the Swedish Methods, and a Summary of the Principles of Hygiene.* New York: American Book Exchange, 1881.

Warren, John C., M.D. *Physical Education and the Preservation of Health.* 2d ed. Boston: William D. Ticknor, 1846.

Wood, Horatio Charles. *Brainwork and Overwork.* Philadelphia: P. Blakiston, Son, 1885.

III. Primary Sources—Journals

The dates given in the following citations refer to years of publication, and to the period covered in the research. In some cases, the collection examined was incomplete or only some of the years were surveyed. That is indicated with an asterisk (*) or a note about the period studied.

American Journal of Education. Boston, 1826–30. Superseded by *American Annals of Education.* Boston, 1830–39.

American Journal of Education. Hartford, 1855–82. Edited by Henry Barnard.

American Physical Education Review. Boston, 1896–1929.

American Vegetarian and Health Journal. Philadelphia, 1850–54.

Arthur's Home Magazine. Philadelphia, 1852–98.*

Boston Journal of Health. Boston, 1887–93.

Boston Medical Intelligencer. Boston, 1823–28.

Boston Medical and Surgical Journal. Boston, 1828–1928. (Surveyed through 1900.) Superseded by *New England Journal of Medicine.* Boston, 1928–current. (Not surveyed.)

Common School Journal. Boston, 1838–52.*

Dio Lewis's Monthly. New York, 1883–84. Superseded by *Dio Lewis's Nuggets.* New York, 1885.

Godey's Magazine. Philadelphia, 1830–92.* New York, 1892–98.* (Title varied.)

Graham Journal of Health and Longevity. Boston; New York, 1837–39.

The Gymnasium. Providence, R.I., 1889–97.*

Hall's Journal of Health. New York, 1854–94.*

Harper's Bazaar. New York, 1867–current.* (Surveyed occasional volumes to 1904.)

Harper's Weekly. New York, 1857–1916.*

Health: A Monthly Magazine. Boston, 1890–94.

Health Journal and Advocate of Physiological Reform. Boston and Worcester, Mass., 1840–42. Superseded by *Health Journal and Independent Magazine.* Boston, Feb. 1843.

Health Reformer. Battle Creek, Mich., 1866–78.* Superseded by *Good Health.* Battle Creek, Mich., 1879–1912.*

Journal of Health. Philadelphia, 1829–33.

Ladies' Magazine. Boston, 1828–36. (Published under somewhat varying names; merged with *Godey's Lady's Book.*)

Laws of Life and Woman's Health Journal. Dansville, N.Y., 1858–93.* (Also known as *Laws of Life and Health Journal.*)

Lewis' New Gymnastics for Ladies, Gentlemen, & Children, and Boston Journal of Physical Culture. Boston, 1860–61. Superseded by *Lewis' Gymnastic Monthly and Journal of Physical Culture.* Boston, 1861–62.

Mary Hemenway Alumnae Association Bulletin. Wellesley, Mass., 1915–37.

Massachusetts Teacher. Boston, 1848–74. Superseded by *Journal of Education.* Boston, 1875–current.* (Known as the *New England Journal of Education* in early years. Surveyed to 1890.)

Mind and Body. Milwaukee, Wisc., 1894–1936.* (Surveyed through 1900.)

Monthly Miscellany and Journal of Health. Boston, 1846–48, 1863–69. (Title varied frequently.)

Moral Reformer and Teacher on the Human Constitution. Boston, 1835–36. Edited by William A. Alcott. Superseded by *Library of Health and Teacher on the Human Constitution.* Boston, 1837–42. Superseded by *Teacher of Health and the Laws of the Human Constitution.* Boston, 1843.

North American Review. Boston, 1815–1940.* (Surveyed 1815–82.)
Peterson's Magazine. Philadelphia, 1842–98.* (Title varied.)
Physical Training. New York, 1901–27.* Superseded by *Journal of Physical Education*. New York, 1927–current. (Not surveyed.)
Proceedings of the American Association for the Advancement of Physical Education. Concord, N.H., 1885–95.
The Triangle. Springfield, Mass., 1891–92. Superseded by *Physical Education*. Springfield, Mass., 1892–96.
Water-Cure Journal. New York, 1845–61.* Superseded by *Hygienic Teacher and Water-Cure Journal*. 1862.* Superseded by *Herald of Health*. 1863–92.* Superseded by *Journal of Hygiene and Herald of Health*. 1893–97.* Superseded by *Omega*. 1898–1900.* Superseded by *Health*. 1900–1914.*

IV. Primary Sources—Reports, School Publications, and Official Documents

Annual Catalogue of the Boston Normal School of Gymnastics. 1891/92–1908/9.
Annual Report of the American Physiological Society. 1837–38.
Annual Report of the Board of Health of the City of Boston. Nos. 1–25. (Published 1873–97.)
Billings, John S., M.D. *Vital Statistics of Boston and Philadelphia Covering a Period of Six Years Ending May 31, 1890*. Washington, D.C.: Government Printing Office, 1895.
Boston Normal School of Gymnastics. 1890–1891. N.p., n.d.
Boykin, James C. "Physical Training." In *Report of the [United States] Commissioner of Education for 1891–92*. Washington, D.C.: Government Printing Office, 1894, I: 451–594.
Buckingham, Charles E., M.D., et al. *The Sanitary Condition of Boston. The Report of a Medical Commission, Consisting of Chas. E. Buckingham, M.D., Calvin Ellis, M.D., Richard M. Hodges, M.D., Samuel A. Green, M.D., and Thomas B. Curtis, M.D., Appointed by the Board of Health of the City of Boston, To Investigate the Sanitary Condition of the City*. Boston: Rockwell and Churchill, 1875.
Chickering, Jesse, M.D. *Report of the Committee Appointed by the City Council; and also a Comparative View of the Population of Boston in 1850, with the Births, Marriages, and Deaths, in 1849 and 1850, by Jesse Chickering, M.D*. 1851, City Document #60. Boston: J. H. Eastburn, 1851.
Constitution and By-laws of the Ladies' Physiological Institute, of Boston and Vicinity. Boston: Alfred Mudge & Son, 1857.
Curtis, Josiah, M.D. *Report of the Joint Special Committee on the Census*

of Boston, May, 1855, Including the Report of the Censors, with
Analytical and Sanitary Observations. 1855, City Document #69.
Boston: Moore & Crosby, 1856.

*Health Statistics of Women College Graduates. Report of a Special Com-
mittee of the Association of Collegiate Alumnae.* Boston: Wright
& Potter, 1885.

*Ladies' Physiological Institute. Semi-Centennial Report. In Memoriam—
Salome Merritt, M.D.* Boston: n.p., 1900?

Massachusetts Homeopathic Medical Society. *By-laws, List of Members,
and Statistics. September, 1890.* Brookline, Mass.: Chronicle Press,
1890.

Massachusetts Medical Society. *A Catalogue of the Honorary and Past
and Present Fellows, 1781–1931.* Boston: The Society, 1931.

*Ninth Annual Meeting of the Ladies' Physiological Institute, May Sixth,
1857.* Boston: Alfred Mudge & Son, 1857.

*Physical Training. A Full Report of the Papers and Discussions of the
Conference Held in Boston in November, 1889.* Isabel C. Barrows,
reporter and ed. Boston: George H. Ellis, 1890.

The President's Report to the Board of Trustees [of Wellesley College].
1883, 1888–1900, 1908, 1909.

Shattuck, Lemuel. "On the Vital Statistics of Boston." *American Journal
of Medical Sciences* n.s. 1 (April 1841): 369–401.

———. *Report to the Committee of the City Council Appointed To Obtain the Census of Boston for the Year 1845, Embracing Collateral
Facts and Statistical Researches, Illustrating the History and Condition of the Population, and Their Means of Progress and Prosperity.* Boston: John H. Eastburn, 1846.

*Synopsis of the Proceedings of the Second Annual Meeting of the Ladies'
Physiological Institute of Boston and Vicinity. With the Secretary's
Report, and the Constitution and By-laws of the Society, with
Catalogue of Library.* Boston: Alfred Mudge, 1851.

Wellesley College Calendar. 1875/76–1909/10.

Wellesley College Circular. 1875–1908, 1913, 1927.

Wellesley College L'egenda. 1889–99.

Wellesley College Prelude. 1891–92.

Wellesley College Regulations. 1876–90.

V. Secondary Works

Ainsworth, Dorothy S. *The History of Physical Education in Colleges for
Women. As Illustrated by Barnard, Bryn Mawr, Elmira, Goucher,
Mills, Mount Holyoke, Radcliffe, Rockford, Smith, Vassar, Welles-
ley and Wells.* New York: A. S. Barnes, 1930.

Banner, Lois W. *American Beauty: A Social History Through Two Cen-*

turies of the American Idea, Ideal, and Image of the Beautiful Woman. New York: Alfred A. Knopf, 1983.

Barton, Helen. "A Study of the Development of Textbooks in Physiology and Hygiene in the U.S." Ph.D. dissertation, Univ. of Pittsburgh, 1942.

Bennett, Bruce Lanyon. "The Life of Dudley Allen Sargent, M.D., and His Contributions to Physical Education." Ph.D. dissertation, Univ. of Michigan, 1947.

Betts, John Rickards. "American Medical Thought on Exercise as the Road to Health, 1820–1860." *Bulletin of the History of Medicine* 45 (March-April 1971): 138–52.

————. "Mind and Body in Early American Medical Thought." *Journal of American History* 54 (1967–68): 787–805.

————. "Organized Sport in Industrial America." Ph.D. dissertation, Columbia Univ., 1951.

Blair, Karen J. *The Clubwoman as Feminist: True Womanhood Redefined, 1868–1914.* New York: Holmes & Meier, 1980.

Blake, John B. "Health Reform." In *The Rise of Adventism: Religion and Society in Mid-Nineteenth-Century America.* Edwin S. Gaustad, ed. New York: Harper & Row, 1974, pp. 30–49.

————. "Mary Gove Nichols, Prophetess of Health." *Proceedings of the American Philosophical Society* 106 (June 1962): 219–34.

————. *Public Health in the Town of Boston, 1630–1822.* Cambridge, Mass.: Harvard Univ. Press, 1959.

Bovard, John Freeman, and Frederick W. Cozens. *Tests and Measurements in Physical Education, 1861–1925. A Treatment of the Original Sources with Critical Comment.* Univ. of Oregon Publication, Physical Education Series, vol. I, no. 1. Eugene: Univ. of Oregon Press, 1926.

Bozeman, Theodore Dwight. *Protestants in an Age of Science: The Baconian Ideal and Antebellum American Religious Thought.* Chapel Hill: Univ. of North Carolina Press, 1977.

Brazier, Mary A. B. "Historical Development of Neurophysiology." In *Handbook of Physiology, Section I: Neurophysiology.* John Field, ed. Washington, D.C.: American Physiological Society, 1959, I: 1–58.

Brumberg, Joan Jacobs. "Chlorotic Girls, 1870–1920: A Historical Perspective on Female Adolescence." *Child Development* 53 (1982): 1468–77.

————, and Nancy Tomes. "Women in the Professions: A Research Agenda for American Historians." *Reviews in American History* 10 (June 1982): 275–96.

Bullough, Vern, and Martha Voght. "Women, Menstruation, and Nineteenth-Century Medicine." *Bulletin of the History of Medicine* 47 (Jan.–Feb. 1973): 66–82.

Bureau of the Census, U.S. Department of Commerce. *Historical Statistics of the United States: Colonial Times to 1970*. 2 vols. Washington, D.C.: Government Printing Office, 1975.

Burnham, John C. "Change in the Popularization of Health in the United States." *Bulletin of the History of Medicine* 58 (Summer 1984): 183–97.

Burstyn, Joan N. *Victorian Education and the Ideal of Womanhood*. New Brunswick, N.J.: Rutgers Univ. Press, 1984.

Caplan, Arthur L., H. Tristram Engelhardt, Jr., and James J. McCartney, eds. *Concepts of Health and Disease: Interdisciplinary Perspectives*. Reading, Mass.: Addison-Wesley, 1981.

Carpenter, Charles. *History of American Schoolbooks*. Philadelphia: Univ. of Pennsylvania Press, 1963.

Coleman, William. *Biology in the Nineteenth Century: Problems of Form, Function, and Transformation*. New York: John Wiley & Sons, 1971.

————. "Health and Hygiene in the *Encyclopédie*: A Medical Doctrine for the Bourgeoisie." *Journal of the History of Medicine and Allied Sciences* 29 (Oct. 1974): 399–421.

Converse, Florence. *Wellesley College: A Chronicle of the Years 1875–1938*. Wellesley, Mass.: Hathaway House Bookshop, 1939.

Cott, Nancy F. *The Bonds of Womanhood: "Woman's Sphere" in New England, 1780–1835*. New Haven: Yale Univ. Press, 1977.

Cowan, Ruth Schwartz. *More Work for Mother: The Ironies of Household Technology from the Open Hearth to the Microwave*. New York: Basic Books, 1983.

Daniels, George H. *American Science in the Age of Jackson*. New York: Columbia Univ. Press, 1968.

Davies, John D. *Phrenology, Fad and Science: A Nineteenth-Century American Crusade*. Reprint ed. Hamden, Conn.: Archon Books, 1971.

Davis, David Brion, ed. *Ante-Bellum Reform*. New York: Harper & Row, 1967.

Degler, Carl N. *At Odds: Women and the Family in America from the Revolution to the Present*. New York: Oxford Univ. Press, 1980.

Duffy, John. "Mental Strain and 'Overpressure' in the Schools: A Nineteenth-Century Viewpoint." *Journal of the History of Medicine and Allied Sciences* 23 (Jan. 1968): 63–79.

Ehrenreich, Barbara, and Deirdre English. *Complaints and Disorders: The Sexual Politics of Sickness*. Old Westbury, N.Y.: Feminist Press, 1973.

————. *For Her Own Good: 150 Years of the Experts' Advice to Women*. Garden City, N.Y.: Anchor Books, 1979.

Epstein, Cynthia Fuchs. *Woman's Place: Options and Limits in Professional Careers*. Berkeley: Univ. of California Press, 1970.

Fellman, Anita Clair, and Michael Fellman. *Making Sense of Self: Medical Advice Literature in Late Nineteenth-Century America.* Philadelphia: Univ. of Pennsylvania Press, 1981.

Frankfort, Roberta. *Collegiate Women: Domesticity and Career in Turn-of-the-Century America.* New York: New York Univ. Press, 1977.

Freedman, Estelle. "Separatism as Strategy: Female Institution Building and American Feminism, 1870–1930." *Feminist Studies* 5 (Fall 1979): 512–29.

Gerber, Ellen W. "The Controlled Development of Collegiate Sport for Women, 1923–1936." *Journal of Sport History* 2 (Spring 1975): 1–28.

————. *Innovators and Institutions in Physical Education.* Philadelphia: Lea & Febiger, 1971.

Glasscock, Jean, ed. *Wellesley College, 1875–1975: A Century of Women.* Wellesley, Mass.: Wellesley College, 1975.

Gordon, Linda G. *Woman's Body, Woman's Right: A Social History of Birth Control in America.* New York: Penguin Books, 1977.

Green, Harvey. *Fit for America: Health, Fitness, Sport and American Society.* New York: Pantheon, 1986.

Grob, Gerald N. *Edward Jarvis and the Medical World of Nineteenth-Century America.* Knoxville: Univ. of Tennessee Press, 1978.

————. "Modernization and Traditionalism in Jacksonian Social Reform." In *Men, Women, & Issues in American History.* Howard H. Quint and Milton Cantor, eds. 2 vols. Homewood, Ill.: Dorsey Press, 1975, I: 192–214.

Hackensmith, C. W. *History of Physical Education.* New York: Harper & Row, 1966.

Hackett, Alice Payne. *Wellesley: Part of the American Story.* New York: E. P. Dutton, 1949.

Haley, Bruce. *The Healthy Body and Victorian Culture.* Cambridge, Mass.: Harvard Univ. Press, 1978.

Haller, John S., Jr., and Robin M. Haller. *The Physician and Sexuality in Victorian America.* Urbana: Univ. of Illinois Press, 1974.

Halsey, Elizabeth. *Women in Physical Education: Their Role in Work, Home, and History.* New York: G. P. Putnam's Sons, 1961.

Handlin, Oscar. *Boston's Immigrants: A Study in Acculturation.* Revised ed. Cambridge, Mass.: Belknap Press of Harvard Univ. Press, 1959.

Hardy, Stephen. *How Boston Played: Sport, Recreation, and Community, 1865–1915.* Boston: Northeastern Univ. Press, 1982.

Hart, Albert Bushnell, ed. *Commonwealth History of Massachusetts: Colony, Province, and State.* 5 vols. New York: States History Company, 1927–30.

Herlihy, Elisabeth M., ed. *Fifty Years of Boston: A Memorial Volume.*

Compiled by the Subcommittee on Memorial History of the Boston Tercentenary Committee. Boston: n.p., 1932.

Hill, Joseph A. *Women in Gainful Occupations, 1870 to 1920.* Census Monographs IX. Washington, D.C.: Government Printing Office, 1929; reprint ed., New York: Johnson Reprint, 1972.

Hoff, Hebbel E., and John F. Fulton. "The Centenary of the First American Physiological Society Founded at Boston by William A. Alcott and Sylvester Graham." *Bulletin of the History of Medicine* 5 (Oct. 1937): 687–734.

Hooks, Janet M. *Women's Occupations Through Seven Decades.* Women's Bureau Bulletin, no. 218. Washington, D.C.: Government Printing Office, 1947.

Howe, Daniel Walker. *The Unitarian Conscience: Harvard Moral Philosophy, 1805–1861.* Cambridge, Mass.: Harvard Univ. Press, 1970.

Howe, Julia Ward, ed. *Sketches of Representative Women of New England.* Boston: New England Historical Publishing, 1904.

James, Edward T., ed. *Notable American Women, 1607–1950.* 3 vols. Cambridge, Mass.: Belknap Press of Harvard Univ. Press, 1971.

Jeffrey, Kirk. "Family History: The Middle-Class American Family in the Urban Context, 1830–1870." Ph.D. dissertation, Stanford Univ., 1971.

Johnson, Allen, and Dumas Malone, eds. *Dictionary of American Biography.* 20 vols. New York: C. Scribner's Sons, 1928–36.

Kaufman, Martin. *Homeopathy in America: The Rise and Fall of a Medical Heresy.* Baltimore: Johns Hopkins Univ. Press, 1971.

Kelly, Howard A., and Walter L. Burrage, eds. *American Medical Biographies.* Baltimore: Norman, Remington, 1920.

Kennard, June A. "The History of Physical Education." *Signs* 2 (Summer 1977): 835–42.

Kern, Stephen. *Anatomy and Destiny: A Cultural History of the Human Body.* Indianapolis and New York: Bobbs-Merrill, 1975.

Kett, Joseph F. *The Formation of the American Medical Profession: The Role of Institutions, 1780–1860.* New Haven: Yale Univ. Press, 1968.

King, Lester S. *The Medical World of the Eighteenth Century.* Chicago: Univ. of Chicago Press, 1958.

Knights, Peter R. *The Plain People of Boston, 1830–1860: A Study in City Growth.* New York: Oxford Univ. Press, 1971.

Leavitt, Judith Walzer. " 'Science' Enters the Birthing Room: Obstetrics in America since the Eighteenth Century." *Journal of American History* 70 (Sept. 1983): 281–304.

———, and Whitney Walton. " 'Down to Death's Door': Women's Perceptions of Childbirth in America." In *Women and Health in*

America: Historical Readings. Judith Walzer Leavitt, ed. Madison: Univ. of Wisconsin Press, 1984, pp. 155–65.

Lee, Mabel. *A History of Physical Education and Sports in the U.S.A.* New York: John Wiley & Sons, 1983.

Leonard, Frederick E. *Pioneers of Modern Physical Training.* New York: Physical Directors' Society of the Young Men's Christian Association of North America, 1910.

Lerner, Gerda. *The Majority Finds Its Past: Placing Women in History.* New York: Oxford Univ. Press, 1979.

Leslie, Bruce. "The Response of Four Colleges to the Rise of Intercollegiate Athletics, 1865–1915." *Journal of Sport History* 3 (Winter 1976): 213–22.

Lockhart, Aileene S., and Betty Spears, eds. *Chronicle of American Physical Education: Selected Readings, 1855–1930.* Dubuque, Iowa: Wm. C. Brown, 1972.

Morantz-Sanchez, Regina Markell. "The Lady and Her Physician." In *Clio's Consciousness Raised: New Perspectives on the History of Women.* Mary S. Hartman and Lois W. Banner, eds. New York: Harper Torchbooks, 1974, pp. 38–53.

————. "Making Women Modern: Middle Class Women and Health Reform in 19th Century America." *Journal of Social History* 10 (Summer 1977): 490–507.

————. "Nineteenth Century Health Reform and Women: A Program of Self-Help." In *Medicine without Doctors: Home Health Care in American History.* Guenter B. Risse, Ronald L. Numbers, and Judith Walzer Leavitt, eds. New York: Science History Publications/USA, 1977, pp. 73–93.

————. *Sympathy and Science: Women Physicians in American Medicine.* New York: Oxford Univ. Press, 1985.

————, and Sue Zschoche. "Professionalism, Feminism, and Gender Roles: A Comparative Study of Nineteenth-Century Medical Therapeutics." *Journal of American History* 67 (Dec. 1980): 568–88.

Mrozek, Donald J. *Sport and American Mentality, 1880–1910.* Knoxville: Univ. of Tennessee Press, 1983.

Murphy, H. B. M. "Historic Changes in the Sex Ratios for Different Disorders." *Social Science and Medicine* 12B (1978): 143–49.

Nietz, John A. *Old Textbooks: Spelling, Grammar, Arithmetic, Geography, American History, Civil Government, Physiology, Penmanship, Art, Music—As Taught in the Common Schools from Colonial Days to 1900.* Pittsburgh: Univ. of Pittsburgh Press, 1961.

Nissenbaum, Stephen. *Sex, Diet, and Debility in Jacksonian America: Sylvester Graham and Health Reform.* Westport, Conn.: Greenwood Press, 1980.

Numbers, Ronald L. *Prophetess of Health: A Study of Ellen G. White.* New York: Harper and Row, 1976.

Palmieri, Patricia Ann. "In Adamless Eden: A Social Portrait of the Academic Community at Wellesley College, 1875–1920." Ed.D. dissertation, Harvard Univ., 1981.

"Pioneer Women in Physical Education." *Research Quarterly of the American Association for Health, Physical Education, and Recreation* 12, supplement (Oct. 1941).

Remley, Mary Lou. "Women and Competitive Athletics." *Maryland Historian* 4 (Fall 1973): 88–94.

Rice, Emmett A., John L. Hutchinson, and Mabel Lee. *A Brief History of Physical Education.* 5th ed. New York: Ronald Press, 1969.

Risse, Guenter B., Ronald L. Numbers, and Judith Walzer Leavitt, eds. *Medicine without Doctors: Home Health Care in American History.* New York: Science History Publications/USA, 1977.

Rosen, George. "Political Order and Human Health in Jeffersonian Thought." *Bulletin of the History of Medicine* 26 (Jan.–Feb. 1952): 32–44.

Rosenberg, Charles E. "The Bitter Fruit: Heredity, Disease, and Social Thought in Nineteenth-Century America." *Perspectives in American History* 8 (1974): 189–235.

———. *The Cholera Years: The United States in 1832, 1849, and 1866.* Chicago: Univ. of Chicago Press, 1962.

———. "The Therapeutic Revolution: Medicine, Meaning, and Social Change in Nineteenth-Century America." In *The Therapeutic Revolution: Essays in the Social History of American Medicine.* Morris J. Vogel and Charles E. Rosenberg, eds. Philadelphia: Univ. of Pennsylvania Press, 1979, pp. 3–25.

Rosenkrantz, Barbara Gutmann. "Introduction: The Concept of Health." In *Health.* Jean Mayer, ed. New York: D. Van Nostrand, 1974, pp. 1–9.

———. *Public Health and the State: Changing Views in Massachusetts, 1842–1936.* Cambridge, Mass.: Harvard Univ. Press, 1972.

Ross, Marjorie Drake. *The Book of Boston: The Victorian Period, 1837 to 1901.* New York: Hastings House, 1964.

Rothstein, William G. *American Physicians in the Nineteenth Century: From Sects to Science.* Baltimore: Johns Hopkins Univ. Press, 1972.

Ryan, Mary P. "The Power of Women's Networks: A Case Study of Female Moral Reform in Antebellum America." *Feminist Studies* 5 (Spring 1979): 66–85.

———. *Womanhood in America: From Colonial Times to the Present.* New York: New Viewpoints, 1975.

Scholten, Catherine M. " 'On the Importance of the Obstetrick Art':

Changing Customs of Childbirth in America, 1760–1825." In *Women and Health in America: Historical Readings*. Judith Walzer Leavitt, ed. Madison: Univ. of Wisconsin Press, 1984, pp. 142–54.

Schultz, Stanley K. *The Culture Factory: Boston Public Schools, 1789–1860*. New York: Oxford Univ. Press, 1973.

Schwendener, Norma. *A History of Physical Education in the United States*. New York: A. S. Barnes, 1942.

Scott, Anne Firor. "On Seeing and Not Seeing: A Case of Historical Invisibility." *Journal of American History* 71 (June 1984): 7–21.

Scott, M. Gladys, and Mary J. Hoferek, eds. *Women as Leaders in Physical Education and Sports*. Iowa City: Univ. of Iowa Press, 1979.

Showalter, Elaine and English. "Victorian Women and Menstruation." *Victorian Studies* 14 (1970–71): 83–89.

Shryock, Richard H. "Sylvester Graham and the Popular Health Movement, 1830–1870." *Mississippi Valley Historical Review* 18 (Sept. 1931): 172–83.

Sicherman, Barbara. "The Quest for Mental Health in America, 1880–1917." Ph.D. dissertation, Columbia Univ., 1967.

————. "The Uses of a Diagnosis: Doctors, Patients, and Neurasthenia." *Journal of the History of Medicine and Allied Sciences* 32 (Jan. 1977): 33–54.

————, and Carol Hurd Green, eds. *Notable American Women: The Modern Period*. Cambridge, Mass.: Belknap Press of Harvard Univ. Press, 1980.

Sklar, Kathryn Kish. *Catharine Beecher: A Study in American Domesticity*. New York: W. W. Norton, 1976.

Smith, Ronald A. "The Rise of Basketball for Women in Colleges." *Canadian Journal of the History of Sport and Physical Education* 1 (Dec. 1970): 18–36.

Smith-Rosenberg, Carroll. "Beauty, the Beast and the Militant Woman: A Case Study in Sex Roles and Social Stress in Jacksonian America." *American Quarterly* 23 (Oct. 1971): 562–84.

————. "The Female World of Love and Ritual: Relations between Women in Nineteenth-Century America." *Signs* 1 (Autumn 1975): 1–29.

————. "The Hysterical Woman: Sex Roles and Role Conflict in 19th-Century America." *Social Research* 39 (Winter 1972): 652–78.

————. "Puberty to Menopause: The Cycle of Femininity in Nineteenth-Century America." *Feminist Studies* 1 (Winter–Spring 1973): 58–72.

————, and Charles E. Rosenberg. "The Female Animal: Medical and Biological Views of Woman and Her Role in Nineteenth-Century America." *Journal of American History* 60 (Sept. 1973): 332–56.

Solomon, Barbara Miller. *In the Company of Educated Women: A History of Women and Higher Education in America.* New Haven: Yale Univ. Press, 1985.

Sontag, Susan. *Illness as Metaphor.* New York: Vintage, 1979.

Spears, Betty. " 'The Building Up of Character Has Been My Aim': A Glimpse of the Life of Mary Hemenway." *Journal of Health, Physical Education and Recreation* 42 (March 1971): 93–94.

———. "The Influential Miss Homans." In *Her Story in Sport: A Historical Anthology of Women in Sports.* Reet Howell, ed. West Point, N.Y.: Leisure Press, 1982, pp. 391–404.

———. *Leading the Way: Amy Morris Homans and the Beginnings of Professional Education for Women.* Contributions in Women's Studies, no. 64. New York and Westport, Conn.: Greenwood Press, 1986.

———. "The Philanthropist and the Physical Educator." *New England Quarterly* 47 (Dec. 1974): 594–602.

———. "Success, Women, and Physical Education." In *Women as Leaders in Physical Education and Sports.* M. Gladys Scott and Mary J. Hoferek, eds. Iowa City: Univ. of Iowa Press, 1979, pp. 5–19.

Stage, Sarah. *Female Complaints: Lydia Pinkham and the Business of Women's Medicine.* New York: W. W. Norton, 1979.

Starr, Paul. *The Social Transformation of American Medicine.* New York: Basic Books, 1982.

Strouse, Jean. *Alice James: A Biography.* New York: Bantam Books, 1982.

Summers, Victoria Frances. "The Historical Development of the Undergraduate Program in Health and Physical Education at Wellesley College." Master's thesis, Wellesley College, 1939.

Taylor, Margery Fitzstephen. "A Historical Study of Professional Training in Hygiene and Physical Education in the Boston Normal School of Gymnastics and at Wellesley College." Master's thesis, Wellesley College, 1939.

Thernstrom, Stephan. *The Other Bostonians: Poverty and Progress in the American Metropolis, 1880–1970.* Cambridge, Mass.: Harvard Univ. Press, 1973.

Twin, Stephanie Lee. *Jock and Jill: Aspects of Women's Sports History in America, 1870–1940.* Ann Arbor: Univ. Microfilms International, 1981.

Uhlenberg, Peter R. "A Study of Cohort Life Cycles: Cohorts of Native Born Massachusetts Women, 1830–1920." *Population Studies* 23 (Nov. 1969): 407–20.

Verbrugge, Lois M. "Females and Illness: Recent Trends in Sex Differences in the United States." *Journal of Health and Social Behavior* 17 (Dec. 1976): 387–403.

————, and Jennifer H. Madans. "Social Roles and Health Trends of American Women." *Milbank Memorial Fund Quarterly/Health and Society* 63 (Fall 1985): 691–735.

Verbrugge, Martha H. "Fitness for Life: Female Health and Education in Nineteenth-Century Boston." Ph.D. dissertation, Harvard Univ., 1978.

————. "The Social Meaning of Personal Health: The Ladies' Physiological Institute of Boston and Vicinity in the 1850s." In *Health Care in America: Essays in Social History*. Susan Reverby and David Rosner, eds. Philadelphia: Temple Univ. Press, 1979, pp. 45–66.

Vinovskis, Maris A. *Fertility in Massachusetts from the Revolution to the Civil War*. New York: Academic, 1981.

————. "Mortality Rates and Trends in Massachusetts before 1860." *Journal of Economic History* 32 (1972): 184–213.

Waite, Frederick C. "Dr. Lydia Folger Fowler: The Second Woman to Receive the Degree of Doctor of Medicine in the United States." *Annals of Medical History* 4 (May 1932): 290–97.

————. "Dr. Martha A. (Hayden) Sawin: The First Woman Graduate in Medicine to Practice in Boston." *New England Journal of Medicine* 205 (Nov. 26, 1931): 1053–55.

————. "Dr. Nancy E. (Talbot) Clarke: The Second Woman Graduate in Medicine to Practice in Boston." *New England Journal of Medicine* 205 (Dec. 17, 1931): 1195–98.

Walker, William B. "The Health Reform Movement in the United States, 1830–1870." Ph.D. dissertation, Johns Hopkins Univ., 1955.

Walsh, Mary Roth. *"Doctors Wanted: No Women Need Apply": Sexual Barriers in the Medical Profession, 1835–1975*. New Haven: Yale Univ. Press, 1977.

Warner, Sam Bass, Jr. *Streetcar Suburbs: The Process of Growth in Boston, 1870–1900*. 2d ed. Cambridge, Mass.: Harvard Univ. Press, 1978.

Watts, Doris Paige. "Changing Conceptions of Competitive Sports for Girls and Women in the United States from 1880 to 1960." Ed.D. dissertation, Univ. of California, Los Angeles, 1960.

Weiss, Harry B., and Howard R. Kemble. *The Great American Water-Cure Craze*. Trenton, N.J.: Past Times Press, 1967.

Wells, Robert V. "Women's Lives Transformed: Demographic and Family Patterns in America, 1600–1970." In *Women of America: A History*. Carol Ruth Berkin and Mary Beth Norton, eds. Boston: Houghton Mifflin, 1979, pp. 16–33.

Welter, Barbara. "The Cult of True Womanhood, 1820–1860." *American Quarterly* 18 (Summer 1966): 151–74.

Weston, Arthur. *The Making of American Physical Education*. New York: Appleton-Century-Crofts, 1962.

Whitehill, Walter Muir. *Boston: A Topographical History.* 2d ed. Cambridge, Mass.: Belknap Press of Harvard Univ. Press, 1968.

Whorton, James C. *Crusaders for Fitness: The History of American Health Reformers.* Princeton: Princeton Univ. Press, 1982.

Wiebe, Robert H. *The Search for Order, 1877–1920.* New York: Hill and Wang, 1967.

Winsor, Justin, ed. *The Memorial History of Boston, Including Suffolk County, Massachusetts, 1630–1880.* 4 vols. Boston: J. R. Osgood, 1880–81.

Wood, Ann Douglas. " 'The Fashionable Diseases': Women's Complaints and Their Treatment in Nineteenth-Century America." *Journal of Interdisciplinary History* 4 (Summer 1973): 25–52.

Woody, Thomas. *A History of Women's Education in the United States.* 2 vols. New York: Science Press, 1929; reprint ed., New York: Octagon Books, 1966.

Young, James Harvey. *The Toadstool Millionaires: A Social History of Patent Medicines in America before Federal Regulation.* Princeton: Princeton Univ. Press, 1961.

Zeigler, Earle F. "A History of Professional Preparation for Physical Education in the United States, 1861–1948." Ph.D. dissertation, Yale Univ., 1950.

Index